The Hogg Family and Houston

Focus on American History Series

Center for American History
University of Texas at Austin
Edited by Don Carleton

The Hogg Family and Houston

Philanthropy and the Civic Ideal

Kate Sayen Kirkland

University of Texas Press ✦ Austin

Copyright © 2009 by the University of Texas Press
All rights reserved
Printed in the United States of America
First edition, 2009

Requests for permission to reproduce material from this work should be sent to
Permissions, University of Texas Press, Box 7819, Austin, TX 78713–7819.
www.utexas.edu/utpress/about/bpermission.html

♾The paper used in this book meets the minimum requirements of ANSI/NISO
Z39.48–1992 (R1997) (Permanence of Paper).

Library of Congress Cataloging-in-Publication Data

Kirkland, Kate Sayen, 1944–
    The Hogg family and Houston : philanthropy and the civic ideal /
Kate Sayen Kirkland. — 1st ed.
        p. cm. — (Focus on American history series)
    Includes bibliographical references and index.
    ISBN 978-0-292-71865-4 (cloth : alk. paper)
    1. Philanthropists—Texas—Houston—Biography.   2. Hogg family.   I. Title.
    HV99.H7K57 2008
    361'7409227641411—dc22

                                                        2008009092

For my father, James Conyers Sayen, 1915–1988, who taught me to love history and showed me by his fine example the value of citizen involvement in our nation's many-layered communities.

An efficient system of public schools is the growth of years, the work of ability and experience, and above all depends on the pride and generosity of a progressive, enlightened people.

—*James Stephen Hogg, January 21, 1891*

All thoughtful citizens, now-a-days, accept the dictum of professional planners that a growing city must have a comprehensive plan, the sooner the better.

—*William Clifford Hogg, 1925*

Throughout the ages . . . man has sought to communicate his richest experiences to his fellowman through various forms of art. This mysterious godlike creative impulse, mankind has translated into the universal language of order and harmony.

—*Ima Hogg, November 1952*

We find a distinct resemblance between the life and practices of a family and the life and practices of a nation.

—*Mike Hogg, 1940*

Contents

A photo section follows page 174

Preface

Ten years after leaving public service, James Stephen (Jim) Hogg, the first native-born governor of Texas (1891–1895), moved his law practice and business headquarters from the state's capital in Austin to Houston, the state's fastest-growing commercial center. Fueled by oil discoveries in surrounding counties and famous for a leadership ethos that welcomed newcomers and their aspirations, Houston had developed a business infrastructure of banks, railroads, and port facilities that encouraged economic expansion. Investors in the infant oil industry like partners Jim Hogg and Joseph Cullinan, whose Texas Company became Texaco after the governor's death, saw Houston as a good location for corporate headquarters because the city also was noted for its attractive residential neighborhoods and stimulating civic life.

The governor did not live long enough to influence Houston's development, but he left a legacy that shaped the emerging metropolis in fundamental ways when three of his four children, Will, Ima, and Mike, made Houston their permanent home after their father's death in 1906.[1] For seventy years the fortunes of the siblings and their adoptive city were entwined. Taking seriously the lessons of their parents, Will, Ima, and Mike joined other far-sighted Houston families to develop a vision of the ideal city, and they invested in institutions that would fulfill their dreams. Until Ima Hogg's death in 1975, their imaginative approaches to commerce, government, and philanthropy allowed them to confront urban challenges and demonstrate the diverse ways in which private resources can be used to promote the public good and sustain a community's quality of life.

When Will, Ima, and Mike settled in Houston, they brought with them strong family values and a heritage of commitment to community service. Jim and Sallie Stinson Hogg taught their children that public service was every citizen's duty, that strong families made stable communities, and that public education at public expense was essential to democracy. They introduced their children to music, art, and history and stressed humanitarian values of concern for others, appreciation of beauty, and stewardship of nature. Governor Hogg transmitted his reformist zeal to Will and Ima, who as children accompanied him on trips to schools, prisons, and mental asylums—expeditions that made indelible impressions on their young minds. The governor, an early progressive, believed the social, economic, and political problems of modern life could be identified and should be solved with proper application of analysis and expert advice. Toward the end of his life, the governor spent hours talking with his children about ways to make life better for all Texans.

Like many progressives who reached maturity before World War I, the Hogg siblings believed social change could be molded and community life improved. Their civic activism was a conscious moral response to industrial growth and urban expansion. Their can-do spirit was informed by strong patriotism and pride in their adopted hometown, a boosterism reflected in the newspapers and promotional materials of the era. They understood that public service through government participation, economic development through responsible business practice, and civic leadership through private philanthropy were all necessary components of healthy community life. The Hoggs invested in Houston's primary industries—cotton, real estate, and oil; they served on local government commissions and held elective office; but they made their most lasting impact as philanthropic entrepreneurs who built civic institutions that have long outlived them. Through these institutions, the Hoggs heeded their parents' admonitions to nurture the community that nurtured them; they empowered fellow citizens to pursue happiness; and they created the Hogg Foundation in the 1930s to be a transformational agent that would prevent, not just palliate, social ills.

Performers know activity on stage is meaningless without an audience. The Hoggs responded to Houston's ethos of progress with ideas that, in turn, shaped the drama of urban expansion in the Bayou City. Acting in concert with other forward-looking reformers, Will, Ima, and Mike inspired a responsive citizenry receptive to pleas for improvement and called upon friends in the community to help shape and explain Hogg family initiatives. Because the Hoggs identified their personal triumphs with their city's destiny, any analysis of their urban ideal perforce includes numerous city scenes and supporting players. Both the Hoggs' opportunity for civic activism and its success can be explained only by placing the family's work in a context that includes the advocacy of fellow reformers and a portrait of the city itself.

This story of individual efforts to improve the quality of life in Houston has not resonated with historians. Journalists may praise public-private alliances Houstonians forge to develop cultural and social service institutions for the city, but scholars too often disparage what they see as an overly cozy relationship among business leaders, local government officials, and philanthropists in shaping the community. Suspicious that the power elite's generosity toward fellow citizens merely masks venal motives, academics have failed to illuminate the synergistic nature of public-private interaction that was particularly powerful during the Hoggs' lifetimes. Scholars also have ignored the idealism that often prompts individual action and suggest instead that civic leaders simply wish to impose social and cultural controls on an unsuspecting citizenry. The Hoggs' dedication to service defies such analysis. They showed a concern for minority voices that was exceptional in their time; they focused attention on education and mental health care to empower fellow citizens; and they urged businessmen to be dutiful civic actors. Like the industry entrepreneurs who chose Houston for company headquarters, the Hoggs used their philanthropy to introduce trend-setting innovations: no museum or symphony existed in Texas when the Hoggs began their advocacy for these institutions; little attention was paid to positive mental health care when the Hoggs established the Child Guidance Center and the Hogg Foundation for Mental Health; few people funded higher education for black citizens or insisted that minority groups be welcomed at cultural events; almost no one understood how material culture could tell America's story when Ima Hogg began collecting Americana and art of the Southwest.

Chroniclers have emphasized the city's phenomenal growth and reveled in its periodic scandals, but they rarely examine how generations of civic-minded Houstonians have marshaled public and private resources to enhance the urban scene and envision a city of destiny. Houston, the fourth-largest metropolitan area in the United States, is a complex urban center that offers a wide range of choices to its citizens. For decades Houston's proactive optimists have understood that aggressive economic expansion and innovative cultural achievement can march together. They have tried to build an urban landscape destined to achieve "world-class" status. Houston's reputation as a free-enterprise heaven in a hot climate tells only part of the city's story. Houston is also a laboratory of cultural experiment where generous patrons have created a climate "essential to the flowering of genius."[2]

The Hogg Family and Houston is neither a biography of three prominent Houston philanthropists nor an urban history of the United States' fourth-largest city. Rather, this study explores how individual ideals and actions influence community development. It examines how philanthropists and volunteers have molded Houston's traditions and mobilized allies to improve the quality of life for all Houstonians. It argues that Houstonians have favored philanthropies that nurture humanitarian values, build community, and encourage inclusivity—even in the era of de jure segregation. Philanthropy as practiced by the Hoggs and numerous Houston families has been a shaping agent and a leavening influence countering the city's commercialism. Houston philanthropists have tried to make their city a decent place to live; they have encouraged the better natures of their fellows; and they have tempered greed and self-aggrandizement with aspiration. The Hoggs believed passionately that everyone can be involved in philanthropic activities: volunteers can pitch in and help dozens of nonprofit organizations; activists can speak up to identify problems and proselytize solutions; donors can give, a little or a lot, to institutions that gain their trust. Philanthropists, while "never a homogeneous lot," are remarkable for their intensity, their self-criticism, and their energetic passion "to transform the insufficiently civil world that is into the world that might be" if their visions could be realized.[3] Understanding the actions of the Hoggs as philanthropists in pursuit of an urban ideal enables us to see ourselves as civic actors and to grasp the role private initiative plays in a democracy. Ultimately the philanthropist's power, if secured by wealth, rests neither in marketplace goals of accumulating nor in political goals of dominating but rather in the authority of a voice that articulates the importance of pursuing a common good.

The Hoggs' embrace of Progressive Era values also makes analysis of their philanthropic contributions problematic for some historians. Progressivism is particularly difficult to understand when examined only as a political or economic phenomenon. In the South, progressives have been tainted because many white southerners used government reform—a critical Progressive Era goal—to separate black and white citizens in the tragedy of de jure segregation. Progressivism as practiced by the Hoggs is best defined not in political or economic terms but rather as a humanitarian attitude, an upper- and upper-middle-class urban response to the transformations in technology, transportation, and communication that created modern America. Progressives like the Hoggs were proactive optimists who understood that change was inevitable but who also respected tradition. To them, social, governmental, and economic structures were fundamentally sound but needed constant revision to strengthen underlying verities. In this view of progress, individuals could and should aspire to improve their lives and partake of the American dream. Progressive leaders like the Hoggs built on the late-nineteenth-century Progressive movement ethos articulated by people like their father: if society was by no means perfected, there was always hope that a better life was within reach and was well worth pursuing.

The Hogg Family and Houston describes, thematically, six ways Hogg family philanthropy, civic activism, and voluntarism framed Houston's development. In the 1920s the Hoggs tried to shape the built environment through business practices, public service, and philanthropy by building planned residential communities, by advocating city planning, and by donating park spaces (chapter 2). In the 1920s and 1930s they adopted the little-understood cause of positive mental health care and established the Houston Child Guidance Center (1929) and the Hogg Foundation for Mental Health (1939) to help fellow citizens build wholesome lives (chapter 3). Like their father, the Hogg children believed education was a many-sided responsibility. In the 1910s and 1920s Will established an alumni organization at the University of Texas and funded student loan endowments at every Texas institution of higher learning; in the 1940s Ima served on the Houston Board of Education; and throughout their lives, the Hoggs supported lectures and faculty at the University of Texas and Rice Institute (chapter 4). Ima fell in love with music as a little girl, studied to be a concert pianist, and decided while still a University of Texas student that the state must have a symphony orchestra. She spent her adult life realizing this dream in Houston as founder, nurturer, and president of the Houston Symphony Society (chapter 5). In 1920 Will and Ima began collecting American decorative arts and paintings and conceived the idea that Houston must develop Texas's first municipal art museum. Will raised money for the original building, and Ima transferred the family's treasures to the museum's care in the 1940s through the 1960s (chapter 6). Finally, in the last decades of her life, Ima imagined the transformation of Bayou Bend, her home and garden, to a house museum and park and undertook several historic preservation projects around the state to transmit America's story to future generations (chapter 7).

The Hogg family's ability to unite politicians, volunteers, and business-people in partnerships of civic responsibility illuminates the power of philanthropic vision to nurture the associations of democracy and provide alternative solutions to society's problems. The Hoggs belonged to a cosmopolitan circle in Houston. Like many of their friends, they traveled frequently, maintained homes in other cities, read widely, and debated issues of the day in extensive correspondence. Like other philanthropists, they recognized social problems often overlooked by economic power brokers and politicians, and they integrated the needs of family, community, state, and nation in an effort to reconcile individual goals and community purposes. Like most successful activists, they secured broad-based support. Through their city planning and residential development projects they tried to create an ideal American city by incorporating design elements and expertise from the East, the South, the Midwest, and the Southwest. Through their education and health care initiatives they hoped to empower Houstonians and Texans to pursue individual goals of life, liberty, and happiness. Through their art collections and historic preservation projects they sought to bring Texans "closer to the heart of an American heritage which unites us."[4] Their every action supports the observation that "philanthropy permeates American life [and] touches each one of us countless times in countless ways."[5]

Acknowledgments

esearch projects, while frequently solitary, are never lonely. Figures from the past who awaken curiosity and friends in the present who offer counsel and critique inhabit the imagination and earn the gratitude of every author. Many friends and colleagues have guided this study. I am grateful to the Hogg family for setting an example that remains as vibrant today as it was during the years Will, Ima, Mike, and Alice Hogg lived in Houston; these friends from the past deserve much fuller attention than is offered here. I particularly value my associations with Professor Ira Gruber, who reintroduced me to the pleasures of academic discourse and demonstrated the tenets of incisive but kindly criticism, and with Professor John B. Boles, whose passion for his students, for history, and for his community inspires emulation. I deeply appreciate the astute comments of Ann H. Holmes, who reviewed a draft of chapter 5; of Terry Brown, who shared her research on the Houston Symphony and pursued symphony data for me; of Joanne Wilson, who loaned me materials collected for her study of Wille Hutcheson; of Michael K. Brown, who read a version of chapters 6 and 7; of Stephen Fox, who generously shared his extensive knowledge of urban planning and Houston history with me; of Susan B. Keeton, who provided me with important materials about the Bayou Bend Gardens plan; of Ann Lents, who discussed current efforts to preserve Houston's quality of life; and of Ann Hamilton, whose understanding of philanthropy and conservation is invaluable. My thanks also to Lonn Taylor and Wayne Bell, whose personal assessments of Ima Hogg and her crusade for historic preservation help define her "particular genius."

At the Museum of Fine Arts, Houston, archivist Lorraine Stuart, curators Emily Ballew Neff and Alison de Lima Greene, and their associates in the Registrar's Office kindly made important information available to me, while Photographic Services Manager Marcia Stein and assistant archivist Amy Scott graciously provided images from their collections. The late A. Edward Groff, MD, while a sustaining docent, prepared a list of objects in the Bayou Bend Collection indicating date of purchase, an invaluable tool for understanding the Hoggs' collecting practices. My thanks to Ann Kelsey, Francita Ulmer, and Shelby Jones for securing permission needed to read the Garden Club of Houston Records and to Margaret Bailey and Bitsey Hail for making available the River Oaks Garden Club Records; both sets of records are in the Museum of Fine Arts, Houston, Archives. June Stobaugh and Mary Beth Staine most graciously directed me to Junior League of Houston histories. At the Center for American History, University of Texas at Austin, Director Don Carleton, former Associate Director Kate Adams, and Winedale curator Pablo Howze led me behind the scenes in their collections, and Steven Williams searched Hogg family collections for images. At the Woodson Research Center, Rice University, archivists Kinga Perzynska, now deceased, and Lee Pecht and their colleagues showed unfailing interest in my project. Librarians at the Texas Room and archivists at the Houston Metropolitan Research Center of the Houston Public Library, staff at the Board of Education, and former Associate Director Ralph E. Culler III of the Hogg Foundation helped me find valuable information, photographs, and maps. Joann Mitchell, former development director of the DePelchin Children's Center, scrambled through a storage warehouse to unearth the minutes of the Houston Child Guidance Center. Portions of chapters 1, 3, and 4 appeared in two articles in the *Southwestern Historical Quarterly*: "For All Houston's Children: Ima Hogg and the Board of Education, 1943–1949" (April 1998), 460–495; and "A Wholesome Life: Ima Hogg's Vision for Mental Health Care" (January 2001), 416–447.

My friends, my daughters, Anne and Jennifer Leader, and my husband, John, deserve special thanks for their support.

Prologue

Rain fell steadily in Houston on Friday, August 22, 1975. Dozens of chairs placed on the North Terrace at Bayou Bend stared empty and forlorn across the sodden lawn toward a marble statue of the goddess Diana standing in a garden framed by native bayou evergreens. For five decades Ima Hogg had welcomed visitors to this outdoor "room" for theatricals, orchestral evenings, garden trails, and weddings. On that dreary Friday, the empty chairs stood mute sentinels as friends crowded inside the house to bid farewell to the only daughter of James Stephen Hogg, remembered eighty years after he left office as one of Texas's most influential governors. Following the 3 p.m. memorial service, Ima would leave the home of her adult years and begin her final journey to Austin, the home of her youth. There, she would join her parents and brothers in the family burial plot at Oakwood Cemetery as Austin city flags flew at half-staff for two official days of mourning.[1]

Journalists sent to record Houstonians' memorial to "the First Lady of Texas" photographed the empty seats and the folded umbrellas leaning against the front entrance. Like the 350 mourners sheltered from the rain in the handsome center hall, they recognized that "an irreplaceable part of Houston's soul is gone." Front-page stories, obituaries, and editorials reprised a family tradition of civic activism; columnists recalled important contributions made by Ima's grandparents, parents, and brothers and recounted anecdotes of a life devoted to "music, art, history and public service." Lonn Taylor, who had worked with her at Winedale, remembered Ima's love of wildflowers, Bach, individualism, folk art, Picasso, and cajolery. "She was a master at getting people to do things; she set an example that others were embarrassed not to follow." But she was also a steadfast friend, showering old and young with recipes, advice, fruit cakes, plants, gadgets, grapefruit, and inscribed Bibles. At ninety-three, Ima Hogg offered young guests Tang because the astronauts drank it in space, and she "remained an active participant in today's world."[2]

Although suffering from arterial disease for some years, Ima had left Houston on August 5 for a vacation in London with friends. While negotiating a taxi in that city on August 14, she slipped and fell. Not strong enough to survive this accident, she succumbed to a coronary occlusion at 7 p.m. Houston time on August 19. As she had planned her many civic projects, so she programmed her funeral, noting in a codicil to her will, "I do not wish to subject my friends and relatives to prolonged eulogies or ceremonies or to require them to listen to music which we have so deeply loved and enjoyed during my lifetime on an occasion of this nature." The Reverend Maurice M. Benitez, at that time rector of St. John the Divine Episcopal Church, read the seventeen-minute Episcopal service. The Reverend Thomas W. Sumners, the church's rector emeritus, noted in brief personal remarks that "Bayou Bend itself is [Miss Hogg's] eulogy." Young pallbearers chosen by Miss Hogg escorted the handsome casket draped in magnolia leaves. Attendees included tearful Bayou Bend docents seated on the curving staircase; her protégé and longtime friend, the concert pianist Drusilla Huffmaster; her lawyer, Leon Jaworski; her general factotum of fifty-five years, Gertrude Vaughn; her butler and chauffeur of twenty-three years, Lucius Broadnax; her friend, executrix, and secretary of twenty-three years, Jane Zivley; Houston's cultural, business, and political leaders; and her successor as overseer and developer of the Bayou Bend legacy, David B. Warren.[3]

Because Miss Ima, as she was known to intimates and family, remained insatiably curious and fully engaged with life, her many friends reacted to her loss as if she had been a young person whose promising journey had been unexpectedly ended. Instead, Ima and her two Houston-based brothers, Will and Mike, had left their adoptive city a broad-based legacy that continues to shape community life. Profoundly influenced by the teachings of their parents and working together, the siblings imagined a beautiful American city supported by a balanced and thriving economy and governed by dedicated public servants. To achieve this dream, they proselytized their causes, prodded their fellow citizens to action, and built institutions that would survive them. For seventy years no aspect of twentieth-century urban life escaped their notice. Their community involvement, their urban vision, and their steadfast leadership enriched the lives of all who knew them and encouraged later generations to follow their examples as philanthropic entrepreneurs.

The Hogg Family and Houston

Chapter 1
A Family Philanthropy

On January 26, 1905, former Texas Governor James Stephen Hogg boarded a train in West Columbia, where he was developing a model farm on the old Patton Place, a property he had purchased in 1901 to renovate as the family home.[1] Like many financially successful Victorian patriarchs who commuted from country haven to urban workplace, the widowed father of four was en route to explore legal and business opportunities in Houston, sixty-five miles to the north. On this wintry morning, the governor was suffering from a nagging cold. While stopped at a station, he and other passengers were jolted in a railroad car coupling "made with more force than usual."[2] Although the governor continued his journey without complaint, camped out in the Rice Hotel, and eagerly returned to his rural retreat when business was concluded, he soon developed several ailments that culminated in his death on March 3, 1906. Jim Hogg's decision to recreate for his own children the antebellum plantation of his romanticized childhood on part of the Martin Varner League in West Columbia while situating the family's business headquarters in Texas's most modern and rapidly industrializing commercial center had far-reaching consequences for city and family. For years, his children gathered friends at Varner-Hogg, the remodeled house and its surrounding acres, to relax and have fun. From a salt dome on the property gushed the oil to secure a family fortune that would ensure the Hoggs' civic influence in Houston. To Houston the governor's children would bring their family's legacy of civil engagement.

FOUNDING A CITY ON BUFFALO BAYOU

Houston's ascent from frontier outpost to twentieth-century oil capital fulfilled ambitions of its founders and generations of determined civic leaders. From the moment of purchase in 1836, New York brothers Augustus Chapman Allen and John Kirby Allen imagined a great city rising on their 6,642-acre investment at the juncture of Buffalo and White

Oak Bayous fifty miles inland from the Gulf of Mexico. Stimulated by the national land craze of the 1830s, these urban entrepreneurs embraced city-building as their route to wealth and Texas's hope for greatness. They formed a partnership in New York financed by family members interested in Texas land speculation, journeyed to Texas in 1832, and settled in Nacogdoches in 1833. Following insurgent Sam Houston's victory over Mexican General Santa Anna at San Jacinto on April 21, 1836, and the subsequent declaration of a Republic of Texas, younger brother John was elected congressman from Nacogdoches, and both men quickly recognized that the self-proclaimed country must have a capital city. Perhaps the Allen brothers were aware of the U.S. Federal District's faltering ability to reach urban status in the early nineteenth century because the struggling United States capital possessed no economic foundation. Perhaps they were slightly appalled by the crass materialism despoiling New York's urban explosion. Perhaps they merely recognized that the buildings and services necessary to a seat of government would be catalysts for wealth creation. Whatever mix of motives underlay their vision, the brothers seemed to understand that no new community would thrive and attract settlers without a firm economic purpose, an ability to establish order, and provisions for civic enrichment.

The Allen brothers searched for a site that could accommodate the Republic's capital but would also serve as a transportation center for produce grown along the fertile rivers emptying into Galveston Bay, and they found "a point on the river which must ever command the trade of the largest and richest portion of Texas." They imagined a "great interior commercial emporium" for Texas and named their settlement after the new nation's liberator, Sam Houston. Immediately they began a concerted political and advertising campaign. On August 30, 1836, the brothers purchased a long column in Texas's only newspaper, the *Telegraph and Texas Register*, and announced that "Nature appears to have designated this place for the future seat of Government."[3] When the first congress of the Republic of Texas convened at Columbia in Brazoria County on October 3, John lobbied nonstop until the legislators voted on December 15, 1836, to designate the Allens' campsite as government headquarters for the legislative term ending in 1840. In January 1837 the settlement was named county seat for Harrisburg (later Harris) County. To ensure that their site would be chosen as the Republic's capital, the hard-nosed entrepreneurs had promised complementary building lots to senators and congressmen. They also had agreed to construct a $10,000 two-story capitol building at their own expense and to provide other amenities including a city hotel. Buoyed by their political success, the Allens broadcast advertisements throughout the United States and Europe and launched Houston's first real estate "boom," which attracted carpenters and mechanics from across Texas and the southern United States.

Accounts differ about the quality and success of this building frenzy. Confident of acceptance by the legislators, A. C. Allen already had hired Gail Borden Jr. and Thomas Henry Borden to make a survey and plat for the flat, muddy site that stretched south and west of curving Buffalo Bayou. Moses Lapham, in the Bordens' employ, completed this work between October 2 and November 19, 1836, and the first land sale was recorded on New Year's Day 1837. Mexican prisoners and black slaves endured mosquitoes and mud to clear streets and building sites. The steamboat carrying Francis R. Lubbock, later governor of the state, struggled through logs and snags for three days on Lubbock's twelve-mile journey up the bayou and then chugged right past the settlement's inconspicuous dock on January 6, 1837, but by March the Long Row of shops had been completed.[4] In April the capitol building was made habitable in fourteen days. Sam Houston may have counted more than one hundred houses and fifteen hundred people by April 28, 1837, but many observers remembered numerous tents and few buildings in these early months. Contemporary accounts record an 1837 temperance meeting, a jockey club, and dancing assemblies, and the April 4, 1837, *Telegraph* includes New Orleans impresario G. L. Lyons's announcement that he would open "the first temple dedicated to the dramatic muse in Texas." The Reverend W. Y. Allen, Presbyterian divine and first chaplain of the House of Representatives, was less enthusiastic, denouncing fifty gambling dens and one hundred grog shops in 1838 to counterbalance his Sabbath School established that year.[5] By 1839, however, retailer John F. Torrey and his brother David Kilburn Torrey had opened their Jewelry and Fancy Store (1839–1849) in a frame house on Main Street opposite the City Hotel. They sold watches, clocks, spectacles, thimbles, cutlery, hairbrushes, perfume, books, musical instruments, and "all kind of Gold and Silver ware manufactured to order at the shortest notice," a confident sign that some residents aspired to both elegance and stability.[6]

The Allen brothers embraced urban living as the site of economic, social, and cultural opportunity, and their vision established a development pattern followed by succeeding generations. Colonial merchants who had gathered products from the hinterland and traded them both locally and abroad had secured North America's first fortunes. Following this example, the Allens chose a site where produce could be floated downriver or dragged by oxcart from the interior and gathered for processing in Houston or for transshipment from Galveston Bay to Gulf and Atlantic ports. Like competitors in Chicago and Kansas City, whose founders also trumpeted their new settlements as gateways to the West in the 1830s, the Allens adopted the popular grid pattern for their city plan. Standard for the era, the grid could be expanded relentlessly across the prairie as the city grew. The Allens platted broad avenues that would accommodate commercial traffic, a Commerce Square on either side of Main Street for trade, and public wharf space. To attract local and national government sponsors, their Borden-Lapham plat included Congress and Court House squares in the town's center. Finally, in laying out the town, the Allens recognized that a successful community was more than a political or economic entity, so they reserved space for church and school buildings.[7]

Houston began auspiciously with well-capitalized entrepreneurs, successful public relations, and the political blessing of first Texas President Sam Houston, but the village quickly experienced the negative consequences of unbridled boosterism. Recurring epidemics of yellow fever decimated the population; falling Texas currency values caused financial backers to withdraw credit; and politicians proved less than enthusiastic about humid weather, flooded streets, frequent gunfights, and inadequate infrastructure. Second Texas President Mirabeau B. Lamar supported a new site for the capital and in October 1839 packed up the government records and moved to Austin, then an outpost on the edge of Comanche country in the rugged hill country of Central Texas.[8] Several Houston merchants recognized that only cooperative action could save their investments, and they took two steps that set precedents for future growth: they formed a voluntary association, and they pressed for transportation improvements.

Because they were dependent on Northern capital, Houston's leading citizens were familiar with the successful promotion of finance, industry, and commerce fostered by chambers of commerce in New York (founded 1768), Philadelphia (1801), and New Haven (by 1801). Houston needed a similar initiative to solve local problems, and business leaders successfully lobbied the Third Congress (December 1838–January 1839) for permission to charter a Houston Chamber of Commerce, officially incorporated January 28, 1840. In 1840 the Texas Congress also empowered Houstonians to build and maintain public wharves, and in 1841 the

City Council authorized the Port of Houston to monitor all facilities along Buffalo and White Oak Bayous and to support efforts to improve access to the sea. This model of government blessing for private initiative and the interlocking private-public relationships such synergy implied proved critical to Houston's subsequent growth. Nineteenth-century civic leaders who maintained access to eastern financial markets, adapted proven institutions to Houston's needs, and focused their attention on political support for port development and transportation perpetuated the Allens' dream that one day a great city would rise along the bayou. Although Texas's delayed entry into the union in 1845, its agricultural economy, its primitive financial structure, and its infant manufacturing sector precluded the extensive urbanization occurring in the Northeast or the Midwest during these decades, Houston's nineteenth-century businessmen competed vigorously to process and ship cotton and lumber products and to improve commercial wharves and storage facilities along Buffalo Bayou. Local merchants formed partnerships to build or attract railroad service and to dredge and improve the waterways. Houston suffered its share of setbacks but experienced continuous growth and economic expansion for fifty years as it developed from a small county seat (1850 population 2,396) to a post–Civil War entrepot (1870 population 10,382) to a vibrant market town (1890 population 27,557).[9]

Houston's animosity toward its seaside neighbor, Galveston, a gracious Victorian port perched on an island sand bar buffering the mainland from the Gulf of Mexico, also spurred the inland city's development. Despite periodic hurricane damage, Galveston had positioned itself as the seagoing port of the region in the 1840s and pursued railroad dominance of the East Texas countryside by supporting state financing for a fan of north-south rail lines terminating at the Galveston docks. Determined to edge out this rival, Houstonians courted proponents of the national east-west system of privately funded lines then beginning construction, and they lobbied the Texas legislature for subsidies and land grants to the transcontinental builders. When state politicians bowed to the national consortium and its local spokesmen in 1856, Houston's boosters celebrated. By building railroad links to America's great cities, entrepreneurs began to develop Houston as a regional gathering, trading, and transshipping point while simultaneously nursing local efforts to create wealth through infant manufacturing operations. In the 1850s Alexander McGowan's iron foundry, A. Bering's sash, door, and blind manufactory, numerous cotton processing gins, and four railroad companies formed an infant manufacturing sector.

Although railroad expansion was temporarily halted by the Civil War, Houston's postwar business leaders and government officials manipulated shipping rates to create a railroad-building boom that favored Houston merchants. In 1860 Houston was the region's rail center; by 1890 fourteen national and local lines crossed in the city; and by 1910 boosters trumpeted "Houston, where seventeen railroads meet the sea," as the ideal gateway to markets in the South and West.[10] Multitracked railyards bustled with trainloads of King Cotton headed for Houston's growing cotton-processing industry or bound for ports around the world. Railroads, cotton factors, and merchants provided excellent jobs and supported the banking, legal, and retail services that would promote Houston's economic expansion well into the twentieth century.[11]

The Civil War years benefited adventurers who carted cotton overland to Mexico to avoid the Galveston blockade, and several merchants prospered at the expense of their island neighbors. Englishman Thomas William House (1813–1880), a baker and ice cream maker by trade, amassed his wealth in cotton transshipments, which he parlayed into Houston's first powerful private banking institution and first public utility, the Houston Gas Works (1866). Mayor during the war years, House and later his family established critical business ventures in railroads, shipping, and sugar and influenced state and national political activity through World War I.[12] William Marsh Rice (1816–1900) also seized the opportunities provided by wartime conditions. He moved operations to Matamoros, Mexico, across the border from Brownsville, and accumulated a fortune by running cotton and other goods through the Mexican port. Although he spent many postwar years in New York, Rice maintained his Houston connections and returned his riches to Houstonians by endowing "an institute for the advancement of literature, science, and art" that became Rice Institute after his death in 1900.[13]

Because Houston had suffered relatively mild hardship during the war years, by the 1870s the city was ideally positioned to embrace a New South faith in future prosperity built on business opportunity. A limited circle of socially compatible competitors assumed business and government leadership functions. Like leaders in other New South cities, they viewed their weak local government as an arm of the private sector and believed its first duty was to promote business. Houston's New South advocates assumed that their clique of city councilmen, lawyers and bankers, business and industry executives, and cotton and lumber barons would dominate politics, keep wages and taxes low, and nurture the processing of raw materials from the surrounding region. Still strapped for capital, these men relied on Northern and British investors to jumpstart their nascent manufacturing sector. Suspicious of government interference, they used city funds only to support infrastructure improvements in the commercial areas of town; little money was reserved for parklands, for street paving or sewer amenities in residential areas, or for social services, still the concern of churchwomen and private charity.[14]

Some local businessmen were alarmed by Houston's uncontrolled growth and seemingly heedless embrace of "foreign" (non-Texas) investors, and they feared the competition of national corporations. These urban populists hoped for government intervention to regulate utilities and transportation outlets and to defray the cost of public services such as sewers, roads, and sidewalks. They were to be disappointed. Municipal government remained relatively passive during these years and intervened only when the leadership clique sought public action to secure private economic advantage. For example, little effort was made to build modern municipal sewerage treatment plants until businessmen realized that a long-festering health crisis resulting from the dumping of raw sewage into Buffalo Bayou was also a business problem. In 1899 business groups seeking funds to dredge a deep-water channel to the sea discovered that they could not secure federal dollars unless they cleaned up the bayou. Immediately, they formed a Sewer Committee and passed a $300,000 bond issue to acquire the newest sanitary technology for the city.[15]

In the mid-1870s Houston began to experience the technological changes and industrial concentration that were transforming commercial centers in the North and East. Businessmen who formed the Buffalo Bayou Ship Channel Company (founded in 1869), the Houston Board of Trade and Cotton Exchange (1874), the Houston Street Railway Company (1876), the Houston Waterworks Company (1879), the Telephone Exchange (1880), the Electric Light Company (1882), and other commercial associations positioned the city to attract manufacturing activity in the 1880s. During this period the Southern Pacific Railroad established its first Houston repair shops for a transcontinental railroad; the city's first steamship office opened; and the area's first suburban development was incorporated in 1887 when the Omaha and South Texas Land Company purchased 1,765 acres northwest of the city to build what became Houston Heights. Double trolley lines ran past several blocks of three- and four-story buildings on Main Street, and numerous telephone poles attested to the new invention's popularity by the mid-1880s.[16] Local unions for typographical workers, railway conductors, machinists, and iron molders defined the thrust of labor activity.

By the 1890s most white Houstonians agreed that their prosperous small city of more than 30,000 residents was a "home of intellectual vigor and refinement, with a past full of interest, a present full of earnestness, and a future full of brightness." I. J. Isaacs, editor of an 1894 business compendium praising the "industrial advantages of Houston, Texas, and environs," described the enterprising building and loan associations that had made good housing available in all income brackets and had thereby "created a class of citizens bound up with the interests of the locality . . . who are content to live and labor here for the general good." Isaacs commended the railroad connections to the whole country, the outlet to the sea, the electric streetcars linking residence to workplace, and the local government devoted to strict economy and secure progress. With rich natural resources, strong credit, and no burdensome taxes, the city's "advance is certain, it cannot be otherwise." Already a leading cotton market, second only to New Orleans in tons shipped, Houston was also headquarters for several lumber companies. Isaacs celebrated the mild climate and enumerated the fifteen public schools, nine for the 2,900 white pupils and seven for the 1,900 "colored" students. In 1894, 180 white and 30 black students attended two high schools in preparation for college. Citing Houston as one of the best-lit cities, with fifty miles of electric wire, Isaacs also noted the Sweeney and Coombs Opera House (opened 1890), where the "cream of the dramatic and operatic profession appears . . . before the Houston public." If Isaacs and other boosters are to be believed, in 1900 Houston was primed for a brilliant future.[17]

Two events that forever changed the demographic and economic balance in East Texas and propelled Houston to major-city status announced the new century. On Saturday, September 8, 1900, a hurricane whipped out of the Gulf of Mexico and inundated Galveston, long Houston's rival for seagoing trade. Historian Elizabeth Hayes Turner describes the devastation that left at least 6,000 of the 38,000 residents dead.

> Not a single public structure in Galveston escaped damage. The hurricane blew away the bridges to the mainland and damaged the central water works system, . . . ships anchored in the bay were sent reeling off in the raging storm to land ten—even twenty-two—miles away from deep water. . . . Hardest hit, ironically, were the churches. African American churches—fourteen in all—suffered the most; every single structure was demolished.[18]

Turner relates the valiant volunteer cooperation that enabled the rebuilding of the city. Never again, however, would Galveston be a major commercial power in the state. Houston, lying fifty miles inland, would quickly capitalize on its sister city's calamity by creating a deep-water port sheltered from the full brunt of wind and water.

Four months after the Galveston disaster and eighty-five miles to the east in sleepy Beaumont, Texas, Captain Anthony F. Lucas realized his prophecy that oil lay beneath a salt dome called Spindletop. On January 10, 1901, the Lucas gusher erupted.

> At exactly 10:30 a.m., the well that made Beaumont famous burst upon the astonished view of those engaged in boring it, with such a volume of water, sand, rocks, gas and oil that sped upward with such tremendous force as to tear the crossbars of the derrick to pieces, . . . For nine days the phenomenon was the wonder and puzzle of the world. It flowed unceasingly and with ever increasing force and volume . . . quite two hundred feet, and spouting in wanton waste 70,000 barrels of oil per day.[19]

Hundreds of men rushed to the scene to build a wall around the well and try to contain its valuable spray of oil that could be seen ten or fifteen miles away. Some 50,000 adventurers poured into the area, and soon "doormat" leases just big enough to sink a well turned the discovery site into a dangerous forest of combustible wooden derricks and spurting oil. Beaumont, reeling from the negative effects of careless wildcatters and inflated money, could not sustain such frenzied activity. As the boom continued, sober businessmen realized that they needed executive headquarters that provided banking facilities, shipping links to industrial regions, and attractive housing for themselves and their employees. Because Houston already boasted the transportation, legal, banking, and retail infrastructure built over several decades, oil entrepreneurs began to see the city as an ideal headquarters for executive staff and their families. Moreover, Houston's business leaders, always ready to welcome newcomers to the power structure, were quick to encourage location of oil-related industries and pipelines along Buffalo Bayou.

Access to the sea had brought the Allens to Buffalo Bayou's headwaters in the 1830s, and hopes for a deep-water port had sustained the long struggle with Galveston for transportation hegemony. Following Galveston's catastrophe and Beaumont's triumph, Houston boosters finally gained deep-water facilities for their city.[20] For thirty years

Houston and Galveston had been maneuvering to develop a deep-water port to accommodate ever-larger commercial ships: Houston used dredging and barge transport; Galveston built jetties in the 1890s to create deep water. While most of this early activity had been privately financed, investors recognized that their limited resources would hamper efficient execution of grand schemes for an international port to rival New Orleans or New York. Willing to partner with federal authorities to fund infrastructure improvements, business leaders approached their congressmen for financial support. In 1896 retiring Representative Joseph C. Hutcheson (1842–1924) of Houston introduced a House bill requesting federal aid to survey and build a twenty-five-foot-deep channel from Houston to the Gulf. Hutcheson then entertained members of the Rivers and Harbors Committee on an 1897 inspection tour and social whirl in Houston; gained support for the project from his successor, Thomas Henry Ball of Huntsville; and shepherded Houston businessmen through congressional hearings.[21]

The 1900 hurricane that swept away much of Galveston tipped the balance in favor of building a protected inland deep-water port and access channel near Houston, but the politically astute Ball palliated both cities. He arranged funding to help restore Galveston facilities to their pre-hurricane level and procured $1 million in the 1903–1904 biennium to begin digging a new channel from Houston to the Gulf. In 1909 Ball devised legislation permitting local areas to create navigation districts with power to issue bonds for improvements. He also suggested that a Houston delegation journey to Washington to propose sharing the cost of forming a deep-water channel with the federal government. This "Houston Plan" for local-federal cooperation stunned the politicians and established a precedent for subsequent improvement projects nationwide. The Houston committee secured $1.25 million from the federal government, the largest subsidy to a local authority up to that time. Committee members then returned to Houston to convince citizens of Harris County, within whose jurisdiction most of the proposed ship channel area lay, to authorize the Harris County Houston Ship Channel Navigation District and vote for the bond issue needed to raise promised matching funds. Voters approved the authority and the bonds in January 1911, but investors proved reluctant until real estate entrepreneur and banker Jesse Holman Jones and lumberman and banker William T. Carter convinced seven Houston banks to purchase bonds in proportion to each bank's assets. Several bank presidents were active ship channel promoters and by November 1911 had agreed to buy half the bonds. City and county governments and private investors took the remainder, and the project moved forward. In 1914 Houston became the nation's newest deep-water port when President Woodrow Wilson flipped a switch at the White House that carried a telegraphic message to set off a cannon blast that inaugurated the facility.

FORMING A SOCIAL CONSCIOUSNESS IN HOUSTON

Many chroniclers of Houston writing from the 1840s to the 1970s imagined their readers as white middle-class advocates of modernity and progress. Steeped in America's classic master narrative of ever-expanding material prosperity, ever-increasing political freedom, and ever-improving social opportunity, these writers focused on the city's economic growth and physical expansion as developed by white middle-class businessmen. Lost in these accounts was the growing uneasiness of a small but powerful circle of white civic visionaries who had begun to question the unforeseen consequences of unrestrained development by the late 1880s and who demanded municipal improvements and civic institutions that would enrich urban life.

Men first tried to improve urban life through the Chamber of Commerce and other industry and professional groups that attracted manufacturing and trade. They established the Lyceum (1848; state charter 1854) as a subscription library and enlivened the social and sporting scene by sponsoring a Bachelors Hall and Club (1871) and the Houston Left-Handed Fishing and Hunting Club (1887), among numerous more serious-minded associations. The city's German immigrants developed Houston's musical culture by founding several vocal and instrumental groups, including the German Quartette Society (1847) and the Saengerbund (1884). While men's groups often looked outward toward commercial or professional participation in national and international markets or sought genial camaraderie, women's associations frequently turned inward to self, home, and community. Hoping to improve living conditions for themselves and their children, women formed parish associations and study groups that came to symbolize reform activism in the Progressive Era (1880–1920) as members broadened their concept of "family" to include every Houstonian.

Discussions in the Ladies' Reading Club (1885), the Ladies' Shakespeare Club (1890), and other literary clubs quickly moved from great books to larger issues of civic and cultural impact for the entire community. Forming a federation of like-minded activists, club women cooperated to secure funding from Andrew Carnegie for a public library (1899) and municipal support for the library's operation. They then over-saw construction and ensured that the doors opened with appropriate fanfare in 1904. Similarly, nineteenth-century churchwomen like the lady visitors from the Christ Church Ladies Parish Association (1871) began to discover unimagined deprivation in poor white, black, and immigrant neighborhoods that threatened the greater public health and safety of all Houstonians.

Tentative nineteenth-century initiatives were followed by a burst of activity after 1900 that paralleled population growth and accumulation of newfound oil wealth. White volunteer women established the Public School Art League (1900) to place art in public schools, the first free public kindergartens (1902), the Young Women's Christian Association (YWCA, 1907) to shelter working women, and the Settlement Associa-tion (1907) to assist immigrant families. They also founded the Thurs-day Morning Musical Club (1908) to study and present classical music, the first Mothers' Clubs to provide amenities in public schools (1908), the Woman's Political Union to secure the vote (1909), the Emma R. Newsboys Association (1910) to care for orphaned or abandoned teenage boys, and the Houston Symphony Association (1913) to bring professional orchestral music to the city. Middle-class black women sought civic improvements by banding together in the Married Ladies Social, Art, and Charity Club (1902), the Art and Literary Club (1906), and numerous church and fraternal groups. In 1915 they formed their own Ladies' Symphony Orchestra and in 1917 founded Bethlehem Settlement to assist residents of the Fourth Ward.[22]

Competing charities and service organizations soon realized that they needed to plan projects and coordinate goals. In 1904 volunteers formed United Charities to make giving more efficient and businesslike. By 1915 municipal officials determined that city government had to play some oversight role in dispensing benevolence, and they created the state's first community foundation. The Houston Foundation, established within the city Department of Public Trusts, investigated and endorsed "charities dependent upon public appeal" and collected statistics about living conditions, unemployment, and delinquency "for the purpose of dis-seminating information relative to the social needs of the community."[23] Houstonians had developed a progressive approach to benevolence. No longer "content to patch and palliate distress," social activists were now hoping "to remove the causes of distress and to prevent their recurrence" by improving living conditions for all Houston citizens.[24]

Men in Houston were often startled and dismayed to learn about the problems their wives and daughters lay before them. Believing low taxes and wages were good for business, they had ignored the consequences for neighborhoods that lacked private sources of funding for up-to-date sewers and roads, effective schools, well-maintained housing, and care of aging or indigent neighbors. Although Houston's male and female leaders maintained gender-specific clubs and activities, they were eager to cooperate when addressing urban blight. Men admired "sweet-voiced" female zealots who paced the sidewalks downtown and buttonholed their male friends on "tag" days—how could any self-respecting man refuse to wear a tag in his lapel to demonstrate support of the "dainty Miss or Mrs." and her worthy cause?[25] Women copied their husbands' business success to run their organizations with impressive efficiency and regard for expert opinion. Men appreciated female ability to identify the elements needed to build a city of recognized national stature. Women understood that no project would flourish without access to male-dominated business, banking, industry, and government resources.[26]

Business leaders and their wives mingled politics, business, social life, and community activism. Rosters of exclusive men's clubs, settlement house boards, city councils, and ladies' improvement societies repeat names in a web of interaction. The Houston Club, founded by socially prominent Houston men in 1894 "for literary purposes; to promote social intercourse among its members, and to provide for them the convenience of a Club House," was a "hub of civic [and] commercial activity." The club headquarters in the so-called Mason Block on the northeast corner of Main at Rusk, owned by Houston Club member, real estate investor, and city Commissioner John T. Mason, also housed the Houston Lyceum and the Single Tax Club. The Ladies' Reading Club, the Ladies' Shakespeare Club, the City Federation of Women's Clubs, and the George B. McClellan Post 9, Department of Texas, Grand Army of the Republic, held regular meetings in the Lyceum hall.[27] The Thalian Club, organized on October 24, 1901, to maintain a library and promote "painting, music, and other fine arts," built a handsome four-story $40,000 clubhouse suitable for social events in 1907. The club boasted as members "the very flower of Houston; men who . . . are the backbone and strength of the city."[28] Will and Mike Hogg and their business partner Raymond Dickson, son of the club's founder, were active Thalians until the club roster of 175 merged with the Houston Club in February 1918.

The success of these and other clubs reinforced the bonds of civic leadership with ties of friendship. In club chambers business deals were settled, civic projects were born, and political careers were fostered. While members often disagreed about operational details, they shared an overarching faith in Houston's future as a great city. They believed in business "efficiency" and "progress," and they harbored no doubts that they could build institutions of enduring value to themselves and to fellow Houstonians. As yet unable to envision a broad-based and inclusive power structure, Houston's paternalistic boosters were at least beginning to sense that economic progress must be wedded to humanitarian concern for fellow citizens. Sophisticated Houstonians, aware of Andrew Carnegie's admonitions to invest surplus private wealth in institutions that would benefit average citizens, began to imagine how they, too, could use their wealth to mold their community.[29]

Author and contemporary social observer Julia Cameron Montgomery, moved by the impressive dedicatory ceremonies that drew an international roster of renowned participants to launch Rice Institute in October 1912, compiled a compendium of Houston's institutions and leading citizens as a "permanent record of the progressive era upon which Houston is entering." She recognized Houston's importance as a commercial center but wanted to describe "Houston as a desirable dwelling place" where "social and moral uplift" would touch "every phase of civic life; where health consideration is vital, and public comfort, pleasure, and recreation receive definite provision." Her vision of community suggests that many Houstonians, newcomers and natives alike, were awakening to the changes commercial success had brought to their lives.[30] In the decades ahead a circle of men and women would emerge who were dedicated to a community that nurtured institutions created and sustained for the public good. Exemplary among these community visionaries were the Hogg siblings, Will, Ima, and Mike, who inherited a family tradition of public service and who worked for seven decades to make Houston a great city.

THE HOGG FAMILY HERITAGE

The Hogg family had been established in East Texas since 1839, when the patriarch Joseph Lewis Hogg (1796–1862) and his wife, Lucanda McMath Hogg, settled near Nacogdoches. A lawyer and planter, Joseph Lewis built Mountain Home in 1846 near Rusk, where he acquired 2,500 acres of timber and farmland and twenty slaves before the outbreak of war in 1861. Here he and his wife welcomed citizens of Republic and State with a cordial hospitality that framed the basis for many nostalgic family tales spun by their oldest daughter, Martha Frances (1834–1920), in later years.[31] At Mountain Home their fifth child and third son, James Stephen Hogg (1851–1906), was born. It was the memory of Mountain Home that James Stephen incorporated in a tribute to "Home! The Center of Civilization: The pivot of constitutional government: The ark of safety to happiness, virtue and Christianity: Home! The haven of rest in old age. . . . Every man should have a home!" It was the loss of Mountain Home after the Civil War that later motivated the retired governor to purchase the old Patton Place in West Columbia as a haven for himself and his motherless children.[32]

Following a tradition of political and military engagement established by his forebears in Virginia, in North Carolina, and across the cotton South, Joseph Lewis served in the Eighth Congress of the Republic, supported Sam Houston's efforts to gain annexation to the United States, headed the Judiciary Committee of the Texas State Constitutional Convention, and was a member of the first Texas State Senate. As a forward-looking pioneer, Joseph Lewis headed a railroad convention in 1854, and as a man of culture he supplemented his children's schoolhouse education with private tutors in music and poetry. Like most members of the planter class, he joined the fight between the United States and Mexico in 1846 and followed his state out of the Union in 1861.

The Hogg family suffered severely during the Civil War. Joseph Lewis perished in Corinth, Mississippi, while leading a Texas brigade for the Confederacy. Lucanda and their youngest child, Richard, died in 1863, leaving household management to Martha Frances, a widow since 1857. Oldest son Thomas Elisha, himself a war veteran, struggled to support the family as a lawyer, newspaper editor, and author of several well-received epic poems, while brothers John and James Stephen sacrificed formal education to help support the family. In the weakened and under-capitalized postwar economy, the young family could not wrest a living from the farm and timberlands and over time was forced to sell the heavily mortgaged land. The proud family heritage of political engagement combined with postwar hardships to inspire in James Stephen and in his children a passion to help Texas rise from defeat and reclaim its rightful place as a great state. As their lives unfolded, the governor and his children would be driven to action by this legacy of duty to family and responsibility to community.[33]

At sixteen, James Stephen—Jim, as he became known—hired on as a printer's devil for the Rusk *Texas Observer*, and he subsequently worked for newspapers in Palestine and Cleburne. Friends remembered him as

penniless, large, and awkward, a poorly educated youth who spent his leisure studying. Boyhood companion Charles Young recalled that Jim did
not go hunting or fishing but instead "feasted" on the stories of old men
lounging at a local hotel.[34] After trying sharecropping and cotton ginning
and being shot by outlaws in 1869, Jim decided to become a lawyer and
fight the lawlessness that still threatened East Texas. In 1869 he also met
Sarah Ann (Sallie) Stinson, the daughter of a successful sawmill owner who
was completing her education at school in Quitman. For the next several
years he read law while publishing his own newspapers, first in Tyler and
after 1872 in Quitman. Serving as reporter, editor, typesetter, distributor,
and salesman, he often slept in his office and soon gained a reputation
for "fearless" editorials that expounded on fairness to all regardless of
station in life. Politics and journalism occupied his days, but he managed
to court Sallie Stinson, run successfully for justice of the peace of
Wood County (1872), and win Sallie's hand from a reluctant father on
April 22, 1874. The young couple moved into a four-room frame house
in Quitman, where their first child, William Clifford, was born in 1875,
and Jim was admitted to the bar the following year. Subsequent
moves took them to Mineola, where Ima was born in 1882, to Tyler,
where Mike was born in 1885, and to Austin, where Tom was born in
1887, as Jim advanced his political career from county attorney for
Wood County (1879–1881), to district attorney for Texas Seventh District (1881–1887), to Texas attorney general (1887–1891), and finally to
governor (1891–1895).[35]

In reminiscences Ima recalled a happy childhood filled with love for
a fastidious, charming mother and adoration for a principled, activist
father. As with any politician, Jim Hogg's conduct and motivation are
subject to varied interpretations. His bitterly fought second gubernatorial campaign and pioneering social and regulatory reforms left a legacy
of praise tempered by angry rhetoric, tall tales, and vicious cartoons
that deeply wounded his daughter.[36] Remembering a loving man who
never bore a grudge and a serious reader who championed higher education and spent hours discussing issues of the day with his children, she
despised accounts of a sweating giant in shirtsleeves gulping water from
a pitcher while railing against his opponents on the campaign trail—and
she denounced such stories in print years later. Yet politics was a spectator
sport in the late nineteenth century; at six feet three inches and some two
to three hundred pounds, Jim Hogg was a massive presence. His girth
was matched by a voice that projected over noisy crowds and a florid

rhetorical style that held spellbound the "little" people whose welfare he espoused against the power of special interests.[37]

Ima found it difficult to reconcile political hyperbole with her memories, and she adopted a protective, even obstructionist, attitude toward historians trying to explain her father's life. She worked closely with her hand-picked official biographer, Robert Cotner, sharing many family papers and stories with him; his detailed and laudatory biography of the governor remains the standard work. Unfortunately, Ima's guarded supervision of the family legacy has deterred subsequent study of an important political figure and limited understanding of how he acquired power, who assisted him, and why his name still carried political weight years after he left office. Nor does the biography satisfactorily explain how "the people's governor" could, as a private citizen, become chief lobbyist for business interests seeking ties to national financial markets. Was it only ironic coincidence that this erstwhile foe of "special interests" should form the Hogg-Swayne Syndicate to participate in the Spindletop bonanza and team with Pennsylvanian Joseph Cullinan and his New York investors to create the Texas Company, forerunner of Texaco?

To their children, however, Jim and Sallie Hogg were above criticism, examples to be emulated in every detail. The parents' actions, teachings, and written admonitions influenced every phase of their children's development in ways that informed the children's outlook on life, their professional choices, and their vision of a healthy community. At every turn, the Hogg children were guided by an insistent moral compass instilled in them by conscientious and engaged parents. Through their devotion to each other and to their family, Sallie and Jim demonstrated their belief that happy family life was the foundation of a strong society. Through their years of government service and their declared love for all Texans, they emphasized their credo that public service was the highest responsibility of each citizen. In their children they instilled the belief that their father's "early exposure to hard work and harsh realities of economic and political life gave him broad sympathy for the problems, frustrations, and needs of his fellow men." In later life, Ima emphasized her father's dedication to the people's business, noting that he worked from daylight to dark, took an hour for lunch at home, and had only a private secretary and stenographer to assist him.[38]

Apparently only Ima set down childhood memories, and she chose her anecdotes with care to illustrate the values she believed marked well-adjusted family life. Except for descriptions of elegant parties at the governor's mansion and mention of family friends with state and national political connections, a reader of Ima's memoirs could mistake her recollections for an idealized vision of any middle-class Victorian household in which the home was man's haven from ferocious competition and woman's domain of social dominance.[39] Certainly Ima's depiction of her mother resembles both the stalwart homemaker of countless advice books and the perfect Victorian lady limned by Elizabeth Brooks in *Prominent Women of Texas*. In 1896 Brooks praised Sallie Hogg as "quiet in her manners, retiring in her habits, unobtrusive in social intercourse, unostentatious in her hospitality, and instinctively humane in dispensing the sweet charities of life."[40] Eighty years later, many would remember Sallie's daughter as modest, quiet-spoken, thoughtful, and Texas's greatest humanitarian.

Sallie Hogg may have been petite at five feet two inches and distinguished by "her tiny, beautifully formed hands" and her "little feet," which "never gave her enough support." She may have always maintained "a sweet and refined appearance," but she also conveyed a steely determination not lost on her daughter. She managed a complicated household and was her husband's "confidant and advisor on all questions." The governor told Ima that "he always discussed everything with her, even his business and felt that a wife should be in every way a complete partner." As Sallie supported her husband's career, cheerfully standing by his side at tedious political receptions and preparing his lunch every day, so the governor relieved her of the noisy children by swooping them up in the carriage for long Sunday excursions while she rested. A remarkable housekeeper and ardent flower gardener, Sallie showed her daughter how to make a small income stretch to provide a bountiful table and welcoming atmosphere. She moved her household often before settling into the governor's mansion, then an old house "in dreadful disrepair . . . cracked and shabby." In fact, she and one or two helpers had to remove "buckets of old chewing gum" from tables, chair arms, and door moldings before completely redecorating. This thrifty woman who was renowned for her fine needlework and musical abilities ran her house like a business. "There were special days for everything and special ways of handling everything. There was complete order and always inventories taken." Yet she made her home the center of social life wherever she lived, hosting Sunday evening hymn-singing, amateur theatricals, and fondly remembered New Year's receptions complete with linen cloths and napkins, catered delicacies, low floral centerpieces, smilax and holly around the windows, mistletoe in the gaslight chandeliers, and dancing.[41]

Ima also remembered her father's attachment to home life. When separated from his family by his business demands or by the children's vacations in the country, he would write poignantly of his loneliness or report on domestic changes.[42] For Jim Hogg no home was complete without a garden; he planted rare specimens, vegetables and flowers, and native trees in Austin, and he boasted proudly of his agricultural experiments at Varner Plantation. Ima recalled that on each Arbor Day, celebrated on Washington's birthday when she was a child, her father would gather his children and their friends to plant trees.[43] Will, Ima, and Mike remembered these scenes of domestic felicity when they developed parklands, planted trees throughout Houston, and planned River Oaks as a residential community of winding esplanades and family-style homes set in landscaped gardens. Will and Ima also recalled frequent trips with the governor to political rallies and visits to hospitals, mental asylums, and schools. From these experiences they developed a willingness to fight for unpopular causes and an optimistic belief that problems could be addressed, that reform within established institutions was a viable path, and that the perfection of society was a goal that must be pursued.

If Ima's recollections of her mother's wifely role and housekeeping duties reflected a traditional nineteenth-century view of woman's work, her depiction of the senior Hoggs' parenting practices suggests that they did not follow the restrictive discipline often associated with formal Victorian child-rearing dictates. "Everything was always done to make our home life attractive to us and every encouragement was given us to stay there. Our grounds were a neighborhood playground," Ima remembered. She and her brothers were included in adult dinners at which guests discussed books and public affairs. Listening to these well-informed leaders stimulated their curiosity and taught them the value of seeking expert opinion. Although Ima had to learn needlework, she was allowed to engage in tomboy romps with her brothers, and all the children were encouraged to study foreign languages, read history and literature, and prepare for college. These indulgent parents laughed at their pranks, took them to cultural events at Millet's Opera House, and did nothing to squelch their rowdy enthusiasm. Sallie also guided her children's spiritual development, making sure they attended Sunday school and teaching gentle values of concern for others and love of order and beauty. A devout Methodist who adhered to prevalent Social Gospel tenets, Sallie taught her children that they must nurture the communities that had nurtured them. A capable musician, she recognized her daughter's musical talent by age three and guided Ima's early piano study until

Ima began lessons with a professional teacher at age six.[44] Will, much older than his siblings, was a favorite with his mother, who hoped he would become a Methodist preacher. During his teenage years, Will often accompanied Sallie on shopping expeditions and developed a taste for nice clothes and beautiful objects. Ima, as the only daughter, was a special companion and helpmate to her frail but dedicated parent.

In these happy family stories Ima alludes only fleetingly to an underlying tension in the household; Sallie did not enjoy robust health and often visited spas to regain strength drained away by pregnancies, household duties, and a fast-paced schedule. To give the tired mother further respite, the children usually spent summers with their maternal grandparents and aunts at their "commodious" old house in East Texas. Ima recalled her Grandfather Stinson as a sweet-tempered, gentle, and merry man with white hair and beard. A Civil War veteran, lay Methodist minister, and legislator who had moved his family to Texas from Georgia in 1860, James A. Stinson was active in the grange and used modern agricultural methods on his experimental farm.[45] Of greater interest to Ima was a mysterious attic full of trunks, a spinning wheel, a loom, and stacks of old books. Here she first learned to love old things and to associate them with her state's history. At the Stinson farm she also began her "love affair" with nature that would culminate in cultivation of a fourteen-acre garden at Bayou Bend, the Houston home of her mature years. Her grandfather Stinson was justly renowned for his flowering fruit trees, an element used in several Hogg gardens, and Ima later replicated the farm's brick-edged flower beds filled with jonquils, bulbs, and roses in her own landscape plans.[46]

Summer relaxation from household responsibility could not conquer Sallie's troublesome ailments; in 1895 she was diagnosed with tuberculosis, and doctors recommended a rest cure in Colorado. That summer Ima accompanied her mother to Pueblo for an extended visit with Governor Hogg's widowed older sister, Martha Frances Hogg Davis. Sallie's condition worsened, her husband and sons were hastily summoned, and she succumbed to the disease on September 20. Jim Hogg described his loss as the "severest shock" of his life and turned to his thirteen-year-old daughter for companionship.[47] The children were devastated. To the end of her life Ima could not speak of these last months when she helplessly watched her mother fade away, unable to bring her relief, but she could honor Sallie's memory by trying to emulate her fierce determination, love of beauty, and concern for others. Will turned inward, immersed himself in study and work, and used the "powerful engine" of imagination to drive "melancholy and dyspepsia" from his thoughts.[48]

Governor Hogg had to begin anew in 1895; his term of office had ended in March, and he scrambled to find a home and set up his law practice while frantically seeking medical advice about his wife's condition. Her death in September left a void he tried to fill by asking his sister Martha Frances (Aunt Fannie) to manage his home and help raise Ima, Mike, and Tom. Will, twenty when his mother died, was rarely home during the next decade because he was completing undergraduate and law school studies and beginning an independent law and business career in San Antonio and later in St. Louis. Indeed, despite the governor's efforts to provide a family atmosphere by purchasing a comfortable house on Rio Grande at Nineteenth Street, the children and their father were seldom together in Austin after Sallie's death. Governor Hogg traveled extensively for his clients; Mike and Tom soon left home for boarding school; and Ima attended schools in San Marcos and Austin before spending two "joyous" years at the University of Texas. In 1901 she traveled to New York City to begin rigorous piano study.[49]

Aunt Fannie's efforts to run her brother's household produced mixed results and caused Ima constant anxiety. Ima later recalled that Aunt Fannie disliked Tom, who had just turned eight when his mother died. Although Ima remembered Tom as "the most outgoing sweet child," she recalled that Aunt Fannie "punished him for everything." Terrified of his formidable, much older aunt, Tom often hid under his bed to escape her censure. He found school difficult and in later life could not settle successfully in an occupation, problems his sister attributed to lack of understanding and helpful intervention in his youth.[50] Equally devastating was Aunt Fannie's often-repeated but medically unfounded warning that the children might contract tuberculosis themselves and transmit the disease to subsequent generations. Her husband had died of tuberculosis, and her son had developed the disease, which he controlled by living in Colorado, so Martha Frances assumed that her brother's children would follow a similar pattern. Although Ima claimed to have had many beaux, she often commented that Aunt Fannie's warnings had kept her from marrying.[51]

The turmoil following their mother's death, the clumsy efforts of Aunt Fannie to discipline carefree spirits, and the cold comforts of boarding school drew the children to each other and to their father. Letters of affection, advice, and anecdote reveal the overpowering importance of Governor Hogg's influence on his children's development and reflect widely held Victorian values. The role of caring family patriarch suited Jim Hogg, and, like other fathers, he admonished his children to exhibit self-control and to be punctual, hardworking, sober, pious, honorable to others, and eager for self-improvement.[52] He also assured his children repeatedly, "No man ever had a more dutiful, decent, loving and lovable set of children than I have!"[53] Writing to Will on the eve of his second gubernatorial race, the governor told his son, "The guiding star of my life has been Duty and fidelity to Trust."[54] In other letters, he affectionately praised Will's exemplary behavior and good judgment, offered advice about college choices, and waxed eloquent when he learned his first-born son would follow him into the legal profession. "Had the wealth of the Vanderbilts been placed at my disposal as the earnings of honest labor I could not have felt happier than by the reception of your splendid letter." Note the implied reminder that riches earned by the sweat of one's brow are acceptable; wealth gained from inheritance is suspect.[55] Clearly Will was being groomed to step into his father's shoes. The governor asked his oldest son to supervise activities of the younger children and proffered advice about dealing with Mike and Tom—teasing Tom is all right because he is "always forgiving," but "jokes, tricks or diplomacy" must not be tried with Mike, who is "as sensitive and unforgiving as he is manly and honorable."[56]

If proud of his sons, the governor developed an extraordinarily close attachment to his daughter, telling her she was "the best friend I have this side of Heaven!" In 1904 he exclaimed, "I think of my God in the deepest gratitude first, then of thee! Your splendid character, your sweet disposition, your charming manners, your fidelity to your young brothers added to your thoughtfulness of me at all times . . . have so impressed me that it is but natural for me to make you second to no living being." Assigning attributes of the precious wife to the daughter, the widower admonished Ima not to study too hard and "to do your part by your health"; he bought her a ring "made after my own design from pearls selected by myself from a lot taken out of the river above Austin" as a mark of the "love and affection of an indulgent father for his ever-deserving, loyal daughter"; and he suggested she purchase a light gray silk dress because "your mother always looked best in that color." When Ima decided to break away from the Methodism of her mother's family, a decision that caused her much mental struggle and anxiety, her father told her he had no objection if she joined the Episcopal Church. Because God had "no choice of churches," he reassured her: "let your own conscience and better judgment be gratified in this question and I shall be satisfied."[57]

In many letters he revealed a protective paternalism that reflected his generation's view that "the daughter is solely an inspiration and refinement to the family itself and . . . her delicacy and polish are but outward symbols of her father's protection and prosperity."[58] At times, however, the governor's effusive affection seems obsessive. Writing to her from New York on her seventeenth birthday, he admitted, "I am not weaned from you. In every feature of your face, in every movement of your hand I can see your Mother! . . . She was honorable, truthful, gentle, faithful, generous, faultless. . . . In you I look for a friend and counselor as wise, as faithful, as true."[59] In other letters, the governor recognized Ima's profound influence over her brothers: "You have always exercised a fine *control* over Will. As to Mike and Tom, you know well, how they idolize you, and yield to your will." He also acknowledged her "ability to 'think'—to study—to investigate—to form your own judgment by process of reason on the facts—[which] has for many years attracted my attention with the deepest interest and pride. This is a rare gift."[60] These messages, while filled with affection and pride, may have produced conflicting emotions in his daughter; how was she to follow her mother's example of domestic perfection, be an independent decision maker, and pursue her own interests? How could she be her father's "worthy daughter" and forge her own identity?[61]

The governor's children found the lessons of his life, politics, and actions clear and consistent. Their father was a man of probity and honor whose word was his bond and who believed that public servants should discover the will of the people and act in their behalf. From him they learned that social issues were the business of every citizen. Like him, they believed that citizen engagement could improve community life. His children remembered him as a great reader who carried history books with him on trips and who believed "public education at public expense" was the foundation of a democracy.[62] They recalled his stories of a glorious Texas past and recognized that his commitment to education was informed by an understanding of the role history plays in shaping the future. The governor acknowledged the force of history at his death when he admonished his children to forgo a marble memorial and instead to "plant at the head of my grave a pecan tree and at my feet an old-fashioned walnut tree." When these trees, with their roots in the past, "shall bear, let the pecans and walnuts be given out among the plain people so that they may plant them and make Texas a land of trees"[63]—a land of greatness in the future. In one simple act, the governor reinforced critical lessons for his children: the values of symbol and simplicity; the importance of the natural world and good husbandry; and his love for all Texans who would build communities in the future. Surely he must have hoped that this request would endear him to posterity and affirm his role as the people's governor. Certainly it profoundly affected his children, who throughout their lives "endeavored to continue our father's concern for the tangible needs of the people" by planting their own trees in a literal and symbolic legacy of civic work and enduring institutions.[64]

WILL, IMA, AND MIKE HOGG

Just thirty-one in 1906 when his father died, Will was now head of the family, and he was quick to assume duties as surrogate parent, estate executor, and confidant. Ima, not yet twenty-four, collapsed after discovering her father dead in the home of his law partner and friend Frank Jones and was "nervous and restless, especially of nights" for several months.[65] Following two years of piano study in New York City, she had returned to Varner when her father's health declined after the train mishap he suffered on January 26, 1905. Despite several operations to repair the damage resulting from the accident, doctors concluded that the governor's heart was failing.[66] Ima remained with her father until his death, and Will, who was working for Mercantile Trust Company in St. Louis, made frequent visits to Varner. Father, son, and daughter enjoyed long talks about the future and developed a vision for publicly funded higher education in Texas. Mike became absorbed in his studies at college and law school after his father's death. Tom had left school "permanently" in 1905 and returned to Varner, where he had been "looking after" the fences and recuperating from ill health and feelings of aimlessness.[67]

In September 1906 Will took Ima and Tom to New York. Music study with her former teacher helped Ima "more quickly find herself." She decided to embark on a course of serious musical training and sailed for Europe in July 1907 for fourteen months of travel and study in Berlin.[68] Will concluded that he could best settle his father's estate and manage his own business partnerships from his father's headquarters in Houston. In March 1906 he opened an office, took rooms at the Rice Hotel, and joined the business elite of his adopted city, falling heir to his father's legal and oil interests as chairman of several advisory committees and assistant to Joseph S. Cullinan, president of the Texas Company.[69] Correspondence with Mike and Tom reveals that Will quickly embroiled himself in numerous "paternal" issues with his younger brothers and by 1909 had decided to establish "a home in Houston for you . . . , sister and myself.

She is all we have left to tie us together, and we owe it to her to fix her up as happily as possible. I know you boys will sanction anything I do."[70] Tom joined the Marines in 1907 and never made Houston a permanent home. After his marriage in 1913 he cited Varner as home but tried business ventures in Tyler and San Antonio before moving to Colorado and later to Arizona. At his death in 1949, Tom left much of his estate to the Hogg Foundation at the University of Texas, but he did not participate with his siblings in their extensive Houston philanthropy.

When Ima returned from Europe late in 1908, she and Will looked for an apartment to share. The pair changed quarters at least twice before Mike joined them in 1912, when the three siblings rented a home at the Oxford apartments. Ima moved to the Marie Louise Apartments in 1915, and the family finally settled in a house at 4410 Rossmoyne (now Yoakum) in early 1917.[71] At first the Hoggs rented from Ross Sterling, who had invited them to purchase in the enclave he was developing. Ima and the architect "contrived a good interior arrangement for the proposed house" by August 1916, so Sterling must have been willing to accommodate the Hoggs' wishes even though final purchase occurred in February 1919. From 1909 through the spring of 1918, Ima taught advanced piano students, some of whom went on to concert careers. In 1912 Mike began his business career in lawyers' quarters in the sixteen-story Carter Building, where Will maintained an office.[72]

Nothing in correspondence from these years suggests that Will, Ima, or Mike imagined lives apart, and friends often noted their mutual devotion. Will was particularly dependent on his siblings for companionship and came to rely on Mike's calm good sense in business and civic matters. After Will's death, an acquaintance told Mike he had "never seen one brother so devoted to another." Mike had been the "apple of [Will's] eye, . . . the source of his greatest pride."[73] However, Will could also be the heavy-handed older brother. According to friends, he "was always yapping about [Ima's] clothes," and he instructed business subordinates to secure his permission before executing Ima's donation requests. Letters to his siblings often included peremptory demands to "Do this now" underlined twice.[74]

Life for the Hogg family settled into a busy and productive pattern as the siblings joined Houston's bustling social and civic circles. Ima was one of twenty women who formed the Chautauqua Study Club in 1909 and, although a relative newcomer to Houston, was named its first recording secretary.[75] She also doggedly marched the streets on tag days for various charitable causes and pursued her professional interest by joining the

Girls' Musical Club (formed 1911), where she served as vice president and president (1913), meeting leader, and performer.[76] Most important, she persuaded fellow music lovers that Houston must have a professional symphony orchestra. Working with local musicians, she organized the first successful symphony concert on a hot June afternoon in 1913. Two years later Ima helped found the Texas Federation of Music Clubs in October and was named second vice president (1915–1917). Ima was elected president of the Houston Symphony Association in 1917 and helped host the Texas Federation's annual meeting in Houston in April 1918.

Will joined the Chamber of Commerce when it was revived in 1910 and focused his attention on social service projects, including support of the local Boy Scouts as vice president and finance chairman, service on the Emma R. Newsboys board, and financial leadership for the Houston Foundation. In 1913 Will supported Joseph Cullinan in a proxy fight that ended in both men's resignation from the Texas Company when they refused to bow to New York investors who insisted that the company move its headquarters to New York. Subsequently, Will, Cullinan, and Judge James L. Autry formed Farmer's Petroleum Company and several other oil and gas industry ventures, and in 1914 Will and Mike opened a cotton brokerage, Hogg, Dickson, and Hogg, with friend Raymond Dickson. The brothers also leased oil production rights on much of the Varner Plantation property.[77] As a member of the Chamber of Commerce Cotton Committee, Will lobbied hard at the local and national levels to stabilize pre–World War I prices by reducing cotton acreage across the South and by encouraging farmers to diversify crops.[78] He gained statewide fame as regent and champion of the University of Texas when he spearheaded the 1917 fight against Governor Jim Ferguson, who was trying to wrest control of the university from its Board of Regents. On January 15, 1918, after years of exploration, the first big oil well blew in at Varner Plantation. Followed by dozens of gushers, the field elevated the Hoggs to Texas's oil aristocracy.[79]

The siblings' civic activity came to an abrupt halt when the United States entered World War I. Mike and Will decided to disband Hogg, Dickson, and Hogg.[80] Mike joined the Army and was shipped overseas on June 13, 1918. After seeing action in the Ardennes and being wounded, Captain Mike, as he was called thereafter, was mustered out in 1919. Will lobbied his father's old friends, Secretary of State William Jennings Bryan and presidential advisor Edward Mandell House, and won a voluntary advisory government post for the duration of hostilities.[81] On July

11, 1918, Will opened an urgent telegram from old friend and Houston business associate Dr. Gavin Hamilton. The doctor advised that Ima, who was vacationing with friends in Delaware Gap, Pennsylvania, was "suffering from a marked degree of anaemia" and was "much run down, . . . particularly her nervous system." Hamilton recommended physical and mental rest and a diet of milk and eggs. Will immediately brought his sister to New York, where he was living, and began a desperate search for medical help.[82]

A sojourn with friends in Maine again ended in illness for Ima, and Will pressed her to consult a doctor. Although she had "positively refused to go to a sanitarium" in July, by October 1, 1918, Will directed that mail be sent to his sister care of Dr. G. W. Ford, Kerhonkson, New York. Almost immediately, Ima began to "see some benefit," and by November 2 she talked of returning home. In fact, she returned to New York on December 4 and to Houston on December 24. However, this episode proved only the first of several that persisted until 1924. After a motor trip with friends in March 1919, Ima again fell ill and on May 3, 1919, left Houston with Will to enter a "rest house" at 1939 Wallace Street in Philadelphia, where she was placed under the care of Francis X. Dercum, a prolific author and well-known specialist in nervous and mental disorders. Dercum followed the teachings of Silas Weir Mitchell, a famous Philadelphia neurologist who popularized the "rest cure" that called for extended and total bed rest, isolation from family and friends, a diet of cream and eggs, and massage. In the decades between 1880 and 1930, physicians frequently recommended this cure to middle- and upper-class women who suffered nervous disorders and melancholia, or "neurasthenia," as the symptoms of what is now recognized as depression were then called.[83]

Ima's condition was complicated by a dreadful mastoid abscess, which she later recalled as a searing pain and knocking sound in her ear. The abscess required surgery and was followed by pneumonia. She remained at the rest house until March 26, 1920, when she and a nurse went to a "pretty house in Ardmore" (Merion) outside Philadelphia, her home until March 1921.[84] During her stay in Merion, she took trips to Atlantic City and Lake Placid with a nurse, visited Will in New York, sat for a portrait by New York artist Weyman Adams, and purchased the eighteenth-century Queen Anne–style armchair of New England origin that inspired her collection of American decorative arts. Will's diary entries and correspondence indicate that he encouraged his sister's collecting as a therapeutic way to reignite her interest in living a full, healthy life.[85]

In March 1921 brother and sister returned to Houston and the excitement of occupying a "proud penthouse" atop the Great Southern Building at the corner of Preston and Louisiana. Built to house the recently formed Hogg Brothers, Inc., a family corporation created to handle the siblings' business ventures, the offices and roof garden became "a showplace of business maneuvering," entertaining, and civic planning until after Mike's death in 1941.[86] Following the company's first annual meeting in April, Ima again traveled to Philadelphia, where she was stricken with appendicitis, consulted Dr. Dercum, and underwent an operation in June 1921. From July 1921 until February 1922, Ima convalesced in Atlantic City, New York, and Lake Placid before going to Houston for a few months. On September 25, 1922, she again consulted Dr. Dercum, underwent another operation in late November, and remained in Philadelphia until December 12, 1922, when she returned to Houston to recuperate.[87]

In April 1923, having pronounced herself well, Ima joined her bachelor brothers and some friends for a trip to Europe. After landing in Quebec on August 1 and enjoying a three-month sojourn at Lake Placid, she was troubled by insomnia and consulted Dr. Austen Fox Riggs, a popular author and pioneering therapist who practiced in Stockbridge, Massachusetts.[88] Similar episodes of ill health—fatigue and "nervous disorders" accompanied by a physical ailment—continued to plague Ima throughout her life. Ironically, the archival record does not disclose a mental health diagnosis despite extensive correspondence between Will and Dr. Dercum. In lengthy interviews later in her life, Ima blames low spirits on physical causes, and records from the pre–World War II decades reveal that the Hoggs and their friends frequented sanitaria and spas for weeks at a time to recuperate from broken bones, pneumonia, rheumatism, and common complaints now quickly quelled by penicillin and antibiotics. These long periods of isolation and idleness in themselves could have induced depressed spirits.

The visit to Austen Riggs's Stockbridge clinic (November 11, 1923, to February 2, 1924) proved an inspiration that profoundly affected the Hogg family's philanthropy. Not only did Ima learn to control her fitful sleeping, but also she acquired a friend and mentor who reawakened her childhood interest in mental health care and taught her that every person "must have a purpose which you believe in and which you will give yourself to."[89] Riggs accepted voluntary patients only and espoused a regimen of therapeutic retraining that stressed "intelligent living," the value of "play," and the relationship of emotions to the nervous system. He believed nervous disorders were "due to some degree of maladaptation of the patient to his environment," and he advocated a "balanced life" of work and play that would enable individuals to achieve happiness as the "byproduct of living wisely." For Riggs, intelligent living required high ethical purpose in society and gave "equal importance" to "physical health, work, play, rest, leisure, and contemplation."[90] Ima later recalled that Riggs introduced her "to the equally important area of positive mental health" and showed her that "all of us can function more efficiently if we learn how to live with our emotions, if they become our allies in achieving important goals instead of complicating factors of inner conflict."[91] Ima shared these revelations with Will and Mike, and the "wholesome life" she and her brothers began to advocate in their philanthropy and business careers expanded Riggs's view of intelligent living beyond the individual to the community. Not only must the Hoggs and all individuals strive to lead purposeful, balanced lives, but also communities themselves must be developed as healthy, beautiful places that provide varied resources to their citizens.

THE HOGGS' PHILANTHROPIC MISSION

The family crisis precipitated by Ima's long illness, Mike's war experience, and the need to manage their newfound oil wealth judiciously turned the siblings toward careers in philanthropy. Unlike Andrew Carnegie, who famously articulated a gospel of surplus wealth management for the public good in his numerous writings, or Jane Addams, who made plain her vision of civic activism through settlement house work and crusades for world peace in several widely circulated books, the Hoggs never defined their beliefs in specific terms.[92] Nonetheless, correspondence with friends and colleagues, publication of *Civics for Houston* and *A Garden Book for Houston*, causes they espoused, and institutional legacies they bequeathed to the city reveal that the siblings were absolutely committed to philanthropy as a vocation that demanded their full attention. They were driven by a well-directed mission to strengthen humanitarian and democratic values explicated by the nation's founders and espoused by their parents. Archival evidence suggests that Will, Ima, and Mike explored two fundamental questions before formulating a consistent philanthropic vision: How could they manage their surplus personal resources effectively for the benefit of themselves and their community? How could they address the complexity of a rapidly changing twentieth-century world? If somewhat inchoate at first, a family philosophy grew ever clearer during the 1920s.

Parental example and family heritage had taught the Hoggs that individuals in a democracy must give back to their communities and defend the "highest ideals of citizenship."[93] They believed their growing wealth meant great opportunity and heavy responsibility. Almost immediately, they formed three convictions that framed their later careers as philanthropists. They concluded that the oil discovered under family land was a natural resource whose proceeds must be held in trust for the benefit of all Texans. They also developed the idea that communities and families could prosper only if each individual acquired the intellectual, emotional, and physical means to lead a "wholesome life" based on "principles of good living" that enabled individuals to "utilize their capacities fully and work with their fellows creatively."[94] Finally, like other contemporary philanthropists, they realized that philanthropy should be managed efficiently and that the process of giving should be organized to effect social change through preventive rather than palliative approaches to public health, education, and welfare.

As their vision matured, the Hoggs examined five critical questions: What should the ideal city look like physically? The great American city they imagined would integrate public parklands, private developments, and civic and commercial zones in carefully planned spaces that would preserve natural beauty and provide recreational outlets for all citizens. How could individuals meet their responsibilities and achieve their fullest potential in this physically beautiful urban space? Agreeing that individual, family, and community well-being were inextricably linked, the Hoggs focused attention and resources on the little-understood and controversial area of mental health care. How could Texans improve their education system? To honor their father's belief that only an educated citizenry could preserve democracy, the Hoggs created scholarships, nurtured Texas universities, and sat on the Houston Board of Education. What cultural institutions would identify Houston and other Texas cities as centers of humanitarian values? Personal inclination and knowledge of great European and American cities provided the answer—a symphony orchestra and a museum of art. And how could Texans participate in their greater national heritage and transmit their story to future generations? The Hoggs collected American art and artifacts and undertook historic preservation projects that underlined a fundamental family belief that only by studying and understanding values developed in the past could citizens of a democracy work effectively in the present and plan for the future. The Hoggs' vision of a wholesome community—a place that supports access to parklands, music, and art, nurtures knowledge of the "American heritage which unites us,"[95] and provides social service and mental health care assistance—links them to generations of American idealists who advanced a moral response to change. The urban ideal they espoused and the institutions they nurtured profoundly influenced their contemporaries and changed forever the city they loved.

The Hoggs' philanthropic vision developed slowly over time as the siblings held "numerous discussions" to execute the "common goals we had in mind."[96] References in statements, diaries, and interviews reveal a close working relationship that encompassed business and philanthropy. Although all three traveled widely, maintained apartments in New York City during the 1920s, and spent many months apart each year, they consulted each other continuously and developed a family approach to problem solving.[97] All three understood that their philanthropies should not be exclusive even if their personal friends formed a restricted, homogeneous circle. "All" Texans meant every citizen of the state, and they specifically set aside funding to support under-served African-American and Hispanic communities. Their demands for fairness to minority groups, while paternalistic, were enlightened and daring in a Southwestern city governed by legal separation of African Americans and whites and steeped in traditions of prejudice against immigrants from Mexico. Although classified as "white" during the Hoggs' lifetimes, Hispanics were systematically excluded from economic, political, and social leadership circles. Childless themselves, the Hoggs placed saving children at the heart of their dreams for family and community, whether through education, child guidance to improve mental health, or mentoring youth.

Once they had identified an issue or problem, they plunged into months of self-education. Books, pamphlets, and study papers accompanied them when they traveled across the country to learn firsthand how others had addressed various issues—from urban planning to historic restoration to school lunch menus. Their ties to political and business leaders enabled them to forge public-private partnerships and bring people from diverse backgrounds together to ensure broad-based support for their ideas. All three siblings proved particularly zealous and vocal in their attempts to persuade the public to support controversial issues such as city planning, mental health care, and a no-third-term drive to unseat Franklin Roosevelt in 1940. Finally, the Hoggs tried to leverage their wealth by developing partnerships with community leaders and other philanthropists. By no means Houston's wealthiest donors, they struggled to ensure that their dreams involved others and were adopted as city or state projects. What a friend said of Will in 1933 applied to his siblings as well: they "had a vision of a great city and a great state and [they] labored incessantly and gave lavishly that this might be realized."[98]

Will, Ima, and Mike worked well together because each sibling brought different strengths to the team, although all three displayed a marked reticence and modesty frustrating to the historian trying to unravel their myriad activities. Reporters did their best to capture the Hoggs in photographs or record Will's far-ranging and often exotic trips, Ima's many good works, and Mike's hunting and flying escapades. The candid poses of most shots suggest, however, that none of the Hoggs courted publicity. Will crept out of town when word reached him that he had been named Rotary Club Man of the Year in 1928; Ima accepted awards but then often shunned congratulatory ceremonies; and Mike seems to have been content to play the "little brother" role of relative obscurity. They did, however, recognize the importance of their family heritage and the seriousness of the civic work they had undertaken, and in later life Ima organized papers pertaining to the family's vast philanthropy and civic activism and distributed them to archives in Austin and Houston.[99]

Playful affection and stalwart support characterize the strong bonds that bound the siblings. Numerous nicknames pepper their correspondence—Podsnapps and Miss Titewadd (variously spelled) were avid collectors; Bilog, Mikandi, and Mikalis corresponded furiously with friends—although most Houstonians knew the Hoggs as Bill or Will, Miss Ima, and Mike or Mickie. To each other, they were Brother, Missima, and Mickey. To posterity the Hoggs remain three siblings who worked feverishly on behalf of mutual and individual interests. Will and Ima urged each other to pursue their newfound collecting passions in the 1920s; Mike and Will were proud of Ima's musical adventures and were closely allied business "chums"; and Ima made her maiden political speech when Mike requested her support for Republican Wendell Willkie during a 1940 no-third-term campaign. Ima developed a circle of friends—librarian Julia Ideson, pianists Eloise Chalmers and Mary Fuller, Austin resident Dot Thornton, Houston Symphony co-worker Nettie Jones, and philanthropist Estelle Sharp, among others—with whom she traveled and shared civic interests. Will and Mike acquired a number of business and hunting cronies, including the popular pre–World War II humorists

O. D. D. McIntyre, Irvin Cobb, and Will Rogers. The exchange of letters among the McIntyres, Cobbs, and Mike Hogg and his wife, Alice, is a touching monument to powerful friendship. For many years the Hoggs traveled with Houston's Sharp, Blaffer, and Cullinan families, celebrated Christmas with them, and engaged them in civic enterprises and business ventures. Guest lists for the Hoggs' frequent parties included the James A. Baker family and members of the Rice Institute faculty as well as fellow workers on their civic projects.[100]

The family built a diversified business empire of investments in insurance, cotton factoring, oil and natural gas, and real estate as well as ventures in shoe manufacturing and flirtations with Hollywood and Broadway. Will was the visionary who always wanted to enlarge any proposed business scheme; level-headed Mike provided the steadying hand and "acted as a brake to the impulsive and emotional outbursts of the dynamic and dominating elder brother."[101] In the 1930s Mike's "superior abilities" and "invariably cheerful and optimistic" attitude increased the value of company properties, even in hard economic times.[102] Opinions vary about Ima's business interest, but she was eager to assume management of Hogg Brothers when Mike died in 1941 and displayed astute business acumen when negotiating purchases for her collections and organizing her estate in later life.

Politics always fascinated and frequently disappointed the governor's children, whose high standards of proper public conduct for their fellow Democrats were rarely met. Will single-handedly drove the campaign that unseated Governor Jim Ferguson in 1917, and every Democratic governor and gubernatorial candidate from 1906 until the 1970s sought the magic endorsement of Hogg family members. Will and Mike also were kingmakers in local politics. Their exposure of perennial Mayor Oscar Holcombe's real estate peculation and their subsequent support for friend and fraternity brother Walter E. Monteith assured Monteith's victory as mayor and "a good house-cleaning" for Houston in 1928.[103] To prepare for the 1928 Democratic National Convention that descended on the city in June, Will and Mike supported the citywide effort to build a convention hall and welcome delegates. Will conceived, financed, and staffed Hospitality House, a fan-cooled tent across from the hall where delegates could meet local volunteers, find refreshments, and rest from their labors on the overheated convention floor.[104]

Mike viewed Prohibition as "the greatest blight that has ever been put upon this country" and represented Houston on a fourteen-member state committee to campaign for the repeal of the Eighteenth Amendment in

Texas.[105] Although ill with the cancer that killed him, Mike launched Texas's "clean upstanding fight" to galvanize "old time" Texas Democrats who hoped to prevent Franklin D. Roosevelt from winning a third term as president. Disillusioned by the president's New Deal policies, Mike and his followers espoused the two-term precedent set by George Washington 150 years earlier as a sound protection against excessive executive or individual power. As state chairman of Democrats for Republican Wendell Willkie, Mike canvassed hundreds of donors all over Texas and spoke to huge crowds about the "real danger to our most cherished institutions . . . the great American tradition of rotation in office" that guaranteed "against the abuses of power" and that "upheld the principles of my father." He even convinced sister Ima to make her first political address to Houston's radio audience—a resounding call to support Republican Willkie that was "bubbling with patriotic fervor."[106] Will never ran for office, but Mike completed two terms in the Texas State Legislature (1927–1931), and Ima won a six-year term on the Houston Independent School District Board of Education (1943–1949).

Will assumed leadership of family affairs from 1906 until his untimely death in 1930. An impulsive, sometimes autocratic man with a hearty voice and demeanor, Will also could be softhearted. He helped his "fellows" attain the good life because of "reverence for the memory of his father and mother." Considered "forthright and fearless," Will avoided recognition of his generosity by often giving anonymously.[107] He was prone to enthusiasms and grandiose schemes, and his explosive temper was well documented by frequent letters of apology. Yet every Christmas he sent dozens of boxes of pecans, candy, and cigars to friends and acquaintances. One youngster received nineteen foreign dolls purchased during his travels in 1930, and Will rewarded five special young ladies with a handsome, fully equipped playhouse—a miniature version of their parents' home.[108] He hated hot weather; he loved to cook, hunt, take long walks, and travel; and he knew how to play, whether in New York, Hollywood, Europe, South America, or yachting at sea. "Intensely civic minded," Will was self-effacing and often betrayed a "wistful desire to be of help."[109] His subscription books became famous. Brooking no refusals, Will would march into his friends' offices armed with blank-paged books bound in blue or black leather and demand pledges in writing to support worthy causes. He promised signatories that no one would pay unless the goal was met or exceeded; of course, no goal ever fell short because Will simply covered any difference himself. Friend

O. D. D. McIntyre recalled his "big heart," love of beauty, and "devastatingly vivid personality." Admirer Nina Cullinan, Joseph Cullinan's civic-minded daughter, noted years later that Will "set a standard" for others.[110] To fellow University of Texas Ex-Students' Association supporter Ireland Graves, Will was independent, generous, warm-hearted, unafraid, and uncomplacent.[111] To sister Ima, Will was a fascinating, complex man whose deep wells of empathy were understood by few who knew him.[112]

Like his father, Will was a large man with erect posture, receding hair, and a square jaw. Sheepish about his weight and looks, Will recorded attempts to diet and visits for hair treatments in his diary.[113] Remembered for his piercing gray-blue eyes, forceful demeanor, and resonant voice, Will was recognized both as a fashionably dressed bon vivant who loved a good joke and as a shy man who often jumped up and left a room when strangers appeared. Trained as a lawyer at Southwestern University at Georgetown (two years) and the University of Texas Law School (LLB 1897), Will wrote letters that resembled well-argued legal briefs animated by vivid imagery or colorful epithet. Known for his strong opinions, Will called one political opponent a "dirt-dauber of discord . . . the apostle of avarice" and despised political grandstanding and business chicanery.[114] A nationally recognized public figure perceived by journalists in the 1920s to share honors with Jesse H. Jones as Houston's most important citizen, Will detested the developer of downtown Houston because he questioned Jones's business ethics. He also felt Jones was self-important and exaggerated his civic deeds by taking sole credit that should have been widely shared. When Jones "allowed" himself to be put forward as a favorite son candidate at the 1928 convention, Will urged Governor Dan Moody not to "proffer as President this ill-fitted pseudo-statesman who . . . is always using the other fellow's chips to his own advantage" and "make yourself and your friends ridiculous."[115] Best known as a "Tender Tempest" who gave "Millions for Learning" and other dreams, Will was praised for introducing a "leavening influence of beauty" that saved Houston from commercialism and for promoting the "spiritual heritage of public service that will always be an inspiration to those who love their city."[116]

Ima—petite, blond, blue-eyed, and soft-spoken—was famous for her stylish hats, early-morning and late-night telephone calls, and clearheaded discernment. Many friends remember that it was impossible to turn her down. With dogged but charming determination she just worked and worked until she got what she wanted. Although Ima was recognized as a leading "Woman of Texas" by 1925, Hogg Foundation Director Robert Sutherland (1940–1970) described her as a humble, self-effacing, non-aggressive patron who shunned the limelight and avoided public appearances.[117] Wayne Bell, Lonn Taylor, and David Warren, young professionals who worked with Ima during the last decade of her life, recall that she was a natural teacher who loved to share her knowledge and a nurturing mentor who encouraged their interests. Always bubbling with imaginative ideas, she would often begin a telephone call with the ominous "I've been thinking" that signaled a new project was brewing. Taylor said "she had the most active, inquiring mind" and "continued to grow intellectually all her life."[118]

Friends believed that "the responsibility of [the family's] wealth was the overriding theme" that drove her life. They remembered her as a self-critical perfectionist with the "capacity to visualize and conceive constructive projects" and "the energy and ability to carry them through to fruition."[119] A strict taskmaster, she expected much of others but was totally committed to philanthropy as a way of life that demanded constant diligent work. Recalled by some as reserved, hard to know, and selective in her friendships, she loved dogs, gardening, and the solace of music. In fact, her lifelong battle with depression, her shy demeanor, and her determined effort to bring dreams to fruition suggest a complex and con-flicted person whose struggles mirror the transition from submissive lady to independent thinker and professional woman limned by historians of Progressive Era women. On the one hand, Ima seemed anxious to appear a charming and well-schooled gentlewoman who fit the conciliatory but supportive image of her beloved and long-gone mother; on the other, Ima was a decisive, outspoken, courageous, and knowledgeable innova-tor who admired professionalism, brooked little opposition to her stated objectives, and espoused causes long before they were widely understood. Although blessed with a talent to sell her ideas to others, she yet displayed "gracious firmness" when explaining any course of action.[120] Archival sources suggest that friends and contemporaries loved the volatile Will and fun-loving Mike, while they stood in awe of the iconic Ima.

In the words of a friend, Ima possessed "more gifts than one little body could handle, and she was a genuine authority on an incredible number of things, from dogs to silver to art and music."[121] This polymath received her formal education at the Coronal Institute in San Marcos, at the University of Texas (1899–1901), and at piano conservatories in New York and Berlin. While a member of the Downtown Club founded by professional and businesswomen in the 1920s, she described herself as a composer (1928) and philanthropist (1940s). In addition to her extensive philanthropic and volunteer work in Houston, she was the first woman president of the Philosophical Society of Texas (1948), a member of the Texas State Historical Survey (1953), and a member of the committee to plan the National Cultural Center (1960, now the Kennedy Center). In 1962 she was named to an advisory panel charged by First Lady Jacqueline Kennedy with redecorating the White House. In 1969 she joined former First Lady Lady Bird Johnson and former World War II leader of the Women's Army Corps and first secretary of the Department of Health, Education, and Welfare Oveta Culp Hobby as the first women named to the Academy of Texas. In later years Ima accepted a number of important local and national honors, always demurring that the accolade should be shared with many others.[122] When she transformed Bayou Bend from a home to a house museum, she worked steadfastly to remove all trace of her presence so visitors could experience their forebears' way of life without distraction.

Mike, also a large, reticent man who constantly watched his weight, was a sweet-tempered, convivial person with a great capacity for friendship. Suffering neither Will's manic highs nor Ima's depressed lows, he was a cheerful, calming influence who helped his brother and sister execute their grand schemes and fulfill their arduous work schedules. Business associates praised Mike's "superior abilities" and "courageous" leadership that enabled him to increase the value of Hogg Brothers holdings during the Depression years. Ever the optimist, he confided to his sister, who was traveling in Germany in 1936, "You and I will live to see the day that people are more prosperous and happier than they have ever been in the history of the world. This is just my own individual fool belief."[123] All his life, Mike had "faith in the ability of the American people to solve all their problems as I have faith in the American family to solve the problems of individual and family life."[124] A gregarious clubman and host who regularly entertained his many friends at home, Mike loved horses and dogs and was consistently among the first to be approached for civic improvements such as the YWCA building (1919) and the Houston City Athletic Club (proposed 1930). Like Will and Ima, he was a life member of the University of Texas Ex-Students' Association and made important contributions to building and academic programs on campus. Law school classmate Palmer Hutcheson remembered that his "beloved friend . . . never failed to place his Alma Mater first."[125]

Mike was educated at the Carlisle Military Academy in Arlington, Texas (September 1901–June 1903), the Lawrenceville School in New Jersey

(February 1904–June 1905), and the University of Texas (LLB 1911); he practiced law at his father's old firm in Houston (1912–1914); and then he devoted himself to business, philanthropy, and politics.[126] More likely to be found in town than either Will or Ima, Mike frequently conveyed Will's wishes to business and civic associates. In December 1929 he became president of Varner Realty and gradually assumed responsibility for all family business.[127]

In July of that year Mike had married Alice Nicholson, described by friends as charming and beautiful, a loving soul mate, gracious hostess, and "treasure" who drew close to Ima after Mike's sad loss to cancer in 1941.[128] Mystery attends Mike's wedding, which took place while Will and Ima were traveling. Ima recalled later that Will was crushed by Mike's defection from the family circle. Perhaps Mike feared his older brother's reaction, but once the family had met his bride, letters of enthusiastic affection flew among them, and Will bought his new sister extravagant gifts during the last year of his life. Family friends called Mike a "lucky stiff" and said Alice "has it all—beauty, charm, sense and sweetness."[129]

Mike met Alice in Austin while he served in the Fortieth and Forty-first Legislatures (1927–1931). As a politician he opposed state control and regulation of the oil and gas industry, opposed running pipelines into the Gulf of Mexico, and delighted in behind-the-scenes kingmaking.[130] He pushed his university friend Dan Moody to victory over Miriam "Ma" Ferguson but opposed a third term for his classmate in 1930, and he supported the liberal Ralph Yarborough in the candidate's losing bid for attorney general in 1938.[131] He was named Outstanding Texan in September 1934. When he died, hunting companion Irvin Cobb lamented the loss, noting that "Dear Mickie" had "died as he had lived—with courage, with unselfishness, with fortitude."[132] Ima and Alice discovered numerous mutual interests after Mike's marriage and continued to work together on social service, garden club, and art museum projects until Ima's death in 1975.

During his lifetime Will dominated family decision making, and journalists extolled his personal generosity, selfless fund-raising, and outspoken fight for a well-planned city. Mike's custody of the family legacy took a gentler turn in the 1930s as he consolidated family business activities, carried on Will's civic projects, and collaborated with Ima to create the state's first professionally managed charitable foundation. In some recollections Ima graciously credited Mike with suggesting a mental health focus for the institution she and Mike established to fulfill terms of Will's testament, but interviews and correspondence reveal Ima as the guiding genius that defined the Hogg Foundation's purpose. Indeed, in the thirty-five years that followed Mike's death, Ima blossomed as the creative standard-bearer of her family's urban ideal. An energetic, imaginative leader, Ima became the city's philanthropic icon. Houston and Texas were the fortunate beneficiaries of a family vision and determination unique in its breadth, persistence, and duration. Through success and failure, the Hoggs provided models for future activism and built institutions of lasting importance.

Chapter 2
Houston, a Domain of Beautiful Homes

During the Civil War young Elizabeth Fitzsimmons often stood at the end of Main Street to get a "clear view" of the high sandy banks across Buffalo Bayou from the gullies and black oozing mud below her perch. She and her friends organized carefree picnics in nearby woods filled with "magnolia bloom or dogwood blossom" or took steamboat rides to "some beautiful spot on the Bayou."[1] As a forceful club woman and outspoken advocate of civic improvement forty years later, Elizabeth Fitzsimmons Ring remembered the simple pleasures of her childhood. When houses, stores, and factories began to clutter favorite picnic spots, she decided to transform the bayou banks into public parkland. In 1899 Ring and an alliance of intrepid female activists stormed the all-male City Council to demand that municipal authorities save the deteriorating but historic Kellum-Noble house and create a city-funded park on the "ragged acreage of underbrush" that surrounded the old homestead.[2]

Mayor Sam Houston Brashear responded to this unusual female agitation by purchasing sixteen pine- and oak-covered acres "full of gullies" straddling Buffalo Bayou to create City Park, later renamed Sam Houston Park.[3] Designed by city engineer J. W. Maxey and dedicated in September 1899, the park proved so popular it had to be reworked in 1906 by the newly elected commission government of Mayor Horace Baldwin Rice. Mayor Brashear also recognized that private companies could or would not provide citywide utility services, so he hired New York civil engineer Alexander Potter to develop a plan for the city to gain control of electricity, water, sewage treatment, and garbage disposal. With these modest but noteworthy steps, Houstonians began a continuing struggle to preserve natural beauty while developing the city's physical environment. For more than seventy years, members of the Hogg family confronted the dual challenges of environmental conservation and urban expansion through their civic activism, their business ventures, and their philanthropy.

HOUSTON IN 1900

When James Hogg and fellow oil men began to transfer business operations to Houston after 1901, they found a prosperous small town where cows, horses, and chickens inhabited utilitarian yards behind rambling turreted mansions or more modest clapboard structures.[4] A residential community of "irregular uniformity" radiated out about one or two miles from the commercial center at Congress and Main Streets, and foreign-born immigrants mingled with white and black Houstonians in the city's six wards that were developing north and south of Buffalo Bayou. By custom, white, African-American, and Mexican residents congregated in clearly defined neighborhoods, a restrictive pattern reinforced by employment opportunities and "whites only" union membership. Not until the city passed an ordinance in 1903 mandating separation of African-American and white passengers in trolley cars did legal segregation canonize tradition in bonds that tightened for thirty years and were not broken until after World War II. In 1901 commercial activity clustered in a few downtown blocks, and a small but growing manufacturing sector was slowly moving eastward along both banks of Buffalo Bayou toward the turning basin and ship channel that were being dredged to accommodate seagoing vessels and access to the Gulf. Pockets of industry also had developed north of downtown where railroads converged and west of City Park around the Freedman's Town African-American settlement south of Buffalo Bayou.

Nineteenth-century Houston residents naturally gravitated to bayou banks outside city limits for picnics, steamboat rides, and "happy hours ... gathering wildflowers and berries" because the ravines and swales shaded by oaks and magnolias broke the monotony and heat of the flat coastal plain.[5] Periodic flooding drove commercial and residential builders southward to the slightly higher ground of the bare prairie farmlands or northward to suburbs on the thirty-foot "heights" above the original city. Immediate bayou environs not reserved for wharves were sold for privately financed cemetery and park development. Hebrew (now Beth Israel) Cemetery, founded in 1844 and the oldest Jewish institution in Texas, and City Cemetery (now Founders Memorial Park) were located outside city limits south of the bayou along the road to San Felipe. Glenwood Cemetery, organized and designed by transplanted English horticulturist Alfred Whitaker in 1871, exploited the site's natural ravines and old-growth trees north of Buffalo Bayou just west of town. Curving drives and parklike vistas attracted subscribers and visitors to Houston's version of the rural cemetery park. Just outside the city limits at the time, Glenwood, like other landscaped memorial grounds throughout the country, became a desirable recreational venue for scenic, meditative strolling. Not only did these serene oases provide recreational space, but also their more remote locations protected nineteenth-century city residents from the unhealthy "miasmas" believed to emanate from burial grounds.[6]

South of Buffalo Bayou and west of downtown, Merkel's Grove attracted members of the Schuetzen-Verein, a German-American riflemen's club, while Anglo settlers congregated at Vick's Park (now Cleveland Park) on the Bayou's north bank.[7] Magnolia Park, south of Buffalo Bayou just two miles east of the city center, became a favorite play and picnic area for white Houstonians. Developed by John T. Brady in 1890 and connected to the city by Brady's Houston Belt and Magnolia Park Railway, the area's 3,750 mature magnolia trees, gravel paths, and water frontage were "better known to Houstonians than any other suburban acreage." Unfortunately, twenty years after the park's establishment, the Magnolia Park Land Company decided to sacrifice natural beauty for commercial gain and promote industrial and residential lots. The Houston Electric Company also hoped to lure streetcar customers to more remote parts of town and developed Highland Park in 1903 as a tourist destination north of the city at the juncture of White Oak and Little White Oak Bayous. Ten-acre Emancipation Park still stands on land purchased by African-American residents in 1872 in a Third Ward residential neighborhood between Buffalo and Brays Bayous. When the space was donated to the city in 1916, it became the first public park available to black citizens.[8]

Newcomers, streetcars, and skyscrapers changed the cityscape after 1900 as the municipality spread fingers of development in all directions into Harris County and began annexing unincorporated neighborhoods. By 1905 the automobile age had arrived in Houston: statisticians counted 80 horseless carriages that year, 1,031 motors by 1911, and an amazing 34,869 cars by 1922. While automobiles remained luxuries for the well-heeled, jitneys, streetcars, and buses connected worker to workplace. In 1908 an enthusiast exclaimed, "There is never a time when our streets are not crowded with busy, hurrying shoppers, men, women and children, white, black and yellow—all are here." Pedestrians admiring "handsome jewels, furs and lace" in shop windows had to "stand out of harm's way" as automobiles and carriages rushed "up and down with their freight of shoppers."[9] The twenty-six miles of pavement noted in 1903 included nine of brick, six of asphalt, six of gravel, three of *bois d'arc* blocks, and one of macadam. By 1908 the county had contracted to build thirteen miles of paved roads, and the city government had floated an ordinance authorizing $100,000 in street-paving bonds.[10] Subsequent agreements bartered a one-third/two-thirds split between city and property owners to spur paving. If these transportation innovations spelled comfort and improvement to most residents, they produced unforeseen circulation and communication problems that intensified as the human and vehicular populations boomed and development spread across the prairie.

In the 1910s skyscraping office buildings began to dominate the commercial sector, and building sites encroached on residential neighborhoods as handsome mansions fell to the wrecker's ball and developers scrambled to build banks, law firms, cotton-brokerage houses, and oil industry headquarters. Hotels and apartments with roof gardens also began to climb several stories into the sky.[11] By September 1909 a *Daily Post* columnist noted that Houston's ten-story buildings could be seen for miles around as they rose boldly on the flat prairie to "puncture the blue firmament—and herald to the approaching visitor the location of the South's commercial center." The columnist then described the sixteen-story Carter Building—the tallest in Texas—under construction and claimed that Houstonians "no longer marvel when a building reaches ten or more stories."[12] The "big, broad buildings" were "bunched toward the center of the city," but in 1910, Boston architect William Ward Watkin "bumped and splashed . . . through a little pine-grown belt to an open, endless, formless swamp" three miles south of downtown where he had been told to construct the campus of the Rice Institute on ten tracts of property (nearly three hundred acres).[13]

As oil industry employees poured into Houston, numerous residential neighborhoods were platted, and the rattle of streetcars resounded farther and farther from the city center. Wealthy Houstonians migrated east of downtown toward the Houston Country Club built on Brays Bayou in 1909 or moved south of downtown to secluded enclaves platted on flat, treeless prairie farmland that had been annexed to the city in 1903. Middle-class residents followed the streetcars to suburban developments. William A. Wilson Realty Company promoted Woodland Heights (1907–1910), a "picturesque woodland" north of the city with "splendid old trees, sandy soil, and perfect drainage." Wilson declared that the 106-acre site provided the "best of improvements and facilities," fire protection, electric streetlights, streetcars, city utilities, fine schools, and graded streets. "Just far enough from the business center . . . to insure the quiet and repose of an ideal residential district," this neighborhood attracted "men of character and standing in the community" and forbade liquor sales or "any other kind of trade or business whatsoever." A moderately priced and hugely popular cottage or bungalow home in Woodland Heights, "sold to white people only," included a modern bathroom and a kitchen equipped with refrigerator, sink, and gas range.[14] Magnolia Park Addition (1909), a community of modest homes east of downtown between Harrisburg and the newly constructed turning basin (1906–1907), was designed to house the families of workers employed in ship-channel industries. Privately operated rail lines carried residents downtown, and within a few years this suburb, too, had been swallowed by the insatiable city.[15] Houstonians bewildered by new neighbors, new industries, and new buildings were attracted to the excitement generated by so much expansion but repelled by the confusion caused by congestion and change. How could individuals find stability, safety, and beauty among frenetic urban activity? How could they balance the demands of a growing economy with desires for an attractive place to live?

In some ways Houston's astonishing growth still seemed controllable in the 1900s and 1910s. Residential developers leapfrogged older neighborhoods to plat suburbs on open farmland. Manufacturers located plants near rail lines and port facilities north and east of downtown. Commercial expansion shot upward into densely packed multistory buildings. A secondary civic center grew around Rice Institute on South Main Street when George Hermann left his estate for park and hospital purposes. It almost seemed as if builders were implementing a spontaneous plan for land use, but by the 1920s, few could ignore the problems created by competing individual initiatives in an urbanizing, industrializing, fast-growing city whose population expanded 74.9 percent in ten years.[16] Rural migrants attracted to high-paying jobs in the oil industry fled exhausted farmlands and poured into an area that already was absorbing trained workers from across the nation. Main Street became impassible as major arteries and electric railways carrying shoppers, deliverymen, and business executives converged on the downtown center. Suburban developers, especially in unincorporated areas outside city jurisdiction, followed no uniform building codes or plat regulations, and many contractors provided substandard amenities or failed to install utilities altogether. Blocks of privately developed streets constructed of various materials did not meet seamlessly, and some areas lacked paved thoroughfares well into the 1920s.

When the growing city incorporated new developments, often under pressure from contractors, the municipal government was saddled with the costly burden of making streets and utilities conform to city standards. Gaps between satellite settlements and the central business district downtown were often neglected and unsightly. Yet William Ward Watkin, looking back in 1927, noted that the 1910s provided a great opportunity to plan a beautiful, functional city. Texans, he concluded, thought "in no small terms." The "amity of purpose, directness of action and fine high-standing enthusiasm" that "are the known attributes of Houston and its leading citizens" assured a high level of civic engagement at a moment when residents and public officials needed to allocate responsibility and resources to build their "glorious" future.[17] Watkin and fellow visionaries like the Hogg family began to ask themselves what kind of urban environment would help Houston thrive. How could the city's energetic population and thrumming economy be contained in a sensible urban plan?

CITY PLANNING IN HOUSTON, 1900–1919

The ongoing planning processes associated with the city planning movement were relatively new phenomena before World War I, although ideas advanced by Frederick Law Olmsted, George Kessler, and others in the nineteenth century had been eagerly embraced by progressive reformers grappling with rapid urbanization. A response to the unforeseen congestion and blight that accompanied industrial, technological, and transportation changes, planning was made possible by the professionalization of American life and the search for "expert" solutions to unexpected late-nineteenth-century social problems. Many Houston reformers were acquainted with Frederick Law Olmsted's defining plans for Central Park, New York (1857–1876), and with his far-flung and seminal planning work in other New York cities, in Chicago (1870–1895), in Boston (1878–1920), and in Washington, D.C. (1875–1894). Because of ties to St. Louis and Kansas City banking, insurance, and railroad interests, businessmen like Will Hogg were familiar with the private-street enclaves of the former city and with George Kessler's extensive and ambitious plan (1893) for parks and boulevards in the latter.[18] As Houston's business and professional leaders grappled with economic expansion, they began to explore planning strategies that might contain change, facilitate growth, and stabilize land values to provide a secure home life for the city's energetic population. Despite Houston's late-twentieth-century reputation as a city of uncontrolled development, today's metropolis also can lay claim to a serious engagement with urban planning processes that were attuned to national trends during the 1910s and 1920s.

The 1900 hurricane that demolished Galveston awakened reformist zeal on the island and in neighboring Houston. Fueled by a desperate need to banish corruption and inaction from city hall, Galveston became the first U.S. city to adopt a commission form of government. Houstonians also embraced this new urban reform as a community ideal and in 1904 elected the second U.S. municipal commission. Viewed favorably by business leaders as "a governing body which should resemble as nearly as possible the board of directors of a business corporation," the small commission or council bypassed the ward system and its perceived control by special interests. Voters held citywide elections for all commissioners so each commissioner owed allegiance to the whole community and oversaw specific government departments and their staffs.[19] In the 1910s and 1920s these commissioners took a broader view of civic responsibility than the ward bosses they had replaced. Step by slow step, they pushed city government to respond to citizen demand for services, to play a pivotal oversight role in the city's development, and to mediate conflicting private agendas. During these decades, municipal authorities structured an infant, professionalized bureaucracy to establish building, paving, and platting codes; oversee public sewerage and utilities; tackle public health issues; project transportation needs and traffic patterns; and organize park and recreation sites.

The influential writings and projects of Frederick Law Olmsted (1822–1903) shaped a vision of the built environment that dominated urban development in the United States from his unveiling of New York's Central Park in the 1850s through the 1920s. Obsessed with organization and planning, Olmsted was an advocate of moral environmentalism who believed parks should provide humanizing vistas for restorative contemplation and democratizing venues where all classes of society could mingle and relax on equal terms. In his urban parks, peripheral suburbs, and connecting parkways, Olmsted tried to recover a feeling of community that was lost in dense, impersonal cities. Using broad expanses of lawn and carefully placed trees, he recreated pastoral scenery, harmonized the city with nature, and separated residential and recreational havens from the turmoil of commercial and industrial zones. These ideas were adopted in hundreds of urban projects in the next decades and played a critical role in Houston's development.[20] Following publication of the massive and widely acclaimed Plan of Chicago, produced by architects Daniel H. Burnham and Edward H. Bennett in 1909, many municipalities began to allocate funds to plan the growth of their cities. These civic reformers imagined a new "comprehensive city, at once thriving and humane, commercial and domestic," that encompassed central business districts, residential neighborhoods, recreational spaces, and civic centers housing educational, governmental, and cultural institutions.[21]

In Houston as in other American cities, progressive citizens who hoped to develop a park system as an antidote to urban squalor were the first to advocate planning processes. These park developers quickly became embroiled in debate about the problems of traffic circulation and the best use of private and public land within a metropolitan area. Their wish to create a beautiful physical environment also meshed with Progressive Era efforts to uplift the entire population by providing safe workplaces, widespread public education, modern health care, proper sanitation, competent child care, and adequate assistance to the needy. Pre–World War I advocates of the City Beautiful and 1920s proponents of the City Functional translated the language of progressive reform into architectural structure and landscape design.

Like Olmsted, advocates of the City Beautiful called for creation of large natural parks joined together by shaded boulevard parkways. Proponents believed that the park-parkway combination would provide ample recreational spaces for the average citizen who could not afford spacious private gardens, while the beautiful park drives would encourage wealthy residents to construct elegant houses and well-tended gardens along their curving byways. City Beautiful architects also called for development of handsome, even monumental civic buildings centered on a formally landscaped square or mall that emphasized the moral significance of these seats of education, government, and culture. Critics of pre–World War I planning complained that too much emphasis was placed on grandeur and beauty and not enough on sound scientific principles. Gathering reams of statistics and applying a "businesslike" analysis to their findings, postwar advocates of the functional city felt that it was not enough to provide beautiful park spaces, shady boulevards, and handsome civic centers. Planners should take a further step and examine the needs of an entire region. Armed with demographic data and analysis of natural resources and business demands, designers of the functional city should develop residential, commercial, industrial, and civic zones to maximize effective and efficient land use. In the 1920s, zoning became a byword for hundreds of municipalities as they quantified needs and legislated use of public and private lands.

Houston's natural environment seemed perfectly suited to Olmsted's theories of park and parkway development. As Olmsted had reclaimed natural features in Brooklyn, Boston, and Buffalo, so Houstonians could retain their bayous as nature preserves that would provide recreational spaces while eliminating "dumps, shacks, and tin can pyramids" and alleviating pollution, erosion, and flooding. In 1906 Mayor Horace Baldwin Rice, nephew of the Rice Institute's benefactor, William Marsh Rice, initiated a systematic park plan and began aggressively acquiring public utilities. Mayor Rice pushed the city to acquire the forty-acre Vick's Park along Buffalo Bayou, five more acres for City Park, and the Houston Waterworks Company property. When the commissioners took responsibility for pumping water throughout the city, they promised eight acres on either side of Buffalo Bayou for park purposes.

In the spring of 1910 Rice appointed the first Board of Park Commissioners, whose three members were to advise him and the municipal government about park acquisition, development, use, and maintenance. Politically astute, Rice assured acceptance of a professional planning process by naming commissioners with economic interests in different parts of the city. George Hermann, bachelor investor and oil man, owned extensive agricultural acreage north of Brays Bayou. William A. Wilson, president of William A. Wilson Realty Company, had partnered with attorney and Rice Institute trustee James A. Baker and other prominent businessmen to develop Woodland Heights as "a charming suburban park" north of White Oak Bayou. Baker, Botts, Parker, and Garwood partner Edwin B. Parker, a powerful railroad lawyer, was an amateur horticulturist with ties to Houston's business and cultural elite.[22] A few months after the park commissioners began work, Houston Electric Company sold its twenty-six-acre Highland Park to the city, which purchased an additional eighteen acres adjacent to the tract at the juncture of White Oak and Little White Oak Bayous and renamed the area Woodland Park in 1914.[23]

Following Park Commission advice, Mayor Rice announced Houston's first park plan, which closely resembled Olmsted's examples. Efforts would be made, he said, to girdle the city with parks joined in a unified, coordinated system by scenic parkways along the major bayous. The commission's recommendations were well received by press and Chamber of Commerce boosters who supported private and business efforts to beautify and landscape bayou banks and who urged city commissioners to approve a public right-of-way along city-owned bayou property. To coordinate these aspirations in a formal park and city improvements plan, the Park Commission, at its own expense, hired Arthur Coleman Comey, an established landscape architect and consultant on city planning from Cambridge, Massachusetts. Comey traveled to Houston in the spring of 1912 and began surveying the city and surrounding areas and gathering data about population, park acreage, neighborhoods, commercial and industrial activity, and growth potential. By March 1, 1913, he was ready to submit a tentative "preliminary report" based on "several months careful study," although he recommended further analysis of social conditions including "education, health, housing, industrial conditions, charities, and the causes of poverty and crime" to ensure a truly comprehensive understanding of urban demands.[24]

Comey combined City Beautiful aesthetic concepts with City Functional analysis to take an all-encompassing view of his assignment that moved far beyond assessment of park needs. He defined three major problems: circulation, use of public property, and restrictions on private property use. He outlined a step-by-step program that could be implemented in carefully orchestrated phases. Noting that by 1910, nationwide 46.3 percent of Americans chose city living because it provided greater job opportunities and better access to educational and cultural amenities, he recommended that commissioners adopt an ongoing planning mechanism. Although Houston's 112.1 acres of parkland provided only 1 acre of park space for every 685 residents, far short of the average 110 citizens per acre in other cities, Comey believed Houston was blessed by the prerequisites of greatness: energetic leaders, a progressive civic government, a large marketing territory, a growing population, radiating railroads, and a unique ship channel resource. Comey explained why park acquisition was only one part of an overarching plan to manage and nurture the city's growth:

> This, then, is city planning,—to study and determine in advance the physical needs of the growing city, and lay out a scheme of development in such a way that each improvement will dovetail into the next, thus gradually forming an organically related whole. The complex activities of a city demand an equally complex plan for development, so that each of its functions may be fulfilled without undue interference with any other.[25]

To Comey, "circulation" meant all forms of communication by water-ways, railroads, streets, electric trolleys, utilities, and "street furnishings" (signs, lights, trees, and bridges). Public property that must be carefully planned included federal, state, county, and city administration buildings; libraries and schools; and recreational facilities such as playgrounds, recreation centers, city squares, neighborhood open spaces, large parks, parkways and boulevards, and forest reservations. Municipal authorities were also told to regulate private property used for churches, cemeteries, institutions, theaters, and hotels; for industrial purposes; and for commercial, apartment, and residential projects. In sum, he advocated a complete civic art movement to coordinate architecture and landscape design in a systematic plan.[26]

Comey made four urgent recommendations: hire a professional superintendent of parks and director of recreation to oversee park activities; create a civic center around the Harris County Courthouse; develop a city gateway entrance of "architectural merit" at the railway station; and purchase the "beautiful pine woods in the vicinity of the Rice Institute and adjoining the proposed Outer System of parkways, where it meanders [along] Bray's Bayou." He also called for playgrounds around schoolyards, a special port or dock board to monitor commercial development along the ship channel, and amendments to the city charter that would empower a strong planning commission and establish uniform building codes. While he stressed the need for playgrounds and recreation centers as healthy outlets for energetic youth and adults and valued city squares and neighborhood parks as "breathing and resting spaces," he placed a system of natural parks along the three major bayous at the center of his plan. Comey suggested that these nature preserves be joined by concentric tree-lined parkway circles within and outside the city limits. This system, he believed, would provide beautiful recreational space and soothing shade, prevent erosion, raise property values of adjacent land, and retain public control over all bayou banks, thereby preventing flooding in low-lying areas, unsightly degradation of bayou banks, and pollution caused by careless private owners. The principles he outlined remained the basis for subsequent planning initiatives through World War II and continue to inform public debate in the twenty-first century.

Perhaps Comey realized that his comprehensive plan contained an overwhelming list of tasks for five city commissioners with minimal staff support. Perhaps the banquet of suggestions was too rich for those who were still suspicious of government interference in daily life. Although voters had authorized $250,000 for park acquisition in July 1912 while Comey was compiling his statistics, no attempt was made to adopt Comey's tentative plans as permanent policy. However, his work did produce several positive actions. In 1912 the city assumed responsibility for public park development and named Clarence L. Brock general superintendent of city parks, a post he would hold until 1943. That year the park commissioners advised purchase of a stretch along the north shore of White Oak Bayou from the Fifth Ward to the Houston Heights line. The city also acquired twenty acres along the shore north of Buffalo Bayou and thirty-five acres south of the bayou east of Shepherd's Dam Road (now Shepherd Drive). In his annual report for 1912 (published February 28, 1913), Mayor Rice advocated purchasing a park "of sufficient magnitude for our people" along Buffalo Bayou, but he was defeated for reelection in April.[27] Happily for Houston, his successor, Ben Campbell, also espoused park planning and city beautification. Campbell's reputation as a park enthusiast was boosted when George Hermann gave the city 285 acres of "beautiful pine woods" north of Brays Bayou and across Main Street from Rice Institute for park purposes.

A lifelong bachelor, George Hermann inherited extensive agricultural acreage from his parents and began his business career by operating a sawmill on land that became the park; he also ran cattle and developed a large real estate business after 1885. In 1903 he participated in the Humble oil field bonanza and became a millionaire. For the next decade he traveled widely in the United States and Europe, studying hospital procedures and befriending physicians. To support Comey's grand plan for a Pines Park, Hermann donated the large area of land along Brays Bayou to the city on May 30, 1914, just months before his death at Baltimore's Johns Hopkins Hospital on October 21. Hermann Estate trustees revealed that the civic-minded benefactor had also bequeathed a square block downtown for a "breathing space" to be called Martha Hermann Memorial Square and had provided $2.6 million to the city for hospital development. Described in Mayor Campbell's 1915 annual report as the biggest event of the year, Hermann's bequests stimulated "beneficial public interest in the movement to develop the playground and recreation centers" and "awaken the people" to the idea that "public parks, the recreation centers of the masses, are as essential to the City as its commercial activities."[28]

Campbell regrouped the Park Commission after Hermann's death and called on Chairman Edwin B. Parker, Sterling Myer, and Jules J. Settegast, executor of the Hermann Estate and owner of considerable acreage not far from city limits, to coordinate the city's valuable recreational resources. In quick succession, Stude Park was bequeathed to the city (May 1915), Hermann Park was officially dedicated (July 4, 1915), and voters approved another $250,000 bond issue for park improvement (submitted 1914, passed fall 1915). In the fall of 1915, the Park Commission asked the city to purchase an additional 122.5 acres from the Hermann estate for the park and hired George Kessler as consulting landscape architect to implement some of Comey's ideas and develop the Hermann legacy.[29] The city commissioners also authorized paving for Main Street from downtown to Bellaire Boulevard in the independent suburb of Bellaire, more than ten miles away.

Of German ancestry, George Kessler (1862–1923) grew up in Dallas but returned to his homeland for training as an engineer and landscape architect. He began an illustrious career in Kansas City when he was hired as superintendent of parks for the Kansas City, Fort Scott, and Gulf Railroad. During that city's 1880s land boom, Kessler designed small parks near upper- and middle-income neighborhoods, and in October 1893 he announced an exhaustive citywide park plan. Initial resistance to his sweeping suggestions gradually dissipated, and he implemented the first stages of a park and boulevard system that remained in place until the 1950s. In 1902 he settled in St. Louis to develop plans for the Louisiana Purchase Exposition.[30] Kessler established park systems throughout the United States and was particularly popular in Texas after publishing the city plan for Dallas in 1910 as the first comprehensive plan for a Texas metropolitan area. His aesthetic vision was informed by bold interpretations of City Beautiful concepts, as he deplored commercial invasions of residential neighborhoods, used playgrounds and parks as "breathing spaces" for poor and working-class neighborhoods, and created boulevards to secure middle- and upper-income property values.[31]

Kessler's plan for Hermann Park owed much to Frederick Law Olmsted's inspiration and to his own ability to reveal nature by selectively winnowing trees and smoothing slopes to create dramatic effects. Designs for the park's primary entrance led the eye along a formal avenue into a natural space carefully manipulated with winding roads, an irregular grand basin, and extensive woodland. In this orchestrated nature preserve linked to downtown commerce by a double-lane esplanade and central boulevard along Main Street, Kessler accommodated both public events and private experiences of natural beauty. Kessler worked on the plan for two years and in 1916 was joined by Herbert A. Kipp, a civil engineer hired by the city to execute the design.[32] By 1917 the park entrance had been completed, but bond money voted for park development had run out, and interest in park acquisition began to flag. Mayor Campbell did not seek a third term in 1917, and strong proponents of city planning and park development like Edwin B. Parker, Joseph S. Cullinan, and Will Hogg were sidetracked by wartime public service duties. Although he remained interested in city projects, Kessler turned his attention to private-sector activities.

It is not clear exactly when Joseph Cullinan and Will Hogg became involved in Houston's nascent municipal planning process. Cullinan, an innovative oil entrepreneur trained in John D. Rockefeller's Pennsylvania oil fields, was quick to take advantage of the Spindletop discoveries. Energetic and forceful, the well-built, self-made Irishman with a penetrating gaze and generous mustache joined Governor Hogg and the Hogg-Swayne Syndicate in a 1901 partnership that became the Texas Company, forerunner of Texaco. In 1905 Cullinan scouted cities for the company's headquarters and refineries and decided that Houston, with its financial infrastructure, railroad connections, and protected shipping facilities, would be ideal. After he resigned from the Texas Company in 1913, Cullinan immersed himself in civic projects, served as president of the Chamber of Commerce during World War I, and purchased thirty-seven acres along Main Street adjacent to Rice Institute for a residential enclave development.[33]

Cullinan was named to a committee considering sites for a municipal park and fairgrounds in 1913 and may have sparked Will's participation in planning activities. In late May 1913, Cullinan gave Will a copy of Arthur Comey's tentative master plan for the city. Will immediately forwarded the report to newly elected Mayor Ben Campbell and urged him to study its tables and maps. When he received no response from the mayor, Will returned the report to Cullinan, scrawling "I wrote the mayor about this and heard nothing. Assume he is not interested" across Cullinan's cover letter.[34] Fortunately for Houston, Will's assumption about Campbell proved incorrect, and Campbell and Cullinan later exchanged copies of Comey's work. In April 1914 Cullinan met George Kessler by chance on a train from Kansas City to Dallas and was soon urging Mayor Campbell to hire the "exceptionally well qualified" Kansas City park planner as a consultant to implement Houston's planning goals.[35] In July 1915 Cullinan called on Mayor Campbell and others to take "prompt action" to restrict land use between Sims Bayou and the San Jacinto Battleground for "agriculture, gardening and residence purposes" only.[36]

In 1915 Cullinan and Will Hogg responded to an appeal from the private-sector Progressive League to organize a Good Roads and Drainage Congress on June 3. Will found guest speakers for the conference and suggested that the chairman concentrate on "City Beautiful propaganda" and the proper development of suburban lands, advice that demonstrated his wide acquaintance with experts in the field and contemporary theories about city building. Forty Houstonians and seventy-eight delegates from thirty-three counties heard Harris County Judge W. H. Ward and Mayor Campbell discuss drainage, flood reclamation, and federal funding for rural improvements as ways to reconcile demands of a growing urban center with needs of the surrounding agricultural hinterland. This early attempt to create a regional plan for the Houston area preceded tentative efforts to coordinate development of the rapidly growing Long Island suburbs east of New York City in the nation's first multigovernment regional plan (1921).[37] In later years, Will occasionally referred to the importance of coordinating regional issues, which were often discussed in the press, but he focused his attention on a plan for Houston.

THE HOGGS AND URBAN PLANNING IN THE 1920S

By the 1920s Will had become Houston's most vocal, tenacious, and organized proponent of city planning, park acquisition, and zoning. He, Mike, and Ima developed a family vision of what the great city should look like, incorporated this vision into their model residential community of River Oaks, and personalized it when they built Bayou Bend, their dream house in the Homewoods enclave adjacent to River Oaks. Will's was always the dominant voice in articulating the Hogg family belief that an ideal urban setting separated commercial and industrial from residential and recreational spaces to maximize land use and preserve investor values. Journalists praised Will and Captain Mike for untiring, "unselfish" lobbying to bring "a measure of architectural beauty and dignity" to the city and disparaged all other downtown landowners as greedy profiteers eager "to exact all that the traffic will bear."[38] In 1961 Ima restated the family's environmental credo for a *Houston Press* reporter. Noting Houston's "amazing vitality and startling growth," its industrial and commercial character, and its "significant . . . artistic, literary, scientific and musical achievements," she concluded, "Houston's urgent need to keep abreast of this phenomenal expansion is an overall plan which would control its development."[39] Although Will's advocacy of city planning and zoning failed in the end to persuade political decision makers, his methods were instructive. Marrying political influence, business interests, and philanthropic vision, he worked doggedly to sway opponents, transfer land from private to public hands, and preserve natural beauty.

Believing that "a beautiful city makes better citizens," the Hoggs drove planning processes forward in three critical ways.[40] As philanthropists who recognized the critical importance of open space and parkland to the city's health, the trio acquired lands suitable for park or civic center purposes and held them until the city could use them. Through complex transfer mechanisms, the Hoggs provided the city with lands that now comprise Memorial Park, the Texas Medical Center, the Buffalo Bayou corridor between River Oaks and downtown, park spaces along White Oak Bayou, and civic center acreage near Hermann Square.[41] As public servants who hoped every Houstonian might someday benefit from the improvements Will advocated, the Hoggs supported Will's work on the City Planning Commission (1927–1929) and actively promoted planning ideas through a multipronged education initiative that drew citizen groups together to examine every issue of urban life. Will's correspondence records a decade of advocacy—against an airport in Memorial Park, for a drainage district for Houston, against vehicular street vendors and buses on Main Street, for a centrally located and handsomely designed civic center, against bus service on parkway drives. As investors who wanted to demonstrate the beneficial effects of planning processes on a grand scale, Will, Mike, and Ima collaborated with their friend Hugh Potter to create an ideal residential neighborhood where they would place their ideal home, Bayou Bend. With formidable energy, they traveled extensively to observe planning processes at work in other cities and absorbed the tenets of national and international trends. No element of the urban landscape escaped the Hoggs' comment and personal attention as they imagined a city that protected its inhabitants, provided beauty in its built environment, and promoted economic growth through efficient land use.[42]

The Hoggs' visionary activism coincided with an upsurge of enthusiasm for city planning that swept Houston in the 1920s when businessmen, politicians, journalists, civil servants, and academics seemed to agree that Houston's severe housing shortages, traffic snarls, polluted bayous, overcrowding, and gyrating land values caused by unrestrained development demanded community solutions. Led by the Chamber of Commerce and its energetic, newly formed Young Men's Business

League, business leaders set up committees, studied issues, and sought expert opinions about ways to make Houston a desirable destination for aggressive industrial investment and healthy family life. While still adhering to City Beautiful tenets espoused by Comey and Kessler, these business reformers demanded demographic evidence to bolster plans for most efficient land use because they wanted a city that functioned well. They also began to explore the rational space solutions advocated by zoning proponents and first incorporated in city plans by New York City authorities in 1916.

In 1919 Mayor A. Earl Amerman (1918–1921) appointed a thirty-member City Expansion Board, headed by the Reverend William States Jacobs, to recommend a planning mechanism. Amerman named J. C. McVea as city engineer (1919–1929). That year the Young Men's Business League set up a Committee of Sanitation to study what it deemed the most pressing urban issue. In January 1921 McVea reported that Houston suffered from three critical problems: no major street plan, no zoning ordinance, and limited power to review subdivision platting.[43] In the same month, Rice Institute initiated an extension course to explore the benefits of city planning. Incoming Mayor Oscar Holcombe revived the Board of Park Commissioners and appointed Lindsey Blayney, a professor of German at Rice, as chairman of a one-hundred-member citizens committee to establish a city planning commission that would be removed from politics and could "carry out a great system of city building."[44]

When businessmen talked, Houston mayors listened, and Houston's business community began speaking clearly about complex urban issues through its monthly magazine, *Houston*, established in the fall of 1919 to detail activities of "the Young Man's Town." Month after month, Chamber of Commerce publicity director George W. Dixon and Young Men's Business League publicity director Burt Rule touted Houston's growth but warned of the need for planning, parks, and zoning to protect and attract investments. Parks, said Rule, were a "show-place for visitors, and a civic asset" that had a "direct and far-reaching influence on the lives of every citizen, both young and old." Statistics, he wrote, had shown that parks decreased juvenile crime, provided "educational value to adults as well as to children" through botany lessons and zoos, represented "rare specimens of the arts and sciences," and were a necessity for Houston's children.[45] Between April and December 1920, seven articles demanded that Hermann Park be improved and emphasized that parks no less than "commercial and industrial advantages" or "churches and schools" are "factors that go to make up a great city" and attract decent citizens.[46] George Dixon caught the "build now" mentality of his construction-business colleagues when he urged them to build homes because every Houstonian should own a home, the "haven to which we return from the daily struggle for existence" and the "center of all that is best in our national life."[47] These homes would boost the economy, but more important they would produce responsible citizens who would work in Houston's port industries and purchase Houston's manufactured goods.[48] Business leaders S. F. Carter Jr. and R. S. Allen called on their fellows to develop a "Houston Spirit" based on cooperation, coordination, and organized effort.[49] Writers addressed salient city needs: expanded hospital care; improved drainage; built more public schools, playgrounds, and parks; improved sanitation; created a street and traffic control plan; and safely lit streets.[50] In 1921 Rule turned his attention to zoning—the "modern art" of city planning needed "on the grounds of business, public health and protection to land values."[51] Houston's major newspapers debated city planning issues in lengthy articles.

By the time Professor Blayney's unwieldy group had united in recommending that the city try a planning process, the civic leadership was attuned to needs and possible solutions. In October 1922 four men were appointed to a City Planning Commission, and in December three more were added.[52] Houston Foundation director and Rice Institute sociologist John Willis Slaughter served as secretary, and city engineer J. C. McVea represented the mayor. Although given purely advisory status, the commission was enjoined to produce plans for a major street system, a civic center, bayou beautification, and zoning as well as to devise a uniform building code. Efforts to establish public-private partnering and communication were reinforced by the commission's mix of municipal officials and businessmen. George Kessler was named consultant, an appointment that ensured continued efforts to carry out the plans first articulated by Arthur Comey in 1913 and developed by Kessler in the intervening years.

The commissioners recognized that the commission's legitimacy rested on actions taken at the state level, and they asked McVea to prepare measures that could be submitted to the state legislature. McVea developed three bills that would enable cities to regulate platting of subdivisions, empower zoning authorities, and make assessments to "facilitate the adequate provision of transportation, water, sewerage, schools and parks."[53] In early 1923, Oscar Holcombe, armed with the commission report, lobbied the League of Texas Municipalities in

Austin to introduce the bills to legislators. The league failed to act, and authorizing legislation was shelved; Kessler died in 1923; the commission lost members, and in July it ceased operations before it had presented plans for city improvements or zoning. In March 1924 Mayor Holcombe, still claiming enthusiasm for planning, tried again. He selected a new commission, requested a modest budget for its operations, and named newspaperman M. E. Tracy chairman. Rice engineering professor Lewis B. Ryon Jr. was appointed planning engineer, and S. Herbert Hare of Kansas City's Hare and Hare began his career as Houston's planning consultant (1923–1960).

Press coverage suggested that this new commission would rally public support despite its lack of authority: the mayor was on board; Ryon corralled Rice students to map improvements, tabulate traffic density, and develop a major street plan; and Hare and Hare announced studies for developing a civic center, zoning, parks, and bayou beautification. S. Herbert Hare should have been an unthreatening figure to Houstonians wary of public interference in private development. Described by an admirer as the "City Doctor," Hare was "a little gray, with a close-cropped mustache and kind eyes, soft spoken, hard-headed," an advocate of order and aesthetics for this energetic city. Hare and Hare, the firm founded by his father, had first platted a Houston subdivision in 1908 and worked in the Olmsted-Kessler tradition.[54] At this moment, with the city poised to address its planning needs, Will, Ima, and Mike advanced the parks debate. In April 1924, they proffered a major piece of undeveloped pine forest three and one-half miles west of City Park to create Houston's largest nature preserve.

THE HOGGS' FOREST PRESERVE

In the early 1920s Houstonians had begun to explore development opportunities along Buffalo Bayou to the west of downtown. Mike Hogg and his law school friend Hugh Potter, while scouting land north and south of Buffalo Bayou, discovered a hunting retreat Mike later called Tall Timbers among the wooded wilds west of Shepherd's Dam. This area south of Buffalo Bayou was accessible by a gravel road (later paved as Westheimer) or bridle paths cut through the trees. Other investors had decided to develop land between Tall Timbers and Shepherd's Dam as a country club in hopes they could lure prominent Houstonians to the uncharted area. Public curiosity about the fate of western Houston had been aroused by newspaper articles asking what would become of Camp

Logan, a stretch of land north of the bayou and west of Shepherd's Dam that had been home to thousands of soldiers during World War I. In October 1923 Catherine Emmott was named chairwoman of a committee to rally public opinion behind transforming the campground into a city park. Tirelessly she rode the streetcar to City Council meetings, visited the Chamber of Commerce, civic clubs, and patriotic gatherings, and canvassed Mayor Oscar Holcombe in her search for a parks sponsor. Such public enthusiasm appealed to the Hoggs, who had been investing systematically in Houston real estate since 1921.

In late 1923, the Hoggs' real estate investment company, Varner Realty Inc., bought 875 acres of old Camp Logan, and by spring 1924, when they purchased an additional 630 acres, the Hoggs had decided the landmark should be preserved as a park. In April the family made an overture to the city that was "absolutely disinterested in any personal profit."[55] The Hoggs proposed a deal for the city that presaged later efforts to conserve prime land for public purposes: Hogg interests would acquire desirable land and hold it until the city could raise funds to gain title to the property; the sales price to the city would be the original cost plus any interest or property taxes that accrued. On July 1, 1924, Varner Realty sold to the city undivided title to 174 acres "for park purposes only" and gave the city an option to acquire more land each July 1 until the entire acreage (1,503 acres over ten years) was in city hands. The land was to be named Memorial Park to commemorate the soldiers of World War I. To help the city make the initial purchase, Will, Ima, and Mike donated $50,000 for the 1924 down payment.[56] Hare and Hare was commissioned to draw up a design for park improvements that would include an eighteen-hole golf course, and the Hogg family retained keen interest in the park and its use.

Time and again until Ima's death in 1975, a family member had to remind the city of reversionary clauses included in each deed to ensure that the city use the land for park purposes only. Efforts to lodge a Presbyterian University, the Astrodome, a restaurant, and oil wells within Memorial Park precincts were defeated by these carefully worded clauses and the persistent oversight of the family. Before her death in 1975, Ima secured promises from conservationist friends Sadie Gwin Blackburn and Terry Hershey that they would continue her vigilance by organizing the Memorial Park Advisory Committee of citizens to protect the park. Typical of Ima's good judgment, she selected young women who had already provided creative leadership for community conservation projects and who would attain regional and national prominence in the environmental field.[57] The oversight group has continued its mission for more than three decades.

The Hoggs acquired other properties considered ideal for parkland or a civic and medical center, and Will began an active campaign to rouse popular support for planning processes. Through Varner Realty in 1923, the Hoggs purchased 133.5 acres south of Hermann Hospital, which they sold at cost to the city a year later and which was transformed into the Texas Medical Center after 1943. Recognizing the logic of associating a civic center with the popular City Park, Will authorized purchase of several downtown parcels on July 13, 1925. These would be transferred to the city "without profit or loss" from Varner Realty when civic center plans matured and funds became available. "We are taking title to this property," Will explained, "hoping that the city will utilize it as part of the Civic Center proposed by the City Planning Commission." The Hoggs offered "cost to us plus carrying charges" (about 6 percent) but were willing to waive any charges or interest "if they quibble."[58] On July 8, 1925, Hare and Hare had explained the importance of a civic center. "Beauty in our cities," Herbert Hare told the Planning Commission, "should not and need not be incompatible with use and convenience, but it should not be forgotten that beauty has a tangible and commercial value."[59] Will's civic center agitation was insistent from 1925 until November 1929, and he persuaded Rice Institute board Chairman James A. Baker and other civic leaders to join his crusade.[60] His frequent letters to Mayor Holcombe explained that a civic center would be economical and convenient, would "advertise our city to the visiting guest," and would be "an enduring stimulus to the civic pride of this town." Also needed, in Will's opinion, were clean streets, removal of billboards, and proper drainage.[61]

Media enthusiasm kept public attention focused on park needs and planning issues and generated another magnanimous gift for park development.[62] In December 1925 Elizabeth (Peggy) Stevens MacGregor decided to fulfill the terms of her late husband's 1923 will by preserving the woodland beauty of Brays Bayou east of the city. She offered the City Commission $225,000 to acquire land for a large park and for a "serpentine" parkway along the bayou that would connect Hermann Park to the newly conceived MacGregor Park. Park and parkway would memorialize her husband, the streetcar executive, ship channel advocate, and suburban builder Henry F. MacGregor, who had developed middle-class subdivisions on East End land owned by the Hermann Estate and served as chairman of the board that planned Hermann Hospital. Working with city officials and the Park Commission, Peggy MacGregor agreed to furnish land and cash for improvements if the city would build the parkway, and she kept a close watch over the ensuing struggle between developers and park supporters to ensure that the city honor the spirit of her gift, announced April 4, 1926.[63] Her vigilance secured nearly three miles of parkland right-of-way north and south of the bayou and 108 acres of "naturalistic recreation," the third-largest forest preserve in the city at that time. To celebrate his friend's civic generosity, Will provided two hundred live oak trees on North MacGregor Drive to form a War Mothers Memorial commemorating Harris County's World War I casualties.[64] Peggy also donated Peggy Park adjacent to Albert Sidney Johnston High School.

While private citizens prodded the city to acquire prime parkland west and east of town, the Planning Commission worked through 1924 and 1925 on a major street plan that specified arteries leading downtown, cross-town connecting streets, bypass loops around the city, and scenic boulevards following the bayous.[65] Although based on Ryon's statistical evidence and explained in extensive press coverage, the plan failed to attract the attention of the City Commission, where it slumbered for nine months after its formal submission on July 9, 1925.[66] The Planning Commission also prepared a comprehensive zoning-enabling ordinance in 1925 and quickly found two voluble champions in Hugh Potter, friend and associate of the Hogg brothers in the River Oaks development, and J. W. Link, lumber executive and developer of the Montrose residential subdivision. Link had discovered that deed restrictions on private enclaves could not prevent encroachment of garages, laundries, and other undesirable commercial establishments that depressed land values in residential areas. Potter waxed eloquent in May 1926: "Will we continue to sit silent while a suburban belt of realty just beyond the city limits is being platted into a jumbled mass of varying and conflicting uses?" No, he continued, "let's make no little plans for this city" but instead adopt zoning, or "the public regulation of the use of private property," to ensure that Houston would become "the great city which she aspires to be."[67] Despite this advocacy, Holcombe indicated that he would not support amending the city charter to enable zoning ordinances because the assistant city attorney advised that such ordinances were unconstitutional. Planning Commission Chairman Tracy moved to New York later that spring, and once again planning efforts collapsed.[68]

As the Planning Commission struggled unsuccessfully to gain legal status and legislate land use, Will turned his formidable energies to educating the public. He, Mike, and Hugh Potter brought Jesse

Clyde Nichols, well-known developer of the Country Club District in Kansas City, to Houston several times to explain planning to skeptical businessmen. Nichols stressed the democratizing effects of planning, whose "primary object is to promote health and the general welfare" by creating "better living conditions and better recreational facilities for working people."[69] In the spring of 1925 Will organized the West End Improvement Association to promote controlled development on the west side of town.[70] He also became active with the Texas Highway Association organized in 1923 and lobbied in Austin to create a coordinated comprehensive road system for the state.[71] By now well known for his civic concerns and generosity, Will was asked to head the Planning Commission in June 1926 but refused because the commission still lacked a budget and enforcement authority.[72] In his November 1926 reelection campaign, Mayor Holcombe promised to press for a zoning ordinance and a budget to support a reauthorized Planning Commission. Will and Mike accepted his assurances and endorsed his candidacy.

WILL'S CITY PLAN FOR HOUSTON, 1927–1929

In 1927 Will and Mike were deeply embroiled in planning issues. For years advocates had understood that without clear lines of authority, a budget, and an ability to enforce planning policy, a planning commission would be ineffective. From January to March 1927 Will wrote letters to friends throughout the state and lobbied hard on behalf of legislation pending in the Texas legislature that would enable municipalities to create planning commissions with enforcement powers.[73] On February 4, 1927, the *Chronicle*'s "Our City" column supported Will's position and challenged "the right of selfish individualism to do what it pleases with its own." The editor declared that "a just regard for the rights of others, for the greatest good to the greatest number, makes up the principle of fairness on which the legal structure of zoning laws is being erected." He then admonished Harris County legislators to work with colleagues to introduce and enact zoning-enabling legislation.[74]

These pro-zoning articles coincided with Mike's campaign to replace a recently deceased Houston representative in the Texas House. Victorious by an "overwhelming vote" on February 20, 1927, Mike left immediately for Austin, where in March he was able to help pass laws that directly affected city planning: to enable municipal zoning ordinances, to control platting of subdivisions, to assess money for park acquisition and development, to require building setbacks, and to allow cities to assess property owners for street widening and improvements.[75] On February 6, 1927, Houston voters approved $200,000 for park improvements, and on April 11, a mere 5,022 citizens authorized nearly $7 million in bonds to develop a civic center, build a new city hall, and make other public improvements.[76] Journalists declared, "Chief credit for the success of the civic center bond issue should go to Will C. Hogg and Captain Mike Hogg, [who] worked untiringly . . . [and] have given generously of their time" to ensure passage. The "onslaughts" of Will's logic "thinned the ranks of doubters." Columnists noted that Will had called on "several hundred citizens" personally to urge their support. Further, the Hoggs had promised to "transfer to the city . . . several lots at their actual cost . . . that could be sold at a big profit . . . in striking contrast with . . . some who are always speculating at the city's expense."[77] The *Press* and *Chronicle* attributed the bond election result to Will's "characteristic energy" and sustained campaign to secure funds for city improvements, and their editors demanded that he be named Planning Commission chairman. "He is for proper zoning and for beautification. We need his services," declared the *Press* editor.[78]

Armed with state support for municipal planning and assurances of monetary support for public improvements, Will accepted chairmanship of a revived seven-member Planning Commission on April 15, 1927. Also named to the commission was Florelle (Mrs. F. Clinton) Murray, in response to Will's insistence that a woman be included in the group.[79] The *Chronicle* gushed that Will's appointment "met with universal approval" because he had "been a leader in every enterprise looking to city betterment . . . an informed and intelligent leader." The *Press* interviewed Will at length and began a series based on his statements to explain the concept of city planning, enumerate Will's goals for the commission, and outline the programs that would be put in place to accomplish those goals.[80]

Although Will had insisted that he would not serve unless the commission were given full powers of enforcement, he accepted the first city planning ordinance, passed June 29, as a start.[81] The ordinance authorized the Planning Commission as an advisory body that could recommend, suggest, and report, and it created a Department of Planning within city government. It recommended that the commission prepare plans for a civic center, for bayou and park beautification, and for zoning; study municipal control of subdivision platting; enforce street rights-of-way and assessments for widening and repair; and submit a major city plan to the city commissioners for deliberation.[82] At their first meeting, on July

9, 1927, the commissioners voted to retain S. Herbert Hare as consultant and Lewis B. Ryon Jr. as city engineer (1924–1930) and secretary of the Planning Commission. Will immediately wrote to Arthur Comey asking for original maps and plans from his 1912–1913 study, and Comey was only too happy to comply.

Will brought an ambivalent understanding of effective public leadership to his tenure as Planning Commission chairman. Although he mimicked the populist rhetoric learned from his father, claimed that his work on the commission was to benefit all Houstonians, and worked hard to sway public opinion, he held all sessions in secret. He noted in the commission's 1929 report that he required secrecy to protect his experts from undue pressure of special interests and to ensure that a complete plan be laid before the people for their deliberation. This impolitic, closed-door approach may have precluded squabbling over undeveloped suggestions, but it immediately made potential opponents uneasy and suspicious and opened the commission to charges of elitism and self-serving cronyism.[83] Equally disturbing were Will's frequent absences from the city. Even if he trusted surrogate Hugh Potter and other committee members to carry out tasks and even if he kept in constant touch through telegrams and letters, his absences ensured miscommunication and deflated enthusiasm at critical moments. By March 1929, Potter reported a "general impatience that the commission doesn't begin to unfold plans." Meetings, he complained, were inefficient and disorganized.[84]

Baffling admirers and critics further, Will countered this top-down, distant approach with democratic inclusiveness as he campaigned aggressively to sway public opinion and to reassure the African-American minority, whose interests were usually ignored by establishment spokesmen. On July 5, 1927, he met with the Inter-Racial Committee and explained that he wanted to involve volunteers in an effort to fan out through African-American neighborhoods with a questionnaire that would pinpoint community needs. Will, who paid for the questionnaire's costs, became a hero to this group when he considered its needs and suggested that he would like to develop an upscale neighborhood for blacks. Yet his survey raised both expectations and fears. Despite a 1924 U.S. Supreme Court ruling that forbade using zoning restrictions specifically to enforce racial exclusion, a new state law allowed de jure residential segregation. Members of the Inter-Racial Committee and volunteers who worked on the survey immediately recognized that zoning ordinances could be used to stymie the African-American community's growth by restricting African Americans to undesirable areas or by forcing them to relinquish established neighborhoods to white encroachment. They wondered if Will's survey would be used for such nefarious purposes.[85] In May 1929 Will outlined his plan for "cooperative or voluntary segregation" that would protect "several districts that are in full possession of the colored people . . . in which the white population will not undertake to reside and beyond which the colored population will not undertake to encroach." While Will did intend that established African-American neighborhoods be preserved, he did not propose avenues for future expansion.[86]

By condemning politicians who ignored the civil rights of African Americans, by considering African-American issues in his citywide plan, and by stating that "the colored population is . . . entitled to civic and economic justice," Will placed himself squarely in the progressive camp on racial issues.[87] But his liberal leanings did not move beyond paternalism, and he never imagined an integrated society, much less a city where all ethnic groups shared social, economic, and political power. Rather, he seemed to believe that minority voices would accept the status quo if white leaders consulted their needs, promised to provide "civic justice" and the same goods and services to all sectors of the city, and secured employment for all. Pledging schools, parks, and a black man's River Oaks did not address underlying issues of racial prejudice and separation, although such actions did blunt racial tension in the segregated city.

In support of planning and city beautification, Will personally coordinated an imaginative public relations campaign directed to children, housewives, and families. Working with nurseryman Edward Teas, he distributed seeds and plants to schoolchildren and garden club members throughout the city to encourage families to create gardens at their homes. Each year between 1926 and 1930 Will paid to have thousands of rose bushes and crepe myrtle, pecan, magnolia, and dogwood trees planted at schools, hospitals, parks, and commercial sites.[88] Gardening along the humid Gulf Coast presented special challenges ignored in publications and catalogs, so Will persuaded writer and River Oaks Corporation employee Ethel Brosius, River Oaks resident Blanche (Mrs. Cleveland) Sewall, and close friend Mary (Mrs. Card G.) Elliot to work with Teas to produce *A Garden Book for Houston*, written in "terms so simple that children may understand them." First published by the Hogg family in 1929, the book has been reprinted several times and continues to serve as a "practical guide book for all those who love the growing of green things." Will believed if he could teach children one by one to love nature, as he had been taught by his parents, they would become adults who took individual steps to make their city beautiful.[89]

Turning from individual to group pressure, Will exerted his greatest public influence by guiding and financing the Forum of Civics for Houston and its publication, *Civics for Houston*. In December 1927 Will explained that he viewed the city and county as "interdependent communities" and hoped the forum would "give impetus to plans and methods for the improvement in attractiveness and usefulness of public structures and private homes and their environment."[90] Will believed Houston had grown to a level of complexity that demanded cooperative and coordinated action of "interested citizens" who owed an "ethical and practical duty to the public and the community." He declared his goal to "make this city more enjoyable, more adequately equipped, more beautiful—and consequently more useful for everyone who lives and works [here]" by seeking the "expert advice and counsel of leading minds in every available field of experience."[91] Housed in the Forum of Civics building, a 1910 schoolhouse at Westheimer and Kirby transformed at Will's direction into a meeting room, civic association headquarters, and library of works devoted to environmental issues, the forum provided a home for its one hundred member organizations.[92] Like other privately funded associations then forming around the United States, the forum was founded to explain the processes of city planning commissions to voters. By making the forum available to citizen groups, Will emphasized his belief that all Houstonians must work together to build their city.

In January 1928 Will began publishing *Civics for Houston*, a yearlong effort to provide "practical ideas about your city, your home and your garden."[93] The monthly magazine included articles by prominent experts, provided a running catalog of national planning efforts and zoning triumphs, and reflected Hogg family beliefs that a great city began as a domain of beautiful homes whose inhabitants could pursue a wholesome life in a stable neighborhood. Edited by Hester Scott, a former employee of the Conde Nast magazine empire, the magazine included columns about home design, interior decoration, garden planning, and domestic activities. Articles devoted to art, music, and architecture were intended to elevate the taste of readers, just as essays about the major street plan, the civic center plan, the Playground and Recreation Association of America, and important public buildings were included to engage citizens in public action. Long discussions of "The Dark Side of Houston"—the poor drainage, unpaved streets, and unsanitary living conditions "in the heart of the city that endanger the life and health of white and colored populations"—and illustrated articles of life in African-American neighborhoods mirrored the Hoggs' understanding that self-interest and humanitarian values must undergird urban development. "Even as a housewife is judged for the condition of her cupboards and closets, for the cleanliness and attractiveness of the seldom used rooms of her house, so may a city be judged by drainage, water mains, lighting, protection, and paving on its less important streets and by-ways," declared the progressive municipal housekeepers of the editorial board.[94] Unfortunately, editor Scott and Will disagreed about presentation and substance. Scott contended that the glossy illustrated format was an unwarranted expense and chided Will for preferring gardening and design articles to hard-driving calls to clean up degraded neighborhoods and provide widespread city services. Unused to female insubordination and annoyed by the intemperate language of her criticism, Will grew exasperated, fired his editor, and finally closed the magazine.[95]

Writers for the city's major newspapers also continued to praise planning activities and explain the beneficial effects of zoning in other cities. This advocacy raised awareness throughout the city. Worried that too much attention was paid to the developments and parks in the South End, where Houston's leadership still resided, citizens north of Buffalo Bayou formed the North Side Planning and Civics group in 1928 and began publishing *North Side of Houston* to support zoning. Sponsors hoped to protect their land values and to secure city improvements for the 65,000 residents of these northside neighborhoods that were largely unprotected by deed restrictions, private wealth, or influence at city hall. When *Civics for Houston* ceased publication in January 1929, the *Post* began a yearlong series about city planning under the aegis of Forum of Civics members, and the *Houston Gargoyle* took on its planning and zoning advocacy. The *Gargoyle*, founded in January 1928 as a "critical news journal for the progressive-minded," continued Will's advocacy of park acquisition and street improvements.

When the Planning Commission began its work in 1927, Will suggested that members take advantage of new state enabling legislation and immediately adopt a minimal set of temporary guidelines for platting residential subdivisions within the city and five miles outside city limits. Although the commission's recommendations were not approved by the municipal government, city engineer J. C. McVea seems to have won developers' voluntary compliance during 1928, and twenty plats within the city and fourteen outside city limits conformed to commission suggestions that year. Will asked Lewis B. Ryon to draft a zoning ordinance. Based largely on earlier models, the ordinance was submitted to the City Commission in December 1927 in hopes its enactment would not have to await deliberations about a complex master plan. Controversy over zoning heated up in the fall of 1928 when word leaked that the Planning Commission had begun developing temporary zoning measures because the City Commission had tabled the December 1927 zoning ordinance proposals. The Planning Commission's new draft measures were meant to protect residential development from commercial encroachment and would be used only until a comprehensive zoning ordinance could be enacted. But real estate broker J. G. Miller complained that such protection discriminated against business development and began an anti-zoning campaign that did not flag until he permanently scuttled the commission's efforts in 1930. Faced with such strong opposition and fearful that a temporary ordinance might undermine support for an overarching zoning law, the Planning Commission dropped its draft measures and continued instead to develop the master plan in secret.

In the fall of 1928, Will became embroiled in the mayoral campaign. In public Will and Mayor Holcombe seemed to be on good terms. In March 1928 the mayor appointed Will to a nine-man committee of "the best brains in Houston" to select an architect for a new city hall that would be built with $1 million in bond funds. Privately, however, Will had known by the 1926 mayoral race that Holcombe was profiting from cozy real estate deals in areas slated for civic center development. Will had kept quiet about activities he considered less than ethical because he thought Holcombe was committed to planning processes, but by late 1928 he and Mike no longer trusted Holcombe's promised support. The Hoggs switched their allegiance to Mike's close friend Walter Monteith and vocally supported his candidacy. Frank letters to friends outlined ten reasons to abandon Holcombe, including extravagance, procrastination, graft, and "disdain of the colored population."[96] After a nasty campaign of charges and counterattacks, Monteith replaced Holcombe at city hall in the December election.

Despite the political squabbles, press coverage in support of planning and zoning continued strong in 1929. A devastating flood that swamped Market Square and most of downtown in June made government control of land use seem the practical answer to many Houstonians.[97] However, real estate developers continued to lobby for untrammeled growth, and lawyer and lumberman John H. Kirby even declared zoning "unwise and un-American."[98] By the time Will submitted his report on October 30, 1929, a small group of opponents led by the real estate claque was ready for a fight. The ten-year barrage of press support and the recent torrent of coverage had failed to generate broad-based interest in planning mechanisms, and public opinion remained generally indifferent to the arcane issues raised by the city planning debate.

THE 1929 PLAN

Report of the City Planning Commission, Houston, Texas, published by Will Hogg's Forum of Civics when the mayor failed to allocate funding, laid out in clear detail not only what Houston was but also what Will hoped Houston might become. On the cover is his concept of the ideal city: a photograph of the skyline etched nobly in the background against a cloudless sky, mediated in the foreground by trees and greensward. Hints of habitation and industry—an elevated roadway and smoke in the middle distance—are partially obscured by nature's bounty and man's genius. If Will had any goal in mind when he took on the task of guiding Houston's planning efforts, it was, in the words of aesthetic philosopher John Ruskin quoted on the inside cover of the report, to do "such work that our descendants will thank us for, and let us think, as we lay stone on stone, that a time is to come when these stones will be held sacred because our hands have touched them."[99] Certainly, Will and his fellow planning commissioners hoped to lay foundation stones for a beautiful, functional city based on continuous, rational, and popular planning processes. They also hoped to establish a tradition of cooperation and excellence by naming the Board of Park Commissioners as collaborators in developing the park, parkway, and boulevard proposals and by hiring special consultants to confer on specific problems.

In many ways the plan, created by S. Herbert Hare, mirrors the recommendations outlined by Arthur Comey sixteen years earlier. City planning is defined as a continuous process or "the art and science of planning in a comprehensive way for the future physical development of a city. Order, convenience and beauty are its watchwords. The practical and the aesthetic must go hand in hand if the citizens are to have the opportunity of living well rounded lives." Its purpose "is to look to the future as well as to the present, to plan with vision, but not be visionary."[100] Like Comey, Hare reviewed current conditions and trends and named traffic circulation, public property, and private property as three critical planning concerns. Unlike Comey, Hare recognized a fourth major issue in the urban planning process: the relationship of urban to regional problems. Hare described urgent challenges, financial constraints, and legislative solutions he believed necessary to secure effective planning mechanisms, and he included sample planning and zoning ordinances.

Like Comey, Hare recognized that a major street plan "is the framework upon which most of the other city planning recommendations rest."[101]

Revealing the deeply embedded racial beliefs of white Houstonians and Will's stated opinion, Hare candidly interpreted the results of the Inter-Racial Committee's survey. The commissioners concluded that the "chief racial problem centers about the negroes," who made up about 18 percent of Houston's citizenry and were a "necessary and useful element of the population." They suggested that "because of long established racial prejudices, it is best for both races that living areas be segregated . . . by mutual agreement."[102] Although the report called for four new neighborhood parks for African-American citizens, it failed to assure space for expansion of African-American neighborhoods. Indeed, in the Fourth Ward areas between downtown and the newly developing River Oaks subdivision to the west, Hare and Hare proposed transforming a blighted but historic African-American neighborhood long ignored by civic authorities into an attractive, white-only parkway development. Despite Will's assurances to the Inter-Racial Committee in May, Hare's final plan actually decreased space "in full possession of the colored people."[103]

The 1929 report announced that "an adequate, comprehensive, and well balanced system of recreation areas for a city is no longer considered a luxury." It recommended the aggressive acquisition of parks to "preserve for the people as a whole the most beautiful scenery," to "reclaim land which is unsightly . . . and which, if not improved, will become a menace to the city," and "to provide adequate recreation areas in the form of playgrounds for children, athletic fields for older children and adults, and places for various forms of active or passive outdoor recreation."[104] Indeed, a complete park system must include large parks and forest reservations, parkways and boulevards, neighborhood parks, playgrounds, and squares. Hare, who was to produce designs for more than twenty Houston parks in the next two decades, included a sample plan for a typical neighborhood playground park in the report.[105]

A civic center or "axis around which to build a comprehensive plan" had long been central to Will's vision for Houston. He hoped to force public officials to plan "with proper aspiration and imaginative foresight" and adopt City Beautiful teachings by gathering Houston's major municipal and cultural institutions around a central downtown plaza.[106] He believed that all aspects of urban life should be included in this civic center: the city hall, the courthouse, the central post office, the public school administration building, the central fire station, the emergency hospital and medical center, a city college, and headquarters for women's clubs and civic organizations.[107] Hare and Hare, which had long stressed that "beauty in our cities . . . need not be incompatible with use and convenience," suggested that the civic center be located around Hermann Square, where the public library had been completed in 1926. The civic center plaza could then link the waterworks site, Sam Houston Park, Buffalo Drive, and two cemeteries on the west with the proposed city market to the east in a coordinated public space.[108] Hare and Hare developed detailed designs for the civic center plaza to be constructed in the Spanish Renaissance style adapted by Ralph Adams Cram and William Ward Watkin in the Cram and Ferguson designs for Rice Institute and the public library building. These Mediterranean interpretations, a nationwide fad in the 1920s, linked Houstonians to a Spanish Texas heritage and its gracious, leisurely lifestyle. In fact, many Houstonians found Mediterranean patios with their soothing fountains and deeply shaded arcades perfectly suited to a hot, humid climate not yet blessed with the refrigerated air available in post–World War II construction. The style's subdued grandeur and suggestion of refinement countered crass commercialism and provided an architectural vocabulary to articulate civic importance and cultural sophistication.[109]

His work on the city master plan completed, Will submitted his report to the mayor on October 30, stepped aside as chairman on November 1, and left town for what he believed would be an absence of two or three years on a tour of the globe—a trip cut short by his death less than a year later. Former mayor A. Earl Amerman was named Planning Commission chairman; Hugh Potter was named vice chairman; and the report was released to the public on December 12, 1929. The report was widely excerpted in the press and received enthusiastically by supporters who praised its thorough but speedy creation and its "intelligent conception of how the growth of a community may be directed, elevated and encouraged."[110] Amerman promised that secret planning meetings belonged to the past and that the commission would hold public hearings to discuss all phases of the report. On December 17 he met with the Houston Real Estate Board, and a storm of protest broke over the zoning issue.

Powerful opponents of zoning launched a furious assault on the 1929 plan. Clarence R. Wharton, a partner in the law firm Baker, Botts, Parker, and Garwood, organized the Houston Property Owners League to protest zoning proposals; J. G. Miller, long a general in the anti-zoning war, was named vice president of the group, and L. W. Duddleston, real estate editor of the *Post-Dispatch*, became secretary. The league solicited 10,000 signatures to stop zoning and charged City Council chambers on January 7, 1930, to shout down supporters. Zoning, they declared, was "an abrupt departure from individualism" and deprived "people of modest means" of the easy access to drug and grocery stores they found convenient and congenial. Elitists, they insisted, were engaging in "dangerous governmental practices and an interference with, if not a reversal of, economic laws." Zoning offered "profitable opportunities for unscrupulous politicians" and placed "real estate . . . at the mercy of the city council."[111] A. L. Hemphill, president of North Side Planning and Civics, defended the plan. Zoning, he said, prevented the confusion of unregulated development, ensured provision of public services, protected the "economic value of investment in homes," encouraged property development, and maintained a balance of values that promoted "the general welfare of our community."[112] For Hemphill, who represented middle- and working-class residents, municipal intervention through zoning seemed a safe protection against rapacious and politically influential speculators. Hemphill's logic failed. Zoning made the council members nervous, and even the Planning Commission was divided. On January 22 the City Council voted to approve all elements of the report except the zoning provisions. The brief but terrible battle left the Planning Commission scarred. On February 1 the City Planning Office closed; platting review was passed to the Department of Public Works, and planning proponents fell silent as the city turned its attention to problems caused by nationwide economic depression.

Subsequent efforts to revive the zoning issue under proponent Hugh Potter in 1938 and again in the 1940s and 1950s also brought explosive opposition and ended in failure.[113] Houston remains the largest U.S. city impervious to the proponents of zoning as a mechanism for land use planning. Ironically the 1929 plan stressed that "the keynote of zoning is protection rather than regulation" to ensure "the health, safety, morals or general welfare of the community." Authorized for the cities of Texas by enabling legislation passed in 1927, zoning was used by 750 cities in the United States in 1929 and was described as the benign "legal expression not only of the golden rule as applied to property, but of a natural economic law which tends to group various kinds of commercial enterprises so as to enjoy the cumulative effect of the concentration of business." Not retroactive, zoning was depicted as good for health, property values, street congestion, utility development, and orderly growth, values espoused by chamber of commerce boosters.[114] Yet so virulent was opposition to zoning that no planning activities succeeded in Houston until 1942, when a newly constituted City Planning Department issued a Major Street

Plan to implement bond funds authorized by voters in 1941. In 1972 Rice University architects founded the Rice Design Alliance to combat a perennial problem, "Houston's lack of civic interest in planning and urban design," and to rectify persistent national ignorance about the city's built environment.[115]

Why was the 1929 plan relegated to oblivion? One answer certainly lies in its emphatic enthusiasm for zoning. Does another answer lie in the seemingly impolitic departure of the commission's chairman on an expedition of pleasure at the moment battle was joined? In the 1920s, planning and zoning were popular instruments nationwide in towns and cities of every description and political persuasion. To be progressive was to espouse zoning as a rational means of ensuring proper land use and successful urban growth. In Houston, the Chamber of Commerce, civic associations from all quadrants of the city, experts, academic spokesmen, many journalists, and important civic activists whose wishes were not easily denied all favored planning and zoning. Two mayors and several city officials claimed allegiance in the pro-planning, pro-zoning camp. However, a vocal minority stirred fears of zoning that scuttled planning efforts as well. Zoning, they suggested, was government encroachment on the rights of the individual; it was anathema to those who equated progress with growth; it was elitist and preserved "good" residential neighborhoods at the expense of demands for commercial expansion. Worst of all, zoning would stimulate corruption and speculation. Clearly city hall vacillated as councilmen tried to please all parties. What of Will Hogg? Did he realize that speculators would seize the day? Because of his untimely death, it is hard to know whether his continued advocacy could have salvaged his years of work. Unfortunately, his frequent absences from Houston, his secret meetings, and his feuds with Oscar Holcombe and others combined to vitiate the power of his generosity and the breadth of his vision.

In a postmortem January 9, 1930, a *Press* columnist concluded that the zoning plan's "sudden and spectacular demise" resulted because friends were "never outspoken nor otherwise active" and because the Planning Commission was divided while enemies were united in their loud warnings of economic disaster if zoning laws were enacted.[116] Friends of planning and its legal avatar, zoning, failed to make citizens understand that planning could be an ongoing process through which all private interests could be heard. If properly constructed, planning processes would balance, not affirm, government power by providing private interests a structured forum. Planning was not a matter of regulation or statutes but "something which can best be brought about through an awakened civic conscience and voluntary work."[117] Perhaps, in the end, the 1929 plan collapsed before Houston's proverbial love affair with individual private initiative. Growth unhampered by regulation triumphed over community concerns for the urban environment to define "progress."[118]

RIVER OAKS, THE HOGGS' RESIDENTIAL IDEAL

The Hoggs fared better with private-sector planning projects. Although neither a philanthropic venture nor a public service, the Hoggs' garden suburb of River Oaks three miles west of downtown had elements of each. Conceived as a civic project to demonstrate the aesthetic and commercial value of sophisticated planning, River Oaks incorporated ideas developed successfully in planned communities across the nation. As philanthropists, the Hoggs and their partner Hugh Potter set aside acreage for a playground park, a school, and pocket parks scattered throughout the subdivision. As idealists, they spent money to create a "rural" haven of peaceful, secure family retreats distanced from the hurly-burly of commercial horse-trading or the clang of industrial produc-tion. As planners, they designed an economically diverse, self-sufficient community to accommodate a mix of customers who sought large estates abutting the bayou, elegant homes on curving streets near a country club, and more modest dwellings on the periphery. They also purchased land along the Westheimer and Shepherd's Dam thoroughfares where they placed small shopping centers, the Forum of Civics community center, and apartments. Potter explained the formative role played by residential developers in shaping their cities: "What City Planning accomplishes . . . throughout the whole city, the modern developer accomplishes by private contract in a particular section of the city. The subdivider is really planning your cities today." Potter and the Hoggs tried to demonstrate "that it costs very little more money to build a beautiful community than it does to build an ugly one."[119] They hoped River Oaks would inspire "beauty and civic efficiency" for Houston's westside development and serve as an antidote to blight caused by "failure to foresee, to gauge, and to direct the dynamic rapidity of [a city's] growth and expansion."[120]

Will, Ima, and Mike brought a broad understanding of residential development options to their Houston realty investments. During his youthful sojourn in St. Louis, Will had discovered the private-place residential neighborhoods that were built in the late nineteenth century. Characterized by broad boulevards with landscaped dividers, protected by substantial gates, and subject to strict development controls, these streets were owned by their residents, not by the city. In these one- or two-block enclaves large houses sat imperiously on small lots and offered their wealthy owners privacy and protection from surrounding urban sprawl. Often built by syndicates of businessmen-residents and particularly popular in the 1870s and 1880s, these private places were controlled by deed restrictions, maintained by assessments, and overseen by associations of residents.[121] The Hoggs themselves experienced private-place living when they moved to the Rossmoyne subdivision developed west of Montrose Boulevard by the Sterling Investment Company in 1914. Ross S. Sterling (1875–1949), a founder of Humble Oil Company (1911) and chairman of its successor, Humble Oil and Refining Company, published the *Post-Dispatch* from 1924 to 1932 and persuaded fellow oil men to become his neighbors. Although Ima worked closely with an architect on plans for the family's home and wrote enthusiastically of the gardens she planted there, the enclave failed to maintain its protected exclusivity, and by the time its deed restrictions lapsed in the mid-1930s, most of the wealthy inhabitants had moved away.[122]

Travels across the country and Ima's prolonged stay in Merion, one of Philadelphia's railroad suburbs, also acquainted the Hoggs with country-place homes set on pastoral acreage. These planned communities were made possible first by railroad and later by automobile, and they were accessible to the larger metropolitan centers from which they took their economic sustenance. Escapes for wealthy executives and professionals, these semi-rural residential parks had several features in common. They used deed restrictions to stabilize property values and sponsored homeowners associations to foster community spirit. Planned as country-like residential communities within easy access of downtown commercial centers, they developed slowly, showcased model homes, and relied on setbacks, landscaping, and minimum pricing to maintain standards.

Jesse Clyde Nichols's Country Club District in Kansas City provided the example of a complete planned community most closely studied by Will, Mike, and Hugh Potter, who frequently visited Nichols's work in progress and conferred with Nichols about their Houston project. Nichols, himself influential in professional real estate circles, began development in 1908 and continued until his death in 1950 to acquire land, open subdivisions, and create a path-breaking large shopping mall accessible to automobile traffic. Not only did he recognize that the automobile had transformed middle-class American life, but also he stressed curving streets to draw homeowners into the womb of community, developed small neighborhood parks, and set aside spaces for schools and churches. Families in the Country Club District could escape the iron grid of congested urban space, relax along "country" lanes in their landscaped gardens, and still enjoy spiritual, educational, and commercial amenities a short drive away.[123] On private streets and in country suburbs, developers provided tranquil escape from urban turmoil, ensured stable land values, and created communal identity with club facilities, neighborhood publications, and unifying landscape design. The Hoggs would remember these examples when creating their own ideal planned community.[124]

River Oaks stands today as the Hoggs' enduring legacy to private-sector residential development, but the large planned community of 1,100 acres was not the first residential real estate activity undertaken by the Hogg siblings. In November 1921, the Hoggs chartered the Varner Company to handle their real estate investments. Through the Varner Company passed all transactions that were later deeded or sold to the city for park or civic center purposes, and in 1921 the Varner Company began buying shares in the Stude Holding Association, chartered in February 1915 by their friend Henry Stude to develop eight tracts of family-held land north of White Oak Bayou and west of downtown. By January 1922 the Hoggs held a majority interest in the Stude holdings and renamed the consortium Varner Realty Inc.[125] They subdivided the land into Norhill, North Norhill, East Norhill, and Norhill Park; they donated land where the James S. Hogg Junior High School (now Hogg Middle School) was built; and within four years they sold more than 90 percent of the property for modest home sites spaced on a traditional grid. Particularly interesting was the Hoggs' civic-minded approach to this development. They demonstrated that amenities could be provided to lower-middle-income residents without decreasing a developer's profits. Houses were tied to city services, and the school, neighborhood parks, and paved streets were linked to the city by a broad parkway along White Oak Bayou.[126]

The Hoggs also expressed interest in Community Place, a Main Street private-place project Houston architect and family friend Birdsall Briscoe (1876–1971) designed for them in 1919, but instead they developed the twelve-acre tract in 1923–1924 as Colby Court. The Hoggs installed paved streets, curbs, storm sewers and gutters, drainage, and landscaping and built a model home of brick veneer. Only three lots sold, however, perhaps because the speculative project abutted retail property. Facing stiff competition from other developments in the area near the Museum of Fine Arts, the Hoggs cut their losses. Will transferred the remaining lots to William States Jacobs, civic leader and pastor of First Presbyterian

Church, and secured the trade on easy terms by a personal promissory note. The congregation eventually moved out Main Street to this property.[127]

Mike first invested in the area west of town when he purchased 118 acres south of Buffalo Bayou in March 1923 as a weekend retreat where he could ride and entertain. Christened Tall Timbers, the wooded land abutted the new River Oaks Country Club golf course. When Mike and his law school roommate and law associate Hugh Potter approached Will in 1924 about buying out the investors who had commissioned the new River Oaks Country Club organized in 1923, Will scoffed at their modest proposal. According to Potter, Will asked, "Why buy only two hundred acres?" He suggested they "make this thing really big, something the city can be proud of." Will then persuaded Potter to relinquish a successful legal career, "take charge of this thing," and create a model of advanced community planning techniques "with the entire resources of the Hogg estate behind it."[128]

In May and June 1924 the Hoggs and Potter took controlling interest of Country Club Estates Inc. (River Oaks Corporation in 1928), which had been incorporated to develop land around the new country club.[129] They hired civil engineer Herbert A. Kipp, an "eminent creator of high-class residential communities," to expand his 1923 subdivision plat for the area and established Widee Realty Corporation to purchase surrounding acreage then owned by truck farmers.[130] Eventually the development spread from Shepherd's Dam Road west to the Southern Pacific Railroad right-of-way and from Buffalo Bayou south to Westheimer Road. In July 1924 tractors broke through scrubby brush to cut River Oaks Boulevard, the first paved street in the area, and all summer workmen cleared the first house sites on the flat, treeless fields. The Hoggs and Potter operated as a team. Hogg Brothers supplied cash to Country Club Estates and Widee, spending more than $1.8 million by late 1930.[131] Will spouted grand ideas but also scrutinized every advertisement and financial report. Mike served as vice president and monitored day-to-day family interests, while Ima worked closely with architects to design speculative model homes and approve plans for subdivision landscaping and custom home designs. Potter, as president, oversaw corporate operations. Described as alert, small, active, and young "in appearance . . . inclination, sympathies, energy, vision," Potter became a power in professional real estate circles.[132]

Will took particular interest in a ninety-acre "parcel of woodland shade and quietude" first called Contentment and later renamed Homewoods. Although advertised as situated "in River Oaks," Homewoods was a separate enclave of "home estates" of three and one-half to fifteen acres. Will conceived it as a "neighborly syndicate of families" who were "brought together solely by invitation and a community of interest." He, Ima, and Mike chose Plot C (14.25 acres) sometime in 1925 or 1926 for their own home, which they later named Bayou Bend.[133] In July 1925 Will wrote "confidential" letters to fifty-three prominent Houstonians, some of whom already lived in exclusive enclaves and several of whom were vacationing at summer retreats, and invited them to invest in the Homewoods project.[134] Thus, the Hoggs' ideal development incorporated both the inclusive garden suburb made famous by Nichols and others and the exclusive private enclave popularized in St. Louis. Through their "distinguished experiment" in River Oaks, the Hoggs hoped to demonstrate the commercial viability of good business practices and astute planning. If successful, they believed their residential development would be widely emulated to set Houston apart as a city of modern design and incomparable beauty.

Although the Hoggs were enthusiastic, esteemed, and influential, their River Oaks scheme seemed a daring speculation. The land beyond Shepherd's Dam Road lay outside city limits "in the country" far from fashionable South End residential areas being developed in the 1920s around Rice University—Shadyside (after 1916), West Eleventh Place (1920), Shadowlawn (1920s), and Broadacres (1923). It was separated from downtown by a slum neighborhood, and it could be reached only by meandering Westheimer Road. To boost curiosity and attract customers, Country Club Estates asked John Staub, Joseph W. Northrup Jr., Birdsall P. Briscoe, and Sam H. Dixon Jr., architects respected for their work in other exclusive neighborhoods, to design fifteen model homes. Briscoe, who had been a classmate of Will's at the University of Texas, and Dixon designed the first model under Ima's aegis—a pink stucco, simplified French Provincial structure on Inwood Drive. Northrup next developed five modestly priced small models in various colonial revival styles popular in the 1920s. The corporation advertised these homes extensively and invited clients to "private showings" of "completely furnished" houses. John Staub, the architect of River Oaks Country Club who later designed Bayou Bend for the Hoggs, began his long collaboration with Ima when the two created a stucco house on Chevy Chase that had been inspired by New Orleans's Spanish Creole Old Absinthe House. With its iron grillwork, arched openings, and pale apricot color, the house seemed perfect for Houston's muggy climate. In later years Staub insisted that Ima invented the term "Latin Colonial" to describe the structure's eclectic style, which she considered an indigenous expression of historic American domestic architecture that synthesized Mediterranean traditions with contemporary home requirements.[135]

Despite the prestige of these architects and the comfort of their model designs, the corporation struggled to compete with South End development in the 1920s and with a Depression economy in the 1930s. River Oaks grew slowly as the corporation opened twenty plats over a twenty-five-year period (1924–1947). To encourage a family "way of life" the corporation tried imaginative approaches. From 1926 to 1932 it employed Charles W. Oliver as project architect and in August 1927 hired Henry Hutchinson, who had been trained in London and Berlin, to landscape common areas and advise homeowners.[136] Potter and Mike encouraged buyers to use in-house staff and assisted homebuyers with financial arrangements. Staff provided maintenance assistance, and the company's partners invited residents to participate in country club, garden club, and Forum of Civics activities. Neighborhood parks, homeowner newsletters, and club membership nurtured community spirit. Like its carefully studied prototypes, River Oaks was separated from surrounding commercial zones by entry gateways and perimeter planting. A broad boulevard (now Allen Parkway) led travelers from the downtown commercial zone to the country club retreat, while curving streets off the main thoroughfares drew residents into an identifiable community. The corporation laid utility conduits underground, paved roads and sidewalks, and installed streetlights and signs. Beautiful old trees shaded the bayou bordering River Oaks, but the Hoggs planted hundreds of trees and shrubs and "35,000 separate rose bushes" to transform the subdivision's flat prairie land into a garden suburb harmonized by uniform landscape design to suggest a forested rural escape from city travails. Detailed restrictions protected investors and prescribed the style, setback, and minimum cost of construction block by block in a balanced overall design.[137]

Houstonians, like most Americans, were susceptible to the blandishments of well-orchestrated advertising campaigns, and River Oaks backers produced masterful propaganda as they worked to create a community identity for their enterprise. Heralded one year after inception as "one more evidence of the surging forces which are lifting Houston to a greater place among the cities of the nation," advertising copy implied that Houston has become "more majestically equipped in the competitive field of commerce and industry" because of this "country club community of homes." High-flown language describing a "panorama of marching green acres, a vista of alluring homesites" and practical descriptions detailing the natural gas mains to every homesite and the only express bus service in the city were mingled in pamphlets and essays that fashioned a creation myth of this "major work of civic development."[138] Other brochures proclaimed, "It is Good for Any City to have its *River Oaks*," or urged buyers to "Build Your Home in a Great Open Garden."[139] Will and Potter carried on extensive correspondence about sales strategy and employed professionals to test market ideas. To promote sales, the partners tried direct mail appeals, pre-development showings of new plats, invitation-only tours of model homes, and a steady barrage of newspaper and magazine spots.[140]

When Don Riddle joined the corporation as publicity director, the sales program became a carefully crafted campaign to build a strong image of River Oaks as a "way of living," not just a place to live. Advertising was disguised as journalism in the home sections of newspapers where River Oaks activities were reported frequently, and the development associated itself with cultural improvements by buying space in theater and concert programs.[141] Campaign word choices reflected Hogg family values about the elements needed to build a healthy community. On romantic curving streets planted with indigenous river oaks and magnolias, publicists claimed, country-place homes harbored men and women who delighted in leisure, athletics, gentility, and community. In River Oaks families could buy "homes for all time," not lots, and be assured of "contentment," "permanence," and "security."[142] To strengthen the myth of River Oaks as a community rooted in long-standing tradition, the corporation ran a series of advertisements on the back cover of *Civics for Houston* linking the development to stories of the "hardy pioneers" and civic-minded settlers who had created cosmopolitan Houston.[143] As the Great Depression set in, Riddle began a series that described life in River Oaks—a father reading to his children, a mother serving tea—and imagined a place that combined the "charms of country life" and "city conveniences in a great protected area." Most important, in River Oaks individuals could choose architectural styles that reflected personal tastes, tied buyers to historic traditions, and provided "harmony without monotony." Built to withstand the test of time, River Oaks real estate would be a buffer against Depression financial fluctuations as well.[144] In the River Oaks domain of beautiful homes, individuals and families could find stability, safety, and beauty far from the bewildering change and frenetic pace of a modern industrial city.

As part of his scheme for the West End, Will lobbied for paved roads leading west from downtown and hired Herbert Hare to design Buffalo Drive (now Allen Parkway) along Buffalo Bayou from downtown to River

Oaks. Begun in late 1925, the parkway allowed River Oaks residents to motor downtown along its scenic byway in ten minutes. Will also prodded municipal authorities and private landholders to develop Kirby Drive as a tree-shaded, esplanade boulevard from Shepherd's Dam to Brays Bayou, thereby connecting Buffalo and Brays Bayous to complete the plan Comey and Kessler had long advocated. Will's approach to the Kirby Drive problems typifies his civic style. In May 1924 Will just happened to be driving past John H. Kirby's property and noticed development activity south of River Oaks. He suggested that Kirby work with the Hoggs to promote and build a drive one hundred feet wide and bordered by double rows of trees on each side from the Kirby estate on Bellaire Boulevard through River Oaks to Buffalo Drive. Will and Hugh Potter then engaged in extensive correspondence with county and city officials and with private property owners along the proposed route to secure public and private funding to develop the right-of-way. Describing himself as "more or less an intermediary," Will reminded Houston's mayor in October 1927 that he and his partners had "put Kirby Drive through River Oaks from San Felipe to Buffalo Drive at a very heavy expense as a part of our conception of what proper planning of that property . . . should be." In March 1928, nearly four years after his initial approach to Kirby, Will announced that all parties had agreed to cooperate, and Kirby Drive became the major north-south corridor between the incorporated suburb of Bellaire and downtown Houston ten miles away.[145]

The serene, parklike idyll of River Oaks had a price. Although Will, Mike, and Hugh Potter could imagine a beautiful built environment that would attract business to and earn praise for their great American city, they could not envision inviting everyone to share this Edenic way of life. River Oaks was intended to be a community of like-minded people who shared standards of taste and compatible views about the structure of society. Deed restrictions specified that African Americans were welcome only in the servants' quarters over the garages.[146] The "gentlemen's agreement" that barred Jews from "exclusive" neighborhoods in the years before World War II was upheld in River Oaks with no recorded opposition from Hogg family members.[147] Will's wish to preserve Buffalo Bayou as a nature preserve is laudable, and his lobbying to construct attractive and safe corridors from River Oaks to downtown made good business sense. His failure to accommodate residents of the intervening low-income neighborhood with housing alternatives shows the limits of his vision. Sufficient evidence exists to support the Hoggs' assertion that harmony, security, and compatibility rather than commercial advantage motivated their projects, but in the hands of enthusiasts less scrupulous than the Hoggs, harmony could quickly become conformity, security could breed exclusion, and compatibility could seem like prejudice.[148]

In the 1910s and 1920s a vision of what Houston could become took form in two master plans and several residential experiments, and the possibility of this City Beautiful and Functional remains lodged in memory today. The Hogg family, who imagined an American city that was heir to traditions from across the nation, articulated a progressive urban ideal. The Hoggs' city would be organized on businesslike principles of efficiency and function; it would adopt an ongoing planning process legitimized by zoning laws and building codes; it would attract individual or corporate investment by separating residential, commercial, and industrial functions; and it would link distinct urban areas by major circulation arteries, scenic boulevards, and local traffic corridors. For the Hoggs, beauty was paramount, and their Houston would nurture bayou preserves, neighborhood and forest parks, and homeowner gardening projects. Most important, the Hoggs' Houston would be a community of homes grouped in well-planned, self-sufficient residential developments graced with every urban amenity. Through education and example, the Hoggs hoped they could sway public opinion to embrace their urban ideal.

Their faith was only partially realized. Arthur Comey and Herbert Hare quantified and explained requirements of a planned city; George Hermann, the Hoggs, and Peggy MacGregor set a standard for park development; Hugh Potter, the Hoggs, and other far-sighted builders stressed residential planning. Efforts to balance individual ambition and community good and to retain old values in periods of rapid transition met strong resistance in Houston. Even visionaries like Will Hogg found it difficult to move beyond personal taste and business interest; even he failed to secure public rights-of-way along the bayous that made his residential projects successful. Faced with a tradition of weak government and a belief that private rather than public initiatives would make Houston a great city, Houstonians fell prey to the propagandists of growth and the grip of speculators. The Hoggs themselves turned from organizing Houston's environment to providing social service stability and cultural meaning for its residents.

Chapter 3
Wholesome Lives for All Houstonians

S pring evenings in 1892 found Kezia Payne DePelchin, then sixty-four, trudging along dusty lanes and through piney woods between her modest lodgings in Houston and the Bayland Orphans Home in Woodland Heights, where she served as matron to Houston's abandoned white boys and girls.[1] One evening after a long walk to save the nickel streetcar fare, DePelchin discovered three homeless toddlers on her porch. Unable to turn them away or take them to Bayland, she and some friends borrowed furniture and a cottage to offer temporary care.[2] Revered as Houston's pioneer teacher, first city nurse, and sympathetic social worker, DePelchin already spent every penny she earned helping others. Legend records that when relatives asked how she would finance a new home for orphans, DePelchin replied that she was "entirely dependent on my faith in God and the good people of Houston."[3] So was born in the last months of her life Faith Home to "care for friendless children." DePelchin's faith that somehow God and his minions on Earth would provide funds and caregivers to protect deserted or orphaned children was rewarded when Ruth (Mrs. T. W.) House, cooperating with *Houston Post* publicists, called one hundred privileged women together at Shearn Methodist Church to discuss ways to realize her dear friend's dream. As so often happened during these years, attorney James A. Baker was asked to assist the project by preparing a charter of incorporation. Patrons, including a male auxiliary of six advisors under Baker's leadership, raised money for two permanent homes that were built in 1893 and 1898 on property at Chenevert and Pierce.[4]

When need outran space in 1912, Kezia DePelchin's friend, the philanthropist Harriet Levy, persuaded her brothers Abe and Haskell to make a joint donation of five lots at 2710 Albany for a new facility. The Reverend Peter Gray Sears, rector of Christ Church (Episcopal), organized a committee and raised $55,000 to build a graceful Italianate villa designed by nationally acclaimed St. Louis architects John L. Mauran and Ernest J. Russell. Constructed of concrete, steel, and brick, this sturdy refuge opened in spring 1913.[5] By 1915 Faith Home was the largest orphanage in Houston and sheltered as many as 150 children at a time. Small subscriptions of $100 to $250 supplemented city funds of $250 a month to care for the children during these early years.[6] By 1926 DePelchin Faith Home had expanded its services to include general child care, and in 1929, as the Children's Bureau Association, the home trained professionals to assist all children who needed protection.[7] For eleven decades the DePelchin Children's Center has been a favorite charity of Houston's elite, its mission to protect defenseless children and repair the family fabric remaining constant as it developed new programs to meet changing needs.

SOCIAL RESPONSIBILITY IN HOUSTON, 1880–1918

Houston's skyline was only one topic hotly debated by civic activists in the 1910s and 1920s. If urban vistas were to be punctuated by handsome structures and softened by lush green spaces to proclaim the City Beautiful and Functional, what should be done for the residents of this great American experiment? How could their lives be improved? Would parks, model neighborhoods, and comprehensive plans for the built environment be sufficient if fellow citizens did not possess the necessary tools to lead happy, productive lives? Made uneasy by the unintended consequences of explosive industrial and urban growth, progressive Houstonians, many of them colleagues and confidants of Will, Ima, and Mike Hogg, came to believe that all citizens should have access to social service resources that would empower them to realize their potential as individuals and participate responsibly in a great democracy. Imbued with serious moral purpose and profound optimism, these progressives began to see that solutions to social, economic, and health questions were fundamentally entwined; epidemics, suffering, and low expectations among some would inevitably impinge on the health, prosperity, and dreams of all. These humanitarian activists, even as they flourished, did not fail to recognize that like every bustling, industrializing city, Houston sheltered its share of the distressed and the dispossessed.

The path to empowerment was not clear to the Hoggs and their friends in the decades before the Great Depression of the 1930s. Most Houstonians favored individual initiative, private problem-solving, and weak local government. Almost no one advocated meddling by outsiders, whether they were New York capitalists, Washington regulators, or benevolent church ladies. Personal charitable acts had long succored the less fortunate with almost no local government oversight or support. While assessed valuations rose 150 percent between 1916 and 1927, city appropriations to Houston's nascent Department of Public Welfare increased only 22.5 percent.[8] However, as the city grew, leaders began to see that community-wide problems like modern sanitation, epidemic control, mass transportation, and low-income housing demanded cooperative solutions. Scholars have noted, sometimes with suspicion, the interlocking relationships among men and women who amassed Houston's first fortunes, managed the city's government, and orchestrated the community's social and cultural life. Ima Hogg, a more compassionate analyst, is reputed to have remarked that the first people in Houston to become rich were "nice" and "set a pattern" by giving money to schools, hospitals, charities, parks, libraries, and the arts.[9] Rosters of civic and service organizations from the 1910s and 1920s confirm that Houston's turn-of-the-century prosperity had fostered a forceful circle of forward-looking men and women who were as willing to confront urban problems as they were to imagine an imposing metropolis. During those decades Houstonians established numerous privately funded social service institutions and reassessed municipal responsibility for the public's well-being.

In the 1910s Will and Mike used their business connections to support social service institutions and woman suffrage, while Ima turned her attention to professional development and the arts. By the 1920s the siblings had begun to see that all their civic enterprises provided "cultural enrichment and a stabilizing influence in the family life" of Houstonians. They also realized that charitable acts to palliate suffering were not enough to dislodge social injustice and build a great city. Before individuals could function responsibly in a democratic society, they must, the Hoggs came to believe, enjoy sufficient emotional stability to overcome frustrations inherent in the harsh realities of daily life. Well-planned communities must, therefore, support service organizations that empowered citizens to lead "wholesome" lives. Anxious to discover underlying causes of the "unhappy conditions which exist all around us," the Hoggs in the late 1920s and 1930s turned their attention to the poorly understood arena of mental health care and espoused the hypothesis that positive mental health was as important as physical well-being.[10]

While projecting a booster spirit of growth and opportunity in the years before World War I, Houston also harbored thousands who needed assistance to manage daily struggles. Women in Houston's religious congregations were the first to recognize that slum areas existed in white,

African-American, and Mexican neighborhoods, and they provided the town's few social services in 1900 when the Christ Church (Episcopal) Ladies' Parish Association, the First Presbyterian Ladies Association, Shearn Methodist Church Women, and the Young Men's Christian Association Ladies Auxiliary are listed in city directories as primary dispensers of aid to widows, orphans, and the indigent. The Christ Church Ladies' Parish Association aided friendless and homeless old women at its Sheltering Arms facility founded in 1893 and opened in 1896. The Beth Israel Congregation Ladies' Aid Society (founded 1895) assisted Houston's immigrant Jewish population. The Florence Crittenden Rescue Home (founded 1896) and St. Anthony's Home provided asylum to destitute mothers, infants, and elderly citizens. But leading activists dissatisfied with palliative charity realized that new approaches were needed to help others help themselves.

In 1907 Alice Graham (Mrs. James A.) Baker decided to attack root causes of social problems. She invited several socially prominent friends to establish the Houston Settlement Association and called on the group to provide basic medical care, day care and kindergarten programs, recreation for youth, and training for young women in home economics and practical crafts. In the years that followed, Baker spearheaded efforts to develop Rusk Settlement, which she organized to assist Jewish and Mexican immigrants living near the noisome cotton mills of the Second Ward. Trying a new idea inspired by advice from University of Texas Professor A. Caswell Ellis, an innovative sociologist and longtime mentor to Ima Hogg, Baker received permission to place her settlement in Rusk Elementary School, "up above the river, with a clear view of the busy workaday life of Houston." This novel approach to social service delivery signaled the critical importance of full-time school attendance to immigrant and poor children living in the surrounding area.

The Settlement Association also staffed North Side Settlement for white residents and supported Bethlehem Settlement, founded by Jennie Belle Murphy Covington for African-American citizens in 1917.[11] Jane Addams's Hull House in Chicago exemplified Progressive Era settlement programs from the 1880s through the 1930s. Typically, men and women of means and education "settled" in buildings in underserved immigrant or slum neighborhoods and attempted to improve conditions through example, classes, and direct assistance. Private philanthropic dollars supported the residents and their programs. In Houston, volunteers from women's clubs and church groups met at nonresidential settlements. Each volunteer served one day a week and organized helping, health care, and educational projects. While still largely palliative, these "effort[s] to aid in the solution of the social and industrial problems . . . engendered by the modern conditions of life in a great city" recognized that many working families could not afford basic social and medical services and lacked the skills needed to succeed in an urban, industrial work environment.[12]

Expanding social service responsibilities demanded coordination and new fund-raising methods. Although generous, few Houstonians welcomed repeated calls on their purses; most wanted efficiency and deplored overlapping programs or poorly managed organizations. A May 1904 solicitation letter expressed the era's growing consensus that "ordinary methods of individual and indiscriminate giving increases pauperism and crime and degrades rather than encourages self respect and self support."[13] After 1910 the Chamber of Commerce Charities Endorsement Committee protected donors by issuing cards to charitable organizations that met chamber criteria. Women also took leadership roles in charitable fund-raising. When the "exceptionally pretty and forceful young" Estelle Boughton Sharp accompanied her brilliant inventor husband, Walter Benona Sharp, to Houston in 1904, the city gained a champion of social welfare reform whose active civic career closed only with her death in 1965 at the age of 92.[14] While her husband, president of Producers Oil Company, worked with Joseph Cullinan and Will Hogg on numerous oil deals, invented the famous Rock Bit and other tools that revolutionized oil drilling, and co-founded the Sharp-Hughes Tool Company, Estelle turned her attention to social service work. She felt inadequate to provide hands-on assistance but excelled at administrative and fund-raising tasks.

Houston friends knew Sharp had participated in Dallas's kindergarten movement and asked her to help them develop United Charities, founded in February 1904 by eleven women to "take charge of the general charity work of the community . . . aid the worthy poor, and check the impositions of the unworthy."[15] Although she demurred at first because she was a "stranger" to Houston, Sharp soon became a leading spokeswoman and "gracious lady of social welfare." She served as president of United Charities several times between 1907 and 1914 and defined its mission to help people help themselves, investigate reports of need, encourage children to attend school, and fight for laws to regulate the workplace and to improve social conditions. She oversaw the group's interaction with the Houston Foundation in the 1910s, its transition to the Community Chest in the 1920s, and its incorporation as the United Fund and Community Council in the 1950s. A woman of strong opinions, Estelle Sharp

forcefully urged United Charities to change its name to the Social Service
Federation and broaden its mission in 1912 so it could more effectively
attack fundamental causes of the problems that marred Houston's social
fabric and better develop the most modern principles of charity work.[16]

WILL'S SOCIAL ACTIVISM, 1909–1918

It is possible that Estelle Sharp, a compassionate woman who established
a fund "to benefit the Negro population of Houston" and who believed
with "courageous fearlessness" that communities must serve "those who
falter along life's pathway," was largely responsible for drawing Joseph
Cullinan and Will Hogg into social service work.[17] The three families
were very close. When Walter Sharp died tragically in 1912 at age 42,
Hogg and Cullinan shared executor duties with the widowed mother of
two boys. Will mentored the boys' progress, and Estelle traveled with
Ima during the latter's illnesses in the 1920s and again in the 1930s. Joe
Cullinan's daughter Nina remembered a slender, tall woman of great
integrity who dressed carefully, "seemed so perfect," was warm but
controlled, and "never stopped working for others despite the travail of
old age"—a "paragon of someone who gave back to her community."[18]

Contemporary correspondence and news accounts frequently recognized Will's generosity, integrity, and devotion to community. Like
Estelle Sharp, Will supported organizations that promoted self-help,
served on the Houston Foundation board before World War I, and advocated Community Chest development in the 1920s. Will quickly established his reputation as a soft-hearted but determined fund-raiser with a
fertile imagination and an inexhaustible supply of blank-paged subscription books bound in blue or black leather that he used to solicit contributions for worthy civic causes.[19] In 1909 he persuaded one hundred men
to purchase second-mortgage bonds to secure Houston Country Club
property, and in 1913 he suggested that Estelle Sharp ask these bond
holders to donate their bonds to the Social Service Federation or YWCA
fund drives, a novel transfer of title often employed by the Hoggs, who
throughout their lives moved large blocks of stock to various nonprofit
institutions. In September 1914 Will and two other Boy Scout supporters
asked manufacturing corporations to participate in an industrial survey
and host three hundred boys on visits to industrial plants throughout
the city—with little cost but much public goodwill to the participants.[20]
By 1916 he was "primarily responsible for just a bit more aggression in
the Boy Scout movement" and spearheaded the effort to select a scout

commissioner and raise $3,000 that year.[21] In 1915 he supported town-lot farming on the Westmoreland addition along Main and Montrose south of downtown; future farmers received a "grub stake" to cultivate undeveloped acreage, learned responsibility and agricultural techniques, and kept the lots tidy until they were converted to homesites.[22]

When YWCA supporters decided they needed a permanent facility comparable to the well-equipped YMCA, they turned to Will to lead the Initial Gifts Committee for a fund-raising blitz in 1919. Will pulled out a subscription book, and he and Mike persuaded friends to pledge $500,000 "as a gift of gratitude . . . to the splendid spirit of service of the women of Houston."[23] Because the construction budget ballooned, Will returned to the funding quest in 1920. In a letter to industrialist and campaign General Chairman Edward Andrew Peden, Will disclosed that he had given $15,000 to the project and would pledge another $5,000 if ten $5,000 subscribers would join him. Forced to leave town before the campaign was completed, Will relinquished his duties to Peden's capable hands and expressed confidence that "a fertile field of unsolicited prospects" would respond "if properly approached by carefully coached committees."[24]

Ima recalled that Will responded to a request to assist the "little newsboys, waifs, on the streets of Houston" by donating maintenance support "as always, anonymously" for a newsboys' home and club.[25] E. Ferdinand (Ferdie) Trichelle, co-publisher of the *Railroad Echo* for area railroad workers, established the Emma R. Newsboys Home for orphaned and homeless boys in 1910 to honor her mother, Emma R. Gilbreath. In 1913 Mayor Ben Campbell gave Trichelle the old Dow School, which was taken down so the materials could be reused to build a "splendid, up-to-date, well arranged" frame structure at 1600 Washington for use as a headquarters home for about 30 homeless boys and a clubhouse for about 400 neglected youth. About 150 boys ages six to sixteen who could not attend public school received onsite manual training and other lessons so they could "improve themselves."[26]

Joseph Cullinan served on the board of the Newsboys Home from 1915 to 1919 and suggested Will and Estelle Sharp as potential donors. Will pledged $12.50 every quarter in October 1915, and he and Sharp visited the facility on November 19, 1915. They urged director Trichelle to apply to the Houston Foundation for support.[27] By November 27, 1915, Cullinan, Hogg, and Trichelle had formed a committee to create a financial plan and raise endowment funds. In January 1916 Will mailed two hundred letters, consigned by the committee, to explain the home's purpose—"to harbor and guide homeless, neglected, and destitute" boys, prevent them from becoming criminals, teach them trades and good citizenship, and prepare them for life in a better world.[28]

Will's affection for the boys inspired a poignant John Lomax anecdote. One Christmas at New York's Claridge Hotel, Will received a box of neckties wrapped in paper "spotted with smudgy fingerprints" from the "damned little rascals" and was overcome by tears.[29] Cullinan sponsored a Newsboys baseball team in 1915 and sent daughter Nina and a friend to arrange Christmas dinner for 259 newsboys and their mothers in 1917. Will helped the boys organize a Newsboys Bank and Trust Company savings account and told the young man in charge to interview cashiers at Lumberman's National Bank about an account.[30] Despite Will's "guiding influence and example" and the financial support of important civic leaders, the Newsboys Home and Club faltered financially during World War I, was found to be "dilapidated" and "untidy" by Houston Foundation inspectors in December 1918, and closed its doors in March 1919.[31]

Probably Will made his most lasting contribution to pre–World War I social service work through his brief tenure with the Houston Foundation, the city's first attempt to address social issues systematically and assume some responsibility for the fate of its less privileged citizens. Certainly the lessons he learned serving the foundation and its operating arm, the Social Service Bureau, in 1917 and 1918 impressed Ima and Mike when they began organizing the Hogg Foundation in the 1930s. The Houston Foundation, or Department of Charity, Benevolence, and Public Welfare, was created by city ordinance on March 22, 1915, to "investigate charities dependent upon public appeal or general solicitation for support," to encourage formation of new private charities to "make life more worth living," and to "foster all worthy enterprises of a philanthropic nature."[32] Although the public had been pushing reluctant city commissioners to assume supervisory responsibility for social services, politicians loath to levy taxes did not want to fund municipal intervention to ameliorate poor living conditions. A community foundation seemed the ideal bridge from private donor to public institution because professionally trained staff would approve recipients and authorize expenditures of the meager municipal resources and the more munificent private-sector donations.

Judge E. P. Hill, founder of Houston Land and Trust Company, inspired fellow citizens to establish the Houston Foundation as a community foundation when he made known his intention to bequeath $200,000 to the city as an endowment for charitable purposes. Hill had urged passage of the ordinance establishing this mechanism to manage donated funds efficiently, and he executed his final testament on April 21, 1915, a month after the ordinance was approved. The foundation was authorized to spend city charity funds "wisely," receive benevolent bequests, investigate private charities, and endorse those that met standardized guidelines. Its seven-member volunteer Board of Public Trusts was also empowered to collect statistics relating to charities, living conditions, unemployment, and delinquency and to oversee all activities to improve the city's quality of life. The foundation replaced United Charities and assumed that body's functions and much of its volunteer support.[33]

Houston Foundation committees changed names frequently, but in general work was divided into departments. Martha Gano, a trained social worker, investigated charities and ran operations during the foundation's early years.[34] In 1916, its first year of operation, the foundation received $26,000 from the city and placed 514 workers in new jobs each month. The foundation also created a Council of Social Agencies to coordinate all white service agencies, and it worked with the Negro Social Service League to better understand African-American living conditions, unemployment, and delinquency. With Progressive Era paternalism typical of enlightened white citizens, the foundation "planned our negro work on exactly the same lines as the work among the white population," formed a joint white-black advisory committee, and created parallel white and black departments. African Americans were asked to raise $50 a month so the foundation could hire an African-American nurse and relief worker. White civic leaders acknowledged African-American service institutions and the ability to care for their own, requested donations from these citizens, and allocated municipal resources to the minority community. They sought advice, but they failed to include African-American spokespeople in final decisions. While eager to raise living standards for all, progressive white leaders did not tamper with the social-political status quo that isolated African Americans from municipal power.[35]

During his tenure, Will supported the foundation in three ways. First, he joined fellow subscribers Estelle Sharp ($5,000), Abe Levy ($2,000), and Jim West, John H. Kirby, and the First National Bank ($1,000 each) with his own gift of $1,000 to support the Texas School of Civics and Philanthropy, incorporated September 29, 1916, by foundation members to train professional social workers and volunteers for public social service in voluntary, civic, and social agencies that addressed urban issues of the day.[36] Next, he served on the Welfare Finance Committee and voted on February 17, 1917, to supplement meager city appropriations with a fund-raising campaign seeking $25,000 from the private sector.

Institutions with strong community support—Faith Home, Texas School of Civics and Philanthropy, Star of Hope Mission, and Bayland Orphans Home—were told to "arrange their own finances." Finally, Will worked closely with Mayor Ben Campbell and his successor, Mayor Joseph Jay Pastoriza, as well as county commissioners to overcome "howling" opposition and secure land for a county-city tuberculosis hospital at Buffalo Bayou and Shepherd's Dam road.[37] In May 1917, when former mayor Campbell declined to serve as chairman of the Social Service Bureau, the foundation's operating arm, Will seriously considered the post. He made sure that finances for the foundation and the tuberculosis hospital land purchase were secure and concluded that he had not "let [his] impulses, good or bad, run away with [him]" before he accepted the job and retired from the Houston Foundation board in June.[38]

As chairman of the Social Service Bureau, Will immediately set to work raising money. By 1914 activists had recognized that the begging pleas of ladies collaring friends on "tag days" resulted in annoyed prospects and small donations insufficient to meet growing urban requirements. Fund-raisers needed large donations from influential wealthy businessmen, and Will's forceful methods set the pace. A July 1918 solicitation letter explained the broad mission of the Social Service Bureau—any activity that enabled citizens to live productively. The bureau purported to oversee all activities of the Houston Settlement Association, the Anti-Tuberculosis League, the Harris County Humane Society, the Kindergarten Association, and the Playgrounds Association with a "corps of efficient trained workers" and volunteers. Bureau workers also attempted to staff settlement and social centers, day nurseries, and fresh-air camps; to teach home economics; to provide anti-tuberculosis nursing and free clinics; to address housing problems; to inspect hospitals; to monitor public playgrounds and kindergartens; to make sanitation inspections; to care for homeless or neglected children and animals; and to prosecute cases of nonsupport, vagrancy, and lunacy. This enormous array of activities cost the city $3,000 per month—of which about $17,000 annually came from tax revenues. It is no wonder that Beulah Bussell, the bureau's chief administrator, reported exhaustion and resigned after Will left office. Will's tenure as chairman was cut short by World War I. Eager to serve the war effort, he anticipated being absent from Houston for at least six months in 1918–1919 and ceded his job to activist Christ Church rector Peter Gray Sears in early 1918. When Abe Levy's three-year term as Houston Foundation chairman expired in 1918, former Mayor Ben Campbell accepted that post and clarified the foundation's expanding role as arbiter of "everything that would assist in improving conditions" in the city, from supervision of charities and philanthropies to management of hospitals to public education and war work.[39]

City and county officials and private citizens struggled from 1915 to 1919 to allocate responsibility for assisting the indigent and disabled and improving quality of life for all citizens. While the public-private Houston Foundation asserted its grand mission to oversee all social service activity in the city and developed the Social Service Bureau to implement policy, it remained sorely underfunded and pitifully understaffed, sometimes employing no more than two or three professionally trained social workers. City officials failed to allocate sufficient resources to Houston Foundation operations, and donations proved inadequate to support all of its programs in these years of transition away from private palliative charity toward proactive public-private efforts to ameliorate causes of poverty and social injustice. Reformers had expanded the meaning of a wholesome civic life but had not foreseen the costs of citywide access to health care, education, and infrastructure amenities. Private citizens wanted to control expenditures, and in the prewar years no municipal bureaucracy existed to challenge or supplant their involvement. Volunteer Houston Foundation board members devoted hours to investigative and supervisory tasks while lobbying large-scale taxpayers to pressure city officials for funds.

POSTWAR SOCIAL SERVICE WORK IN HOUSTON

World War I was a turning point in Houston as in the rest of the nation. Volunteers rallied to sell war bonds, hold meatless weekdays, plant victory gardens, and entertain troops stationed at Camp Logan. The war energized municipal government and was a catalyst for its bureaucratic expansion and professionalization. The war also turned attention away from long-term humanitarian reform, and in the immediate aftermath of the armistice, civic activists discovered that unifying Progressive Era values had been challenged by a new ethos of progress focused on material well-being and fueled by explosions in the automobile, home appliance, and construction industries. Nationwide, the years following World War I shattered illusions about Anglo-Protestant traditions that had shaped American Victorian culture. Violent labor strikes in 1919, anti-Communist red-scare hysteria inflamed by a revived Ku Klux Klan, and a severe recession in 1921 were succeeded by eight years of unprecedented intolerance, conformity, and prosperity during which Americans amassed two-fifths of the world's wealth, attempted to legislate morality by banning alcohol, and discovered a generation gap. Youthful Houstonians, like their peers elsewhere, found cheap cars, radio broadcasts, jazz, short skirts, short hair, and illicit gin much more exciting than earnest discussions about the health and welfare of downtrodden but distant neighbors; and many of their elders were similarly seduced by easy money, unexpected leisure, and fundamental disinterest in humanitarian concerns.

Despite this new materialism, Houston's female and male reformers did sustain their search for new approaches to social service welfare issues. The Hoggs applied progressive values to their city and residential planning activities. Joseph Cullinan and John Henry Kirby organized the American Anti-Klan Association to shut down the Houston klavern, which operated in the city from September 1920 until sometime in 1924. Marcellus Foster (Mefo), publisher of the *Chronicle*, debunked the Klan's racism, moral certitude, and resistance to change in two simple questions: "Why anonymity, if the common good is sought? Does decency need a disguise?"[40] Journalists kept Houstonians informed about an array of postwar problems even while trumpeting economic triumphs and exploding growth. Columns in *Houston*, the Chamber of Commerce mouthpiece after 1919, in *Woman's Viewpoint*, published by Florence M. Sterling from 1923–1926, in Will Hogg's *Civics for Houston* (1928–1929), and in the *Gargoyle* (1928–1932), backed by Estelle Sharp and banker William A. Kirkland, made readers aware of issues littering the "thorny road of civic and social reform" as they attempted to build "phalanxes of solidarity" among prewar humanitarians.[41]

Articles explained the "new morality" of young America, reviewed the tragedy of drug abuse, and applauded Margaret Sanger's "stormy" fight to introduce birth control, deemed by *Gargoyle* editors "one of the most necessary aids to decreasing misery and raising economic levels among the ignorant and poverty-stricken."[42] *Civics for Houston* devoted its August and September 1928 issues to "Houston's Colored Citizens," while the *Gargoyle* examined poverty in the Third and Fifth Wards, prison conditions, and child welfare.[43] Blasting the *Houston Post-Dispatch* for its "distinctly conservative and very, *very* Dry" stance against repeal, the *Gargoyle* crusaded against Prohibition, "with its Federal police enforcement, its interference in the lives, liberty and pursuit of happiness of the citizens of the states." Citing the impossibility of enforcing such moral legislation when some states utterly repudiated the infringement on personal rights, *Gargoyle* editors reprinted James Stephen Hogg's 1880s peroration against the "evil and inevitable results of Prohibition":

"Morality, sobriety and religion spring from a different source than brute force or the lash of the law. Men cannot be made moral, forced into temperance, or whipped into religion." Hogg warned that efforts to suppress saloons would only "scatter the traffic and use of intoxicants and force them into low dives and high places alike, without the attendance of law or the burdens of taxation." Self-styled "Liberal" voters Joseph S. Cullinan, John E. Green Jr., Palmer Hutcheson, E. A. Peden, and Harry C. Wiess joined advertisers on May Day 1932 to urge defeat of the "Reactionary Dry Minority" at precinct conventions.[44]

During the 1920s the Social Service Bureau continued to connect clients with appropriate agencies for assistance, and city leaders began to address public health care needs.[45] Early in the decade, the Young Men's Business League, a subsidiary of the Chamber of Commerce, set up a Home Welfare Department supervised by Lou Stallman, a "food expert and dietitian." She published periodic reports about health conditions, vital statistics, child welfare, proper diet, and malnutrition.[46] In 1919 a municipal hospital opened at Camp Logan, and a Social Health Committee that included prominent business leaders, religious leaders, and several doctors studied ways to enforce Texas's new Venereal Disease Act. Jefferson Davis Memorial Hospital, Houston's first municipal hospital entirely funded by a bond issue, opened on March 1, 1925, with 150 patients and a psychopathic ward that ended confinement of the "insane" to the county jail. By 1928 writers deemed the facility "woefully" overcrowded and in 1931 regarded it as inadequate and poorly located. Hermann Charity Hospital, built with a $2 million gift to the city of Houston from the estate of George Hermann, raised its fireproof Mediterranean tower east of Rice Institute in 1925. That year Allie K. (Mrs. James) Autry donated funds to the city for a school and hospital to treat white tubercular children ages four to thirteen.[47]

Although municipal and charity hospitals reserved a few segregated beds for African-American patients, it was not until June 19, 1926, that Houston's first hospital devoted to its African-American population opened its doors at the corner of Ennis and Cargill. The fifty-bed Negro Hospital (later renamed Riverside General) was made possible by Joseph S. Cullinan in honor of his son, John Halm Cullinan, "one of the millions of young Americans who fought in the World War to preserve and perpetuate human liberty without regard to race, creed, or color." The hospital was dedicated to "the American Negro to promote self-help, to inspire good citizenship, and for the relief of suffering, sickness and disease amongst them."[48] Ironically, this modern, fully equipped monument to humanitarian values, built on two city blocks provided by the City Council, sparked strenuous controversy. Carefully planned by benefactor Cullinan and managed by an African-American medical board supervised by a white advisory council that retained full power to approve all policies, the hospital pleased no one. White citizens complained that their African-American neighbors were incapable of responsibly running such an important institution; black spokesmen and disaffected *Houston Informer* editor C. F. Richardson bitterly attacked the "high-handed and czaristic" white oversight board. Cullinan's friends at the *Gargoyle* called Richardson's angry criticism "inexcusable" and noted that visitors found the plant clean, quiet, orderly, and up-to-date.[49] Although the hospital provided safe health care delivery, its oversight provisions failed to ameliorate race relations.

Jazz and gin may have addled some young minds, but many Houstonians were as eager to apply new approaches to civic problems as they were to build new industries and try new gadgets. The municipal Board of Health sponsored a cleanup week each spring and fall during the decade to raise public awareness; Houston's branch of the National Council of Catholic Women opened a free clinic for Mexican residents in 1923; and several churches sponsored day nurseries for working mothers. Anxious "to make a difference," twelve young women, the daughters of Houston's prewar civic leaders, met on January 22, 1925, to form what became the Junior League of Houston. First president Adelaide Lovett Baker, daughter of Rice Institute President Edgar Odell Lovett, recalled years later her excitement when she learned about Junior League activities to harness the energies of privileged young women for civic work in New York, where the movement had been founded in 1901. Adelaide, Mary Cullinan Cravens, Margaret Cullinan Wray, and their friends charted a new course for educated young women when they opened a luncheon club in the basement of the Gibraltar Savings and Loan to raise funds to establish a well-baby clinic for indigent children. Volunteer women would manage the lunchroom and assist clinic medical personnel by assuming managerial and clerical duties. Following concepts already established at the national level, the Houston league recruited young women, trained them to identify social service needs, assigned them to projects throughout the city, and raised funds to support social service initiatives. The founders were well acquainted with the pioneering work of Adelaide's mother-in-law, Alice Baker, and eager to encourage their friends to contribute to the community. Continuing a Progressive Era tradition, they advocated projects that would help less fortunate women and children expand their horizons, improve their health, and enrich their lives.[50] Once trained to understand civic needs, many of these women later assumed leadership positions in the city's social service, cultural, and educational organizations.

Serving as a catalyst for these and other social service projects was a new approach in community fund-raising—the Community Chest. An outgrowth of World War I War Chest bond drives, community chests engaged businesses and individuals in broad-based support of local philanthropic organizations. No longer were a few rich philanthropists supposed to shoulder the charity burden; rather, on a "democratic basis," all citizens of a community were called upon "to care for its members who are in need" by cooperating to alleviate suffering. Community Chest advocates embraced progressive beliefs that "privation is abnormal, temporary and remediable" and that all citizens have "the right . . . to an opportunity to live and grow in the modern sense of the word."[51] The Community Chest was organized in Houston in 1922 upon recommendation of a 1921 Chamber of Commerce study committee to carry on the work of United Charities and regroup civic activities interrupted by wartime demands.[52] Developer Jesse H. Jones and banker John T. Scott obtained the original charter, and attorney Clarence R. Wharton served as first Community Chest president. With the return of prosperity and with support from the Chamber of Commerce, citizens adopted the format of one brief, citywide charity campaign as a device to cut solicitation costs, to improve delivery of services, to relieve donors from irritating repeated solicitation, and to provide adequate funds for all institutions. In short, businessmen wanted a system that was efficient and effective. When the first fund drive, managed by a professional fund-raiser, fell short, a group of leading citizens met, raised the necessary money in a few weeks, and established November as Community Chest Month when prominent businessmen would "ramrod" Houston's citizens to ever-higher levels of giving.[53] Each year the chest added agencies to its approved list as the budget climbed to $600,000 by 1931.

Will, Ima, and Mike embraced the modern fund-raising technique in 1922 and gave $2,000 apiece to the inaugural $400,000 campaign, in aggregate the largest Community Chest donation. After Will's death in 1930, Mike and Ima each contributed $3,000 to keep the annual Hogg family gift at a steady $6,000 per year into the 1940s. Will wrote to business acquaintances in Houston and around the state to endorse the Community Chest concept and urge other cities to examine its advantages. Ima served on fund-raising committees over the years; Mike was a board member during the late 1930s; and Alice joined the board soon after Mike's death in 1941.[54] In 1928 a Council of Social Agencies (1928–1976) was organized as an arm of the Community Chest to discover what underserved groups needed by conducting research on social conditions. Data in hand, the council acted as advocate for the powerless and helped agencies implement new ideas. Estelle Sharp served on the council for years, watched it expand to include all Harris County communities, and guided its efforts to coordinate Community Chest, municipal, and volunteer groups. In 1956 Estelle and Ima provided funding through the Walter Benona Sharp and Hogg Foundations for the council to conduct a six-year child welfare study.[55]

Houston's post–World War I experiments in voluntarism coincided with redefinitions of professional and public views of psychiatry, mental health, and youthful delinquency or social maladaptation—issues of particular interest to Ima and her brothers. Ima frequently recalled visits to mental institutions with her father, and in 1968 she presented Henry Maudsley's prescient *Responsibility in Mental Illness* (1878) to the Hogg Foundation. Well-worn and much-marked, this volume had been given to Governor Hogg in 1891.[56] By 1920 the application of scientific principles to the study of social problems had inspired both increased acceptance of and greater confusion about mental hygiene precepts. The science of mental hygiene originated in the United States in 1909 when Clifford Beers, himself a victim of mental illness, founded the National Committee for Mental Hygiene. An outgrowth of the public health movement and the revolution in psychiatric practice that sought prevention rather than institutionalization, "mental hygiene symbolized and advanced the application of science to social life." Mental hygiene's mission became the "study and application of principles of personality development" to help "all individuals utilize their capacities fully and work with their fellows creatively."[57] Its greatest challenges were the definition and perception of "normal" behavior and the discovery and embrace of practical therapies. Mental hygiene activity was predicated on three assumptions: that "well-adjusted" children were the best guarantors of a stable, productive adult population; that "normal" behavior patterns in children could be identified and taught; and that children were malleable and greatly affected by environmental factors, which could be ameliorated or changed. In the progressive tradition espoused by the Hoggs, mental hygiene advocates believed that if the problem could be identified, it could be solved.[58]

Nationwide, the mental hygiene movement corresponded with and was nurtured by the development of "scientific" philanthropic foundations that adopted efficient management practices to organize the process of giving and to effect social change through preventive rather than palliative approaches to public health and welfare issues. Philanthropists like John D. Rockefeller, Elizabeth Milbank Anderson, Olivia Sage, and Kate Macy Ladd had transformed giving from a tradition of personal charity that assuaged specific tragedy to a business of planned support that analyzed causes of social problems and guided change. Alarmed by social and economic transformations resulting from industrial growth, immigration, urbanization, and rural poverty and armed with social-gospel religious tenets that urged a moral response to change, they recognized new demands to husband their wealth and to address broad community issues.

Rockefeller organized seven philanthropies between 1901 and 1913 and brought them together under a reconstituted Rockefeller Foundation in 1929 to address education, medical research, and disease prevention. Elizabeth Milbank Anderson focused work of the Milbank Memorial Fund, founded in 1905, on public health, broadly interpreted. Inspired by her physician daughter and moved by the plight of freed slaves and immigrants plagued by epidemic diseases and poverty, she advocated preventive community health care projects.[59] Olivia Sage founded the Russell Sage Foundation in 1907 to influence social welfare policy. She emphasized the importance of discovery and diffusion of knowledge, supported demonstration projects, published studies, and in the foundation's early years emphasized child-helping, the role of play, and the training of professional social workers. Kate Macy Ladd, who believed "no sound structure of social or cultural welfare can be maintained without health, that health . . . resides in the wholesome unity of mind and body," founded the Josiah Macy Jr. Foundation in 1930 to concentrate on "fundamental aspects" of health, sickness, and relief of suffering. Like the Hoggs, Ladd asserted that "in an enlightened democracy, private organized philanthropy serves the purposes of human welfare best, not by replacing functions which rightfully should be supported by our communities, but by investigating, testing, and demonstrating the value of newer organized ideas." Like Ima, Kate Ladd inherited strong family habits of service to mankind and suffered long periods of ill health.[60]

Not to be outdone by the social science experts staffing private-sector philanthropies, government, too, had begun to shape social and family life. By the 1920s, newly enfranchised women and socially conscious men were pressing governments at all levels to redress social inequities and address personal difficulties. The traumatic dislocations and nationwide economic collapse of the 1930s made all but the most ardent individualists grapple with ways government agencies, individual philanthropists, and privately managed institutions could cooperate to address social problems. At the onset of World War II, a symbiotic public-private process had emerged: foundations and private institutions tried to influence social policy and government spending by identifying a need, financing and organizing pilot programs, garnering public enthusiasm, and then turning to government agencies for continued funding and maintenance. These national trends influenced the Hoggs' two most important contributions to social service philanthropy—creation of the Houston Child Guidance Center in 1929 and establishment of the Hogg Foundation for Mental Hygiene a decade later.

IMA AND HOUSTON'S CHILD GUIDANCE CENTER

Philanthropists and experts interested in shaping social progress had first turned their attention to child-saving initiatives to assist "maladapted" or delinquent children. Juvenile courts, introduced in Chicago in 1899 and adopted by all but three states by 1920, developed a nonpunitive separate system of justice designed to keep young offenders or neglected and dependent children out of institutions by encouraging education, treatment, and rehabilitation. To many observers, however, juvenile courts acted too late because their jurisdictions covered only those who had already displayed severely maladjusted behavior or had been the victims of abuse. What about the child at risk, the child for whom intervention and guidance could ensure a happy, productive life? Founded in 1918 by Anna Harkness, widow of Standard Oil of Ohio investor Stephen Harkness, with an initial gift of $10 million to "do something for the welfare of mankind," the Commonwealth Fund recognized that maladapted children needed careful professional evaluation. The fund studied competing approaches to delinquency prevention and in 1920 sponsored a "program of psychiatric treatment, research, and field work."[61] Fund professionals teamed with the National Committee for Mental Hygiene in 1921 to inaugurate a four-pronged, five-year pilot program in 1922. As a first step, the fund collaborated with the New York School of Social Work to open a Bureau of Children's Guidance to train psychiatric social workers and examine "unadjusted" children. The fund established seven demonstration child guidance clinics, including one in Dallas, to help "normal" children overcome temporary problems. A committee on visiting teachers cooperated with schools and community agencies to work with children and families, and a committee on methods developed publicity to educate the public and combat stereotypical fears of mental illness and mental health care.[62]

Scholars of the child guidance movement, while generally praising attempts to assist children with various mental health difficulties, point out the pitfalls of the mental hygiene approach. Experts found they could not define "normal" behavior, and they assumed, without sufficient evidence, that their paternalistic policies would ameliorate what were, in effect, socially constructed "maladaptations." Mental hygiene became a "catch-all for problem-solving through prevention," and by enhancing the status of professionals, the movement reinforced middle-class values and views of "normal" behavior.[63] But parents and reformers who were worried about social change and family deterioration hailed the child guidance clinics enthusiastically as expert answers to the unsettling effects of industrialization, urbanization, and "the revolution in manners and morals" unleashed in the 1920s.[64]

At first, the clinics tried to incorporate both the preventive models of community education and family support and the palliative prototypes of patient treatment and professional training by coordinating all health and cultural resources to promote the emotional well-being of every child. By 1930, however, many clinics, headed by psychiatrists, had narrowed their goals to the treatment of "children with mild behavior and emotional problems."[65] The goals of protecting community mental hygiene and intervening to prevent social problems were largely forgotten. In formulating her mental health care philanthropy and discussing it with her brothers, Ima experimented with both preventive and palliative models but never lost enthusiasm for prevention as the primary goal. Although the Houston Child Guidance Clinic came to privilege medical treatment and professional training in the 1960s and 1970s, the Hogg Foundation has never wavered in its mission to bring the message of prevention and early intervention to cities, towns, and rural areas throughout Texas.

During Ima's 1923–1924 sojourn in Stockbridge, Massachusetts, Austen Riggs was organizing a child guidance clinic in Pittsfield, Massachusetts, and introduced her to the pioneering concept. Riggs told Ima about the Dallas demonstration clinic that had been established by the Commonwealth Fund in 1923 and proposed that a similar institution could benefit Houstonians.[66] Ima embraced Riggs's ideas with enthusiasm. Had not her parents demonstrated the importance of family, and had not they emphasized the link between family and civic life? Would her brother Tom's volatile career and her own struggles have been avoided if the motherless children could have consulted experts at a child guidance clinic? Like her father, Ima had come to believe "that in every head there is a good idea hidden like the jewels of the Ocean," but she understood that individuals often needed appropriate tools to extract the gems and use them in everyday life.[67] Just as they merited access to natural parkland, open spaces, and adequate housing, so Houstonians deserved services that would empower them to lead wholesome lives.

Encouraged by Riggs, Ima embarked on a program of self-education in 1924 and devoured available literature describing mental hygiene and guidance clinic goals. She also discussed the possibility of a clinic with Will, Mike, and their circle of friends familiar with the city's social welfare needs. She recalled later in life that psychiatrist Will Menninger's belief that "no one is perfectly balanced in life—that everyone needs help" influenced her thinking about guidance clinic goals, and she drew several conclusions from observing Will's and dear friend Estelle Sharp's social service activism with the Houston Foundation.[68] The foundation's broad definition of social welfare responsibilities fit Ima's growing understanding that all quality-of-life issues—from sewers to symphonies—contributed to positive individual, family, and community mental hygiene. She agreed with Houston Foundation efforts to collect data, educate the public, and disseminate information as broadly as possible. Houston Foundation attempts to coordinate all services under one umbrella and foster public and private-sector cooperation paralleled Ima's struggles to deliver mental health care and engage municipal and state officials in the use of positive, preventive, therapeutic approaches.

Ima invited Dr. George Stevenson, director of the Division of Community Clinics for the Commonwealth Fund, to visit Houston and consult community leaders about organizing a fund-sponsored clinic for the city.[69] In 1926 the Community Chest authorized $7,500 for a child guidance clinic, but Stevenson concluded that municipal interest was insufficient to warrant a clinic sponsored by the Commonwealth Fund. Undaunted, Ima kept up her propaganda and worked with like-minded volunteers to strengthen community services. In 1929 when Stevenson paid a second visit, he told Ima and other philanthropists that the social service infrastructure was at last sufficiently mature to support the referral program fostered by child guidance clinics.[70]

In the late 1920s, child-saving issues were given good press, especially by *Houston Gargoyle* publisher Estelle Sharp. Columnist Ruth West suggested that the "Root of Evil" lay in a failure to understand and guide small children during their formative years. In a 1929 article, West outlined goals of a steering committee hard at work to establish "a Mental Hygiene Clinic" whose "most important function will be an educative one, to make the public fully aware of the powerful influence of mental hygiene in erasing crime, insanity, disease." According to spokesman John Willis Slaughter, professor of sociology at Rice Institute, parents attending the clinic would be trained to raise their children "happily." Slaughter also announced the steering committee's dream: a headquarters "in a dwelling house, with a yard where 'problem' children may be observed at play, with comfortable waiting rooms where harassed mothers may await a conference hour," and a staff composed of a psychiatrist "trained in mental diseases," a psychologist who understood emotions and the mind, two or three social workers, and secretaries. Referrals would come from "every organization, every individual charged with the care or education of minors."[71] On October 20, 1929, West devoted three columns to preschool and adolescent children, "about whom a mass of specific information has been gathered in recent years." She noted that "science has reduced the business of child rearing to practical, or nearly practical terms" and advocated companionable parent-child relationships based on positive discipline where "Dos" replace "Don'ts" to open a "new line of thinking, instead of merely closing an old one."[72]

Although Ima gaveled the organizing meeting of the Houston Child Guidance Clinic to order in her home at seven o'clock in the evening of April 23, 1929, she never served as president of the organization. Instead, she exerted influence through unwavering financial support and energetic committee work. Because she believed it was important to attract male leadership in the business community to this privately funded organization, Ima asked neighbor John E. Green Jr. to read the steering committee report. Founders recommended that the clinic be established and estimated that it might take $25,000 a year to operate successfully. John Willis Slaughter, at the time executive secretary of the Community Chest and head of the Houston Foundation, suggested candidates for the founding board. Representatives from Faith Home, the Family Service Bureau, and the Probation Department; several doctors; school district administrators E. E. Oberholtzer and J. W. Mills; businessmen Kenneth E. Womack, Leopold Meyer, and John Dorrance; public-spirited members of the Junior League and Parent-Teacher Association; and civic leaders associated with other city projects comprised the original board.[73]

By October 16, the thirty-three-member volunteer board had pledged $10,000 (including $2,000 from Ima), signed Dr. James Cunningham as director, hired two social workers, and rented a headquarters house at

703 Gray at Louisiana.[74] On November 1 the Houston Child Guidance Clinic was ready to embark on its dual mission as stated in the constitution and bylaws of its charter approved by the state of Texas: "The diagnosis, treatment and guidance of problem children. The study of the principles of mental hygiene, and the application of these principles to problem children and other persons connected with or related to such children."[75] A memorandum inviting guests to the first open casework conference to demonstrate clinic procedures, held after one year's operation, further explained the clinic's purpose:

> The clinic is a community agency designed to act as a bureau for mental health work for children. Its aims are the study, treatment and prevention of childhood behavior problems which may be forerunners of chronic physical illness, nervousness, mental disorders, delinquency, crime and other social problems of importance. In other words, it is an agency which protects and conserves human material.[76]

To attract supporters, the board invited three hundred Houstonians to partake of donated tea and sandwiches, visit the clinic, and meet the staff on January 20, 1930.[77] *Gargoyle* columnist Ruth West praised the nascent organization in long articles November 10, 1929, and April 17, 1930. She listed board and staff members and explained that the clinic would provide free service to any child whose behavior was a problem. She announced the goal of producing happy, healthy citizens through an ounce of prevention that would "supplant wherever possible the more expensive and less effective pounds of cure, our 'houses of correction,' prisons, insane asylums." Two case studies illustrated how practical advice had produced tangible results in some two hundred cases over the first six months of clinic operation.[78]

Study, treatment, and prevention remained overarching goals during Ima's association with the clinic, although the institution changed programs over the years to accommodate community needs. By 1957 the clinic's purpose was encapsulated in a pamphlet for parents and teachers, "Every Child Has a Right to Be Happy." Created by the board's education committee, the general information brochure announced that the renamed Guidance Center of Houston would "help children with emotional problems reach well-adjusted relationships with other people in everyday living."[79] By the 1950s the center's approach to helping children form these well-adjusted relationships encompassed four goals: to operate a psychiatric clinic for the treatment and study of children with "emotional problems"; to educate and train mental health care professionals; to conduct research in the fields of human behavior, mental disorders, and interpersonal relationships; and to promote understanding of mental health issues in the community.

Participation in the programs was always voluntary and was open to "children of all colors, creeds, [and] economic and social levels" who were under eighteen years of age and lived in Harris County and to their parents. Referrals came from parents, schools, social agencies, courts, clergy, and friends. About 80 percent of cases in 1956, for example, were children ages six to thirteen. In that year the psychiatrist, psychologist, psychiatric social worker, and assistants counseled 325 children and 440 parents and provided information about sister agencies to 644 members of the community; they conducted 266 interviews with children, 3,225 with parents, and 1,139 with care providers for their young clients. The staff also lectured and supplied general information to the public; organized in-service training for child-care professionals and teachers; and consulted with other agencies to address community needs.[80] Typical treatment included weekly psychotherapy with the child and interviews with parents; this process usually lasted about fifteen months, with a range from four to twenty-three months. Problems believed to inhibit the child's ability to "mobilize his inner resources and strengths and to find healthier and more constructive ways of dealing with inner stresses and the external pressures of everyday life" included poor adjustment to school, unhappiness, excessive fears, rebellious and withdrawn behaviors, truancy, destructiveness, excessive daydreaming, temper outbursts, sex and eating problems, depression, stealing, fire-setting, and an inability to get along with family or peers.[81]

During Ima's forty-six years on the center's board, she worked actively with colleagues Estelle Sharp, Nina Cullinan, Leopold Meyer, and others to stabilize the institution's finances and define and disseminate its mission.[82] Unfortunately, the center's early funding records cannot be found, and memoranda in archival sources are confusing. It seems clear, however, that Ima guaranteed financial support of up to $10,000 per year from 1929 through 1932 and during that period dispensed at least $10,200 from personal funds and $4,250 from Hogg Brothers Inc. In November 1930 Ima outlined an "acute" financial crisis to George Stevenson in hopes that the Commonwealth Fund could assist the "young and struggling clinic," that year largely supported by her $10,000 gift. In 1931 Treasurer Leopold Meyer explained why the center needed Community Chest money, noting that he doubted that Ima would give more than the $8,000 already donated to center projects. Correspondence shows that Mike joined his sister with enthusiastic endorsement of the center and generous gifts to the struggling project.[83]

Unable to secure financing from the Commonwealth Fund, which had switched from funding to oversight functions in 1927, Ima defended the board's October 14, 1930, decision to explore Community Chest support. In 1932 the Community Chest defrayed $15,000 of an $18,000 budget for the first time; gifts from Ima and Mike made up the difference that year. Even with Community Chest funding, Depression-era shortfalls necessitated staff and salary cuts that seriously threatened program development.[84] By 1941, Community Chest donations covered all operating costs, and the center's financial stability for daily operations appeared more secure, although Ima occasionally made gifts for special purposes. After 1948 the center also received $20,000 a year from the Texas Department of Health through the National Mental Health Act, and from the mid-1940s on, Ima funneled Hogg Foundation support to the clinic for training and research programs. Always concerned that poor families might not be able to afford clinic services, Ima fought to keep fees low and scaled to a family's income. In 1961 she pledged $8,000 on the condition that the fee schedule remain unchanged. Her gift and conditions were accepted.[85] In April 1962 Ima funded a formal review of center activities, and at the September 10, 1962, board meeting she proposed that a committee be established to receive endowment gifts. In 1970 she wrote to U.S. Senators John Tower and Ralph Yarborough requesting continued federal support of the Texas Department of Public Welfare, whose allocations supported the center's programs.[86] Despite these tenacious efforts, board minutes during these decades indicate that funding remained an acute problem.

For thirty years, the Guidance Center also struggled to establish a permanent facility and made do with grossly inadequate and unsuitable quarters that restricted program development and effective delivery of services. The center was frequently ejected from rental properties on short notice, and its board unsuccessfully tried to locate a site at the Texas Medical Center, which was being developed after World War II. Finally, in June 1959, stockbroker Edwin K. Dillingham, his wife Lottie, and their children alleviated the housing problem by donating the family's large neoclassical house on Austin Street for a permanent home.[87] Ima served on the building committee that oversaw remodeling, provided "a very generous" gift of $10,000 anonymously to begin a fund drive for building renovation, and relentlessly pursued recalcitrant prospects.[88] Refusals by two major Houston philanthropies, the M. D. Anderson Foundation (established in 1936) and the Houston Endowment (established in 1937 by Jesse H. Jones), goaded Ima to counterattack. On June 14, 1960, she wrote Judge John H. Freeman, chairman of M. D. Anderson, to express her "genuine regret" that the foundation had refused to fund the center; she noted that after three decades in "impossible quarters" the clinic "desperately" needed facilities to treat "children . . . suffering from behavior problems." She then mentioned her own "substantial" donation and requested reconsideration. On June 23, 1960, a check for $25,000 arrived at the center. Similar pleas to John T. Jones Jr. elicited a like response from the Houston Endowment. In appreciation for these efforts, for securing $18,000 from the Hogg Foundation, and for her decades of service, the board named the facility's new wing for the Hogg family and honored Ima herself with a bronze and marble tablet acknowledging her contributions.[89]

Ima made her most important contributions to the center's success by supervising the board's public education and long-range planning activities. She shaped the board's character by heading the nominating committee in 1931, 1932, 1937, and 1944 and took direct responsibility for hiring and firing personnel and reviewing performance while serving on the personnel committee in 1948–1950. Always interested in young professionals with stellar academic credentials, Ima supported hiring the youthful James Morrow Cunningham as founding director of the clinic. Described by contemporaries as "applying a keen, earnest, hopeful intelligence to the problem of correcting bad habits," the bespectacled, newly minted psychiatrist had completed a fellowship at the Institute for Child Guidance in New York. A lover of golf, bridge, music, and cabinet making, Cunningham was praised because he talked to juveniles "without using a lot of lumpy, indigestible words."[90] Other original staff members also had proven track records with the child guidance movement: psychologist Mary Lasater had been a Commonwealth Fund fellow at the Institute for Child Guidance; chief social worker Charlotte Henry had completed the Family Service Course at Western Reserve University; and social worker Lucretia Brewer had trained with the child guidance clinic in Cleveland.[91] Typically, Ima had gone to the best sources to recruit the center's initial staff.[92] Ima served on the selection committees that searched for new directors in 1934, 1938, and 1943 and was instrumental in hiring Dr. Harry Little as director in 1948. Little proved one of the center's most enduring and successful leaders, serving from 1949 to 1966, but during Ima's lifetime the center had difficulty hiring professional staff because the board could not offer competitive salaries due to funding shortfalls.

In June 1944 Ima organized a special planning and policy committee to review the clinic's mission and programs with the new director, John H. Waterman (1944–1948), and to develop a mutually acceptable plan of action better to serve community needs. Under her tutelage, this committee, which met frequently at her home during 1944 and throughout 1945, presented formal proposals on January 28, 1945, that articulated two critical goals: to operate a psychiatric treatment clinic for children and adults and to maintain a community-wide preventive mental hygiene program. Focusing on the prevention of juvenile delinquency, Ima stressed the need to implement a visiting teacher program in the schools, to cooperate with the Houston Independent School District and the juvenile court system, to reach out to the public, and to support professional training, which she considered "key." Then she went to work to implement her recommendations.

Through Ima's efforts as a Board of Education trustee, Houston schools inaugurated a visiting teacher program in 1945. Ima worked closely with Hogg Foundation Executive Director Robert Sutherland to structure a professional training program at the Guidance Center in cooperation with the University of Houston and the University of Texas and to provide financial support for the project through the Hogg Foundation. After several discussions, Ima approved the course by the late fall of 1944 and applauded the "galaxy of stars" promised as instructors in 1945–1946. Ima could not contain her delight that the center, the University of Houston, the University of Texas, and the Hogg Foundation would be associated in a unique and mutually beneficial partnership. Finally, Ima invited representatives of the juvenile court, the probation department, and the Houston Police Department's Crime Prevention Bureau to meet with Guidance Center committee members on November 4, 1945. The group discussed ways to stem the growing incidence of juvenile delinquency and crime. Ima told her colleagues about a successful cooperative program in Baltimore that was funded by that city's Guidance Clinic, the Johns Hopkins University Hospital, and the county government. The Houston committee decided to emulate the Baltimore program and employ a psychiatrist to work full time with the probation and crime prevention bureaus, the salary to be defrayed by the center and the two city departments.[93]

Ima's records during the 1940s make clear her concern that counseling and training take precedence over research because she felt the staff could not effectively discharge all three functions.[94] Most important to Ima were community outreach efforts to explain the center's work to the public. She served as chairperson of the education committee (1930–1933 and 1936–1937) and remained active on the committee for many years, helping the director set up community educational outreach programs and staff a speakers bureau. Minutes reflect her attempts to inform board members, as she brought books to meetings and bombarded members with reading lists of mental hygiene materials. She gained permission to reprint *Commonwealth Fund Hygiene Bulletin* articles in the *Child Guidance Center Bulletin* published by the committee, and she created other promotional materials. She tried to educate college club women to the need for a citywide mental hygiene program by reaching out to the Panhellenic Council in 1930, and she developed a joint Clinic-YMCA summer camp program in 1939.[95] Ima arranged public lecture series, invited guest speakers to annual meetings, placed articles in the *Gargoyle*, and arranged speaking slots on KTRH public-interest radio broadcasts.[96] She frequently brought groups to clinic headquarters or entertained care providers and civic leaders together in her home. Periodically she supported efforts to broaden the clinic's mission and make it a mental health care facility open to all age groups.[97]

In December 1948 Ima announced her intention to retire from the board to make way for new supporters. Instead, board members persuaded her to accept lifetime honorary active status and invited her to serve ex officio on all committees. She remained an active participant on the personnel and building committees, obtained publicity in local newspapers, and served as the center's delegate to the Texas State Department of Health meeting in Austin in 1951. In 1950 she outlined her vision of the organization's future at the annual meeting. She urged supporters to widen the center's scope of interest, to stay informed about state and national trends in mental hygiene, and to lobby for passage of legislation that supported eleemosynary and mental health institutions.[98]

In later years Ima became Houston's preeminent spokesperson for mental health care. In 1953 she hosted meetings to discuss forming a local mental health society, and in 1954 she joined business executive John C. Flanagan, Nina Cullinan, and others to found a local affiliate of the state association that became the Mental Health Society of Houston and Harris County (later the Mental Health Association of Greater Houston). She served on the society's board for two terms, advocated mental health education, and counseled with social service and mental health professionals and volunteers about dozens of projects.[99] A typical admirer, Dr. Henry A. Cromwell, chairman of the Youth Guidance Program for the thousand-member Council of Churches of Greater Houston, wrote warmly to thank her for discussing council efforts in 1957 to stem juvenile delinquency with "sympathetic interest, excellent insights, and constructive suggestions." From 1940 until her death she supported the Texas Society for Mental Hygiene (later Health).[100]

Despite Ima's diligence and generosity, the Guidance Center struggled to meet Houston's growing demands for juvenile mental health care services. A "Blueprint for Health" developed by center personnel in 1952 called for ten treatment teams by 1962 to meet projected growth; when a study committee examined the center's programs and structure in 1959, it found that Harris County's exploding population would require eleven teams. At the time of the study, the center operated with "slightly less than two teams." From September 1958 through March 1959, the center alone treated 374 children, while the five other Houston agencies that addressed the problems of "disturbed children" handled no more than 170 cases together. Desperate need notwithstanding, the center could not meet demand because it lacked qualified personnel and was plagued by uncompetitive salary schedules, inadequate operating funds, and unsuitable facilities well into the 1960s. Even with these chronic problems, the center garnered high marks in the 1959 study, whose authors concluded that the "quality of service provided . . . is superior" and outlined a series of new programs to train personnel and improve therapies.[101]

Gaps in the archival sources make it difficult to evaluate the center's achievement during Ima's lifetime, but the unending struggle for funding, the frequent change of directors, the acceptance and rejection of program ideas, and the attempts to define "mental health" suggest a mixed reception of the center and its mission. From the 1930s through the 1960s, when Ima was most active, professional approaches to mental health care and child development were harshly contested and underwent fundamental changes. During this time the public was still hesitant to embrace family therapy, and advocates of palliative efforts to treat patients warred with those who attempted to prevent problems through programs emphasizing public awareness and education. Nonetheless, Ima's determination to build public interest through a privately managed institution and her flexible approach to community needs continue to inspire staff and volunteers at the nonprofit DePelchin Children's Center, which merged with the Child Guidance Center in 1992. DePelchin's mission to sponsor services for children and families in crisis echoes the pioneering dreams of Kezia

DePelchin and Ima Hogg to provide children the love and guidance that would enable them to lead wholesome and happy lives.[102]

IMA, MIKE, AND THE HOGG FOUNDATION
FOR MENTAL HEALTH

The Child Guidance Center of Houston and the Hogg Foundation for Mental Hygiene (changed to Hogg Foundation for Mental Health in December 1957) embody contrasting attempts to create a wholesome community through mental health care philanthropy.[103] In founding the Child Guidance Center, Ima relied on Commonwealth Fund guidelines that favored a psychiatric treatment model. She shared planning and vision with a group of leading Houstonians, deferred presidential duties to others, and worked in the volunteer trenches day by day to ensure the center's acceptance. When Ima and Mike established the Hogg Foundation in July 1939 as a memorial to brother Will's dynamic life, they benefited from Ima's accomplishments in Houston but brought a family interest in mental health care to a statewide constituency. The foundation's mission reflected their shared vision that optimum mental health care could be achieved through education and prevention and that the well-being of family and nation were forged together.

Ima and Mike spent a decade discussing their plans for an institution that would commemorate their brother and fulfill the demands of his last testament. Once a decision had been made to create the foundation, Ima worked with a small committee of top university administrators to assert her vision of the foundation's purpose. Mike strove to maximize the value of Will's estate in the depressed economy of the 1930s while fulfilling his brother's far-flung civic goals. Both Ima and Mike sought financial stability and effective professional leadership by adapting the foundation model, and from inception they foresaw only advisory roles for family members. Sadly, Mike had little time to enjoy the results of his hard work and generosity because he succumbed to cancer in 1941. Ima was left to define the family's wishes alone.[104]

In the summer of 1930, Ima had joined Will on what proved to be their last trip to Europe together. While staying in Baden-Baden, Will underwent unsuccessful emergency gallbladder surgery and died on September 12, 1930. As Ima frequently recalled, during their trip she and Will discussed ways to support mental health care in Texas, and these conversations proved critical to establishing the Hogg Foundation and to interpreting Will Hogg's final testament.[105] Setting aside a portion of his

$2.25 million estate for family and loyal employees and for scholarship endowments at eighteen state colleges and universities, Will left the residue of his estate to be used in Texas in a manner to be determined by his executor, Mike, "counseled by [Ima's] good judgment and opinion." The testament suggested three possibilities: a vocational school in Brazoria County for training "poor" boys and girls as a memorial to his parents; a lecture foundation at the University of Texas to attract scholars of "proved learning" to explain mankind's experience; or a foundation "for the common good of all or any part of Texas" to which Ima and Mike would also bequeath significant portions of their estates.[106]

After lengthy discussions with attorneys for the Hogg estate and with university representatives, Ima and Mike combined elements of options two and three to fulfill their fiduciary duty. Remembering Will's devotion to the University of Texas as graduate, founder of the Texas Ex-Students' Association, and regent, they settled on the university as the appropriate recipient of his funds. Mindful of conversations with Will and eager to advance mental health care services on a broad scale, Ima and Mike decided that the common good of all Texans would best be served by establishing a foundation devoted to a broad program that promoted positive mental health and nourished the individual through social intervention, education, and community programs.[107] This disposition of Will's estate reflected the Hoggs' devotion to Texas, to education, and to the stability an endowment provided, and it underscored their long-standing argument that mental health care formed the basis for wholesome community life. The foundation became the first major philanthropy in the United States to focus attention on the broad issue of family mental health and the first professionally managed foundation in Texas. In later years Ima funneled financial assistance through the Hogg Foundation to mental health care facilities in Houston and Harris County, and she helped Houston agencies participate in foundation initiatives.[108]

Ima wrote to foundation experts for advice and worked closely with University of Texas President Homer Rainey and other top administrators and regents to refine terms of the gift. She convinced university officials that a foundation, still a little-used vehicle for transferring private wealth to public programs, would be a valuable university asset.[109] The ideas were essentially hers, but Ima usually spoke of discussions with "my brothers" or referred to decisions made in concert with Mike; in later recollections she sometimes credited him for the foundation's mental health care focus. By July 1939 the letters of transmittal to the University of Texas had been signed, and the university announced the formation of a unique institution funded by an initial grant of more than $1.8 million. A private foundation, housed within the university and administered under the supervision of the university's Board of Regents, would be established to provide a broad program of mental health education to communities throughout the state. Other Hogg family members also would bequeath funds to the foundation and could therefore guide its mission.

Children of a famous politician and themselves attuned to government's possibilities, Ima and Mike saw the critical importance of engaging the public sector and awakening state and local governments to their social welfare responsibilities. Ima's work in Houston had taught her the difficulty of raising money for mental health care, and she well knew the value of careful stewardship. By endowing a foundation, she and Mike ensured that funds would be available for controversial work. By placing the foundation under the control of publicly appointed regents, they assured public-sector engagement with mental health issues. By linking the foundation to a major state university system, they provided an avenue to make the latest scholarship available to all Texans. Community spokespeople, government leaders, and university researchers would thus be forced to work together to address mental health care issues effectively. Through such cooperation, no single agenda would dominate the delivery of high-quality mental health care.

The unique structure—a private foundation within a public institution—cleverly sidestepped the vexing question of public accountability for private philanthropy. The Hoggs' private wish to nurture a broad vision of positive mental health would be carried out by professionals within an academic setting and administered by stewards who were public officials ultimately answerable to the foundation's beneficiaries, the people of Texas. The foundation would serve three critical functions of philanthropic organizations: it would assist those in need; it would address a broad public constituency; and it would provide a public forum for advocacy and reform of mental health care delivery. Most exciting, the Hogg Foundation would both operate programs of its own and make grants to communities, institutions, and individuals throughout Texas. Immediately Texans showered the Hoggs with praise, and newspapers across the country headlined the family's "munificent contribution." University President Rainey, in consultation with the Commonwealth Fund's George Stevenson, established an advisory committee to search for a director. Search committee members included Ima, several doctors, Houston Child Guidance Center Director J. P. Malloy, Irene Conrad of the Houston Community Chest, Gaynell Hawkins of the Dallas Civic

Federation, and experts on nutrition, health education, home economics, and family life.[110]

The foundation's purpose as Ima restated it over the years remained quite consistent: "educating people in the art of better living" through prevention, community outreach, and cooperation.[111] First, Hogg Foundation money would support services that reached all Texans. Remembering the lonely rural families she met while traveling with her father and recalling the insights of her mentor and favorite University of Texas professor, Caswell Ellis, about the desperate needs of poor farmwomen, Ima stressed the obligation to develop programs in rural communities and small towns. Nor were African-American or Hispanic Texans forgotten. From the foundation's inception, gifts were made to projects targeting these groups. Second, positive mental health became and remained the foundation's central mission. Recalling brother Tom's childhood problems and believing that individuals must learn how to live with their emotions, Ima encouraged the foundation to create resources that adopted new methods of treatment and prevention or helped individuals, families, and groups secure assistance in times of trouble to increase emotional stability and ensure effective functioning. Third, Hogg Foundation work was based on consultation, integration, and cooperation at the local level. Reviewing her work in Houston and believing that problems could be addressed only when local groups worked together, Ima encouraged building mental health care resources in communities and supported the policy of granting aid only to pilot programs that could be matched by community funds. In this way, the influence of foundation money, modest by some standards, could be stretched and its significance as a catalyst for action multiplied. Moreover, community values would be respected and nourished, and no attempt would be made to mandate standards set by experts housed in a central bureaucracy. Instead, foundation meetings, modeled on the three-day inaugural Home and Family Life Conference, would convene social service practitioners, academics, and civic leaders to explore strategic questions of mental health care. Finally, the foundation, although not a research institute, was to adopt scholarly practices, share information, collaborate, and retain all use of endowment income.[112]

At the foundation's three-day inaugural conference held in the Hogg Memorial Auditorium February 11–13, 1941, Rainey affirmed the Hoggs' vision of positive, preventive, therapeutic mental health care and told guests they were witnessing "some real history in the making with the inauguration of a mental hygiene program for the state of Texas . . . one of the first in the nation." Echoing beliefs long espoused by the Hogg family, Rainey continued:

> The home lays the foundation for the whole of American democracy in its individual, group, and institutional relations. It is therefore most important that we give recognition to the family and to family problems. . . . This concept of mental hygiene . . . is going to play the most important role in the redirection of education in the next 20 years—mental health for the normal man.[113]

If some disputed Rainey's hyperbole, none could deny that expectations for the new institution were high, that university leaders fully endorsed its mission, or that the Hoggs' persistence was about to pay great dividends to all Texans. At a time when Texas was ranked last in the nation in mental health care standards, the foundation energized reformers and sponsored legislative initiatives. In the next three decades its staff worked to shape policies that would underpin healthy communities, expand services throughout the state, educate citizens about available public and private resources, and reorganize the state system of mental health care delivery. The search for appropriate delivery of social services, including physical and mental health care, has long been cause for debate. In a complex, highly technical society, elite trained experts are needed to address controversial issues, and accountability to a poorly informed public can become a serious issue. The Hogg Foundation's convening mechanism provided a new way to resolve the conflict between democratic participation and expert management by bringing together men and women of many viewpoints at the community level, where programs impact daily lives.

If the Hogg Foundation was blessed by founders of broad vision, it also has been fortunate in its professional leadership—only four directors since 1940.[114] Described by admirers as a man of "compassion, empathy, and modesty" whose "remarkable capacity for detecting common ground" enabled him to form lasting and warm friendships, Robert Lee Sutherland, director from 1940 until 1970, was undoubtedly the ideal partner for Ima Hogg because both believed "there was nothing more productive than the creative abilities of human beings." Together they built an institution that today leads the state's mental health care activities and shapes the role of private-foundation philanthropy in community life. Formerly associate director of the American Youth Commission and dean of men and chairman of counseling at Bucknell University, Sutherland had written extensively on social problems affecting African Americans, and he shared many concerns with the Hoggs. In a 1941 resume he listed as hobbies "helping groups see the importance of group morality" and teaching individuals how to avoid personality disorders that "limit one's effectiveness in his field of work and in his community relationships." A memorial tribute eulogized Sutherland's "pervasive influence and innate ability to draw people together in a common cause, regardless of background and political persuasion." Because of Sutherland's activism, statewide mental health care advanced from forgotten stepchild to robust adult during his thirty years with the foundation.[115]

Sutherland immediately understood Ima's grand vision to promote positive mental health and nourish "the individuality of each person through social intervention, education, and community programs." He articulated her ideas to others and devised programs relating abstract concepts to specific needs.[116] Sutherland gradually expanded the foundation's definition of mental health care to include assistance with all facets of daily living, and he supported community demonstration projects targeted at issues as diverse as housing, crime prevention, health hazards, and delinquency—anything that related to the "optimum functioning of the personality in its social, familial, and vocational roles."[117] Slowly he overcame Ima's reluctance to spend money on research and developed partnerships with faculty on University of Texas campuses statewide. In this way he assuaged administrators' concerns about university support of community outreach projects and provided these programs firm scholarly grounding. He expanded counseling services for children and college students and nurtured interaction among employees at state facilities for the mentally ill.

From the beginning the Hoggs and Sutherland worked well together. No sooner had Sutherland arrived in Texas than Ima invited him and his wife and daughter to her home to discuss the inaugural conference, a harbinger of the frequent visits that punctuated their relationship and fostered free-ranging exploration of ideas. Letters composed on trains, aboard ships, and while bouncing over rutted Texas roads detail a synergy and mutual enthusiasm that never waned. In November 1940 Ima, Mike, and Alice introduced Sutherland to Houston's social service leadership at a dinner for two hundred during which the new director explained foundation goals to empower individuals "to get complete enjoyment out of community life."[118]

Ima came to trust Sutherland implicitly, and he soon learned to appreciate "the daring and breadth of [her] ideas," her "wisdom and skill in thinking through practical methods for their attainment," and her willingness to introduce him to key players whose friendship he needed. In turn, he kept her informed, invited her to address the biennial conferences of the foundation's national advisory committee, and encouraged her to participate on city- and state-sponsored mental health boards in the 1950s and 1960s.[119] He frequently sought her advice and was grateful for her moral support in battles with the university administration. She defended him to regents and university presidents who questioned the community service orientation of a foundation managed by an academic institution, and at crisis moments she restated at length, clearly, and in writing the purposes of her philanthropy. She took his family to symphony concerts and sent him books, flowers, and grapefruit.

Sutherland's prodigious energy must have impressed Ima. During the war years he traveled everywhere in Texas, provided services in 152 communities that included 2,000 groups, and touched the lives of more than 400,000 people. Sutherland was active at the national level as well. He established the Conference of Southwest Foundations in 1948–1949 (formal charter 1956), helped to charter the Foundation Center in New York, and served on the Council of Foundations board for many years. In February 1969, with Ima's enthusiastic endorsement, Sutherland became president of the foundation, and he continued to serve as emeritus professor after his retirement in 1970.[120]

In 1941 Ima anticipated an advisory role in shaping the foundation's mission. She wrote Board of Regents Chairman Leslie Waggener, "My active interest in the foundation was never anticipated after the estate was turned over to the University authorities. It is only through the courtesy of Dr. Rainey and Dr. Sutherland that I have been drawn into discussions of any plans."[121] While this modest description of her intentions belies the avid interest with which she supervised each of her philanthropic projects, Ima did not foresee, nor did she follow, a day-to-day involvement. So successful was her advisory approach that Sutherland praised her for "rigorously" avoiding unwanted interference. Instead, he lauded her responsiveness to "requests for counsel." Her "years of service to educational work, . . . special regard for the field of mental health, and . . . remarkable organizational experience" made her comments "indispensable." Three decades of correspondence and Sutherland's observations to others make clear that between patron and professional lay bonds of true friendship and mutual respect.[122]

Typical of Ima's approach to advisory planning was a January 6, 1958, letter to Sutherland reiterating her "conviction that the greatest good could come from a mental health program which was designed to prevent and allay some of the unhappy conditions which exist all around us." She went on to praise the foundation's work and suggested "with some temerity" a comprehensive new program designed to goad the state into legislative action and civic responsibility. She noted that she knew of no "instance where a comprehensive Mental Health Program on a community or state level has been organized and projected which possessed all the factors to make it effective," and she urged Sutherland and the Hogg Foundation to select a major city for a pilot program to arouse public interest and "insure a united effort of all civic forces . . . so that with the facilities of the required number of well-staffed public and private agencies, a sustained and successful plan of action could be evolved." She concluded that the Hogg Foundation's dynamic leadership, the university's prestige, and the governor's cooperation would ensure success. She then announced a gift of 395 shares of General Dynamics stock to underwrite development of the plan.

Such a letter would have come as no surprise to Sutherland; instead, it reflected many months of thought, long discussions between them, and trial balloons floated past community leaders whose cooperation would be needed. Ima's imprimatur and financial support would pave the way for Sutherland to seek acceptance for the plan among University of Texas administrators and local agency personnel. From correspondence, it is hard to say with whom these ideas originated; in this case, Ima had long lobbied for a coordinated pilot program uniting all agencies in a broad effort, but Sutherland, too, favored this approach. Probably, he was inspired by her general wish and devised a plan to implement specific goals; she then restated their thinking in a long letter to him. Sutherland had an ability to shape issues discussed in meetings and telephone conversations to reflect his own ideas while expressing Ima's thoughts as well.[123]

During Ima's lifetime, two outside committees were established to oversee strategic planning for the foundation. Since 1959, a national advisory council has held two two-day planning sessions each year. The council's work was augmented in the 1960s by a medical advisory committee that holds two daylong sessions each year to discuss the medical aspects of mental health programs. The foundation offices have long maintained a library of mental health publications and since 1962 have been a repository for the Foundation Center of New York, which provides information to the public about all national philanthropies.[124] Today, Hogg Foundation program priorities reflect Ima's goal to help all Texas families and children achieve a wholesome life.

After Mike's death in 1941 and Tom's in 1949, Ima strengthened the foundation and expanded its mission through continued financial support. In the 1950s Ima, Alice Hogg Hanszen, and the estates of Mike and Tom Hogg made substantial gifts to the university that doubled the foundation's income and enabled Sutherland to hire Wayne Holtzman as director of research, a goal pushed by university administrators. Several other gifts followed, and in the 1960s Ima established a fund, administered by the foundation, to provide fellowships for training in psychiatric social work and visiting teacher programs at the University of Texas School of Social Work.[125] Ima and Mike were reluctant to use the family name in the foundation's title because they wanted others to contribute. To Ima's disappointment, few donors who were not family members supported the foundation directly during her lifetime. However, the foundation's matching-grant philosophy generated considerable additional support for mental health care initiatives from national grantors such as the Ford Foundation and from local philanthropists in communities throughout the state.[126]

On October 2, 1964, Ima expanded the Hogg Foundation mission by incorporating the Ima Hogg Foundation with an initial gift of shares and property valued between $500,000 and $600,000. Into this endowment would be placed the residue of her estate, and the income from its investments would be allocated to children's mental health agencies in Houston and Harris County. Like the Hogg Foundation endowment itself, this fund was to be managed by the University of Texas and supervised by the Board of Regents.[127] Although Ima considered endowing the Child Guidance Center, she decided that the stability and investment expertise provided by the state university would better protect her gift and provide funds to an array of Houston-area institutions. Moreover, the Ima Hogg Foundation's endowment fulfilled the commitment she had made in 1939 to bequeath substantial money for mental health care services to the Hogg Foundation at the time of her death. On May 3, 1976, a "Day of Celebration" for Ima Hogg's life, University of Texas System Chancellor Charles LeMaistre announced activation of the Ima Hogg Foundation. The fund's first grant, $604,349 to the Houston Child Guidance Center and the University of Texas Health Science Center at Houston to be paid from 1977 to 1983, established a child psychiatry training program that embodied Ima's mental health care goals. The program emphasized education, meshed academic expertise with community outreach, and reinforced the mission of a valued civic institution, Ima's beloved Child

Guidance Center. In subsequent years, the fund supported numerous Harris County organizations that targeted "at risk" groups or pursued well-planned mental health care programs, but it focused major grants on the Child Guidance Center, the DePelchin Children's Center, and the Family Service Center, institutions created to help children succeed.[128]

Family goals for the Hogg Foundation and the subsidiary Ima Hogg Foundation suggest that while the Hoggs advanced a moral response to social change, they wanted to avoid imposing personal values on others. They preferred to provide individuals and groups the resources with which to identify local problems and develop homegrown solutions. In the 1920s and 1930s promoting mental health by helping individuals realize their potential and by turning victims of poverty or clients of welfare agencies into productive citizens was a relatively new idea.[129] The Rockefeller, Milbank, and Macy Foundations had begun to apply proactive approaches to physical well-being, and the Commonwealth Fund had supported child saving through professional guidance, but Ima and Mike were the first philanthropists to establish a major endowment devoted solely to positive mental health care. Believing no individual or institution could act alone, the Hoggs brought volunteers and professionals, businessmen and academics, government officials and private-sector care providers together in cooperative partnerships. At a time when cultural philanthropy garnered social acclaim, they turned to the little-understood arena of mental health care and used their social position and wealth to publicize its needs. Their optimistic activism paved the way for others to imagine and pursue personal visions of life, liberty, and happiness. Hogg family initiatives in mental health care clearly emanated from a profound concern about the ability of individuals to sort out the complex problems of a changing America.

Ima had long ago internalized Austen Riggs's dictum that every mentally healthy person must have a serious purpose in life. Contemporaries honored her dedication to community mental health; in April 1956, the University of Texas regents gave her a volume of letters from citizens throughout Texas who had been touched by her generosity.[130] In retrospect, critics may justifiably contest definitions of "normal" or "maladjusted" behaviors. Skeptics may feel that the Hoggs' reliance on professional experts to solve social problems was misplaced and has led to increased government intervention in everyday life. Yet doubters should not disparage the Hoggs' attempts to confront the social cleavages that plague America. It is a mark of their foresight that the mental health care institutions they founded continue to prosper. Unlike many of their contemporaries, Ima and Mike recognized the link between a wholesome, purposeful life and good mental health. They both understood that individuals who possessed the tools to solve family problems would be prepared to address the challenges of a great democracy.

Chapter 4

The Public's Education, a Many-Sided Community Responsibility

The year 1912 is still remembered as the year of commercial shipping's most tragic—and perhaps most unnecessary—loss at sea. On April 12, White Star Line promoters launched *Titanic*, its very name trumpeting the hubris of its owners. Two nights later, an orchestra playing, the unimagined happened as the colossus scraped an iceberg and sank to the ocean floor, carrying two-thirds of its passengers and crew to watery graves. Subsequent investigations revealed that overconfidence, greed, haste, and poor judgment had marked this magnificent maiden voyage. Six months later, on October 10, seven ebullient trustees of a fortune accumulated by entrepreneur William Marsh Rice welcomed residents of Houston, luminaries of academe, and citizens of the world at the launching of another well-publicized enterprise, the self-proclaimed world-class university rising on the prairie west of Houston, on that day a small commercial city on the frontier of cultural progress. Weeks earlier, lacquered wooden cylinders girdled with blue ribbon and closed with a silver seal had arrived at institutions of learning and repositories of culture wherever they existed on the globe, inviting representatives to a three-day intellectual festival that would celebrate the birth of the William Marsh Rice Institute.

All Houston rallied to greet the 152 dignitaries who journeyed to the unfinished campus at the end of a dirt road. Elegant "programmes," commemorative versions sheathed lavishly in suede, announced twelve inaugural lectures, which were subsequently bound in three handsome volumes. Political and social leaders addressed visitors at breakfasts, banquets, receptions, and garden parties, their oratory linking the nascent seat of learning to civic improvement. A special train whisked guests to Galveston beaches for an overnight stay at the Hotel Galvez that featured a "shore-supper and smoker." Clubmen provided participants two-week passes to enjoy Thalian, Houston, and Houston Country Club amenities, while hostesses from Houston's most influential families assisted Rice Institute Board Chairman James Addison Baker and President Edgar

Odell Lovett and their wives with the important business of proffering Southern hospitality and introducing Houston's citizens to institute guests.[1] Musical interludes by a New York quartet, a "popular illustrated Lecture" by acclaimed naturalist Hugo de Vries of the University of Amsterdam, and a citywide "service of song and prayer" attended by "some six thousand souls" including "the clergymen and choirs of practically all the churches of the city" proclaimed the institute a cultural treasure. Formal ceremonies culminated in a grand Procession of the Delegates and Guests gowned in academic regalia, preceded by a band, and admired by crowds of proud Houstonians who assembled to hear President Lovett explain the purpose and goals of the new institution. The dynamic young leader, already a popular fixture at Houston events, announced "the first alignment of the Rice Institute . . . on the map of the earlier universities" and promised to build a "community distinguished by high standards" of scholarship, self-government, and service.[2] This alliance of intellectuals, civic visionaries, politicians, and businessmen proved a potent force for the city's development in succeeding decades.

TRADITIONS OF LEARNING IN HOUSTON

Vaguely conceived by William Marsh Rice (1816–1900), a merchant, cotton broker, and Civil War–era millionaire, the institute had been much in the news by 1912. Houston's civic leaders greeted with enthusiasm word that Rice had counseled with his six most trusted friends and incorporated an "institute for the advancement of literature, science, and art" on May 19, 1891.[3] Although parameters of the institute and its role in the city's civic life were not defined by Rice's trust documents, Houstonians immediately grasped the possibilities inherent in Rice's vision. They followed the unfolding saga of the institute's organization and construction of its first buildings with avid curiosity. Since Houston's founding, citizens had tried various educational models—privately funded and publicly supported schools, self-improvement groups, lending libraries, and reading clubs. When Rice Institute opened its doors and invited its neighbors to join the inaugural celebration, participants knew that at last Houston could boast an institution that would advance the city's reputation as a seat of culture and expand educational opportunities for its residents.

Houston's men had been first to seek self-improvement when they founded the Philosophical Society of Texas among a huddle of tents in 1837 and established a members-only men's lyceum as a lending library in 1848. Late-nineteenth-century Houston women had eagerly opened their "close, observing eye[s] and fertile brain[s]" to study all subjects that would improve life. Adele Briscoe Looscan and Caroline Ennis Lombardi inaugurated the woman's club movement in Houston when they formed a Ladies' History Class in 1885. Quickly rechristened the Ladies' Reading Club, this popular activity was followed five years later by the Ladies' Shakespeare Club, founded by Louise Cohn Raphael. Only the next year (1891) did Cesar Lombardi and Emanuel Raphael counsel with William Marsh Rice about building an institute of literature, art, and learning. Like club women across the nation, Houston women thirsting for knowledge quickly moved from self-culture to civic reform, and their activism had become "a mighty factor in the development of our present civilization" by 1912, when city directories estimated a population of 109,000. Chamber of Commerce and professional men's study committees, women's literary and civic clubs, the Houston Lecture Association (organized 1908), and a Houston Chautauqua (organized 1909) had led hundreds of men and women up "the mountain side of culture and learning" by the time Rice Institute offered its first extension lectures to the public in 1912–1913.[4]

Contemporary commentators praised the city's historic support of public schools. Early settlers had quickly opened Sunday schools and numerous short-lived private academies to provide rudimentary instruction, and in 1851 Zerviah M. (Mrs. Abraham W.) Noble began her life's work teaching Houston children, first as proprietor of a private academy in her home, and after 1871 as principal of the county's first free public school. When the city passed an ordinance authorizing municipal control of all county schools within city limits in 1877, Mrs. Noble continued her career as teacher and principal for the city's racially segregated school system. By 1912, 372 public schoolteachers taught 15,000 students, double the staff and enrollment of the previous decade. Costs at these segregated schools reached nearly $331,000 that year because city officials had begun to incorporate Progressive Era reforms into the curriculum and the rapidly expanding physical plant. New schools were surrounded by spacious, well-equipped playgrounds and housed recreation gymnasia. Twelve schools offered modern manual training and domestic science to "prepare the boys and girls to meet new conditions in life." Night schools for adults and children over twelve helped immigrants learn English and citizenship, taught illiterate adults to read, and provided practical classes in stenography, typewriting, bookkeeping, cooking, and sewing for all ethnic groups. By 1912 the public schools ran four kindergartens for those who could pay the tuition, maintained mothers clubs and Parent-Teacher Associations in most schools, and provided music and art classes.

City overseers had recently ordered new fireproof buildings designed by established architects. Handsomely constructed of concrete, steel, and brick, they boasted the latest technology for sanitation, ventilation, heating, and lighting. Houston supported several private academies that catered to the children of Houston's leaders and a segregated parochial system that maintained schools for white, African-American, and Mexican Catholic children.[5]

Like the entrepreneurs who had envisioned a great city on a muddy bayou bank, the founding trustees of the William Marsh Rice Institute imagined a great seat of learning. In 1908 they hired Edgar Odell Lovett, a vigorous young scholar of great promise at Princeton College, and gave him wide latitude to build an institution that would combine seminal research in the arts and sciences with practical application in the urban environment. Lovett and the trustees chose the nationally renowned Boston architect Ralph Adams Cram of Cram, Goodhue, and Ferguson to create "a measurably new style" for the campus as a worthy monument to the founder's vision.[6] Lovett and the trustees recognized a dual responsibility: to tie the new institution to its host community while simultaneously linking the nascent university to worldwide educational leaders. In turn, Houstonians immediately understood that the institute would shape its host city—economically by attracting and nurturing technically advanced industries and an educated workforce, physically by spurring development, and culturally by offering residents opportunities for self-improvement through exposure to scholarly inquiry.

Situated on farmland southwest of the business district, Rice Institute proved a catalyst for urban expansion. Hermann Park, residential enclaves, and the Museum of Fine Arts established a community at the end of Main Street in a setting that harmonized residential and public spaces to create "a center of learning, culture and the humanities" praised by journalists.[7] In April 1910, President Lovett assured 250 "influential and thinking men" of the business community that the institute would be a "vital part of the life of this city."[8] The institute would be no isolated ivory tower. Professors would be urged to participate in civic activities, and the community, still lacking an expert infrastructure of its own, could rely on the institute's trained professionals to address increasingly complex urban issues.[9] Lovett introduced a complete curriculum of extension lectures in 1912–1913, and institute professors played critical roles in the development of the Museum of Fine Arts, in the creation of Houston's parks and transportation systems, and in the delivery of social services.

The civic activism of the institute's original faculty members delighted Houstonians who were proud of the handsome institution and grateful to these pioneering scholars for their eager embrace of municipal life. In November 1918 Rice announced a series of lectures made possible by Estelle Sharp, who provided funds to place work of the Texas School of Civics and Philanthropy under Rice Institute aegis. Sharp underwrote salaries for a visiting lecturer and a resident lecturer, and she persuaded Will Hogg, oil man Joseph Cullinan, retailer Abe Levy, and banker John T. Scott to sponsor four scholarships each year to attract students who would prepare for careers in social welfare work in the South.[10] Sociologist John Willis Slaughter was named resident lecturer and began a frenetic life of undergraduate teaching, public speaking, and civic activism. During the 1920s and 1930s, Slaughter served as president of the Houston Foundation (1921–1938), executive secretary and chairman of the Community Chest annual fund drives (1922–1937), executive head of Jefferson Davis Hospital, and secretary of the City Planning Commission. In January 1925 Slaughter helped Joseph Cullinan make an "anonymous" donation to build a "Negro hospital" and in 1926 served with Susan Vaughan (Mrs. W. L.) Clayton as vice chairman of the all-white advisory committee that managed the institution.[11] In 1938 Slaughter became director of the Houston Community Trust created by James Baker, Rice trustee Harry Hanszen, and five others to navigate New Deal tax codes. The founders worked with eleven Houston banks to encourage wealthy donors to establish trust instruments for bequests or make outright gifts to expand Houston Foundation resources and benefit designated civic institutions. Slaughter's wife, a noted horticulturist, was active with the Garden Club of Houston and introduced amaryllis, crinum lilies, and other plant materials to Houston gardeners.[12]

Town and gown interaction continued into the 1920s when Curtis Howe Walker, professor of history and government, persuaded Houstonians to launch an Open Forum to debate the "leading problems of the times" and "to seek the truth persistently and bravely, no matter how arduous and painful the search."[13] From 1926 through 1938 lumber industrialist James J. Carrell presided over an Open Forum board and fifty-member advisory council that included Ima Hogg, librarian Julia Ideson, *Post* publisher Oveta Culp Hobby, and school Superintendent Edison E. Oberholtzer. Men's and women's clubs, the Forum of Civics, the League of Women Voters, and the National Council of Jewish Women joined Rice Institute as institutional supporters. Crowds from a few hundred to more than six thousand heard speakers debate such controversial issues as Prohibition

(Clarence Darrow), birth control (Margaret Sanger), and socialism (the "strikingly handsome . . . cultured, brilliant" Norman Thomas).[14] Pledged to "throttle no idea," the forum provided Houstonians a formal venue to engage the era's most advanced defenders of personal freedom, social justice, and international understanding.[15]

HOGG FAMILY SUPPORT FOR HIGHER EDUCATION IN TEXAS

Advocacy of higher education, calls for universal public schooling, and debates about controversial issues were not widely supported in Texas in the early twentieth century. A rural population continued to be skeptical of "book learning," and persistent fiscal conservatism dampened enthusiasm for lavish expenditure on abstruse disciplines whose practical value was sharply contested. Indeed, the Hoggs and their circle of friends recognized that the battle for excellence in education was only beginning in 1912 when the Rice Institute opened its doors. In proselytizing their view that public education was a "many-sided community responsibility," the Hoggs continued a long-established family tradition. From colonial days, Hogg family members had stressed the value of education and recognized its role as a foundation stone of democracy. An ancestor had helped establish the institution that became the University of North Carolina; their grandfather, Joseph Lewis Hogg, taught his children that churches, colleges, and newspapers held equal sway over the public mind, and he donated property for a school and hired a teacher.[16]

In campaign speeches, in two gubernatorial addresses to the legislature, and in his 1895 farewell address, Jim Hogg insisted it was the duty of the state and its people to mandate and pay for the best education for all children in Texas. He pledged a fully funded six-month academic year for schoolchildren and endowments for the University of Texas and Texas Agricultural and Mechanical (A&M) College.[17] The governor's rhetoric exceeded his ability to persuade the legislature to enact enabling legislation for his educational reform agenda, but he worked hard to convince fellow Texans that universal public education was critical to the state's future growth as an industrial power in the mainstream of national life. The governor also hammered home his definition of the university as a "forum of reason" to maintain liberty and justice, as a sanctuary for scholars who preserved past accomplishments and generated knowledge, and as a site to train teachers of the young, engineers of modern economic life, and leaders of the state.[18] When the capitol was destroyed by fire in 1881, the state's library of books, maps, and papers perished with the building. In

1891, three years after the new capitol was completed, Governor Hogg reopened the library and appointed a historical clerk. He also added a Spanish translator and archivist in 1893, steps that eventually led to creation of the Texas State Library and Historical Commission in 1909. Perhaps as significant, the governor instilled in his children the belief that it was their duty to nurture public education for all Texas children, regardless of race, religion, or economic condition.

During the last months of his life, the dying former governor spent hours rocking on the veranda at Varner, formulating plans with his oldest son and his only daughter to make Texas a leader in public education. The governor well understood that Texas was hampered by its rural heritage, but he also realized that citizens and government officials must be made to see the urgent need for a fully funded public education system. Father and children reached critical conclusions. Like other progressives, they believed only educated citizens could effectively participate in and safeguard democracy. They viewed education as a many-sided responsibility demanding individual, community, and state support. For them, the education process from kindergarten through postgraduate enrichment needed to be a seamless continuum of opportunity open to all. Philanthropists, they realized, could help ambitious young people by guaranteeing financial support for higher education and providing scholarship assistance. Finally, the Hoggs recognized that an effective educational system was the slow work of years and depended "on the pride and generosity of a progressive, enlightened people." Two barriers threatened educational excellence: securing adequate financial resources and protecting intellectual integrity and freedom. The Hoggs recognized that these challenges were interrelated: financial independence would enable educational administrators to retain control of their institutions and would protect scholars in their pursuit and dissemination of knowledge.[19]

In his new role as Hogg family spokesperson after his father's death in 1906, Will was the first to act on these principles. In 1911 he tackled the issues of control and funding at the University of Texas, which at that time was also the contested overseer of the Texas Agricultural and Mechanical College. Recognizing that politics played havoc with university attempts to attract established scholars, Will conceived the idea of a Texas alumni group that would promote school spirit among alumni, raise money to educate the public about the need for a great university, provide funding to the institution, and develop a strong body of informed and loyal former students to lobby legislators for university support.

Will prepared his "Texas Exes" Alumni Association initiative carefully. He studied the university systems of other states—and discovered some unflattering statistics about Texas's position in the academic horse race. He persuaded university President Sidney E. Mezes to serve as chairman of the Organization for the Enlargement and Extension by the State of the University Plan of Higher Education in Texas. Mercifully this cumbersome title was quickly shortened to Hogg Organization, much to Will's dismay. To manage the organization, Will created a nine-member standing committee that included the president of the Board of Regents and an eight-member advisory committee with non–University of Texas luminaries such as Rice Institute President Lovett. Then he began to solicit his friends for donations.

By June 1911 Will had prepared pamphlets for distribution throughout the state and was ready to lay his plans before the newly formed Ex-Students' Association at its annual meeting. He explained how he would fight "prejudice against higher education" in the state: he would raise at least $25,000 and not more than $50,000 per year for five years by securing pledges of $25 to $250; he would stimulate thought and "arouse aspiration" for higher education in Texas by engaging the public; he would call on others to expand and maintain the faculty and facilities with a "carefully adjusted financial provision"; and he would demand that all state-supported educational institutions be removed from political influence.[20] Banking on his famous name and his father's connections, Will wrote and visited hundreds of Texas graduates or friends of education and raised 443 subscription pledges totaling $149,000 in a whirlwind four-month tour of the state. By February 1912, the Ex-Students' Association had hired F. M. Bralley, state superintendent of public instruction, as executive secretary and Arthur Lefebre, former state superintendent of public instruction, as secretary for research. Lefebre's work resulted in a series of articles distributed to newspapers across the state that compared Texas's inadequate funding and decentralized administrative system to funding and programs in other states. Will was rewarded for this imaginative initiative with a term on the reorganized Board of Regents (August 1913–January 1917).[21]

Although Will had phenomenal success gaining and retaining subscribers for the Hogg Organization, as a regent he immediately embroiled himself in controversies that culminated in a long-running battle with Governor Jim Ferguson (1914–1917). What ended as a war to control public education in Texas began peacefully with a chance meeting on September 23, 1914, and a follow-up letter a few days later. With his usual optimistic enthusiasm Will expressed pleasure that Ferguson would "give much thought and attention to the educational situation." He responded to Ferguson's "willingness to discuss educational affairs" by listing three critical ideas that would modernize and improve the state education system. All would prove later sources of conflict. Will asserted that all county schools should be locally controlled through "non-political supervision" selected on "a professional basis." He argued that constitutional amendments should ensure "permanency and dependability" in funding the University of Texas, the A&M College, the state's normal schools, and the College of Industrial Arts. He believed that the "petty jealousy" and "brambles of misrepresentations and personal abuse" existing between the University and the independently managed A&M College should be resolved either by passing a constitutional amendment to separate the two institutions and provide each with permanent funding sources or by uniting the two institutions firmly under one board of regents. Will Hogg, an idealistic statesman of education, understood the pitfalls of political interference; Jim Ferguson, a crafty demagogue whose populist rhetoric far exceeded his willingness to deliver, soon proved he had no wish to divest himself of the political plums provided by control of a state school system.[22] Amity between Will and Ferguson was short-lived. The governor did not accept Will's offer to obtain "disinterested expert advice," and Will quickly realized Ferguson lacked visionary policy ideas.

Will and Ferguson went to war when the governor criticized University of Texas budgets in an attempt to wrest control of university business from the Board of Regents.[23] Not satisfied with undermining the regents' authority to approve budget requests, Ferguson locked horns with acting President W. J. Battle over academic appointments and use of funds. When the belligerent governor attempted to influence the regents' choice of a permanent president and demanded that the new man, Robert E. Vinson, fire six professors in June 1916, the regents refused to buckle to the governor's interference. The governor then foisted three political cronies on the Board in the January 1917 regent rotation. Almost immediately House and Senate committees began investigating Ferguson's activities. Although the committees' findings substantiated charges of malfeasance and bullying lodged against the governor, the House and Senate ultimately exonerated Ferguson of wrongdoing in March. Unchastened, Ferguson demanded that the regents fire President Vinson, Ex-Students' Association Secretary John Lomax, and three faculty members. When Ferguson summoned the regents to the Capitol on May 28, 1917, to threaten a veto of the university appropriations bill if regents did not bow to his will, the students rose in protest and marched en masse down Congress Avenue to the Capitol, brandishing "We oppose one-man rule" banners and demanding that the governor leave university business to the regents.

At every turn in this drama, Will resisted Ferguson's attempts to destroy the university's independence and insisted that politics had no place in academe. After his Board of Regents term ended in 1917, Will provided anti-Ferguson data to alumni and legislative committees, and when the governor packed the Board of Regents and vetoed the university appropriations bill in June 1917, Will decided to fight.[24] Organizing a coalition of faculty, students, and alumni, Will took rooms in the Driskill Hotel in Austin, appointed himself secretary of the Ex-Students' Association, and teamed with prohibition advocates, suffragists, and "Mothers of Texas" to rouse the people and rid the state of its governor. Will saturated the media with details of Ferguson's financial peculation and other malfeasance and spearheaded calls for impeachment.[25] He financed a pamphlet that was sent to every University of Texas graduate in August 1917 and used Ferguson's statements to condemn the governor "through his own mouth." Will also funded an Ex-Students' Association chronology of "Ferguson's War on the University of Texas" and paid for two thousand copies of the Record of Investigation that included a colorful introduction penned by Will himself. Dedicated "To the People in their hour of humiliation, this record of shame" outlined the governor's misdeeds: Ferguson had violated the Texas Constitution, falsely accused faculty members, "maliciously and mendaciously traduce[d]" the university, "attack[ed] the freedom he was elected to preserve," dismissed from eleemosynary boards appointed officials who disagreed with him, misappropriated government funds and misused properties, and violated civil and criminal banking laws.[26] Will's cogent legal briefs, relentless exposure of greed, and impassioned press propaganda that decried Ferguson's "putrid paw of patronage" and his "paltry personal prejudices" carried impeachment forces to victory.[27] Once Will had secured the House's bill of impeachment in August, he packed his bags and, "whistling cheerfully," slipped quietly out of town and headed for New York, content to allow the Senate "court of justice" to reach judgment without him.[28] Will's "bear fight" with Ferguson proved only the first of several battles Will fought to keep politics out of university business. In 1923–1924 he rallied public opinion and Texas alumni to deny former governor Pat Neff the university's presidency. In 1927 he declined to be nominated for another term on the Board of Regents because ultraconservative neo-Klansman J. Lutcher Stark, who had promoted Pat Neff's candidacy as university president, remained regent chairman.[29]

While Will's battles for excellence in education at the University of Texas did not directly affect institutions in Houston, they did focus attention statewide on his goals for educational philanthropy and did establish his reputation as a fund-raiser without equal. Working closely with lifelong friend and Texas Exes Secretary John Avery Lomax, Will developed the concept of a Texas Exes Student Loan Fund endowment after World War I and drew up a charter for its incorporation. Texas graduates and friends were invited to assist students who could show any kind of financial need with loans made on very generous terms. Over the years, Will helped hundreds of students with unrecorded thousands from his private account. Insisting on anonymity, Will authorized Lomax to provide funds to any students "in distress" and to bill him after the fact; any repayments were returned to the Texas Exes to increase endowment of the permanent loan fund. Will threatened Lomax that he would withdraw all support if word of his generosity were leaked. Will also set up student loan funds at all other Texas institutions of higher learning, provided bequests to each in his will as memorials to his parents, and helped develop other alumni support groups around the state.[30] Certainly his most enduring legacy, the loan funds boosted students up the ladder of success, goaded every university in the state to provide financial assistance to students, and taught Texans who had benefited from their own college experiences to assist future generations.[31] In a posthumous tribute, Rice Institute President Edgar Odell Lovett recalled Will as "one of the first citizens of the commonwealth to recognize the need felt no less by state-supported than by privately endowed colleges and universities . . . for supplementary resources above and beyond their ordinary channels of income."[32] Will failed to persuade legislators to enact laws that assured funding to the university or removed its governance from politics, but he began a tradition of private generosity that continues to sustain innovation, construct buildings, support students, and counter political horse-trading.

During the 1910s and 1920s advocates of educational innovation could always count on Will to "advance progress and reform" by lobbying legislators and governors and by speaking out in public forums and the press.[33] Admirers "acknowledged the inspiration of his educational outlook, which was as broad as the state itself, and the influence of his campaigns in season and out for the education of public opinion in Texas."[34] Family members and fellow Houstonians were quick to follow his example. Mike, also a devoted graduate of the university's law school, became an invaluable propagandist for university expansion in the 1920s and 1930s and a member of the Ex-Students' Executive Council in 1937–1938. With friend and old business associate Raymond Dickson, Mike led the 1924 fund drive for a memorial stadium financed by the University of Texas Memorial Stadium Association incorporated by the Texas alumni association, and in the 1930s he raised money for the Hogg Memorial Auditorium dedicated in 1933 to the memories of his father and brother Will as a performing arts center.[35] The three siblings befriended university professors, established lectureships on the Austin campus, and endowed chairs in several departments.[36] Mike's will stipulated that the residue of his estate be given to the University of Texas to establish a department of municipal government. As residuary legatee, the Board of Regents was directed to perpetuate the principle of local self-government, support research pertaining to municipal issues, train men and women for careers in local government, and make information and counsel available to Texas municipalities. Finally, Ima and Mike realized, without much hesitation, that only Will's beloved university provided a site appropriate for their memorial Hogg Foundation.[37]

Although most of the Hoggs' philanthropic dollars and volunteer time went to their alma mater, they did not forget Rice Institute. In late April 1922 Ima charmed President Lovett at a dinner party by telling him she wished to endow a lectureship anonymously "to stimulate an interest in, and love for music on the part of the student body of Rice, and . . . the people of Houston generally."[38] She hoped her "experiment" would introduce formal music study to Rice students and produce an informed Houston audience for the professional performances she yearned to encourage. Ima may have been an anonymous donor, but she worked hard to find prominent musicians for the lecture-recitals and approved many choices personally. Lectures were well attended, and Rice officials distributed tickets to musical clubs, alumni clubs, journalists, politicians, Chamber of Commerce officials, and Rice students, faculty, and friends.[39] Even when Ima was out of town, Will and Mike supported her generosity by entertaining lecturers and guests at post-performance receptions.[40] Bright and intellectually curious, the Hoggs associated with institute professors, enjoyed their social conversation and professional opinions, and found them congenial partners in numerous city planning and cultural initiatives.

Despite President Lovett's announced intention to nurture town and gown ties, not all institute activities were well received by Houstonians.

Several battles were joined when religion, politics, open discussion, and academic freedom made uncomfortable bedfellows after World War I. Houstonians considered the institute "their" university, and some felt justified in trying to influence policy. Trustees found political and press comment intrusive and unwelcome even as they sought funding for institute programs from city philanthropists. The general public wallowed in ignorance. In a *Chronicle* article on April 1, 1929, John Willis Slaughter reminded readers that "their" institute had no oil wells in West Texas, no state treasury support, and no rich alumni but was "absolutely dependent upon the generosity of Houston citizens for its future." Each year, after all, young Houstonians received $200,000 in free tuition, while civic committees of every kind received untold hours of labor and expertise from the Rice faculty. In September Slaughter told Kiwanis members, "Rice belongs to Houston and we should back it up" by creating "endowments for its progress in years to come."[41]

By the late 1920s the institute's vision had begun to outpace its generous endowment, and supporters were discussing the need for supplemental funds. Well aware of the services Rice provided "our city, our state, and our nation," Will responded imaginatively to Slaughter's warnings about Rice's endowment predicament. In May 1929 he presented a novel funding idea to institute trustees, and in the fall, he prepared a petition to city hall that he hoped would reinforce the bonds between city and institute and reimburse the institute for educating Houston's young people. By October 1929 he had gathered 815 signatures for this petition in a Memorial Book from the Citizens of Houston. The petition he had proposed to the Rice board and to Houston's public recommended that the City Council adopt an ordinance to provide $250,000 a year to support Rice for at least ten years beginning in 1930; it also called for a special election to amend the city charter "to permit municipal support for this institution of learning which is so essentially a part of our city."[42]

Ima, Mike, and a roster of Houston's leaders endorsed the idea, and Will set up a Protective Campaign Committee before he left town for his world tour in November 1929. Committee members included Mike, Hugh Potter, and other business associates. After Will's death in September 1930 the initiative collapsed. The contested benefits of public support, the strained Depression-era municipal budgets, and the movement to create a University of Houston ended further discussion of municipal funding for the institute, although town and gown continued to cooperate on mutually beneficial projects, and city philanthropists became generous supporters of construction projects and academic programs on the Rice Institute campus. Twenty years after Will's initiative, in March 1951, the centennial of her father's birth, Ima chose Rice Institute as the repository for the family's copy of the transcribed collection of James Stephen Hogg's state papers because "we have followed with the deepest interest and a sense of civic pride the progress of the Institute since its inception."[43]

IMA AND HOUSTON'S BOARD OF EDUCATION

During the 1930s Mike and Ima focused their educational activism on projects at the University of Texas that culminated in creation of the Hogg Foundation, but in 1943, less than two years after Mike's death, Ima turned her attention to Houston's public school system.[44] At one o'clock on Monday afternoon, April 5, 1943, a small, elegantly dressed woman with sparkling blue eyes and softly curling hair entered the meeting room of the Houston Independent School District's Board of Education at Sam Houston High School. Dr. Ray K. Daily, who had been reelected to Position 4, introduced the newly elected representative for Position 3, and board President Holger Jeppesen extended the "best wishes and good will of the Board members" to Ima Hogg, who at age sixty-one was beginning her only term of elected office. Ima thanked them graciously and stated in her firm but soft-spoken manner that she would like to meet with each member of the board and with the superintendent and business manager "to get the benefit of their counsel so that she may become better acquainted with the workings of the Board and better prepared to become an active member."[45] As Will had tried to imbue the processes of city planning with the family's vision of a City Beautiful and Functional, so Ima would endeavor to inspire Houston's Board of Education with the family's belief that high-quality public education formed the foundation for engaged citizenship in a viable democracy. Through a term of public service, Ima hoped to transfer lessons learned during her career in philanthropy to the public sector and fulfill her father's admonitions that the public school system was every citizen's responsibility.

Houston's public schools had been supervised by the city after 1877, but in 1923 citizens authorized a separate taxing entity, the Houston Independent School District, and created a Board of Education to manage district programs and personnel.[46] Houston's population grew 111 percent in the 1920s (from 138,276 in 1920 to 292,351 in 1930), and citizens realized that the school system needed a major reorganization and modernization. Edison E. Oberholtzer, who had overhauled the rapidly expanding Tulsa, Oklahoma, system, came to Houston in 1924 after the district conducted a "conscientious and painstaking" national search. He quickly built a new administration committed to programs that adapted to social change, were managed frugally, and provided broad training for citizenship in a democracy.[47] Taking advantage of 1920s prosperity and responding to the city's astonishing growth, Oberholtzer embarked on a much-needed building program that benefited all areas of the expanding city and added 950 classrooms to district schools between 1924 and 1931 at a cost of $11 million in bond indebtedness.[48] Like other progressives, Oberholtzer believed democracy demanded an informed, educated public, and he pointed with pride to curriculum innovations that stressed pupil-teacher cooperation and parent involvement and that prepared students for the "complicated civilization which will confront" graduates in the 1930s.[49] The superintendent's innovations, while praised by many, were received with skepticism by critics who protested rapidly rising costs and feared that "structure has been literally thrown out of the window" to accommodate new theories that "integrated" (a new-fangled expression) "subjects for the pupil and . . . the pupil with his . . . community."[50]

By the 1940s the all-white Board of Education was composed of seven members elected for staggered six-year terms in nonpartisan citywide contests. Two places had traditionally been reserved for women. Citizens well known for their civic, professional, or business accomplishments vied for all positions, which demanded serious commitment because members were responsible for the daily affairs of all schools in the segregated system and oversaw all business of the University of Houston and its affiliated College for Negroes.[51] Members were expected to attend at least two regular meetings each month and were frequently asked to add specially called sessions and conferences to their schedules. A typical biweekly Order of Business covered petitions from citizens, letters and other communications to the board, committee reports, and lengthy statements by the superintendent and business manager. All personnel changes, leaves of absence, vacations, bills, and contracts required board approval. Meetings lasted for hours, often adjourned before all matters could be covered, and frequently were continued to the following day. Each member visited schools and served on several standing and special committees, most of which met at least once each month. During one typical week in 1945, Ima attended the board meeting, visited nine schools, and fulfilled obligations to six other organizations.[52]

Ima was not fooled by her cordial welcome at the April 5 meeting. She joined a board deadlocked between forces loyal to reformist

Superintendent Oberholtzer and those partial to the district's entrenched business manager, Hubert L. Mills. Well aware of the power struggle forced on outsider Oberholtzer by Houstonian Mills, whose service to the Houston public schools antedated the superintendent's by more than a decade, Ima was prepared to tackle the "problems which have torn the school board for some years."[53] When Oberholtzer came to Houston in 1924, he discovered that Mills's ties to city and state officials left him impervious to supervision. For several years, the rivalry slumbered while Mills strengthened his position by placing friends and relatives in jobs throughout the system and gained board members' support by pleading "fiscal responsibility" in arguments with the superintendent. Oberholtzer endeared himself to Will, Ima, and their circle of progressive friends by developing a strong academic program and by supporting the city's cultural institutions. In the late 1920s the Hoggs, Hugh Potter, and Estelle Sharp organized River Oaks mothers in a telephone campaign to pressure Oberholtzer to build River Oaks Elementary as a model school attuned to the "child-centered" philosophy of "interest and effort" espoused by philosopher and reformer John Dewey. As Principal Eva Margaret Davis explained, the River Oaks approach taught the child, not the subject. She believed interested children would make an effort to learn. Ima and Davis became close friends as Ima built up the school library, underwrote landscaping for the grounds, and urged parents to support the school, which was built on land donated by the River Oaks Corporation.[54]

The rift between Oberholtzer and Mills widened in 1937 when newly elected board member Holger Jeppesen formed an anti-Oberholtzer clique that lasted until 1945. Described by fellow board member Ray Daily as "a man of no education" who was only "interested in athletics," the tall and imposing Jeppesen found two influential board allies in Henry A. Petersen and Ewing Werlein, who were elected in 1938 and 1941, respectively. Daily thought Petersen, an "elegant and brilliant" brain surgeon, was "disappointed" and "frustrated" because he was forced to perform general surgery since there was little demand for his specialty during most of his career in Houston. No such frustrations marred lawyer Ewing Werlein's self-assured conservatism. The silver-haired and voluble Werlein was an imposing figure who in 1943 was both a practicing attorney and professor and dean of the Houston Law School. In the 1950s Werlein, son of the pastor at First Methodist Church, led the ultraconservative anti-Communist Committee for the Preservation of Methodism founded in December 1950 to dislodge Methodism's perceived "pink fringe."[55]

Dr. Ray Karchmer Daily, who led the moderate group that usually supported Oberholtzer's educational reform programs, was "a lively, brilliant, little woman, whose charm and staccato manner of speech, punctuated by infectious, merry smiles have won her legions of friends." A feisty ophthalmologist who had practiced with her husband, Louis, since 1914 and had been elected president of the Baptist Hospital staff in 1931, Daily joined the Board of Education in 1928, when she replaced the appointed female incumbent who chose not to seek election. An outspoken critic of fellow board members, Daily later claimed the men believed that "the man with a Ph.D. was a fool" and that "a masters wasn't worth a hundred dollars more a year than anybody else." She recalled that several board members would not shake the hands of African-American teachers; so at the dedication of (black) Wheatley High School in 1950, she gave an address and shook hands with everyone. Accustomed to periodic accusations of Communist affiliation, the liberal Daily championed special education, equalization of pay for black and female district employees, reading programs, and industrial arts instruction to support the war effort and to provide training for those not going on to college. After twenty-four years of service, she failed to gain reelection in 1952 because she advocated federal funding for the school free-lunch program, which her opponents condemned as a Communist plot.[56]

Insurance executive E. Dale Shepherd Sr. voted with Daily on many issues. Fair-minded and deeply religious, Shepherd was appointed to the board in 1928 and reelected twice, and he served as its president from 1935 until 1940. He retired in 1945 to devote more time to his business. George D. Wilson, a prominent civic leader, was a moderate. He was elected to the board in 1933, served as president in 1944, and retired in 1945 after two terms. Concerned about the effects of war on Houston's youth, Wilson was chairman of a 1943 Houston Symphony program that attempted to discourage delinquent behavior by providing twelve free concerts in city parks during the summer.[57]

In the 1945 school board contest, Holger Jeppesen was reelected, and two new members, William G. Farrington and Charles W. McPhail, replaced Shepherd and Wilson. Farrington, a conservationist, was president of his own real estate development company, director of the University State Bank, and president of the Southampton Civic Club. He advocated updated property evaluations and promoted economical construction methods.[58] Charles McPhail, vice president of Houston Lighting and Power, was endorsed by conservative businessmen. A former chief of police and FBI agent, McPhail stressed safety education, fought juvenile delinquency, favored "the removal of politics from the school system," and supported additional school construction.[59]

IMA'S ELECTION CAMPAIGN

By seeking membership on this contentious body, Ima made an unusual civic commitment. Houston women had long been indispensable leaders of Houston's cultural, educational, and health care initiatives, but in the 1940s few held elective public office. Moreover, Ima consistently denied any affinity for politics, as she stated in a 1946 letter:

> Causes interest me. Strange as it may seem to you, I dislike politics—at least the negative way the world has continually gone about it. I had been hoping the time would come when men sufficiently wise and strong, could draw others to them through agreement on common needs, not because of agreement on some defiance or accusation. The only cure for a torn world, I am confident, will be a new mental attitude in our human relations.[60]

Ima's public advocacy in the 1940s belies this disclaimer. Her typewriter was rarely idle as she prodded reluctant public officials to assume some responsibility for the social and health care services she continued to support through personal philanthropy. Letters in 1943 to legislators in Austin, to Governor Coke Stevenson, and to fellow citizens urged passage of the aid to dependent children act, argued for a school to train social workers, and demanded creation of a dental college at the University of Texas. In May 1945 Ima endorsed adoption of the Prairie View State College budget; in June 1946 she supported the National Mental Health Act; and in 1948 she wrote numerous letters calling for federal appropriations for community mental hygiene clinics. She also protested removal of Houston's Division of Crime Prevention from police headquarters.[61] In 1943 the demands of war weighed heavily on Ima's conscience, and when asked to stand for election to the school board, she saw a way to serve Houston's children in a time of crisis.

World War II produced an economic explosion that was welcome after the stagnation of the previous decade. A world at war, battling for ships, munitions, oil, and cotton products, brought new industries and immigrants to Houston. Population jumped from about 384,000 to nearly 600,000 during the 1940s. Designated the "citadel of defense" by its Chamber of Commerce propagandists, the city stood "on the threshold of unprecedented industrial and business activity" in 1941.

Already first in manufacturing in the South and eleventh in the nation, Houston attracted new refineries and related businesses every month that year. By 1943, when Ima launched the liberty ship SS *James Stephen Hogg* on April 23, Houston industries employed 114,000 in war-related work, paid a $5 million weekly payroll, could turn out a new ship in sixty-six days, and produced 50 percent of America's wartime energy needs.[62] As the startling increase in chemical workers attests—from 180 to 20,000 between 1940 and 1949—the war gave birth to whole new industries that transformed Houston into a modern manufacturing giant. Less gratifying were the pressures on Houston's school system. Schools were crowded well beyond capacity. Teachers and staff decamped for the military or for high-paying jobs in industry. Family dislocations caused a sharp rise in juvenile delinquency and a demand for nurseries and other extended-care facilities for young children whose mothers were working in war industries. New industries demanded curriculum development. But financing the war effort dampened taxpayers' ability or desire to increase inadequate school budgets.[63]

In the summer of 1942 school board attention was focused not on war-related crises but instead on the continuing battle for control waged by the district's business manager. Hubert Mills created a board deadlock by offering Eletha (Mrs. B. F.) Coop, a board member since 1928 and an Oberholtzer ally, the lucrative position of assistant director of the district lunchroom department. After her departure, most contested school business ground to a halt. The remaining six board members could not agree on Coop's replacement and decided to await results of the scheduled April 1943 election for the seats held by Coop and Ray Daily. Dr. C. M. Taylor, the well-respected former president of the Houston District Dental Society, had filed for the post, but a group of "women from all sections of the city" formed the Citizens' Educational Committee to promote female candidates for the two positions and combat a potential shift toward Mills's more conservative camp. The committee persuaded Ima to challenge Taylor in Position 3 and endorsed incumbent Daily for Position 4. Committee members stressed "the necessity of having two able women on the school board," in keeping with district tradition; they acknowledged Dr. Daily's "proved" value and noted Ima's long-standing interest in education.[64] While Ima occasionally appeared at campaign meetings alone, made her own statements to the press, and conducted a solo radio appeal on KPRC on April 2, she and Daily were linked as a moderate-to-liberal slate in the public mind. On February 27, 1943, the newly organized East End Children's Educational Forum responded to the Citizens' Educational Committee's action by endorsing Taylor for Position 3 and Irene Davis, wife of Houston oil man Sam H. Davis, for Position 4.[65]

In the businesslike way Ima approached any new enterprise, she studied the issues and prepared a statement that she elaborated at coffees and meetings held in homes and businesses throughout the city and restated in her April 2 election-eve radio address. She outlined three reasons for running: first, Houston deserved two women representatives on its Board of Education; second, Ima's time could be devoted to "the welfare of the Houston public school system"; and third, service to education provided "an opportunity . . . to answer the challenge which this war makes to every man, woman, and child on the homefront." Viewing elected office as a "privilege and an obligation," she continued:

> It is my belief that any person elected to the school board should regard himself or herself as a representative of all citizens of Houston, regardless of class, color, or creed. If elected, I would not look upon myself as promoting the interests of any special group or section of the City. It would be my desire, therefore, and hope, to perform a service, however modest it might be to my community as a whole.

She concluded by declining to say how she would vote on any issue since "one who is not a member of the Board of Education could hardly pretend to have sufficient information to know the answers to the many questions which have arisen and which will come before the Board."[66]

Ima's major opponent, Dr. C. M. Taylor, ran a similarly high-toned campaign and advocated "four freedoms" for teachers: "freedom from fear of losing their jobs . . . freedom from salary discrimination . . . freedom from coercion in political campaigns . . . and freedom from want in old age, . . . already achieved through the teacher retirement law." Ima responded to these catchy slogans by saying she, too, would fight for "salaries commensurate with the service [teachers] render to society," for their financial security, and for freedom from interference in teaching.[67]

In contrast to this civil competition, Daily's chief opponent, Irene Davis, attacked the incumbent bitterly. Davis accused Daily of advocating controversial books for the junior high school curriculum and insinuated that Daily's postgraduate medical study in Europe was anti-democratic and had somehow fostered ideas dangerous to young Houstonians. Davis further charged that "our children's education is too general, too much social this and social that. Let us get back to essentials."[68] Daily, lauded by her supporters as patriotic, courageous, and public-spirited, bluntly retorted that Davis "shows a profound lack of familiarity [with] the mechanics of the curriculum . . . Not once during these two years has any textbook or reference book been discussed by the board. The selection of these books is an administrative function and is handled by competent people in the superintendent's department."[69]

Intensely derogatory undercurrents that foreshadowed the demagogic school politics of the Cold War era in the 1950s roiled the campaign.[70] Both candidates saved an anonymous campaign leaflet that attacked Ima as "very old, very rich—no children, and all she knows about children is what she has read in a book" and Daily as a "Russian born Red Jewess—she has been investigated by the F.B.I. and they no doubt have their eyes on her now."[71] On March 8 one writer told Ima she was the "victim of a wily scheme to exploit you that Dr. R. Daily may continue to be perpetuated in office on the School Board, by riding in on your skirts." In her reply of March 11, Ima defended herself and Daily as patriotic Houstonians.[72]

These scurrilous accusations were dismissed by the many prominent citizens who rallied to Ima's support, impressed by her long-standing civic consciousness, her executive ability, her willingness to serve, and her belief that teachers formed "the heart of the school." Every few days, new endorsements were announced in a carefully orchestrated effort to counter negative rhetoric with positive statements. Her dear friend Estelle Sharp, speaking for "civic and social club circles," stressed the importance of female representation on March 21. Longtime friend and fellow cultural philanthropist F. M. Law, president of the First National Bank, endorsed Ima's candidacy on March 24: "Miss Hogg has frankly stated that if elected she would enter upon her duties without commitment and bound by no preconceived ideas. She is a woman of broad viewpoint, generous and sympathetic in her nature." On March 30 University of Houston attorney Palmer Hutcheson and thirteen men from the "city's educational committee" pledged to push the Hogg-Daily slate. Finally, former school board president and prominent attorney Colonel William B. Bates addressed the KXYZ radio audience on Ima's behalf on April 2, the same day as her address on KPRC.[73]

Houston's three major white-owned newspapers united in affirming the judgment of business, cultural, and social leaders. On Friday, April 2, the *Post* noted that Ima "has taken an active interest in civic and educational affairs for years, is well informed on such matters, and has a sympathetic understanding of the problems of the schools. She has no ax to grind, but only a patriotic desire to render a public service." In a lengthy editorial on

March 30, the *Houston Press* asserted that Ima should be elected "by virtue of her native ability, her background of cosmopolitan experience and her long devotion to the cause of education," which "should be of invaluable assistance on the board." In its election-eve endorsement, the *Chronicle* held "with many friends of the school system, that we should have at least two women on the board." The *Bellaire Breeze,* a neighborhood newsletter, departed from its nonpartisan policy to urge support for Hogg and Daily "simply because they are highly recommended by those most likely to know: the majority of the teachers, the YWCA, and the community leaders of every type who we have found trustworthy in such matters."[74]

White middle-class and elite leadership stood solidly behind the Hogg-Daily ticket, but support was mixed in blue-collar and black neighborhoods. Labor lawyer Arthur Josephus Mandell and his partner Herman Wright got the Oil Workers International, the United Steelworkers, and other labor unions to endorse Ima and distribute leaflets in blue-collar areas. Writing to congratulate Ima on April 13, 1943, Mandell noted that the unions had supported her because "we believe that you will give progressive and intelligent leadership on the School Board. We know you will do your utmost to raise the teachers' pay to a level where they can live with economic security, and provide for all Americans regardless of race, creed, or color equal educational opportunities as befits our system of government."[75] Apparently without studying Daily's board record, R. R. Grovey, president of the Third Ward Civic Club and black organizer for the CIO, claimed that Daily was unsympathetic to blacks and gave his support to Taylor and Davis. The Negro Advisory Committee to the City Council endorsed Taylor and Daily. Carter Wesley, editor and publisher of the city's most influential black newspaper, the *Houston Informer*, repeated the "unfortunate" underground rumor that Ima was a surrogate for Superintendent Oberholtzer, who was "not the friend of Negroes" because he set salaries for black teachers well below salaries for whites and hired "substitutes and supernumeraries at starvation wages to teach in the negro schools."[76] Ima's statements did reassure J. B. Grigsby, member of the board of the Houston Negro Hospital, who wrote to her that he would get "a large number of my racial group" to vote for her.[77]

Given the restrictive poll tax that severely limited black participation and the habitual apathy of voters in school district elections, it is not clear that the extensive press coverage or the hard work of the Citizens' Educational Committee swayed many voters on election day, April 3. When the ballot count was officially announced at the April 10 meeting of the Board of Education, only 7,515 voted in Ima's contest and 7,442 in Daily's, less than 10 percent of the more than 85,000 eligible voters. In Position 3 Ima received 4,369 votes, Taylor polled 3,034, and three others 112 votes. Daily routed Davis, 5,097 to 1,959, while a third candidate received 386 votes.[78] With this endorsement, Ima Hogg began her career as an elected public official and spent a busy month gathering information, reading, and visiting schools.[79] By the board meeting on May 24, she was ready to turn her attention to school board business.

IMA'S CONTRIBUTION TO PUBLIC SCHOOL EDUCATION

During the campaign Ima had adroitly avoided discussing two newsworthy matters: equal pay for black teachers and the renewal of Superintendent Oberholtzer's contract. With business booming, population soaring, and labor at a premium, some Houston entrepreneurs began to change their views about race relations, and conditions improved for African-American Houstonians.[80] Spurred to action by *Informer* publisher and attorney Carter Wesley and by a Dallas lawsuit that had won equal pay for African-American and white teachers in that city, Houston's black teachers discovered the value of organized protest during the waning days of the 1943 Board of Education campaign. Although the district had built two high schools for African-American students and had established the Houston Colored Junior College (later the Houston College for Negroes and now Texas Southern University) these schools suffered from lower pay scales and larger classes. Only white schools provided advanced classes, many extracurricular activities, and swimming; African-American students often lacked supplies and textbooks, and in 1943 the starting pay for black teachers was $675 and for white teachers $1,125. When victory in the Dallas case was announced in March 1943, Houston's black teachers decided to seek redress. A three-part plan emerged from several secret strategy sessions: a citizens committee was formed to shepherd a Houston lawsuit through the courts; a fund-raising committee began canvassing African-American business and professional leaders to raise $5,000 needed for legal expenses; and attorney F. S. K. Whittaker agreed to prepare a petition and to represent the teachers before the school board and in court, if necessary.[81]

Sensing that the Dallas decision might prompt court action to equalize the salaries of Houston's African-American and white teachers, the school board met on April 1 and decided to hear Whittaker and to consider the black teachers' petition on Monday, April 5. Oberholtzer estimated that $297,500 would be needed in 1943 to equalize white and black pay scales for more than four hundred black employees in thirty schools.[82] On April 5, the day Ima was introduced to the board, Whittaker and eleven teachers and principals appeared at the specially called meeting to present their proposal for salary equalization. Whittaker stated that he represented all black teachers and principals and hammered three critical points: first, "that negro teachers in the Houston school system receive at least a third less than white teachers for the same type of work"; second, "that this schedule, based on race, is a violation of the 14th Amendment to the Constitution"; and third, "that colored teachers for a number of years have met the standards required by the Board for white teachers." He noted that "precedents for equalizing salaries of negro and white teachers have been set in several cities, including Dallas, since 1935."[83] Whittaker then introduced the teachers and principals and listed their salaries and qualifications.

After some general discussion the board retired to executive session to discuss two related issues: pay raises for all employees so the district could compete in the tight labor market and equalization of black and white pay scales. While no record of the closed-door meeting exists, members must have been persuaded by Whittaker's argument, by the lawsuit he had filed simultaneously in federal district court, by the Dallas decision, and by the knowledge that they could not replace hundreds of teachers at a time when labor shortages were already a district-wide problem. Finally, Ima's campaign statements favoring improved salaries for all teachers and her frequently repeated promise to treat all sectors of the community in the same way made it clear that she would give a majority to the Daily-led group that favored black-white parity and pay raises for all employees. Delay was pointless.[84]

When the board met again on April 12, Melvin E. Kurth, attorney for the Board of Education, reported that he had met with Whittaker "as directed by the Board" on April 5. The lawyers had agreed that salaries of African-American teachers would be slowly raised and would reach parity with white salaries in September 1945. Retroactive to March 1, 1943, the agreement would be effective when "signed by each and every colored teacher and principal." In a show of unity, Werlein, seconded by Shepherd, moved to adopt the resolution, and the motion passed unanimously. *Informer* editors, recognizing the drama of the board's voluntary action, devoted front-page space to the historic decision:

In the most inspiring example of racial cooperation and democracy at work, . . . the School Board of the City of Houston distinguished itself by the forthright manner in which it faced the fact of the inequality in the pay of Negro teachers, and the dispatch with which they took steps to adjust it. The action not only argues courage and character, but establishes the willingness of the board members to represent all the people and to so act to increase racial amity and confidence in the city.[85]

Houston thus became the first large Southern city to equalize pay scales for white and African-American teachers without a courtroom fight. On May 3 James H. Law, president of the Colored Classroom Teachers and Principals Association, brought the school board thanks from 445 African-American teachers for a "second emancipation" and assured those present that every teacher would give "undivided support to the school system."[86]

If the issue of pay equalization for black teachers and principals could be settled without Ima's official sanction, the question of Superintendent Oberholtzer's contract renewal awaited her tie-breaking vote. In response to requests from high school students who wanted a publicly supported local avenue for further education, Oberholtzer had created a segregated junior college system in 1927 that was administered by the Board of Education, with the school superintendent doubling as system president. The segregated colleges quickly developed four-year programs, and in 1933 the Texas legislature approved expansion to a segregated four-year university system, still under Board of Education authority and still managed by a superintendent-president.[87] Almost at once it became clear that the demands of a school system and a growing university system were too great to be handled effectively by one man and one board. When Holger Jeppesen joined the board in 1937, criticism increased, and by 1939 it was obvious that the dual administration was destined to change. War distractions delayed the creation of a freestanding university, but on May 18, 1942, board members voted to study the university's status.[88] At the May 24, 1943, meeting, the first Ima attended as a voting member, the full seven-member board, in closed executive session, debated Oberholtzer's contract renewal and the related issue of university management for nearly two hours. When the public was readmitted to the board room, George Wilson moved that Oberholtzer be given a five-year contract identical to his existing agreement with the school board. Daily, Shepherd, and Ima supported Wilson. Petersen and

Werlein opposed the motion because they felt a three-year contract was more appropriate in wartime. Jeppesen abstained.[89]

Subsequent events revealed that a deal had been struck during the contract battle to ensure that Oberholtzer would eventually be named president of a separated University of Houston (with its segregated College for Negroes), while Mills continued in a position of power in the school system. On July 26, 1943, the Board of Education authorized the formation of an advisory board of fifteen prominent citizens under the chairmanship of multimillionaire wildcatter and school dropout Hugh Roy Cullen, who already had poured thousands of dollars into the local university system because he believed the university's mission was committed to the practical needs of working men and women.[90] Board of Education members, in their roles as trustees for the local university, "agreed to abide by all decisions of [the] Advisory Board" and authorized it to oversee daily operations of the segregated campuses and to secure legislative approval to separate the university from the school district. At a Board of Education meeting on May 29, 1944, Ima and all other members present voted to approve a bill drafted by school board lawyer Melvin Kurth and University of Houston advisors Palmer Hutcheson and Colonel W. B. Bates to complete the separation.[91]

Disagreements immediately erupted. Ray Daily, who did not attend the May 29, 1944, meeting, joined faculty, politicians, and citizens in criticizing specific provisions of the bill relating to hiring and curriculum development. Ima clashed with the Daily faction when she sided with personal friends who had drafted the legislation. In an interview years later, Daily asserted that Ima was "taken in" by men on the board. It seems more likely that Ima agreed with friends who had supported her frequent requests for help with civic causes like the Child Guidance Clinic and Symphony Society. On March 12, 1945, the bill that separated university from school district passed and was signed by Governor Coke Stevenson; on March 13 Edison E. Oberholtzer became the first president of a freestanding University of Houston that included the segregated College for Negroes campus. On March 3, 1947, the state legislature granted autonomy to the renamed Texas State University for Negroes, and the entity became Texas Southern University on June 1, 1951.[92]

Deputy Superintendent William Ernest Moreland, a modest, quiet man who had served tirelessly on community projects, was appointed acting superintendent of the school district. Ima hoped the board would pursue a candidate of national standing, but to her disappointment,

Moreland was given a permanent appointment in July 1945. Having been promoted through the ranks of district administration, he was no match for the powerful Mills and the board's conservative faction, even though he favored the enlightened academic policies inaugurated under Oberholtzer.[93]

If the squabbles over Oberholtzer's contract and the creation of a separate university system offered glimpses of the politicking that Ima found distasteful, the vexing problems of wartime challenged her ability to address school issues with imagination. In July 1943, Ima was named chairwoman of the Lunch Room Committee and member of the New School Properties Committee, assignments that forced her to address the district's severely crowded classrooms and exploding school enrollments, which climbed from 65,198 in 1940 to 83,090 in 1944–1945.[94] In fulfilling her duties as lunchroom chairwoman for two years, Ima oversaw the minutiae of a freestanding business operation that comprised one hundred cafeterias, provided forty thousand meals each day, and was expected to support operations from meal sales. No detail escaped Ima's attention, and during her chairmanship, she operated the lunchroom department with a surplus that was used to upgrade equipment, to provide raises and bonuses for the department's staff, and to teach proper nutrition and hygiene by providing low-cost, healthy meals for all children.[95]

The New School Properties Committee presented different burdens. The Houston Independent School District had used Public Works Administration (PWA) largesse, steered to the city by Reconstruction Finance Corporation Chairman Jesse H. Jones (1933–1939) and Houston Congressman Albert Thomas, to expand and rehabilitate its physical plant during the 1930s, but the 1940s population surge and wartime inability to maintain school properties produced crisis conditions by 1943.[96] Threats of half-day double sessions, stories of children standing in the aisles, and pictures of cooks preparing meals in kitchen-classrooms appalled board members. Worse still were the complaints of parents who brought tales of falling plaster, standing water, faulty plumbing, and unsafe fire escapes to meeting after meeting with board members.[97] Following visits to Foster Place and Southmayd Elementary Schools in March 1944, Ima confirmed parent complaints: water was standing in the school yards although no rain had fallen; at Southmayd six toilets served three hundred girls; and students at Foster Place ate lunch in a room nineteen by twenty-four feet that doubled as a classroom. "When you visit the schools and see that every one of them needs something—it's baffling. . . . I don't see how we're going to keep up with the rapid growth of the city," she told a reporter. In 1943 Ima voted to use federal funds to pay for temporary and prefabricated rooms, and she pressed voters to authorize $7.5 million in bonds in 1945 and another $25 million in 1947.[98] Although Houstonians voted for the funds and the board authorized construction, rehabilitation, and land purchase between 1945 and 1948, the district was unable to keep pace with the city's growth, and Ima's term ended much as it had begun, with a struggle to provide safe facilities adequate to serve Houston's exploding school population while containing budget growth.

When the board was not preoccupied with "an urgently needed building program" that "overshadow[ed] curriculum concerns," it often seemed mired in personnel disputes regarding the district's 3,500 employees.[99] By 1943 pay scales had been stagnant for years, and increases were completely inadequate to meet the 69.9 percent cost-of-living increase that hit Houston between 1939 and 1948. Ima at once demanded fair and equitable treatment for all employees in salary matters, noting that an African-American tool-room keeper received only forty-five cents an hour in 1943, while a white employee performing the same tasks received sixty-five cents an hour. For years journalists had exposed teachers' "meager" financial rewards, their "nerve-racking" work environment, and the failure of parents to appreciate classroom dynamics or cooperate with teachers' demands.[100] Low pay and pressure to manage larger classes meant constant calls for higher salaries, although many teachers were improperly trained, and some lacked bachelor's degrees. Ima seconded a motion to affirm board opinion that "teachers must be assigned in their area of expertise," but in matters of hiring and promotion, she "made it a policy . . . never to make any suggestions to the Personnel Department, as I feel that is purely an administrative matter."[101] She did, however, support "increasing teachers' salaries . . . to see that we get the best teachers available," and she pressed the superintendent to improve training standards and develop "a forward looking program" so the district could compete with the more financially rewarding, less stressful jobs offered in the commercial sector.[102] During her term of office salaries rose dramatically with starting contracts moving from $1,125 in 1943 to $2,300 in 1947–1948. Teachers viewed Ima as their champion and wrote to express "deep and sincere appreciation" for her "independent, thoughtful judgment and . . . genuine objective approach."[103]

Although Ima dutifully oversaw the Lunchroom Department and valiantly struggled with personnel and facility issues, she had greatest success when she adapted lessons learned from her privately funded philanthropies to school district needs. Made aware of rising levels of juvenile delinquency associated with war-related distress by reports from Child Guidance Clinic, Houston Symphony, and Community Chest volunteers, board President Ewing Werlein initiated a long discussion in January 1944 about ways the Board of Education could aid Houston's youth. Ima agreed with Ray Daily and George Wilson that school playgrounds and athletic facilities should be available to groups free of charge, but she stressed the need for well-planned, well-supervised programs like the one being tried at John Marshall Junior High School, where nine youth-service agencies cooperated on a plan implemented by paid workers who conducted all activities. The board placed Ima, Daily, Oberholtzer, and Mills on a committee to investigate the use of school facilities for community needs and named Werlein chairman.[104] With all factions in agreement, committee work moved quickly. On February 15, 1944, Werlein reported meetings with school physical education personnel and with representatives from the city Parks and Recreation Department, from social service organizations and Parent-Teacher Associations, and from other groups who might use school grounds. His committee recommended offering "without cost . . . school buildings and play grounds for recreational purposes, under policies and with activities approved by the Board of Education."[105] The board approved these recommendations, and during her term Ima continued to endorse requests to use school facilities.[106]

While Ima urged cooperation between the school board and the Parks and Recreation Department, she also prodded her colleagues to aid Houston's youth by studying underlying causes of student maladaptation. Building on her work with the Child Guidance Clinic, Ima pressed citizen groups to petition the Board of Education for a visiting teacher program so problem students could be identified and helped. Visiting teachers, really trained social workers who visited homes and classrooms, had been used successfully in school systems since 1906 and had been incorporated into the Houston curriculum from 1929 until 1934, when the program lapsed due to lack of funds. On October 9, 1944, the Youth Service Committee on the Youth Problem, a coalition of school, church, civic, and welfare groups, school principals, and Parent-Teacher Association representatives, followed Ima's leadership and petitioned the Board of Education for reinstatement of the visiting teacher program. Board members were shocked to learn that nearly 14 percent of children ten to seventeen were "known to the police department" in 1943.[107] Convinced that it must take preventive measures, the board named Ima chairwoman of a committee to study the issue.[108] Primed for action, Ima sent a thirty-four–item bibliography and excerpts of published material to local presidents of the Houston Teachers' Association, the Council of Parents and Teachers, and the Texas Congress of Parents and Teachers. Tactfully crediting Oberholtzer as host, she invited Carmelita Janvier, nationally known director of special services for the Orleans Parish school district in Louisiana, to Houston and arranged meetings and dinners so Janvier could share her knowledge of visiting teacher programs with public school staff and representatives from community agencies, with the Board of Education, and with the "colored Principals to discuss their needs and problems."[109] Significantly, Ima made sure all constituencies met with the expert.

Drawing on her long-held beliefs about the psychological factors that foster a wholesome life to illustrate the way visiting teachers could help "promote the welfare of the child as a whole," Ima explained the program to members of the Houston Teachers' Association who had not met with Janvier. Ima reassured the classroom teachers that visiting teachers do not interfere, that they only "aid and supplement" other personnel in a preventive program "focused on salvaging as much human material as possible, and mobilizing every resource in the community to that end." Taking a practical approach, Ima noted that the classroom teacher cannot teach and the taxpayer loses money when children fail because of emotional, physical, or mental difficulties that go untreated. Since the term "visiting teacher" was a misnomer, Ima carefully explained that a visiting teacher was "an expertly trained, psychiatric social worker, or school visitor, . . . with an ingratiating personality . . . skillfully trained in the art and techniques of interviewing." This staff member would help teachers recognize problems, study individual children, recommend therapies, visit the child's home, guide severe cases to proper social service agencies, and "cooperate with all individuals or agencies concerned with the welfare of children." After studying curricula from all over the country, Ima concluded that such programs succeeded only when social service staff and teachers worked together.[110]

On November 27, 1944, Ima made her formal report to the board. In addition to the visit from Janvier, Ima had digested readings from the research department of the school system, the Council of Social Agencies, and the Hogg Foundation, and she had made these materials available to the Board of Education. She had interviewed school administrators and representatives of community agencies to see how a program could be implemented in Houston, had met frequently with the superintendent to formulate recommendations, and had called a November 20 conference to discuss the proposals. Impressed by her diligence, the board gratefully accepted the report and voted to adopt the superintendent's suggestion that a coordinator be hired to set up a program. Delighted by these results, Ima sent copies of her report to Beulah Wild at the Bureau of Mental Hygiene, to Robert L. Sutherland at the Hogg Foundation, and to Carmelita Janvier, thanking them for their "invaluable service."

During the search for a visiting-teacher coordinator, Ima relentlessly prodded district administrators to hire staff, and she finally reported that the program had been launched in September 1945. Eleanor Craighill, "a very personable woman, young enough, modest, with ability," was named coordinator to supervise six visiting teachers—three white and three black. Given the usual pace of school business and the grave problems finding trained personnel, Ima's ability to push the program through the board and system bureaucracy was remarkable.[111] The search convinced Ima that trained visiting teachers were "impossible to find." To remedy the deficit, she established three scholarships at the University of Texas, through the Hogg Foundation, to support candidates for social service training who promised to work in Houston.[112]

Ima championed school district programs for child care and for disabled children as well. Mike Hogg's widow, Alice, was chairwoman of the Working Mothers Advice Center during the war years and kept her sister-in-law apprised of private-sector initiatives to care for children left unsupervised while their mothers worked in war industries. Nearly nineteen thousand women, many with small children, took jobs in Houston's essential industries, and many of them lobbied school officials and civic leaders for help with child care. Congress responded to wartime demands by passing the Lanham Act, which provided federal funds for locally administered nursery schools. Houston's first Lanham Act nurseries, opened in 1943 for children ages two to five, were immediately successful, and additional nursery programs, summer care, and after-school supervision were introduced in 1944. Although run by the school district, these care centers often were located in housing that had been built for war workers with federal funds.[113] When the Board of Education had to approve extension of Lanham Act funds in April and September 1944, Ima and Ray Daily eloquently defended the use of federal money to meet wartime needs for social services not provided by private agencies. Working mothers, led by Kathleen E. Houston, begged the board to continue funding and include after-school care in its peacetime planning. When federal financing ceased in August 1945, several private agencies recognized the critical need for day care and continued to fund nursery, after-school, and summer camp programs initiated during the war.[114] Ima and Daily believed that young children gained essential social skills and parents retained peace of mind when nurseries were available. As her final act on the Board of Education, Ima joined Daily to make sure six free kindergartens were organized in black elementary schools for the 1949–1950 school year.[115]

In 1939 surveyors for Houston's school health department and department of special classes discovered a significant population of physically and mentally disabled children who needed special services but who were being overlooked because programs addressing their needs had been discontinued or reduced in the mid-1930s. For lack of money, little was done until Ima took action in 1943. In June Ima met with Margaret Caillet, a specialist who wanted to start a school in Houston for children with special needs. Ima carried Caillet's plans to the superintendent and in July persuaded her friend Susan Vaughan (Mrs. W. L.) Clayton to donate $1,000 to the Board of Education to equip a school for disabled children. In September, classes opened at the one-story Eastwood School with Caillet, a program assistant, and a nurse on staff.[116] Serving as board liaison, Ima organized a support group of prominent women including sister-in-law Alice Hogg. On October 1 members of the group toured the new school and talked with the district superintendent and other officers about issues confronting the disabled. Everyone agreed the committee could best serve the program by educating the public about the problems of special needs children.[117] After the state began funding special education in September 1945, Houston's program developed swiftly. By the time Ima left the board, the school system was implementing recommendations made in an extensive 1947 report. Attuned to the latest thinking about children's issues because of her ties to the Houston Child Guidance Clinic and the Hogg Foundation, Ima mustered support in the community for an overlooked sector of the school population. By initiating a pilot program, she made sure the district and Houston's parents were prepared to take advantage of state funding as soon as it became available.

Dear to Ima's heart was the wish that all children could experience the joys of great art and music. In her frequent school visits, she attended art classes and noticed that many schools had no fine art displayed on their walls. To remedy this deficit, she revived a popular pre–World War I tradition by giving the schools a collection of reproductions "to acquaint our boys and girls with various masterpieces of art."[118] These prints circulated through the district's schools, and Ima made sure African-American schools were included in the program. She insisted that art programs be part of the curriculum in African-American schools, and in later years she provided easels to display prize-winning school art projects in public spaces.[119] Ima studied the district's music program and noted in 1945 that most schools lacked trained teachers, instruments, and proper practice rooms. She argued for a district-wide program with proper instruments, teachers, and music rooms provided to all elementary and secondary schools. Drawing on her contacts at the University of Texas, she arranged for members of its College of Fine Arts to study the district's needs and formulate a program, a seventeen-month process begun in January 1948. Although no longer on the board when it met in May 1949 to discuss results of the study, Ima wrote her former colleagues and urged them to accept the report's recommendations.[120]

Endless other questions, large and small, confronted Ima during her years on the Board of Education: budgets, bond issues, property condemnations, summer classes, libraries, athletic programs, even typewriter purchases and travel accounts.[121] As 1948 drew to a close, rumors circulated that Ima would not run for reelection to the board. Responding to a crisis at the Houston Symphony Society, her "old and I might say first love," Ima had agreed to serve as president in June 1946. At that time she told a friend, "I would be tempted to resign from the School Board, but I am endeavoring to go on with both organizations."[122] In February 1949 she did announce her decision to retire and made known her desire that a woman "who would uphold something of the same philosophy of education and the principles which I cherish for the welfare of our children" replace her on the board. She expressed regret that she could not devote more time to the ever-present problems of district business. Her decision not to run drew testimonials from fellow board members and sparked a front-page press battle as eight candidates, four of them women, filed for the post.[123]

Many considerations undoubtedly influenced Ima's decision not to seek reelection. In another six years, she would have been seventy-three years old, and the wartime crisis was past. The political aspects of school board business troubled her. To close friend Margaret Patrick, director of physical education in the elementary schools, Ima confided, "I do not think I am particularly fitted for many of the phases of school board membership, though I have enjoyed participating in the work."[124] Other interests commanded her attention. She remained president of the Symphony Society until 1956, and in the postwar years she returned to serious collecting of Americana, a pursuit she had neglected for more than a decade.

Although retired from the Board of Education, Ima did not forget Houston's children. Working through the Symphony Society, she continued to foster district-wide music programs in the 1950s and 1960s. During these decades she dispersed large collections of books, records, magazines, and sheet music to the Houston and Austin public libraries, to the Hogg Foundation, and to Rice Institute, the University of Texas, the University of Houston, and Texas Southern University. Among her most endearing gifts to the public libraries were hundreds of beautifully illustrated children's books in several languages, which Ima had purchased on her travels abroad—a poignant reminder that although she was childless herself, young people were never far from her thoughts. The Hoggs had all been inveterate readers and book collectors. Governor Hogg frequently described books he was reading in letters to his children, and the siblings often recommended books to each other or exchanged volumes at Christmas and birthdays. Inventories of books at Bayou Bend made in the 1930s and 1940s reveal the family's eclectic, voracious reading habits. In every room, piles of books and magazines relating to civic projects, to spiritual growth, and to literary interests cluttered tables and crammed bookcases. Boxes of books sat on closet shelves, but all these collections gradually found their way to city and university libraries.[125]

During the politically polarized 1950s Ima reminded Houstonians that educating Houston's young people must be separated from politicking. In the summer of 1954 she joined an informal group of leading citizens— among them philanthropists Nina Cullinan and Ella Fondren, Marshall Plan overseer Will Clayton, banker William Kirkland, Rice Professor Radoslav A. Tsanoff, and former University of Houston president W. W. Kemmerer—to combat the red scare tactics that had paralyzed the school board since its 1952 election.[126] Generated by sensational press coverage of red-baiting school board campaigns and lurid reporting of Senator Joseph McCarthy's House on Un-American Activities investigations, the anti-Communist hysteria further exacerbated the split between the longtime incumbent business manager, Hubert Mills, and Oberholtzer's successor as school district superintendent, James Moreland.

In October 1954 Ima tried to blunt the hatred and fear stirred by press agitation when she described the qualities needed in effective school board members: intellectual and emotional maturity, integrity and independence from any faction, a sound philosophy of education based on current needs, and a regard for spiritual and cultural values. Most important, a school board member must understand that a school board is "a judicial policy-making body," not an administrative department. She closed her letter to the editor of the *Post* with a strong restatement of her wish that Houstonians would impose a "sacred trust" on everyone connected with the school system to see "that our children are fitted . . . to recognize and fulfill the obligations and privileges of democratic citizenship in a world which strives toward peace, harmony and prosperity."[127] Ima's letter marked a change of heart at the *Post*, where publisher and former governor William P. Hobby had condoned publication of vituperative attacks. By late 1954, his more liberal wife, Oveta Culp Hobby, had convinced her husband that this coverage only inflamed hate-mongering, damaged Houston's reputation, and destroyed the public school system.

In 1956 Ima spoke at a televised town meeting on public education about "the obligation and opportunity" of educators "to equip our children, not only scholastically, but emotionally to live as useful and happy adults in a changing world"—a summation of her crusade to support positive mental health care. She went on to emphasize the importance of music appreciation and visiting-teacher services to nurturing this well-balanced life. Board of Education President Verna Rogers declared, "You should be a television star" and praised Ima's "vivid manner" and "effective" voice.[128]

In 1943 Ima told her supporters that she would represent all Houstonians. In her fight to equalize pay for district employees, in her insistence that all schools—black and white—be given copies of fine art works for classroom display, and in her care for the disabled, she persistently pressured the school board to serve all of its constituents. In her 1949 retirement speech, Ima stressed her belief that educating the whole child for a lifetime of community involvement laid the foundation for a vibrant democracy. Through the visiting-teacher program she brought principles of sound mental health to the classroom. By listening to the needs of school district personnel and by maintaining close ties to privately funded community organizations, she broadened the support system available to schoolchildren and their parents. By advocating programs that nurtured physical, emotional, cultural, and academic well-being, she tried to ensure that every child would be given the tools to live fully and that every school employee would be treated with fairness and dignity. In an era of change, her vision of excellence never wavered. She served at a time when the board's superintendent and business manager often seemed more intent on destroying each other than on improving the school system. She served on a board that was overwhelmed by the conflicting demands of war and peace and hindered by innate conservatism that made its members reluctant to raise taxes and resistant to federal financial support.

The Hoggs espoused educational reform and activism at a moment of dramatic development. Texas's population moved from rural to urban during the first decades of the twentieth century, and even citizens resistant to change recognized that the shift demanded new approaches to school administration and academic curricula. The Hoggs tried to address the era's complexity by balancing public and private initiatives and by recognizing the importance of each. Will understood that private money and unified public opinion could topple governors and sway administrators. Mike and Ima discovered a unique way to support public improvements with private money in their Hogg Foundation. Ima's school board service demonstrated the valuable contribution nonpolitical citizens can make to publicly funded institutions. Heeding their father's admonition that good citizens must act with "pride and generosity" to ensure that young people "be capable of self-government and the preservation of their rights and liberties," the Hoggs devoted years of service to bring an "efficient system" of "common free schools" to all Texans.[129]

Chapter 5

The Symphony, a Constructive Force in Houston Civic Life

June 21, 1913, like most Houston summer days, blazed by five in the afternoon. A ladies' committee of classical music devotees, eager if apprehensive, stood in the sweltering lobby of the city's new Majestic Theatre, an ornately decorated vaudeville house adorned with mirrors, statues, and frescoed ceiling that seated six hundred, boasted loge boxes, and cooled its audience with open windows and wall fans.[1] Theater owner Karl Hoblitzelle of Dallas had donated two hours between regularly scheduled matinee and evening performances for a great experiment. Julien Paul Blitz, a Belgian cellist with dreams of forming a symphony orchestra, and Ima Hogg, a professionally trained pianist who believed a "vigorous center of commerce" like Houston must support symphonic music, had lobbied friends and musicians to attempt a trial concert. Ima corralled the audience, and Blitz gathered thirty-five musicians to rehearse a modest program of popular favorites that featured an unspecified "ebullient" Mozart symphony in E-flat, the fantasia from Bizet's *Carmen*, and the "Waltz of the Flowers" from Tchaikovsky's *Nutcracker Suite*. Blanche Foley, a Houston soprano, sang Gluck's "Divinités du Styx" from *Alceste* with "purity" and "clarity," and Rabbi Henry Barnstein,[2] a member of the Houston Music Festival board, described the goals of a civic movement to bring great music to the city. "Dixie" triumphantly concluded the performance. *Houston Post* music critic Wille Hutcheson, who used her newspaper columns to promote musical culture, gave equal space to the "intensely warm" conditions, the socially prominent attendees who almost filled the hall, and the musical effort. "Cordially enthusiastic" supporters agreed with her conclusion that if the ensemble had not perfected the performance after three rehearsals, the evening did offer "far more to enjoy and admire than to condemn or sharply criticize." Encouraged by this guarded enthusiasm, the ladies' committee voted to continue its efforts to build a resident symphony orchestra after the summer heat had subsided.[3]

EARLY HOUSTON'S MUSICAL TRADITIONS

The trial concert represented a culmination and a beginning. Entertainment had always been central to Houston's civic life. G. L. Lyons's 1837 promise to build a "temple dedicated to the dramatic muse" introduced visiting performers to makeshift stages in the frontier outpost. As the town grew, entrepreneurs lured professional troupes to gaslit vaudeville houses, and local amateur singing groups and theater bands provided music for appreciative concert audiences and dancing assemblies in the years before Spindletop. With the trial symphony concert, however, Houston's civic leadership raised the bar of cultural ambition. No longer would visiting artists or talented amateurs satisfy the city's cultural demands; cosmopolitan Houstonians now aspired to build homegrown professional cultural institutions of the highest quality.

In the century after Spindletop, Houston achieved cultural maturity as a world center that supports acclaimed symphonic and chamber music, opera and musical theater, classical ballet and modern dance, repertory and commercial theater, comprehensive and specialized visual arts museums, an array of subject-specific museums, and experimental performing and visual arts groups, schools, and galleries that create a "climate essential to the flowering of genius."[4] If remarkable for the breadth of its cultural offerings, Houston also provides an exemplary legacy of civic cooperation. Although Houston's activists and philanthropists have had mixed success in their long struggle to shape the built environment, wrest parklands from the grasp of private speculators, provide social services, and ensure educational excellence, these same socially conscious leaders have enjoyed almost unqualified triumph in their efforts to link Houston to cosmopolitan centers of creative expression.

Time and again, citizens, usually female, have identified a missing piece of the cultural scene, banded together to test popular interest, and generated support from enthusiastic donors. Houston's women have framed the city's cultural development as volunteers, spokespeople, and patrons of experimental activities that became major civic institutions. Husbands and fathers have been quick to recognize that cultural organizations are "an essential of modern life" and good for business.[5] After its reorganization in 1910, Houston's Chamber of Commerce encouraged members to support the arts and participate on volunteer boards and chamber committees that addressed arts issues. This early activism gave rise to a continuing tradition of business-volunteer participation and funding. Houston's business elite has long believed that a vibrant commercial city should also aspire to cultural sophistication. As volunteers and benefactors in the 1910s and 1920s, Will, Ima, and Mike promoted this nascent cultural activism and formed an association with two institutions that would benefit from their vision, oversight, and generosity for seven decades: the Houston Symphony Association and the Museum of Fine Arts of Houston. Both organizations bear witness to the Hogg family's attempts to infuse civic life with physical and moral excellence; both established development patterns that were replicated again and again as Houston's cultural philanthropists marshaled private resources to design and manage institutions for public purposes.[6]

Houston's cultural impetus coincided with the city's commercial ascendancy as a cotton, rice, and petroleum capital during two decades of population growth and urban expansion in the 1900s and 1910s. Well-heeled Houstonians had traditionally sought refuge from the summer heat by retiring to the countryside or traveling north, but improved rail and steamship access and unexpected wealth accumulation at the turn of the twentieth century permitted more frequent journeys to distant cities in the United States and to destinations in Europe and Asia. The elegant vistas of Paris, the glories of Rome, the beauties of Florence, the imperial collections of London, and the music festivals of Berlin and Vienna trained the eyes and ears of these travelers, who were able to spend months away from home or business indulging their growing awareness of the arts. When back at home, Houstonians joined musical and literary clubs that provided lectures, concerts, and discussions to strengthen their aesthetic taste and shape emergent civic goals. Like other Americans, Houstonians began to see arts institutions as avenues to provide personal and social regeneration, as beacons to edify public opinion, and as catalysts to help artists and craftsmen infuse commercial products with aesthetic value. Art, architecture, theater, and music became visual and auditory expressions of a Progressive Era civic consciousness, whose proponents were eager to improve urban life; clean sewers, paved streets, forest parks, museums, well-designed buildings, civic orchestras—all became essential elements of an ideal city.[7]

Critical to the development of Houston's cultural institutions was the emergence of leisure as a phenomenon that was changing daily life for all social and economic groups. Turn-of-the-century urban Houstonians discovered they had more discretionary income and time to devote to pleasurable pursuits. Arts institutions in some cities may have been perceived as preserves of the elite, but Houston's Progressive Era idealists saw the arts as democratizing forces that could consolidate civic identity and promote social goals of civic responsibility and harmony. Houston's museums, theaters, and concert halls—much like the city's parks where everyone could mingle to enjoy natural beauty—would also welcome all Houstonians. Concerned that fellow citizens might fritter leisure hours in "unhealthful" saloons (311 in 1910 Census reports), pool halls, or moving-picture shows, guardians of culture hoped to instill the "moral fastidiousness and cultural refinement" of "elevated leisure pursuits" that placed classical music, Shakespearean drama, and Old Master oil paintings at the acme of a cultural hierarchy.[8]

German immigrant Gustav Dresel recorded Houston's first musical performance in 1837, and Madame Louise Thielman sang "serious and comic songs" in the Capitol Building's Senate Hall on December 17, 1839. Fleeing religious persecution and political upheaval, Germans emigrated to Texas in large numbers in the half-century between 1830 and 1880 and were the first Houstonians to promote musical culture. Houston's German minority congregated in "Germantown" south and east of Buffalo Bayou and organized dancing, singing, militia, and athletic groups that began meeting in the Turnverein, or Turner Hall and Garden, built on the corner of Prairie and Caroline in 1854. Germans retained a strong cultural identity, but they developed an equally vigorous civic consciousness in their new surroundings, introduced classical concert programs, and presented open-air instrumental and vocal concerts to all Houstonians.

In May 1884 Professor Carl Zeus and his students established a Singing Choir, or Saengerbund, drafted a constitution for the group, and developed plans for a clubhouse.[9] Chartered as a state institution in June 1890, the Houston Saengerbund provided recreation, lectures, vocal and instrumental recitals, drama, patriotic celebrations, and "other elevating and laudable" activities. Houston's Saengerbund joined the German-Texan Singers' League (Saengerbund), which held statewide saengerfests (music festivals) from 1854 through 1916. Houston hosted the league's annual Saengerfest in 1885, 1894, 1902, and 1913—a grand prewar occasion when musicians entertained for three days at the City Auditorium.[10] A driving force behind the civic music movement in Houston, the local Saengerbund maintained Saengerfest orchestras from 1885 to 1918 and invited the St. Louis Symphony Orchestra and singers from the Metropolitan Opera to enhance festival performances.[11] From 1899 to 1909 Professor E. Lindenberg directed the thirty-two–piece Houston Symphony Club, which had been formed to stimulate demand for a professional orchestra, and he led the group at Saengerfest activities.[12]

German choral and instrumental groups, Lewis's Military Band and Orchestra (founded 1883), and Gilbert and Sullivan productions (after 1886) encouraged music-loving Houstonians to gather "for pleasure and enjoyment" at dances, parades, and picnics. Professional musicians, unionized in 1897, provided ensemble music for restaurants and movie houses and formed a nucleus for band and orchestral concerts. In the 1890s reformist enthusiasts joined the nationwide club movement "to educate and improve the public taste by giving the best music only."[13] The pioneering Treble Clef Club, organized as the Ladies' Singing Society in April 1896 to hire a coach and provide "concerts of a high artistic standard," enjoyed five successful seasons under three directors at the Light Guard Armory or at the Beach Auditorium on Main and McGowen.[14] Following a brief hiatus, the club reorganized in 1904 and quickly grew from twenty-three to seventy-five singers; it included 672 associate members by 1911 and attracted 4,000 to that year's closing concert. By 1912 Julien Paul Blitz was directing the group's productions.[15] For a decade the club sponsored an annual concert series featuring its large chorus and "an imposing list" of "big musical names."[16]

Not to be outdone by female enthusiasts, a group of men formed the Houston Quartette Society in 1900 to incorporate remnants of short-lived English men's singing clubs and bring the "world's best vocal talent to the city."[17] In the fall of 1903 Quartette Society members invited the presidents and musical directors of Texas singing clubs to a concert in Houston and suggested that attendees form the Federation of English Singing Societies of Texas to complement the well-established statewide German saengerfest movement. In 1904 and 1905 the Quartette Society sponsored state festivals that attracted four hundred singers, featured performances by the stellar New York Symphony and the well-known Pittsburgh Symphony orchestras, and filled the old Beach Auditorium "with splendid melody."[18]

In 1911 the Quartette Society asked the Woman's Choral Club to co-sponsor the festival. Brainchild of music mavens Ione Allen Peden and Wille Hutcheson, who served as founding president in 1901, the Woman's Choral Club had fifty active members in 1911; they paid $5 dues, provided three annual concerts, and brought well-known singers to Houston. Peden, a keen musician, was married to Houston industrialist and arts supporter Edward Andrew Peden, while Hutcheson, an incorrigible club woman and member of a prominent Houston family, wrote a *Post* cultural column for twenty years (1904–1924) and was the first accredited music critic in the South.[19] Other choral club members included Katharine Blunt (Mrs. Edwin B.) Parker as musical director, much-praised singer Mary Root (Mrs. William H.) Kirkland, and music promoter and soprano Edna Saunders, three women who became formidable advocates of Houston's civic music movement for the next four decades. Associate members included oil men Will Farish and Robert L. Blaffer, artist Emma Richardson Cherry, and civic activists Henry Barnstein, Harriet Levy, the Reverend Harris Masterson, and Estelle Sharp, all supporters of Houston's blossoming cultural scene.[20] Other musical clubs and several church choirs also stimulated interest in musical performance.

When music-loving civic leaders met with the manager of the Chicago Symphony Orchestra in March 1907 to discuss forming a Houston Music Festival Association, they represented a well-informed public eager to join a movement then sponsoring May festivals nationwide. In 1908 and 1909 the Chicago Symphony Orchestra teamed with local choristers to produce May festival concerts at the Prince Theatre. The New York Symphony Orchestra under Walter Damrosch provided an orchestra-only festival on April 25, 1910, that featured Houston pianist Helena Lewyn. In May 1911 Damrosch returned and joined a massed chorus of local singers ably trained by conductor Hu T. Huffmaster, music director of the Woman's Choral Club and for years an important leader of Houston's music scene.[21] Leadership Houston comprised a patrons' roster that grew to five hundred and listed musician Ima Hogg, suffragist leader and businesswoman Annette Finnigan, political leader Joseph C. Hutcheson Jr., prominent doctor Gavin Hamilton, and business leaders Robert L. Blaffer, Howard R. Hughes, and John H. Kirby.[22]

The increased musical activity convinced Mayor Horace Baldwin Rice to add the City Auditorium to his building program for a new County Court House and City Hall Market. In 1910 Edna W. Saunders, daughter of former mayor John D. Woolford, was named booking agent for the $235,000 auditorium that seated 3,400, and she launched a five-decade career as Houston's premiere impresario (1910–1963) by bringing sixteen symphony concerts to Houston for the hall's opening season. In her subsequent career, Saunders placed civic improvement and artistic merit before commercial gain and frequently booked acclaimed artists without regard to cost because she felt their appearances in Houston were important to the development of Houston's musical culture.[23]

Inspired by the May 1908 festival, a group of the "best amateurs and leading professionals" met on May 25 to establish the women's Thursday

Morning Musical Club, an aggressively serious study and performance club that would "stimulate greater achievement through rivalry."[24] Members elected Treble Clef Club musical director Margaret (Mrs. Robert L.) Cox president and named Katharine Parker chairwoman of its board of examiners. Candidates were required to pass a stringent exam, and the course of study included early and modern French, Italian, and German composers as well as sessions devoted to Slavonic composers, Grieg, American composers, and famous women composers. Contemporaries anticipated that the group "would doubtless have developed into a conservatory," but the club struggled to retain a director and seems to have withered after World War I.[25]

IMA'S FIRST LOVE

Ima Hogg fell in love with music when she was a little girl.[26] Years later she recalled dancing in the aisle during a concert in Austin—and she was, she thought, perhaps three years old. At ninety-three she could be caught off guard singing cheery ditties to herself. Grand pianos graced the drawing room and upstairs sitting room at Bayou Bend, and a big old radio hidden in a sitting room cupboard attested to hours of listening enjoyment. In fact, Ima loved all kinds of music, and she and Will were avid theatergoers. She often argued for fine arts festivals that combined music, art, and theater activities and in the 1960s asked teenagers to take her to rock 'n' roll concerts.[27]

Grandfather Hogg had insisted that his children study piano, violin, and voice, and Ima remembered sitting with her father at the piano while he sang in all the voice ranges, even lampooning a falsetto. Ima's mother taught her daughter's first piano lessons at the age of three. At six Ima began formal piano training with professional teachers that continued through her years at the University of Texas. Her family and teachers considered her a prodigy and proudly noted her almost perfect pitch. Great-aunt Lizzie Stinson Philips invited the little girl to play duets during summer visits with the Stinson grandparents, and Jim Hogg often asked his daughter to accompany Sunday evening hymn singing with visitors at the Governor's Mansion on the piano, banjo, or guitar. As a teenager and college student in Austin, Ima performed at several musicales in private homes, attended every available musical performance, and noted breathlessly the "always great" Ignace Paderewski after his March 3, 1900, Austin triumph.[28] Recounting university experiences, she remembered the "red-letter evening" when a "beautiful" small orchestra from Mexico performed a classical program on campus. "From that night," she recalled, "I never rested until we had a symphony orchestra in Texas."[29]

Ima continued professional-level study with the renowned but "kindly, patient" Adele Margulies during sojourns at the National Conservatory of Music in New York from 1900 through 1904, and she performed a Grieg solo in recital there.[30] Carefully chaperoned, the eager young musician attended dozens of concerts, jotted impressions on her programs, and kept meticulous notes in a theater record book. Comments on her programs made during these and subsequent years reveal her maturing comprehension and her emphasis on technique and "sympathy" as qualities critical to successful performance.[31] Ima's musical training culminated with rigorous coaching in Berlin during 1907 and 1908.[32] Encouraged by Will to take "any opportunity to improve myself," Ima rented rooms with a German family, immersed herself in language study, and began lessons at the popular music school managed by Franz Xaver Scharwenka, a Polish-German composer, pianist, and teacher, and his brother. After a few months there, she switched to a more compatible taskmaster, Martin Krause. Krause, protégé of Franz Liszt and famous pianist and teacher, wanted to present his talented pupil, but Ima relinquished a concert career, returned to Houston in late 1908, and began training advanced piano students. There is no archival evidence to explain Ima's decision to forgo a concert career, although she apparently felt unqualified to perform at the highest levels. It seems likely that family pressures, societal constraints, and a streak of perfectionism as well as her desire for a rooted home life brought Ima back to Houston.[33]

When Ima returned from her European adventure, still a young woman of twenty-seven in 1909, Houston's musical leadership welcomed her warmly. Her enthusiasm, her expertise, and her acquaintance with stars of the international concert circuit drew admiration, and she joined the well-regarded Woman's Choral Club; in 1910 she was named to the club's executive committee. Ima attended musical evenings, performed in local musicales, acquired several advanced pupils, and showcased their talents at formal recitals in her home.[34] Often described as both modest and determined, she worked with other young women to found the Girls' Musical Club, whose bylaws stipulated clearly that "girls shall be given preference" as active members and as officers.[35]

Associated in January 1911 under the guidance of Corinne Abercrombie (Mrs. Gentry) Waldo "for the purpose of study and self-improvement along musical lines," the club met first at the home of Alice (Mrs. James A.) Baker and included "an invited group of twenty-five young ladies"; Miss

Alice Baker was named president.[36] Ima served as president for the 1911–1912 and 1912–1913 seasons, and the yearbook during these years lists eight officers, only one of whom was married. Membership was a serious commitment, with club dues ($3), fines for tardiness, and expulsion after three unexcused absences. Active members in 1919 included established cultural leaders such as artist Emma Richardson Cherry and music patron Katharine Parker; daughters of prominent families such as Nina Cullinan and Emilie Stude; and talented musicians such as Blanche Foley and Mary Fuller. Bessie Griffiths, Ima's star pupil and a promising local music teacher, was a "privileged" member that year, as was Mrs. Baker, whose patronage had become essential to the success of cultural and civic endeavors. Because privileged, neither lady was required to perform.[37]

Extant yearbooks narrate the club's ambition and showcase the talents of dozens of women who had pursued musical studies since childhood. In 1911–1912 members linked painting and literature to musical traditions in several nations.[38] At a meeting on Tuesday, January 9, 1912, attended by Rice Institute President Edgar Odell Lovett, members explained the life and contributions of Franz Schubert: Ima Hogg described "Schubert—the Lyric Tone Poet," while Wille Hutcheson interpreted "The Erlking" and "The Wanderer." Others performed songs and an impromptu.[39] In 1912–1913 members met every other Tuesday from November 19 through June 3, and they conducted two open meetings at Katharine Parker's home, where members and guests presented lengthy programs that included lecture presentations and instrumental and vocal performances. That entire year was devoted to the study of classical periods in music and their representative composers. A leader, who presented a paper and performed, presided at each meeting. Ima took charge on February 11 and February 25, 1913, for two of four sessions devoted to the music of Bach and Handel. On February 25 she described "Bach's Perfected Fugue Form" and performed the "Well-Tempered Clavichord" (G-minor Fugue, no. 16) and the Prelude in B Minor, no. 22, selections she repeated at the March 18, 1913, open meeting. As the club matured during the next two decades, it organized a Junior Girls' Musical Club for schoolchildren, began Sunday-afternoon musicales at the Museum of Fine Arts during its 1928–1929 season, and sponsored concerts by established visiting recitalists and by string quartets from London and New York.[40]

In an action that would become typical of her philanthropy, Ima started a Trustees' Musicians' Fund in 1925 to secure "special benefits for [Girls' Musical] Club members" or for those local performers who "identified with the club through common purpose and aims." As chairwoman of the fund and of the benefit committee, Ima worked with soprano Blanche Foley, music columnist Mary Elizabeth Rouse (club president 1925–1926), and others to organize a benefit concert on April 16, 1925, at the Main Street Auditorium. Proceeds helped local women pursue professional careers in music. The fund was Ima's first use of an endowment to stabilize an organization financially and was a tool she developed for other philanthropic interests. Ima also understood the value of gala benefits as a way to broaden the support base and introduce potential donors to new institutions. In 1930 the club, no longer predominantly unmarried girls, rechristened itself the Tuesday Musical Club, an organization that continues to provide musical education to its members. Ima remained an active member; she held club musicales in her home and encouraged her friends to maintain ties with the Museum of Fine Arts, the Houston Symphony, and other cultural organizations.[41]

FOUNDING THE HOUSTON SYMPHONY

Edna Saunders, the Treble Clef Club, the Thursday Musical Club, the Girls' Musical Club, the Saengerbund, the combined Quartette and Woman's Choral Clubs, and the Houston Music Festival Association—all were sponsoring programs for a growing city of 78,800 (1910 Census). For nearly a decade Wille Hutcheson, as musical editor of the *Post*, had trumpeted news of recitals and concerts, detailed club activities, and explained Houston's historic musical interest dating to the city's founding. Her witty, lengthy articles reflected broad appreciation of classical and popular music, and it is not surprising that they inspired ambitious dreamers to imagine building a resident symphony orchestra. In later years, Ima was credited as founder of the Houston Symphony Orchestra Association (the Houston Symphony Society since 1936) and lauded as its guardian angel from 1913 until her death in 1975. The scant extant records bear witness to her pivotal role in launching the symphony movement in 1913, in reorganizing the struggling association from 1929 to 1931, in pushing the established regional orchestra to national and international prominence during her 1946–1956 presidency, and in hiring top-flight conductors during the 1950s and 1960s. At every juncture her vision and tenacity propelled the organization forward. However, she was always quick to insist that she was "a," not "the," founder of the association. She always acknowledged and pursued broad-based community support and recognized the continuing struggle of many vigilant music lovers dedicated to bringing symphonic music to the city.[42] To Ima must go credit for articulating a grand vision and discovering ways this dream could become real, but her determination met receptive patrons eager to develop a musical legacy. Without the sustained enthusiasm of countless performers, audiences, and angels, Houston would have been unable to nurture a vibrant musical culture that has continued for more than a century.

Music inspired and stimulated Ima and brought her "release from daily care and frustration," and she wanted to share this personal joy with all Houstonians.[43] Years after the symphony was a well-established institution, she recalled that the "basic theory upon which the Symphony was founded was that it should serve the best interests of all people in Houston, regardless of age, status, or religious faith."[44] As a volunteer for, activist promoter of, and donor to the Symphony Society, Ima served these best interests in four important ways. Her vision informed the symphony's mission to maintain the highest standards of artistic achievement while responding to the "practical needs" of musicians: great music, she believed, must be "available and understandable to every age and type of individual," especially to children; and the symphony must have ample financial and community support to ensure its place as "a constructive force in Houston civic life."[45] Ima's generosity sustained the symphony financially: she provided support through large personal donations; she recognized the dangers of dependence on one or two funding sources and inspired volunteers to broaden the donor base through subscription and maintenance fund drives; and she established an endowment fund and solicited other donors to invest in the organization's future. Her devotion nurtured effective Symphony Society leadership: for forty-five years its members turned to her each time the organization needed a new conductor, president, or chairman, and she looked for individuals who were builders, not consolidators, who grasped practical constraints, and who could be flexible enough to "grow with the Orchestra" as it improved.[46] Finally, her musical knowledge defined programming strategy: she worked with conductors to unite artistic excellence with popular taste in a contentious marriage of convenience because she believed "a symphony . . . is a necessary component . . . of every great city just as are schools, universities, libraries and museums."[47] Her struggle to bring great music to the banks of Buffalo Bayou is a saga of one woman's determination to wrest harmony from the cacophonous disharmonies of conflicting constituencies.

Groups touring the United States recorded their most successful year nationwide in 1912–1913. Visiting performers, local chamber ensembles, and club recitals taxed Houston's limited theater space, but dinner-party conversation that year often centered on Houston's stimulating theater scene. When Modeste Altschuler, conductor of a Russian symphony orchestra, absconded and left his musicians stranded in the city in 1912, talk turned to forming a resident symphony orchestra. Local musicians did not receive the foreigners' overtures with enthusiasm, and potential supporters resisted voluble lobbying from musical club women because they were satisfied with touring celebrities who brightened the social scene during their brief engagements but required no long-term local financial commitment. Still, musicians and music lovers kept talking. Julien Paul Blitz, at the time musical director of the Treble Clef Club and conductor of a popular ensemble that entertained at Gus Sauter's Viennese-Victorian restaurant, approached several music club leaders. Every time he mentioned his dream of a symphonic orchestra for Houston, he was referred to Ima Hogg. In the spring of 1913, Blitz met with Ima, Wille Hutcheson, Katharine Parker, and several other women to develop a plan using Houston's homegrown talent. Blitz volunteered to select and rehearse thirty-five musicians from local cafes and hotels for a trial concert, while Ima and her friends in the Girls' Musical and Woman's Choral Clubs secured 125 guarantors. The June 21 concert convinced musicians and organizers that a professional symphony orchestra could succeed in Houston.[48]

When summer travelers returned to Houston in the fall of 1913, the ladies' committee that had organized the June experiment began formulating a modest and logical plan to create a resident symphony, develop a regular concert schedule, and build an audience. Speaking the language of business, these women secured good press coverage and favorable editorial opinion. Readers of the Sunday-morning *Post* on November 9 learned that "those who had the pleasure and privilege of hearing the concert given by a highly trained body of Houston musicians" would soon again enjoy a symphony season. Quick to dispel civic concerns about "aim, scope and expense," *Post* cultural critic Wille Hutcheson listed several premises critical to orchestra promoters' thinking: a modest three-concert season; music selections of wide appeal; local musicians who would "send their children to our schools and [be] loyal to Houston's interests and enthusiasts for its future"; and low ticket prices "so that the orchestra may be really claimed as a people's orchestra." Hutcheson summarized

Houston's music scene and noted that musical clubs, the Music Festival Association, and local promoters already were spending large sums on musical attractions: they imported "expensive soloists," "great Eastern orchestras . . . at a prodigious expense," and grand opera on "a most sumptuous scale." Despite this financial outlay, Houston would never be "fully musically equipped and in line with the great musical centers of the continent until we have our own symphony orchestra" to "attract the best class of people." There is no question that Ima and her friends sincerely believed symphonic music could and should be the heritage of all Houstonians. There is also no question that they well understood the necessity of appealing to commercial self-interest. Common sense or their training as Southern ladies suggested the importance of wedding musical appreciation to social prestige. Expensive boxes, festive parties, and formal attire ensured that Houston's elite would nurture "the city's latest and sturdiest infant."[49] This formula of artistic appreciation, business acumen, and social acceptability continues to inform Houston's cultural philanthropy.

Buoyed by growing support, the ladies' committee organized by Corinne Abercrombie Waldo met in preliminary discussions at Katharine Parker's home and then gathered potential guarantors in the Chamber of Commerce rooms in early November to explain their program, elect officers and directors, and name Julien Paul Blitz conductor.[50] The women clearly knew that their persuasive powers could carry them only so far, and they sought an alliance with Houston's business brokers to ensure financial backing among those who might only respond if they could believe music would be good for business. Katharine Parker somewhat reluctantly accepted the office of president because she was not completely wedded to the idea of a resident company. Ima considered her the natural leader both because she symbolized the woman's music movement by virtue of her roles in the Woman's Choral Club, the Thursday Morning Musical Club, and the Girls' Musical Club and because she was married to prominent lawyer and music enthusiast Edwin B. Parker, associate of lawyer-banker James A. Baker, Houston's most important prewar power broker. Ima was named first vice president; Frantz Brogniez, an amateur composer of oratorical and orchestral works, became second vice president; Caroline (Mrs. A. F.) Lillard was elected recording secretary and Mary (Mrs. William M.) Abbey corresponding secretary; and developer Henry F. MacGregor accepted the duty of treasurer. A galaxy of Houston civic leaders and Hogg family friends formed the original board of twenty-five directors. Will Kendall volunteered to serve as business manager, and religious and civic leaders joined a seven-member advisory board. Ima Hogg, Katharine Parker, Mary Abbey, Corinne Waldo, and Julien Blitz signed the charter petition for incorporation.[51]

The list of symphony founders reflects Ima's ability to unite musical factions and her understanding of a board's role as promoter and guarantor of the worthy cause. Most female members had already demonstrated their passion for music and their ability to organize and proselytize through music club participation. The men were officers or patrons of the Houston Music Festival, represented important power bases, or were respected civic actors and close business and personal associates of the Hogg family. If Will and Mike did not share Ima's passion for music, they understood her project and proudly urged their friends' support.

The new board ratified proposals of the women's committee, and the first season began with three twilight concerts performed by local musicians at the Majestic Theatre, again available free through the kindness of Hogg family acquaintance Karl Hoblitzelle. Volunteers exceeded the announced goal of 100 guarantors at $25 each and signed 138 socially prominent supporters to secure a comfortable $3,450 to begin operations and keep ticket prices low ($0.25 to $1.00). Years later Ima recalled how hard she and others worked to convince these pioneers. "We took the telephone book and talked to everybody we thought might be interested. Not many had ever heard of such a thing" as a municipal symphony orchestra; if they had, they thought it was "impossible in Houston."[52] Ima enlisted brother Will, whose talented fund-raising schemes were well known. He made up a pledge letter and canvassed dozens of prospects, "at the instance of my sister," to "raise the financial foundation" for a symphony orchestra.[53]

On Friday afternoon, December 19, 1913, Ima triumphantly joined the capacity crowd to hear baritone Arturo Lugaro inaugurate the twilight season under the direction of Julien Paul Blitz, who "gave a full program of extraordinarily great merit."[54] In large part, this audience was generated by Abe Levy and the Levy Brothers Dry Goods advertisements, which encouraged customers to "do something 'For the good of Houston' . . . and so pack the Majestic Theatre that there can be no doubt in the promoters' minds that Houston wants such an orchestra."[55] Press articles assured readers that Houstonians were about to join an elite group of American cities offering resident symphony seasons. High school students formed a pupils' orchestra, and the Girls' Musical Club announced that it had chosen orchestral instruments for its field of study during 1913–1914. The first season proved a success; the public attended faithfully, the players were enthusiastic, and the criticism was muted. Ima had realized her dream; she had placed Houston "in the list of symphony supporting cities," and the "enthusiastic audience" had demonstrated "the musical progressiveness of Greater Houston."[56]

Houston continued to attract touring soloists and ensembles during the 1914–1917 period. The Houston Art League sponsored concerts at the City Auditorium; the Woman's Violin Orchestra attracted critical acclaim; the Girls' Musical Club, the Woman's Choral Club, and the Treble Clef Club all guaranteed concert seasons; while in May 1916 the New York Philharmonic, America's oldest symphony orchestra, founded in 1842, drew responsive audiences. So crowded was the concert schedule that visiting soloist Reinald Werrenrath exclaimed in May 1916, "Why, Houston has musical indigestion. Your city isn't large enough to properly assimilate all the good things you have here during a season."[57] In 1916–1917 Marcellus Foster (Mefo), publisher of the *Post*, sponsored Diaghileff's Ballet Russe (December), the Minneapolis Symphony (January), Maud Allan's forty-piece orchestra (February), and Metropolitan Opera tenor Giovanni Martinelli (April). In February and March 1917, the Houston Symphony Association, the Treble Clef Club, and the Woman's Choral Club joined forces with the Grand Opera Committee chaired by Edwin B. Parker to bring Boston's National Grand Opera to Houston for performances of *Aida* and two other operas.[58]

Despite the guns of August in Europe, Houston Symphony Association planners repeated their formula of three twilight performances at the Majestic in its second season, which opened on November 26, 1914, Thanksgiving Day. Blitz asked to be relieved of his conductor's post after the third season, and Paul Bergé, a violinist, replaced him for the fourth season of three twilight concerts, again opening on Thanksgiving Day, November 30, 1916. The season, described as "the most flattering in its whole existence," closed in March 1917, only weeks before the United States declared war on Germany on April 6, 1917. In a *soiree d'art* during Easter week 1917, Houstonians tried to palliate the horrors of war headlines through the solace of music. Ima played the orchestral accompaniment for Liszt's Concerto in E Flat Scherzo finale, cellist Julien Blitz and violinist Rosetta Hirsch performed solos, and Henry Stude provided a reading.[59] At this terrible and uncertain moment, Ima assumed the presidency of the association and began planning the 1917–1918 concerts.

The next twelve months must have been very stressful for Ima. President of the Symphony Association, chairwoman of the State Symphony Committee charged with "investigating the possibilities of a

State Symphony Orchestra" for the Texas Federation of Music Clubs, mentor to her advanced piano students, and participant in several civic clubs, it is no wonder letters to Will are rushed and abrupt.[60] Her life was filled with meetings, including as hostess for the third annual meeting of the Texas Federation of Music Clubs April 3–5, 1918, at which the Houston Symphony "gave what was probably the most artistically finished program in its history."[61] Despite fervent musical club activity, Ima had begun to realize that the time was not opportune to inaugurate a civic symphony orchestra movement. Her beloved Germany had become the enemy, and works by her favorite composers were stricken from association programs. Even before the United States declared war, some musicians had joined the armed forces. Friends later remembered how she tirelessly trudged up and down Houston's streets seeking support, and contemporaries praised the remarkable strides made by the struggling orchestra in difficult times. Association officers and directors worked unceasingly to gain the musicians' confidence, build an audience, and provide appropriate instruments for their musicians. Blitz and Bergé drilled local performers in the essentials of orchestral technique, and dress rehearsals were opened, free of charge, to high school pupils.[62] But when the fifth season ended on April 3, Ima was faced with a terrible decision. Although several groups announced ambitious musical seasons that included patriotic sing-along concerts for soldiers stationed at Fort Logan, the Symphony Association was silent. No plans for a 1918–1919 symphony season ever materialized, as more and more young men left for the front and Ima fell ill that summer. How could the association know an armistice would be declared in November 1918?[63]

Always generous with her energy and her purse, always turning every performance into a festive social occasion, always counseling, planning, prodding, Ima exhausted herself trying to sustain the civic music movement. It is hard to say whether Ima's subsequent illness and absence from the city for long periods (1918–1924) or new entertainment diversions in the immediate postwar years most affected the Symphony Association's development in the 1920s. For more than a decade the association maintained a presence in civic affairs and sponsored touring ensembles, but the drive to form a resident symphony lay dormant. In its first five seasons, however, the association had laid the foundation for work that would follow: it had shown that Houston audiences did enjoy symphonic music; it had proved that the business community would support a resident orchestra as a civic asset; it had demonstrated the importance of music education to build an audience; and it had shown that a symphony association could unite professional musicians and music lovers in a project that brought pleasure to many and stature to the city.

MUSICAL HOUSTON IN THE 1920S

Ima was asked to stay on as president of the Symphony Association in 1919, but by 1921 it had become clear that her illness and prolonged absences from Houston interfered with civic responsibility. Huberta Garwood, married to prominent judge and Houston Music Festival patron Hiram M. Garwood, assumed the association's presidency for the next decade. Although the association maintained membership and sponsored chamber orchestra recitals, its members were discouraged by the tepid response of postwar audiences to numerous attractions brought by Edna Saunders and various musical clubs. Did all Houston prefer Chicago's Isham Jones, king of jazz, and his fourteen-piece "international" recording orchestra to recitals by Metropolitan Opera soprano Alma Gluck and pianist Nadia Boulanger or concerts by the revered Philharmonic Society of New York? Was the "cool top-of-town Rice Roof" more suited to boomtime Houston's Roaring Twenties excitement than a staid concert hall?[64] If recitals and symphonic concerts had lost their luster in the 1920s, opera and ballet still captivated audiences. Citizens wrote lengthy letters to the editor explaining exactly how Houston could foster "a school of opera . . . with a gala week all our own."[65] Edna Saunders received accolades for bringing ballet troupes, singers from the Metropolitan Opera, and a season of Chicago Civic Opera performances in March and April 1927. A *Chronicle* reporter noted that Saunders's "one tremendous musical event of the year . . . will draw more people to Houston from surrounding cities and towns than will a convention of the first class."[66]

So popular were these opera seasons that Houstonians attempted something truly daring in March 1930. Recognizing that Houston was known "throughout the length and breadth of the land" as the fastest-growing southwestern city and home of one of America's engineering triumphs, the Houston Ship Channel, a citizens' group led by the Chamber of Commerce made a bid for recognition as one of the nation's elite cultural centers. Chamber officials, impressed by the German Grand Opera Company's "notable" 1929 U.S. tour, asked to be included as the only southern city on the company's second coast-to-coast visit to the United States in 1930. Engaging impresario Sol Hurok to bring the German company to Houston, chamber sponsors presented *Der Ring Des Nibelungen* at the City Auditorium on March 3, 4, 5, and 6. Richard

Main Street, Houston, ca. 1910. MSS 114–685, Houston Public Library, Houston
Metropolitan Research Center.

Childhood portrait of Will Hogg, ca.
1895. Photo by Journeay. MS 21: Ima
Hogg Papers, Museum of Fine Arts,
Houston, Archives.

Childhood portrait of Ima Hogg, ca.
1895. Photo by Journeay. MS 21: Ima
Hogg Papers, Museum of Fine Arts,
Houston, Archives.

Childhood portrait of Mike Hogg, ca. 1895. Photo by Journeay. MS 21: Ima Hogg Papers, Museum of Fine Arts, Houston, Archives.

Tom Hogg, ca. 1895. Photo by Journeay. MS 21, Ima Hogg Papers, Museum of Fine Arts, Houston, Archives.

Tom, Ima, and Mike Hogg at South Egremont, Massachusetts, August 1903. CN01538, Ima Hogg Papers, 1824–1977, Center for American History, University of Texas at Austin.

Ima and Will Hogg at Varner
Plantation, ca. 1906. MS21: Ima
Hogg Papers, Museum of Fine Arts,
Houston, Archives.

Portrait of Will Hogg, ca. 1910.
MS21, Ima Hogg Papers, Museum of
Fine Arts, Houston, Archives.

Ima Hogg at the piano,
1920s. CN06573, Ima Hogg
Papers, 1824–1977, Center
for American History,
University of Texas at Austin.

Mike Hogg, ca. 1930.
CN06235, Ima Hogg Papers,
1824–1977, Center for
American History,
University of Texas at Austin.

Portrait of Alice Hogg, undated. Photo by GITTINGS. MS21: Ima Hogg Papers,
Museum of Fine Arts, Houston, Archives.

Portrait of Ima Hogg, ca. 1940. Photo by GITTINGS. MS 21: Ima Hogg Papers, Museum of Fine Arts, Houston, Archives.

Bayou Bend: aerial view from the southeast. Photo by Landiscor Inc., 1999. Bayou Bend Collection and Gardens, Museum of Fine Arts, Houston.

Downtown skyline, Houston, ca. 1970. MSS 157–40, Houston Public Library, Houston Metropolitan Research Center.

Wagner's four-day Ring Cycle demands an attentive and sophisticated audience; Houston was game to try.

The project probably thrilled Ima Hogg. A passionate Wagner devotee who would attend the Ring Cycle at Bayreuth and elsewhere several times during her life, Ima was one of 231 prominent women marshaled as the Houston Committee to secure underwriting and audience support. Chamber leadership and female advocacy ensured success. Hugh Potter, president of River Oaks Corporation, served as general chairman of the event; Chamber of Commerce President R. C. Kuldell and Mayor Walter Monteith presided as honorary chairmen; and prominent chamber members and staff formed the working committee. Front-page newspaper coverage and praise by Rice Institute Professor S. A. Nock declared "Opera Debut Big Success," detailed the singers' triumphant performances, praised the splendid orchestra, and lauded the chamber's "good judgment and courage." Mixing politics, society, and drama, Nock described the special train that brought performers and stagehands to the station where hundreds of Houstonians led by Hugh Potter welcomed them. He noted the "fashion on parade" at the performances and included photographs of Governor Dan Moody and his party in their evening finery. Chamber of Commerce organization, social approbation, and musical excellence had worked their magic and proved that Houston was the "musical center of the Southwest."[67]

Civic leaders and cultural journalists did their best to stimulate public interest in "serious" music during the 1920s. Ima Hogg recognized the importance of an audience attuned to the beauties of classical music when she underwrote her first music lectureship at Rice Institute in 1923. Reporters described the minutiae of every activity when the Texas Federation of Music Clubs held its convention in Houston March 20–23, 1927. Dressed in her azalea best, the city offered musical meetings and social engagements to nearly three hundred delegates whose presence enlivened the somnolent music scene. Choir director Ellison Van Hoose marshaled a mass chorus of convention participants for a Tuesday-evening songfest, and Edna Saunders sponsored pianist Mischa Levitzki at a concert honoring the delegates. Scholarships to the New York School of Music and Art were awarded to students of voice, piano, and violin. Delegates were treated to tea at the headquarters Warwick Hotel, breakfast hosted by past presidents of the Girls' Musical Club, luncheon presented by the St. Paul's Methodist Church Choir, an excursion to Ross Sterling's Bayshore mansion for tea, a reception given by the Girls' Musical Club at the Museum of Fine Arts, concerts and recitals, and several "other entertainments." Special trains, front-page newspaper coverage complete with flattering portraits of convention leaders, and a "royal" welcome from Mayor Oscar Holcombe and school Superintendent E. E. Oberholtzer advertised Houston's status as a "well-balanced" artistic center.[68]

In general, however, journalists found Houston's musical culture sadly mediocre. Ruth West complained that Houstonians in 1928 swooned over international stars who had been well advertised for weeks in advance but were indifferent to local talent and seemed ignorant of well-known artists not announced effectively in the press. Critic Hubert Roussel suggested that his fellow citizens preferred Lucky Strike cigarettes to Beethoven suites. "It was impossible," he railed, "not to be impressed by the size of the audiences that stayed away from" two concerts played by the "brilliant musicians" of the Minneapolis Symphony Orchestra, brought to Houston by Edna Saunders in April 1929.[69] Mary Elizabeth Rouse expressed shock that Elizabeth Rethberg, "one of the greatest sopranos of all time," had attracted fewer than five hundred people in 1926; she declared in December 1929 that "Houston is going backward musically."[70]

Commentators suggested several difficulties to surmount in building popular sentiment for a municipal symphony orchestra. So-called good music was difficult—to study and appreciate, to perform properly, and to support financially. Jazz and radio were spoiling America's ear for high-quality performance by "spreading a lot of racket everywhere in the name of music."[71] To one jaded columnist, music teachers were failing to set high musical standards for their pupils, were aggressive self-publicists, and were often poorly trained themselves. Another writer suggested building civic taste by purchasing a concert organ for the City Auditorium and supporting a municipal band.[72] Advocates of classical music believed several concerts each year by first-class touring orchestras, lectures at Rice Institute, musical afternoons at the new Museum of Fine Arts, and recitals sponsored by Edna Saunders and the Girls' Musical Club would create demand for symphonic music.[73] Some appealed to that suspect character, civic pride: if Dallas could present a symphony orchestra of seventy-five musicians to an audience of nearly four thousand willing to hear new work by a Dallas composer, how could Houston lag behind?

THE SYMPHONY REBORN

Despite editorial doomsayers, Ima must have sensed stirrings of interest in a rejuvenated symphony orchestra in the late 1920s. In 1928 Josephine Boudreaux had returned from six years' study in Europe and formed a string quartet that quickly gained press and audience attention, and Foley Brothers department store began sponsoring Wednesday musicales that year. In February 1929 Ima began a discreet survey of orchestras throughout the United States to discover potential candidates willing to wield the conductor's baton in Houston.[74]

Then in late 1930 Houston entered a season of symphonic soap opera. As recounted by critic Hubert Roussel, Houston gyrated from no interest in a local symphony orchestra to three contending organizations to one triumphant victor during twelve titillating months. The furor started when voice coach and piano teacher Noma (Mrs. John Wesley) Graham decided she wanted an opera company and training school in Houston and set off for Europe in August 1930 to find a director. Described as a "personality of rare color, temerity, and impulse," the legendary choir director of the First Methodist Church at first gained promises of support for a civic opera company from Mayor Walter Monteith and the Chamber of Commerce, but her "saturation technique of publicity" seems to have repelled the cultural elite, and plans faltered.[75] Undaunted by establishment indifference or Wall Street tremors, Graham dragooned Milan opera maestro Uriel Nespoli and, with some difficulty, carried him through immigration hassles to Houston in January 1931. Ensconced in Graham's "new and elaborate studio" on Westmorland Boulevard, the "short, stout, nervous little man, who paced about . . . flinging his arms in Italian outbursts," began to train singers for a proposed *Aida*. Needless to say, his opera would require an orchestra.[76]

Meanwhile, a group of musicians had begun practicing with Victor Alessandro, music director of public school bands and orchestras, first in the Carter Music Company salesroom and later in the basement of the First Christian Church. By late 1930, Alessandro had attracted forty dues-paying players—$5.00 per annum to buy music—who were ready to perform. Somehow he was introduced to cotton and real estate broker N. D. Naman, who quietly promised financing and produced a charter signed by himself and four other supporters. With $350 to cover one concert, the Houston Philharmonic announced plans for a 1931 concert series on Sunday afternoons at the Scottish Rite Cathedral Auditorium, to begin on March 15.[77]

Stunned that Houston was about to hear a resident orchestra supported by "a number of people who had not heretofore been associated with the symphony movement at all,"[78] an association committee, with Ima Hogg as pivotal spokesperson, invited Naman and W. H. Hogue to a meeting in the Chamber of Commerce offices. Pointing out the association's years-long, if currently slumbering, effort to cultivate a symphonic movement, Ima and her friends suggested that the two groups work together under the established association banner to create a "truly representative" orchestra. Naman and Hogue, feeling justifiably that their orchestra, organized by the musicians themselves, was already representative, declined the association's offer.

Galvanized by rejection, the association began to play hardball. First, it buried its decade-old argument that World War I had interrupted its work and left Houston disinterested in symphonic music. Next it reorganized and in early April announced new leadership: a "wise," quiet, and dignified pillar of the association, physician Joseph A. Mullen, was named president; Huberta Garwood stepped down to first vice president; and Ima Hogg was named second vice president.[79] Then association members hired the "colorful and dynamic" Uriel Nespoli as conductor.[80] Although Ima Hogg later claimed Nespoli "didn't know anything at all" about symphonic music, board members were quick to retain his services when Noma Graham proved unable to finance her opera dreams and was willing to release him from contractual obligations.[81] With a conductor on board, the association organized an orchestra of some seventy-five local musicians who would be paid to rehearse and perform—unlike Philharmonic members, who played for free.[82] Finally, the association announced two introductory and complementary concerts at the Palace Theatre on May 6 and 7.[83]

To further roil the musical stream, internationally acclaimed tenor Ellison Van Hoose, former director of the Treble Clef Club, choir director at First Presbyterian Church (1916–1936), and intimate friend of Edna Saunders, publicized formation of a "strictly commercial" Little Symphony of twenty-two musicians who would present concerts featuring vocal soloists. The ensemble would make its debut April 28, 1931, at the Palace Theatre. Apparently Saunders, who had been cooperating with the Symphony Association for a decade to present orchestral and chamber music, resented Ima's attempts to reorganize a resident orchestra that would compete with her own touring attractions. Saunders left a fall 1930 meeting called by Ima to discuss a restructured symphony orchestra and refused to support association efforts thereafter.[84]

It is not hard to sell tickets when Houston's social elite, its popular musicians, and its honest music mavens are engaged in mortal combat for the heart and mind and purse of the concertgoing public. Healthy crowds witnessed the fight, which was vividly recounted in press reports. First to the mat was the forty-piece Philharmonic, whose modest program was warmly applauded March 15; next came the well-attended debut on April 28 of the Van Hoose gambit. Then on Sunday May 3 the Philharmonic tackled the second movement of Beethoven's Fifth Symphony at its second afternoon concert. Praised by critic Roussel for its "well-shaded interpretation," the orchestra showed promise and the effects of hard work.[85] Encouraged by critical and audience acclaim, the Philharmonic announced a five-concert season for 1931–1932, to begin in October.

When Nespoli mounted the podium before the seventy-odd "hastily gathered and quickly trained" musicians of the Symphony Association, did he intend a direct confrontation with the Philharmonic, or was it coincidence that his debut May 6 and 7 featured Beethoven's entire Fifth Symphony? The press waxed poetic about the rejuvenated orchestra and accompanying chorus of 110 church and amateur singers. Under Nespoli's internationally acclaimed baton, the musicians produced "some of the most beautiful music [heard] in the city in many a day" in "truly impressive demonstrations of musical zeal."[86] The lengthy program featuring Wagner and Beethoven was probably overzealous, but the association had filled the theater and "demonstrated . . . that [Houston] is a metropolitan city." A delighted Ima Hogg sent President Mullen her check for $602 to defray expenses of the two trial concerts.[87]

Mullen, with Ima's support, quickly secured Nespoli's services for a full 1931–1932 season of six concerts to be held in the 3,400-seat City Auditorium. Although the Philharmonic and Van Hoose orchestras bravely soldiered on, advertising their seasons and launching campaigns to sell tickets to an additional eighteen concerts, neither group could withstand grim reality: the three orchestras would have to share performers; national economic storms dampened funding ardor; and the association, once roused, was too powerful to combat. Association members belonged to Houston's civic and economic power structures, and they could withstand attack from poorly financed and socially obscure contenders. Houston had room for only one symphony society, and the challengers succumbed to summer's doldrums. Determined to succeed, the association undertook a bold membership campaign, sold six hundred season tickets, consolidated its gains, and lured rival patrons and musicians to its camp. The Chamber of Commerce insisted the association "should have the cordial support of the business and professional interests" to broaden musical culture and "establish a higher order of living" for all.[88] Harmony may not have replaced discord, but by November 1931 Florence Hogue, wife of Philharmonic sponsor W. H. Hogue, had been named the association's recording secretary.[89]

Houston's symphonic rebirth occurred at a moment of personal trial for Ima and Mike. Will, head of the family since their father's death in 1906, had died unexpectedly in September 1930 while undergoing emergency surgery in Baden-Baden. Although prostrated for several weeks by the tragedy, Ima rallied bravely in the last months of 1930, fortified by brother Mike's steadfast support and sister-in-law Alice's warm affection. Mike stepped into Will's role as family mentor and president of Hogg Brothers and other business interests, and Alice began to work closely with her sister-in-law on several projects. Perhaps energized by the symphony's tribulations, Ima did not at first succumb to the demons of depression that had immobilized her for so long in the early 1920s. In 1931 and 1932 she threw herself into association activity, searching nationwide for musicians, selling ads and tickets, and recruiting patrons. In 1932 she participated in musicales, and she performed in concert at the public library with Adele Margulies's students on January 14, 1933. But in July 1933 her health betrayed her. Accompanied by Estelle Sharp, Ima traveled to the Mayo Clinic in Rochester, Minnesota, for orthopedic surgery. Setbacks followed, and in October she began a long recuperative visit in Tucson, Arizona, with brother Tom. During her absence, Mike held long "confabs" with the conductor and kept his sister apprised of "the ins and outs and intrigues of your Symphony Orchestra." He reassured her that subscription sales seemed to be doing well. Letters from friends detailed successful fall 1933 concerts and other symphony activity.[90]

The Symphony Association, whose members hoped Ima would become its president in September 1933, refused to let her resign from the board during this period of enforced absence because any hint that she was not actively engaged "would disturb the confidence of the public and delay subscriptions." Clearly, Ima's "counsel and guidance" had become indispensable to the symphony's continued development.[91] In the public mind, "Miss Ima" was the Houston Symphony, and she would remain its symbol long after her death in 1975. Symphony historian Hubert Roussel called her the orchestra's "exigent Juno, never easy to please, and at the same time its most devoted evangel."[92] Ima understood that the symphony had to move slowly in its climb toward excellence; only gradually and through hard work could audience, musicians, and conductors be brought to the highest standards of performance and appreciation. As Houston's musical history unfolded in the next four decades, successive music directors had to please Ima and her highly trained ear, urge musicians to ever-higher levels of performance, charm Houston's social elite, and provide "melodious" music preferred by "people of average taste."[93] Only a rare conductor could manage these conflicting requirements.

Although the *Press* congratulated association directors at the end of Nespoli's 1931–1932 season for the symphony's artistic success, for giving jobs to unemployed musicians, for providing tickets at low prices, and for completing the season with "less than a $300 deficit," board members were not happy with his performance.[94] Programs were too long, too unfocused, and often "woefully under-rehearsed," and apparently Nespoli lacked social skills to endear him to sponsors, although he believed he and his wife "had made very dear friends" in Houston.[95] The Executive Committee decided the Italian must be replaced. Nespoli took his case to the press in a barely comprehensible letter and filed suit for breach of contract, but he finally accepted the board's decision and continued his career in New York.

Association Treasurer Bernard Epstein suggested that the committee consider Frank St. Leger, the "charming and cultured" junior conductor for the Chicago Opera Company. The fortyish graduate of the Royal Academy of Music made an excellent impression, and on June 4, 1932, President Mullen, Ima Hogg, Huberta Garwood, Florence Hogue, and Treasurer Epstein offered St. Leger a contract, which he accepted and the full board ratified on June 8.[96] St. Leger, a piano prodigy who had conducted at Covent Garden and led Chicago's opera orchestra, was a success socially, and he and his wife found shelter in apartments over the garage at Ima's home.[97] He enchanted luncheon groups and ladies' musical clubs with earnest propaganda and relished card games and hunting or fishing trips with wealthy businessmen whose financial support was critical; but he seems to have misinterpreted Houston's musical taste and pampered audiences with unchallenging repertoire. Critics noted "steady improvement" in the musicians and "a new high in vitality, in tone quality, . . . in tone color" and in "expressiveness," but they often seemed more impressed by the "smartly-groomed audience [that] more than half filled the spacious auditorium" than by the music.[98]

Half-filled auditoriums and boring fare made board members restless after three seasons. Once again, it was time to find a conductor who would challenge musicians and audience to reach higher levels of musical sophistication. New president Joseph Smith (1934–1936), an insurance executive, revamped business operations and encouraged donated support so Houston could compete for the best musical talent. When it came time to renew St. Leger's contract in the summer of 1935, Smith hesitated. He knew Ima Hogg and two friends, who were vacationing together in New York, had "already taken steps" to discover a replacement for the lackluster St. Leger. The conductor must have understood that all was not well, and he challenged Smith with stringent demands that Smith refused to meet. Although Smith urged St. Leger to reconsider his stipulations, it is clear that both sides wanted important changes. St. Leger secured a position with the Metropolitan Opera Company, and the association's Music Committee, after studying twenty-three applications, recommended that the board hire three guest conductors for the next season—Vittorio Verse, Modeste Alloo, and Alfred Hertz—and continue its search for a resident conductor.[99] The press lauded the well-known maestros whose hiring was a "significant step forward," and large audiences during the 1935–1936 season enjoyed programs "replete with musical beauty" that raised expectations.[100] If not all reviews glowed, if some conductors were shocked by the amateur quality of Houston's musicians, still orchestra and audience benefited greatly by exposure to the stringent demands of three directorial styles.[101]

IMA'S SEARCH FOR MUSICAL EXCELLENCE

In the spring of 1936 with the conductor's job still unfilled, Ima engaged in a little self-confessed chicanery as chairwoman of the recently renamed Houston Symphony Society's nominating committee. One afternoon she invited several prominent Houston men, including friend and lawyer Walter Walne, to her home to discuss candidates for society president. As each guest entered the house he received a note saying he had been named president. After several rounds of Ima's famous well-laced fish-house punch, much laughter, and considerable cajolery, Walter Walne accepted the post, which he held until the summer of 1942. Ima Hogg and oil man Harry Wiess served as vice presidents. On May 26, 1936, the board announced Walne's election, a season ticket subscription goal of $30,000, and a search committee to select a permanent conductor. Prominent attorney Jesse Andrews was made chairman of the search committee because Ima wanted to ensure business support, but minutes and correspondence reveal that her leadership and opinion were decisive.[102]

Costs had been steadily increasing, from $12,000 to $16,000 to $24,000 between 1930 and 1936, and board members realized that their search for a well-known conductor must be accompanied by an aggressive campaign to find solid financial support. Press articles recounted efforts to build a donor base: On May 27 the Chamber of Commerce pledged its cooperation because "the people of Houston have given conclusive evidence of their interest in and appreciation of good music." On June 2 the board announced that William L. Clayton of Anderson Clayton would lead a group of powerful businessmen to raise needed funds and meet the budget, and on June 14 a membership group met at Bayou Bend to announce results of a whirlwind subscription campaign. Finally, on July 3, following a June 30, 1936, meeting of the search committee hosted by Ima at Bayou Bend, the board announced that Ernst Hoffmann would be the new orchestra conductor.[103]

A slender, handsome man, brisk, businesslike, and analytical, Hoffmann was dedicated to fine musicianship and had studied at Harvard and the Berlin Conservatory for Music. Son of a German violinist, Hoffmann conducted the Commonwealth Symphony Orchestra, a Works Progress Administration project in Boston. Longtime Houston Symphony Concertmaster Raphael Fliegel remembered Hoffmann as a great conductor who was much beloved by the musicians because he "did everything" for the orchestra and "asked for nothing in return."[104] Ima had been busy in May and June as she secured her choice for president, organized a subscription campaign, and wrote experts around the country to request information about candidates for conductor. Her gift of $1,000 led a July 4, 1936, list of contributions and was one of only fifteen donations of $100 or more.

With the advent of Walter Walne as president and Ernst Hoffmann as conductor, the Houston Symphony entered a period of stability that allowed board members to focus on improving the orchestra. In a May 1935 letter Ima stated that the symphony wished to move beyond "the best material among our citizens" and recruit musicians competitively with $10,000 set aside for that purpose.[105] Ima also turned her attention to audience-building and fund-raising. She believed firmly that everyone who wished to should be able to attend symphony concerts. As early as 1931 she was purchasing tickets for music teachers in public schools, for pupils who displayed "meritorious work," and for charitable groups so citizens throughout the city could enjoy fine music during the economically stressful times. While these "free" tickets suggest a need to paper the house during lean economic times, they also reflect Ima's insistence that fine music be available to all citizens.[106] By 1937 Ima was providing complementary seats to "several hundred underprivileged music lovers" at every concert and had helped the society develop a pricing structure that included low-cost subscriptions for adult students, matinee concerts for children at twenty-five cents a ticket, and sections reserved for "negroes at popular prices."[107] Ernst Hoffmann supported Ima's efforts to build an audience by introducing a series of pop concerts, made popular in his native Boston as a way to "indoctrinate young people with the critical importance of fine music."[108] By 1938 the symphony season included six regular concerts, six lower-priced pop concerts, four concerts for schoolchildren, and four engagements in Beaumont and Galveston.[109]

To guarantee the orchestra's financial security, Ima energized Houston's corps of volunteers by inviting young women to her home to form a Women's Committee (renamed the Houston Symphony League in 1978). She served as chairwoman during the committee's first two years (1937–1939) and set a course still followed seven decades later. A veteran volunteer of twenty years ascribed the committee's lasting success to Ima Hogg: "like the conductor of her own orchestra . . . and with the greatest of artistic perfection [she] was able to evoke the best possible performance from each of the players."[110] Combining social enjoyment with serious purpose "to build an ever greater Orchestra," Ima inspired volunteers and organized each subcommittee around a particular function. She held meetings in lovely homes or interesting civic venues and rewarded hard work with box seats, orchids, and friendship.[111] After sorting address cards, planning fund-raisers, entertaining musicians, or working with children in the schools for a season or two, many of these women became devoted advocates of their resident symphony, connoisseurs of fine music, and financial supporters.

Extensive coverage of committee activities in the *Post* and *Chronicle* reflected community belief in the symphony as a "cultural force."[112] The Women's Committee took over the subscription drive, then the symphony's only source of assured revenue, and immediately introduced innovations that allowed the board to increase its goals year after year, even in the slow economic times of the late 1930s. In the 1937 campaign, more than three hundred workers were divided into committees covering all women's and civic clubs, businesses and industries, churches, schools, and residential areas; it would have been hard to miss any likely subscriber. An article describing the 1938 campaign estimated that women working for three weeks were able to check 22,000 prospect names in 700 hours of volunteer labor. Even Ima's terriers Gilley and Bonney were "overworked" as they greeted and "bid a canine Godspeed to all who leave."[113] In 1939 the Women's Committee adopted bylaws, produced its first gala fund-raiser—a Viennese ball at Houston Country Club that netted

$1,057.20—and created a Children's Committee to supervise youth-oriented activities. Before handing the Women's Committee's gavel to her successor, Ima announced plans for a Maintenance Fund drive. As the Women's Committee prospered, subcommittees expanded responsibilities to include numerous fund-raising special events, youth concerts, student and Young Artists auditions, a Junior Patrons Committee to provide funds for the orchestra and educate young members, and docent outreach to children in schools, hospitals, and libraries.[114] Today the league continues operations as one of Houston's most powerful volunteer support groups.

As war clouds rolled across the globe, the Symphony Society again questioned whether it could sustain a full season. Far less timid than leaders of the infant association had been when confronted by World War I dislocations, society planners decided civilians and men in the armed forces needed their symphony to assuage the "stress of war."[115] After six years as president, Walter Walne wanted to retire in 1942, and the executive committee, guided by Ima's firm hand, asked Hugh Roy Cullen, king of the wildcatters and possibly Houston's richest citizen, to form a committee to find Walne's successor. Cullen, a bluff but kindly man with decided opinions, had no interest in music, but his wife, Lillie, adored the symphony. Cullen announced there was no need for a committee; he would sign on for the duration, and moreover he would underwrite operations, as much as $125,000 in 1944–1945 alone.[116] In her report of a long-range planning committee that had met three times during Christmas week 1943, Ima praised Cullen's "leadership, guidance, and very generous contributions" and noted that his prestige advanced the symphony's cause with the Chamber of Commerce and other donors.[117]

Cullen viewed his job as a civic duty and the symphony as a public morale booster, and he reorganized symphony management to separate artistic and business functions.[118] Also sponsor of Houston's Wartime Youth Council to combat juvenile delinquency during wartime, Cullen pushed conductor Ernst Hoffmann to expand the repertoire and touring season and persuaded the City Council to appropriate $5,000 for free summer concerts in neighborhoods where delinquency rates were high.[119] During the war years, concerts began with the "Star-Spangled Banner," and the symphony became an important regional symbol that catered to servicemen by touring military bases and distributing free pop-concert passes to soldiers. Cullen personally persuaded NBC to broadcast its national Cities Service weekly radio concert live with the Houston Symphony on January 15, 1943, and for the first time, a national radio audience heard the city's symphony in concert. Impressed by the broadcast's audience-building potential, Cullen then challenged Texas Gulf Sulfur's commercial self-interest and civic pride and signed the Houston company to underwrite free Saturday-afternoon concerts to be aired live across the Southwest.[120] The 1944–1945 season listed seventy-four engagements: ten subscription concerts, one special event, four operas, eight student performances, twenty-eight tour stops, and twenty-three visits to military bases or USO halls. It is hardly surprising that Cullen told his successor, Joseph S. Smith, that Hoffmann had "worked like a dog" during the war.[121]

Stimulated by Houston's wartime prosperity and population boom, Houston's boosters announced that the city was entering an era of greatness. A world-class symphony seemed within reach at last. Cullen kept his word and resigned at war's end, although no formal action was taken by the society until January 1946, when Joseph S. Smith was recalled as president and Cullen promoted to chairman, both terms to begin May 1. Almost immediately Houston's music world was plunged into crisis. Although Cullen accused Smith of starting "a row" with the conductor, Ima may have been the source of the trouble. In the next three decades neither she nor the executive committee would discover how to replace conductors whose usefulness had been exhausted without causing a firestorm. By 1946 Ima, who had been named society vice president in 1944, wanted to move the symphony from regional to national status, and she felt that after ten years, Ernst Hoffmann, beloved as he was by audience, musicians, and donors, had done all he could with the orchestra. Cullen, recalling Hoffmann's yeoman service during the war, stood behind the hard-working conductor and blamed Smith for stirring up trouble and failing to raise money. On April 23, 1946, Cullen resigned as chairman-elect, made public a letter strongly urging retention of Hoffmann as conductor, and challenged Smith to "assume full responsibility for raising money."[122] Realizing he could not withstand Cullen's animosity, Smith resigned on May 8, having served for one week.

Ima rushed back from a vacation in Mexico, appointed a committee to choose a new president, and called on Cullen to discuss the crisis. "Shocked" that Ima "wanted to discuss firing Ernst Hoffmann, giving him $10,000, and getting a new conductor," Cullen threatened to withdraw his vital financial support.[123] In the end, the committee and Cullen turned to Ima and demanded that she become president. She took the reins provisionally in mid-May but insisted that insurance magnate Gus Wortham be asked to serve as chairman to ensure strong financial backing from business leaders. Glad to be rid of Smith and confident that the new team would build the symphony's reputation, Cullen told Wortham he would "subscribe 20% of the budget" and "continue his interest." By December friends assured Ima, "if you and Mr. Wortham will carry on for the next year, the success of the symphony ... is assured."[124] In February 1947 the board voted to find a new conductor. Ima broke the news to Hoffmann that the 1946–1947 season would be his last and initiated a search to find a replacement of national standing.[125] Although correspondence and press accounts suggest that Hoffmann was treated cavalierly, he and Ima continued to exchange friendly letters until his death in a tragic automobile accident in 1955. Ima told Hubert Roussel that Hoffmann was "very sweet" about his dismissal and "always so reasonable." She would never forget how painful the interview had been.[126] The wish for improvement had been hers, and the finesse with which she weathered the crisis restored harmony without alienating Cullen's critical financial support, even though the loyal Hoffmann was pushed aside.

TOWARD INTERNATIONAL ACCLAIM

Ima's election as president inaugurated a long period of stability (1946–1956) for the society administration that continued under Maurice Hirsch, who served as president from 1956 to 1970. The society hired Tom Johnson as business manager in 1948, and he immediately enlarged the professional staff. Formerly the youthful manager of the Austin Symphony, Johnson held a bachelor of music degree and had considerable experience as a military band conductor and as a publicist.[127] He had asked Ima to support the Austin orchestra; she had countered by suggesting he invite the Houston Symphony to perform in Austin. Although they "agreed to disagree," Ima sent him $100 and remembered him in the fall of 1947 when she decided Houston needed a new business manager.

Johnson came to Houston to "deal with the financial responsibility" that Ima had handed to Chairman Gus Wortham when she became president. During Ima's decade of service, four prominent chairmen—Gus Wortham (1946–1948), F. M. Law (1948–1950), Warren Bellows (1950–1953), and Harmon Whittington (1953–1956)—built strong ties to funding sources in the business community that helped stabilize the orchestra's finances, but trouble continued to plague relations among conductors, board members, and musicians.[128] Ominous rumblings often marked Ima's efforts to engage the ideal conductor and develop programs acceptable to disparate constituents. Civic-minded patrons with no ear for music like Hugh Roy Cullen could dispense money and leave musical matters to experts because they viewed a symphony orchestra as a civic asset, not as a source of personal pleasure. But to Ima, the symphony brought delight and consolation. Trained as a musician herself, she held strong views about musical quality and appropriate programming. For her, financial patronage was insufficient; more important was the aesthetic imprint she hoped to stamp on the orchestra.

To ease the transition from Hoffmann to a new man and to allow the board time to test several candidates, the executive committee decided to rely on guest conductors for the 1947–1948 season. Among the recruits were Leonard Bernstein (January 1948) and Efrem Kurtz, who was offered the job of resident conductor late in March 1948. Correspondence between Ima and Bernstein reveals that she hoped he would come to Houston as music director. In a charming letter, the prolific composer explained that "the prospect of Houston was a bright and hopeful one; I had fallen in love with the town and many of its inhabitants," but New York must remain home if he wished to pursue a Broadway composing career.[129]

Efrem Kurtz seems to have been the universal favorite. Wortham and Ima already had approached him in the spring of 1947, but the ongoing management crisis with Cullen and Hoffmann made further discussion impossible until March 1948.[130] Carefully vetted by several members of the board and well received during appearances in January 1947 and March 1948, Kurtz would remain in Houston until 1954. Like Hoffmann before him, Kurtz began his tenure with high hopes, much praise, and great plans for expansion and improvement. At first all went well for the tall, elegant former conductor of the Ballet Russe de Monte Carlo orchestra. Houston's symphony attracted musicians and guest conductors of high quality; the season expanded to include 103 performances by 1950–1951; and the new conductor was a popular attraction at luncheons, dinners, and committee meetings.[131] At the close of the 1950 season, Sir Thomas Beecham declared Houston's orchestra, hitherto "virtually unknown and on the verge of collapse," to be "one of the very best in the country." A *Christian Science Monitor* article said the season had "made musical history in the Southwest" as ushers turned away "hundreds," crowds cheered, and Kurtz "stumped the country" for fresh talent. Ima had achieved her goal of national recognition.[132]

Kurtz did not, however, develop a repertoire that satisfactorily sustained audience interest, and ticket sales began to flag during his third season. A less-than-enthusiastic executive committee renewed Kurtz's contract in 1951, but only for two years. Attendance did not improve, and when the 1953 season closed, new chairman Warren S. Bellows told Kurtz his contract would not be renewed. Instead, during the 1953–1954 season, the society would rely on Kurtz, by letters of agreement, and on several guest artists. Once again, Ima and others felt the popular conductor had accomplished what he could, and it was time to move the symphony to a higher performance level in the long quest for national and international recognition. Critics had begun to complain that Kurtz's programs were unchallenging musically, while society leadership feared the maestro's marital difficulties and growing intimacy with a young orchestra flutist might explode in scandal.[133]

In trying to sidestep Kurtz's personal and musical difficulties, the society's executive committee found itself embroiled in failures of communication that reached melodramatic, if not scandalous, proportions. A rising European star, the thirty-nine-year-old Hungarian Ferenc Fricsay, had dazzled Houston with his "gymnastic baton style" and "magnificent muscularity" as a guest artist in November 1953.[134] Negotiations for a yearlong trial residency in Houston began immediately.[135] Implicit in the sixteen-concert engagement announced January 16, 1954, was the promise of a permanent contract, provided Houston audiences reacted well to Fricsay's dynamic style and Fricsay and his wife enjoyed their stay well enough to make Houston a permanent home. Although the search committee hoped to hire someone of international repute, possibly, therefore, of European background, it was adamant in requiring a full-time commitment to the Houston community as well as to the city's symphony.[136] Board members wanted the new music director to devote most of his time to building the orchestra's skills, repertoire, and reputation.

When Fricsay arrived for his first concerts in the fall of 1954, it seemed that he would propel the orchestra to new levels "in closer connection with American and European musical life."[137] Ima entertained him "at home" October 24; musicians loved his vigorous style; and audiences responded enthusiastically to his "stunning" performances. But relations between the conductor and the society's inner circle quickly soured and by December 1954 had reached a crisis.[138] Unfortunately, Fricsay found Music Hall acoustics deplorable and said so volubly. Ima and other board members, who had supported the hall's expensive renovations, took strong exception to his criticism.[139] Fricsay also seems to have believed that the executive committee wanted him to outline his wishes for an ideal orchestra in November 1954. When he submitted an elaborate long-range plan that included requests for a new music hall designed specifically for symphonic performance, for extensive touring in Europe and America, for better instruments, and for higher salaries, board members balked. Although the board commended "his desire to look to the future and visualize a superior orchestra for Houston," the finance committee stated that his requests could not be met; his wish list was interpreted as a series of demands, and the imbroglio was aired in the press.[140]

The storm worsened when rival *Post* and *Chronicle* publishers, editors, and critics seemed to be telling different stories. Longtime critic Hubert Roussel, then writing for Oveta Culp Hobby's *Post*, had grown very friendly with symphony business manager Tom Johnson; Johnson fed Roussel an expurgated version of the board and administration viewpoint and ignored *Chronicle* critic Ann Holmes's requests for information. Trying to untangle the rumors, Holmes hired an interpreter, invited the misunderstood Hungarian and his wife to lunch, and listened attentively to his story, which she then retold to the public. According to Holmes, Fricsay "stoutly insisted" that Tom Johnson had solicited the maestro's vision for a great symphony. She stressed that the Johnson-Symphony Society report conflicted with Fricsay's statements and noted anguished telephone calls from musicians and the public praising the conductor.[141]

While a semantic misunderstanding centering on "wish" or "demand" may have triggered the December explosion, it is also possible that a Fricsay-Houston union was not to be. Ima objected to Fricsay's "phrasing," and business manager Johnson grumbled about his attitude and cost projections. Fricsay's promoter, Andrew Schulhof, warned the conductor that his failure to ask what the public wanted or to understand financial constraints of privately funded community projects would alienate American music supporters. By January 1955 Fricsay found himself without an agent and without a job.[142] Ima and Chairman Harmon Whittington came to believe Fricsay had "endeavored to disrupt the morale of the musical employees of the Society" by making his grievances public.[143] The Symphony Society's public statement announcing Fricsay's departure said merely that the board had "learned with regret" that a "serious rheumatic condition" would preclude the conductor's return in February. Although she stood firmly with the forces arrayed against Fricsay, Ima may have been personally upset and affronted by the emotional explosion that pitted musicians and music lovers against music patrons. F. M. Law, who had been out of the city during the fray, tried to comfort her by complimenting her as "a great woman and a great citizen" and concluding, "Mr. Fricsay was not for us, and it is just as well for all concerned that we found that out early." Unhappily, business concerns and personalities seem to have trumped pursuit of musical excellence in relations with this acclaimed conductor.[144]

Musically 1955 proved an exciting year for Houston. The Symphony Society prevailed on world-renowned maestro Sir Thomas Beecham, then seventy-six years old, to leave retirement and finish the 1954–1955 season.[145] Elva Lobit founded the Houston Grand Opera, and a group of ballet aficionados established the Houston Ballet Foundation to support creation of a professional school and resident company. In the fall of 1955 charismatic maestro Leopold Stokowski, then seventy-three, began an engagement that seemed to herald the symphony's acceptance by the national and international music world. Ima had followed Stokowski's career faithfully since 1920, when she had attended concerts of the Philadelphia Orchestra led by the dynamic young conductor. When Ima retired as president of the society in 1956, she must have felt confident that the orchestra would prosper under the combined guidance of music lover and business leader Maurice Hirsch and world-acclaimed eminence grise of the symphony world Leopold Stokowski.[146] In negotiations leading to his letter of agreement with symphony officials, Stokowski indicated that he would encourage talented young conductors, make recordings, begin a scholarship program, and be available to critics and music departments at Rice Institute and the University of Houston.[147]

While Stokowski's tenure certainly added luster to the orchestra's reputation, his stay was not untroubled. Although Ima befriended him, attended all his rehearsals, and often invited him to dinner, he seemed to her an unhappy and lonely man. His formal personality and his chilly criticism of Houston's Music Hall and musical taste did not endear him to friendly Houstonians who were proud of their efforts to build a musical culture accessible to everyone. Struggling through a divorce from socialite Gloria Vanderbilt and separated from his young sons, Stokowski failed to make friends and visited Houston only for rehearsals and concerts. His passion for contemporary music fell on untutored ears and drove traditionalists from the hall. However, his potent reputation and ability to raise performance standards overcame any disquiet, and when his three-year contract expired in 1958, both sides agreed to continue on a year-to-year basis. This solution proved unsatisfactory; Stokowski spent less and less time in Houston, and Houstonians began to wish for a conductor willing to reside in the city.[148]

When Sir John Barbirolli stopped in Houston on February 1 and 2, 1960, as part of a nationwide tour, he provided "dramatic and spellbinding" revelations to an eager audience.[149] Critics acclaimed a thrilling evening, and board members began to think that Sir John might be just the figure to follow Stokowski. Well known to Americans through radio broadcasts as the youthful genius confident enough to follow Arturo Toscanini to the New York Philharmonic's podium from 1937 to 1943, Barbirolli had been knighted by George VI for returning to war-torn Manchester and restoring the Hallé, Britain's oldest symphonic orchestra, to its prewar reputation. Once again Ima guided efforts to find an appropriate conductor. Who exactly had the idea to approach Barbirolli is unclear, although Ima's confidant, business manager Tom Johnson, executed the request. Speculating that Barbirolli would never leave his beloved Hallé orchestra but might want to vary his conducting duties, Johnson pursued the Barbirollis to Atlanta in March 1960 and suggested what was a novel idea at the time: would the maestro consider bridging the Atlantic to become head conductor in Houston while retaining his position in Manchester? Barbirolli was intrigued.

The Symphony Society's inner circle kept negotiations secret but continued an eager transatlantic pursuit. Finally, the executive committee signed a contract with the star in August but postponed announcement of its coup until after the fall 1960 season had begun. Nonetheless, rumors of impending change in Houston had been leaked to the press by April. Displeased by seeming treachery, Stokowski forced the board's hand by telling his final April audience that the 1960–1961 season would be his last in Houston and that he was departing for "personal" reasons. Stokowski returned with appropriate fanfare in the fall, but between his October and November concerts, the society announced Sir John Barbirolli's appointment, effective in the fall of 1961. Given little warning of the board's plan to make a formal announcement, Stokowski received this news coldly, packed up his bags, and notified the administration that he would not return. Once again the society had failed to effect a smooth transition and was forced to complete the season with a series of guest conductors.[150]

Houstonians welcomed Sir John Barbirolli, an "adorable" man, according to Ann Holmes, with warm enthusiasm. He returned the compliment during six happy seasons that saw the orchestra placed securely on the national stage.[151] A January 1971 memorial to his genius explained his success in Houston: "the magic of the maestro was that he could get his musicians to see his vision and project it to the audience. . . . [He] recreated the miracle of music for the multitudes of many lands."[152] Tours to Washington, D.C., and New York City in 1963 to celebrate the society's fiftieth anniversary made other Americans aware of Houston's impressive musical scene. Inspired by the orchestra's new level of proficiency, John T. Jones, Jesse Jones's nephew, proposed to the city on June 11, 1962, that the Jones family foundation, the Houston Endowment, underwrite the cost of a $6 million symphony hall. Since 1938 patrons had been pleading for a performance hall that met a symphonic orchestra's acoustical needs and an audience's comfort. Neither the City Auditorium nor the much-renovated Music Hall had satisfied critics.[153] Jones Hall met every aesthetic expectation when it opened to great fanfare in 1966, and it has been the home of Houston Symphony ever since. In her December 1966 program message, Ima enumerated symphony blessings: a beautiful performance hall; a Ford Foundation grant of $2 million to build the endowment that would be matched by Houston dollars; and a Rockefeller Foundation grant to the University of Houston and the Symphony Society to support open rehearsals and a concert featuring American composers in April 1967.[154]

Not everyone was so content with symphony management and programming. When Barbirolli finally announced his retirement in 1967, he took emeritus status and oversaw a smooth transition to his successor, Andre Previn, a rising young star of the international music circuit. However, Previn's tenure was short-lived for reasons personal and musical, not least among them that he offended Ima and others by parading about in hippie costumes with his paramour, Mia Farrow, while his wife languished in Los Angeles. Previn's dismissal in May 1969 shocked *Post* music critic Carl Cunningham, who wrote an article condemning the "secrecy and duplicity" of the executive committee that "destroy the confidence of serious mature conductors who might otherwise come and build an ambitious enterprise in Houston." Cunningham said Houston was "not getting a full artistic return on investment" because the society was controlled by four people. Although unnamed, he could only have meant Ima, Gus Wortham, Maurice Hirsch, and Tom Johnson, who, Cunningham believed, had failed to make "efficient, intelligent, imaginative and artistically meaningful decisions." The four immediately counseled and decided to beg for harmony between critics and Symphony Society patrons. Ima mailed a letter to the *Post*'s Sound-Off editor in October to explain the symphony's "vicissitudes" and the frustrations of board members who had to fight Houston's reputation as a "hick" town "so rich it could afford impossible salaries, extensive tours abroad, and palatial furnished residences"—the demands of several conductor candidates.[155] An uneasy truce seems to have been arranged, and during Ima's last years, Lawrence Foster wielded the symphony's baton in relative calm.[156]

IMA, THE SYMPHONY'S EVANGEL

Ima was an activist president who worked with conductors to shape season programs and select guest artists. Deeply interested in each incumbent maestro as a musician and a friend, she attended all rehearsals when she was in town and proffered advice about personal matters. She kept abreast of the international music scene, encouraged the compositions and performances of Texas artists, and urged patrons to commission works for the orchestra. Each December during her presidency and for years afterward, she addressed the audience at Christmas with a message in the program that reaffirmed her dream of a civic symphony of highest quality accessible to all citizens.[157] Leopold Stokowski noted that she believed in "indigenous creative talent" and conceived and organized the Texas Composers Commission to help composers pursue professional careers.[158] When she relinquished presidential duties in 1956, fellow music lovers praised her "evangelism for a broad program" that drew "every segment" of the Houston–Harris County population to symphony concerts.[159] While she was president, the symphony announced Music for Everybody, which encompassed free outdoor summer concerts, radio broadcasts from the Music Hall sponsored by Texas Gulf Sulphur, special events, subscription and student concerts, and ensemble performances at junior and senior high schools.[160] Ima nurtured "cultural progress" and institutional cooperation by organizing the Texas Creative Arts Festival in March 1948. Sponsored by the Symphony Society, for several years the festival attracted support from music clubs, the Museum of Fine Arts, the Public Library, Houston's Little Theatre, and the River Oaks Garden Club. The festival featured an Azalea Trail, exhibits, concerts, and plays.[161]

Ima loved watching students develop and "as a silent benefactress of many young people" gave financial and moral support to numerous aspiring artists. In 1947 she announced a student auditions program to reward children in Harris County ages nineteen or under who could perform a concerto from memory. Winners performed with the Houston Symphony at student concerts.[162] Ever eager to bring the joy of symphonic music to new constituents, Ima inaugurated promenade concerts for young adults and a program to drive the handicapped to concerts in 1948.[163] That year the society persuaded board member W. D. Sutherland, president of the

Henke and Pillot grocery chain, to underwrite free concerts on Saturday evenings during the winter season, with the tickets to be distributed at Henke and Pillot outlets.[164] In 1949 an Activities Committee took closer control of public relations and related issues, and in November 1951 Ima fulfilled a long-standing dream by establishing an endowment fund to ensure the organization's future.[165] A conduit for her own donations, the fund became a critical source of income in later years. During her tenure as president, the symphony also increased the number of season ticket holders and donors.[166] In 1952 she inaugurated a Painting to Music program to award prizes for art inspired by student performances. Winning entries were displayed in the foyer during performances, and in 1955 this art and music program was expanded to include exhibits provided by the city's leading museums and galleries.[167]

In the seventeen years following Ima's presidency, her interest in symphony activities never waned, and she remained active on the Women's Committee and as a revered counselor to the society's executive committee.[168] Possibly her most rewarding musical experience during these years was her work with Carlos Chavez, founder and director of the National Conservatory of Music and Symphony Orchestra of Mexico (1928–1952). Over the years Ima had nourished the ambitions of contemporary composers and had encouraged the symphony to commission works for the orchestra.[169] She often begged others "to keep ears and minds open to new, strange innovations," and in 1969 she realized a personal dream when she asked Chavez to compose what became the symphonic *Ode to Clio*. She had met Chavez on her frequent trips to Mexico, where she attended many musical events, and she had developed a warm friendship with him. In November 1946 she had worked closely with Gus Wortham to welcome "the great patriot" and "distinguished representative of our good neighbor to the south" at a Chamber of Commerce dinner during Chavez's residency as a guest conductor.[170] In February 1948 she had approached him about "building a great orchestra" in Houston. In his gracious refusal, Chavez told her he was tempted but could not leave his beloved orchestra and Institute of Fine Arts. He also shared with her his opinion of steps Houston must take to achieve greatness: better salaries, a concert hall dedicated to symphonic music, broad-based support, and no semiclassical offerings.[171]

For several months in 1969, muse and composer corresponded about the genesis of Chavez's ode. Ima was drawn to his work because she and Chavez were united in their understanding of history and of music. Ima had long been a student of history, and in August 1969 she wrote to Chavez that she had been "startled" by an article in *Life* magazine that "set me to thinking of Cleo [*sic*], the Muse of History, the subject you are now preparing for the Houston Symphony." Clio, Ima noted, had two masks: "one is hideous and frightening. The other is infinitely beautiful." Ima "felt impelled to write" Chavez and suggest that the ode presented "an opportunity . . . to declare the exaltation which has inspired men to great achievements." Chavez replied in November that the ode was finished, and he told her about his feelings that "the historic process of mankind is reflected in the development of music through the ages." Following the March 1970 premiere concerts, Ima expressed herself as "completely satisfied" and proud to have Chavez's composition in Houston's repertory.[172]

In a December 1953 speech thanking members of the Symphony Society for reelecting her president, Ima remarked, "we are custodians, all of us, of a very precious trust."[173] She viewed the symphony as an enterprise that must have "unwavering loyalty and support of . . . civic forces and individuals who influence public opinion,"[174] and late in life she admonished the municipal government "to contribute sufficient financial aid . . . for this benefit to its citizens."[175] Volunteer, civic activist, philanthropist, board leader, no one took more seriously the sacredness of her civic quest to nurture a resident symphony and make it a constructive force in Houston's civic life during the sixty-two years she fought to build a great orchestra for Houston. As a volunteer, no task was too small for her attention, whether sorting prospective donor cards, shopping with conductors' wives, or supporting the committee work of others. She "taught several generations of young women [on the Women's Committee] the meaning and rewards of disciplined service" by encouraging them to develop programs and expand ideas introduced during her two years as founding chairwoman of the committee.[176] As a civic activist, Ima overcame innate reticence and went on the stump and on the air to advocate the civic benefits of a world-acclaimed orchestra. She used economic, social, and aesthetic arguments to convince the business community that its support of a resident orchestra made sound business sense. As a philanthropist, she gave generously year after year, often supporting new programs and plugging deficits. As a board manager Ima ensured that her vision for the symphony was adopted, and she relied on a small group of insiders who supervised and managed the orchestra and board subcommittees, reviewed all contracts, and approved programming. Theoretically, this tight control should have ensured smooth operation, but it does not seem to have averted miscommunications among musicians, conductors, critics, and public.

In a May 16, 1956, farewell report to the board, Ima summarized her experience with the symphony. "When I say that I have gained more than I have given, I am not being humble. Responsibility is rewarding. Association through so many years with hundreds and hundreds of men and women who are workers for something beyond themselves has given me a glow of love for Houston beyond measure."[177] Her gratitude was reciprocated. To celebrate Ima's interest in young musicians, Maurice Hirsch and his wife, Winifred, "absolutely overwhelmed" her by endowing the Ima Hogg Scholarship Fund in her honor—"the most beautiful and gratifying tribute I could imagine."[178] Symphony League volunteers recognized her "inspiring leadership" and "intelligent, enthusiastic insistence upon ever higher standards of excellence," which made her a "high priestess of beauty in all its varied forms."[179] In 1976 they memorialized Ima's love affair with music by establishing the Ima Hogg National Young Artist Competition, open to performers on all instruments who wished to compete for valuable awards and a chance to perform in concert with the Houston Symphony.[180]

Ima's lifelong devotion to the cause of symphonic music in Houston illuminates the parameters of her philanthropy and reveals the complexity of her personality. She insisted on the orchestra's civic mission, wanted ticket prices to be kept low, and opened performances to all citizens, but she also demanded the highest possible standards, in musicians, in musical instruments, in performance selections, and even in audience attention. She believed support for the symphony should be broad-based and feared reliance on one or two major donors; yet she encouraged Hugh Roy Cullen to plug massive deficits during the 1940s and frequently stepped in herself to meet budget projections. She personally assisted many musicians, befriended conductors, and inspired volunteers, but among the hundreds of men and women with whom she shared musical joys and sorrows, only a few individuals stand out as confidants and companions. While she shunned publicity, she used her social position and insistent charm to persuade dozens of admirers to fulfill her dreams by making her passions their own. People could not deny her requests. By the 1930s Houston leaders realized that Miss Ima was critical to the symphony's success; by the 1940s she had become an icon.[181] For nearly forty years no decision was taken without consulting her wishes. Although she demurred when others wished to honor her and frequently found excuses to avoid award ceremonies, she accepted the accolades and enjoyed the approval of others. If she sought expert advice from a wide array of music supporters, in the end she worked doggedly to make sure her vision of excellence would prevail so the symphony's "universal language of order and harmony" could provide "some spiritual life and wholesome recreation for future generations" and reveal the "mysterious godlike creative impulse" inherent in the arts.[182]

Chapter 6

A Museum by the People for the Use of the People

"You of the City of Houston, in setting apart this building dedicated to the arts, are initiating a work of vital importance," declared Homer St. Gaudens to civic leaders who had gathered on the evening of Saturday, April 12, 1924, to swing wide the doors of the first municipal art museum built in Texas. The orator, who was director of fine arts at Pittsburgh's Carnegie Institute and son of renowned sculptor Augustus St. Gaudens, predicted that "if this country is to continue to go forward through coming ages, it must nourish and stimulate its imaginative and emotional side, as it has already trained its practical sense." Houston Art League President Florence Fall, director Ima Hogg, ex-officio trustee Mayor Oscar F. Holcombe, and other league officers, directors, and trustees welcomed hundreds of Houstonians eager to hear speakers praise project organizers and define the functions of an art museum. Newspaper accounts recorded that a "stream of humanity" braved mud and skimpy board sidewalks before it "poured through the doors" for an open house from five to six o'clock in the evening. Reporters estimated that more than one thousand citizens were turned away from the crowded dedication and reception at eight thirty. The central cultural problem, St. Gaudens told his audience, was "not confined to what you shall put upon your walls, but what you shall put into the hearts of your people. . . . You must reassure your public . . . that it must not feel the need of putting on felt slippers when it approaches art."[1]

Civic leaders had struggled for twenty-four years to reassure the public that everyone could enjoy fine art. When appeals for financial support to house a public collection of paintings and sculpture in a permanent museum fell far short of funds needed to construct the city's art palace, "a coterie of businessmen" stepped forward to defray the deficit and assure completion of the building "as originally planned." Subscribers to the fund were told their names would not be announced when the "high-minded use of their wealth" to cultivate "the spiritual and cultural side of life" was made public to loud applause at the opening ceremonies.[2] Despite this guarantee, one subscriber did not attend the festivities anyway: Will Hogg, who had conceived and executed a three-week campaign to raise more than $200,000, had, as usual, avoided the accolades of his friends by absenting himself from the ceremony.

ARTISTIC ASPIRATIONS IN HOUSTON

Music was Ima's passion, but collecting and enjoying works of art were pleasures pursued by Will, Ima, Mike, and Mike's wife, Alice. The Hogg family association with the Museum of Fine Arts, Houston, began in the 1910s, was paramount in securing the institution's original galleries in 1924, and provided the largest single gift made to the institution at the time of Alice Hogg Hanszen's death in 1977—the Bayou Bend Collection and Gardens. Like Ima's determined desire to build a great symphony for Houston, the Hoggs' collecting fervor advanced a didactic and civic purpose. The Hoggs believed that if Houston were to be a great city, its leaders must collect and display examples of humankind's creativity in a comprehensive municipal museum that would give every citizen opportunities to appreciate, understand, and participate in artistic achievement. Like others who espoused Progressive Era ideals, the Hoggs believed art museums could promote civic identity, enrich urban life, and democratize culture by opening their doors freely to everyone. In developing their attitudes toward the role of artistic expression in civic life, the Hoggs were responding to national trends, but in forming their own collections, they were daring pacesetters who challenged traditional concepts of "fine" art. As collectors and as advocates of public access to all art forms, they provided exemplary leadership and inspiration to Houston's nascent arts community. The Hoggs' visionary generosity ensured Houston a prominent place in the nation's cultural boardroom.

America's barons of industry may have gone west in the nineteenth century to build their fiefdoms, but they turned east to Europe to recover ancestral habits cast off by the Revolutionary generations and to sheathe their newfound wealth in a patina of cultural polish. London's monumental repositories attested to Britain's global hegemony. French and Tuscan palaces engorged by royal and ducal acquisitions but liberated by Parisians and Florentines weary of exclusion from power illuminated the ties that bound the arts to politics as individuals struggled to build just and nourishing societies. Should not America's mercantile princes create their own collections? Should not America's great cities maintain palaces for the people to showcase civic pride and commercial success?

Art museums, as they are known in the twenty-first century, arose in the 1870s at a moment when great wealth, urban density, and civic confidence merged with idealism. Charles Willson Peale had introduced his gallery of Revolutionary War portraits, curios, and natural wonders to Philadelphians in 1786 and had initiated the Pennsylvania Academy of Fine Arts in 1805. Yale had opened the first college museum in 1832, and the Hartford Athenaeum had revealed its antiquarian treasures in 1844, but the comprehensive public museum with its departments, lectures, and studio courses was achieved after 1870 when New York businessmen and Boston aesthetes incorporated the Metropolitan Museum of New York and the Boston Museum of Fine Arts with the premise that these cities would build collections to engage the general public.[3] The immediate popularity of these institutions led to eager emulation around the country.

Art quickly followed commerce south and west. In many growing cities, citizen groups "who saw in the arts the leavening force that would make their cit[ies] truly great" fostered civic art movements that culminated in dozens of incorporated art museums in cities across the country in the years between 1870 and 1910.[4] Celebrated poet, journalist, and arbiter of culture William Cullen Bryant spoke for these groups and for individual collectors at a public meeting called in 1869 to discuss formation of the Metropolitan Museum in New York. This museum, he said, was a patriotic necessity that proclaimed America as a world power and New York as the "third great city of the civilized world." Museums were needed to display works by American artists, to house collections donated by munificent citizens, to offer training to art students, and to provide "alternative entertainment of an innocent and improving character" to burgeoning urban populations.[5] The Hoggs later espoused these tenets and found in Houston a receptive audience for their enthusiasm. The city's quest for a civic art museum replicated national cultural reform initiatives and was heralded by the work of an intrepid committee of women.

Emma Richardson Cherry, a professional artist trained in Chicago, New York, and Paris, "brought art to Houston" when she and her husband, oil broker Dillin Brook Cherry, settled in the city in 1898.[6] Encouraged by her father and husband to pursue her vocation as a painter, Cherry communicated her vitality and appreciation of beauty to hundreds of students who were also struck by her embrace of several media and her willingness to explore new art forms. While teaching art in Denver in the early 1890s, Cherry helped found the Artists Club of Denver, an exhibit and support group that became the Denver Art

Association and eventually the Denver Art Museum. When she arrived in Houston, Cherry discovered no art clubs, no studio courses for aspiring artists, and no classes in the public school system. At once recognized for her "poetic temperament and charm of manner," Cherry plunged into Houston's cultural life as a founder of the Ladies' Reading Club, sponsor of twilight musicales, and member of the Girls Musical Club. Her studio home in a historic antebellum house on the corner of Fargo and Hopkins Streets became Houston's first salon where artists and musicians mingled with the city's social elite.[7] Cherry also conceived the Houston Public School Art League established in 1900 to bring replicas of great art works into the classroom.

At four o'clock in the afternoon of March 17, 1900, Cherry, three Houston schoolteachers—Lydia Adkisson, Roberta Lavender, and Cara Redwood—and "a number of ladies and two gentlemen" met at the home of Lavinia Abercrombie Lovett, wife of prominent railroad lawyer Robert Lovett, and heard Jean Sherwood of Chicago explain the purposes and benefits of an art association. Enthusiasm for Sherwood's eloquent advocacy "subsided into a deep earnestness and the election of officers." Lavinia Lovett assumed the presidency; Robert Lovett, Mary B. Hill, and Adele B. Looscan were appointed to write a constitution; and a general meeting was called for March 24 at Houston High School to launch a membership drive.[8] Forty-two men and women, including teachers, mothers, and socially prominent couples, joined the Houston Public School Art League at the March 24 public meeting and pledged to enrich children's lives by advocating "art culture in the public schools."[9]

The first order of business was building membership, especially among mothers of schoolchildren. Parent and teacher organizations were becoming important school support groups at the turn of the twentieth century, and the Public School Art League seems to have served as a catalyst for parent action in Houston's schools. The "awful storm" that devastated Galveston in September 1900 and made "it necessary for every one to contribute to the material needs of suffering humanity" sidetracked efforts to "anticipate the spiritual needs of all future generations," but by March 1902 the league had attracted 164 members.[10] In January of that year league volunteers had raised enough money ($402.10) to begin placing replicas of great works of art in public school classrooms as their first step to build art programs in the schools. Years later, Emma Richardson Cherry recalled loading her buggy with reproductions of famous paintings and trotting up and down Houston's dusty streets to every school in town.[11]

By 1908 the league boasted six hundred members, many of whom had purchased $1 family memberships so their children could display buttons that proclaimed they belonged to an important civic movement.[12] That year the league played host to sculptor Lorado Taft of Chicago for a school demonstration and public lecture. Deemed "one of the best things we have ever attempted for the children," Taft's demonstration inspired in his audience of five thousand a "wave of childish modeling, in crude clay" liberated from excavations for a new city sewer system. "Citizens" of Houston failed, however, to "appreciate the opportunity" to hear the world-renowned artist at a paid evening event, leaving the league sadly in arrears. Despite this setback, in 1908 the league was able to purchase twelve sets of thirty-five pictures needed for each grade school. Cooperating with parents, teachers, and children, the league exhibited a framed set in the Pagoda at the corner of Capitol and Fannin and raised $950 through ticket and refreshment sales. The Pagoda was owned by Jesse H. Jones, who loaned the space for the exhibit and thereby began a long association with league and museum activities. The league also created a fund to bring art lecturers to the city so parents could "grow with the children in art knowledge."[13] The league's goals of public education were quickly emulated in the African-American community, which supported separate cultural activities. Art Club members hosted Mrs. Booker T. Washington as guest speaker in 1908, and pioneering African-American teachers provided limited art instruction in cultural clubs and segregated public school art classes.[14]

BUILDING A MUSEUM

In 1913 the Art League's activist president, Corinne Abercrombie (Mrs. Gentry) Waldo, called on members to develop programs of citywide significance. Dropping "Public School" from its name, the Houston Art League secured a charter from the state and began a campaign to build a permanent civic art museum as a community focal point where creative activity, collecting, patronage, and art education would converge. Artistic activities had fragile roots in Houston and in Texas. As early as 1837, A. Andrews advertised his talents as painter and miniaturist in the *Telegraph and Texas Register*. The *Galveston Weekly Journal* reported in 1851 that Englishman Thomas Flintoff (circa 1809–1892) had begun his career as portraitist of prominent Texans and their families, and the same year German-trained Herman Lungwitz (1813–1891) settled in the Hill Country as Texas's first landscape artist. But it was the Texas Federation of Women's Clubs, with its goal of self-education, that promoted the first Traveling Art Gallery, a collection of reproductions that toured ninety-five cities and towns in Texas between 1900 and 1903. Attempts to establish galleries in Galveston (1878), San Antonio (1888, 1894), and Fort Worth (1909) did not lead directly to full-fledged museums until the Art League's persistent efforts after 1900 made Houston's municipal museum the model for other Texas cities.[15]

During the league's early years members rented headquarters space in a Victorian mansion at 1896 Main Street where they held classes, gave monthly lectures, and displayed their first loan exhibit.[16] Members took an active interest in city planning debates and efforts to develop a centrally located civic center that would include a museum of art. In 1913–1914 league President Corinne Waldo and a committee began discussions with George Hermann about a long-term lease of land adjoining Rice Institute, but Hermann's unexpected death in 1914 occurred before a contract could be signed.[17] While these negotiations were under way, Mayor Horace Baldwin Rice, whose wife, Caroline, was league vice president in 1914–1915, tried to provide city property for a museum, but the city attorney ruled the transfer illegal. Rice German Professor Thomas Lindsey Blayney, league president from 1915 to 1917, then worked with trustees of the Hermann estate to acquire property at the juncture of Montrose Boulevard and Main Street, provided a building worth at least $20,000 could be constructed there within ten years. Joseph Cullinan, who was platting his Shadyside enclave community nearby, and his wife, Lucie Halm Cullinan, paid $3,300 to the Hermann estate on the league's behalf. The league promised to build a permanent facility within the stipulated time, and the sale was executed in August 1916.[18]

A committee led by Mary Hale Lovett, wife of Rice Institute's president, assisted by ten men and women including Corinne Waldo, art lecturer Stella Shurtleff, architect William Ward Watkin, and league President Florence Fall, mailed 1,500 engraved invitations to celebratory dedication ceremonies to be held at the site on April 12, 1917. Setting a precedent followed at future dedication ceremonies, the league called on member and Rabbi Henry Barnstein for an invocation and invited Rice Institute Professor Stockton Axson to address supporters. Speeches by Florence Fall and Mayor Ben Campbell underlined the new institution's civic purpose, while the singing of "America" and a benediction completed the ceremonies. Thereafter, the league held an annual Founders' Day celebration with formal exercises, speeches, and music every April 12.[19]

Although World War I interrupted construction plans, the league did receive its first major collection in 1919 from the estate of George M. Dickson, a bachelor manufacturer of iron locomotive wheels. Lacking permanent exhibition space, the league placed works by William Merritt Chase, Jean-Léon Gérome, and other well-known artists in offices of the mayor, the City Council, and its own members. By 1920 Houston had become a vigorous port and manufacturing city of 138,000 whose leaders lobbied for national recognition. League members believed it was finally time to build their museum, and they hired William Ward Watkin, project architect for Rice Institute and professor of architecture there, to develop plans. His mentor and former employer, Ralph Adams Cram, renowned Boston architect responsible for the design of the institute's campus and many large civic projects nationwide, served as consulting architect.[20]

The Cram-Watkin design for a classical temple that would house a comprehensive collection was composed of a central exhibit space and wings on each side that could be adapted as classroom, office, or exhibit space when the museum's collections grew and its educational outreach programs developed. Rather than use the Mediterranean Renaissance style made popular for civic structures on the institute campus and in plans for the new city library, Cram and Watkin distinguished the museum and elevated its importance by linking its design both to significant temples of art in major U.S. cities and to the sublime traditions of Greece and Rome. Cram created a publicity pamphlet illustrated with conceptual drawings in which he justified the municipal art museum as a "shrine . . . wherein . . . we test and evaluate a past civilization." Collections, he claimed, provided "a criticism of existing social conditions and a stimulus to better living" because "art and beauty are inseparable from life."[21]

With complete plans and a budget of $200,000 in hand, league President Florence Fall, a popular club woman of "queenly stature," turned the "man-sized task" of fund-raising over to a new all-male museum board of trustees led by Joseph Mullen as president and John T. Scott as treasurer. Banker Scott "anticipate[d] no difficulty in raising" needed funds. Believing the museum to be as important as "harbors, banks, and factories" to a "well-balanced, complete metropolis," he drafted an army of volunteers and turned to the community for funds in early 1922. Despite many small donations and a few "patron" supporters at $1,000 apiece, a "year of drudgery—hard work and tense" brought only $80,000 to league coffers.[22] Watkin scaled back his plans, and in February 1923 Don Hall was awarded a contract for $115,000 to begin work on the central portion of the plan only.

By early 1924, with completion of the building in sight, league officers still had raised little more than $80,000, including large donations from Will, Mike, and Ima Hogg, Estelle Sharp, the Cullinans, the Dickson family, and Susan Vaughan Clayton.[23] Prospective donors needed to be reminded, forcefully, that an art museum heralded the city's cultural maturity and raised "standards of refinement and beauty" critical to a "wholesome environment."[24] Fortunately, the museum found a champion in Will Hogg. Will had been following the museum project since 1918 and had immediately agreed to support the construction effort in 1922, but he had left initial fund-raising to others. Contemporaries provide various accounts about Will's decision to complete the fund drive. His friend Henry Stude recalled years later that Will had sought his protection from a "committee" of Art League Treasurer John T. Scott and cotton magnate William L. Clayton, who had requested an appointment to discuss the flagging campaign. Susan Clayton McAshan recounted a more dramatic legend that reveals Will's explosive temper, quick remorse, and boundless generosity. Desperate for funds, McAshan's charming mother, Susan Vaughan Clayton, called on Will, who was finishing a meeting before he dashed to a train. He peremptorily refused her request for an additional donation. Overcome by remorse only a few hours later, he apologized profusely when he returned to town and told John Scott he would raise the necessary money himself.[25]

In three weeks between March 24 and April 12 Will bullied and flattered and shamed his friends until thirty-one associates pledged $5,000 apiece, the Claytons pledged $25,000, the Cullinans pledged $20,000, and Will himself promised another $30,000, thereby raising the Hogg family gift to $40,000. The funds would enable the league to complete the central block and begin work on the east and west wings immediately. When results of the whirlwind campaign were announced to the public at the opening ceremonies on April 12, the generosity of the anonymous donors "thrilled the lovers of art" and "stir[red] the pride of every citizen in Houston devoted to the community welfare."[26] Burke Baker wrote effusively to his friend Will, noting that no names were mentioned "but everybody knew that there is only one man in Houston who has the spirit and the ability to successfully put over that sort of thing. You have done a service of permanent and incalculable value to the City and the State; and as a citizen I want to express to you my own grateful appreciation." Edgar Odell Lovett protested to Will the next day that he had called home and business numbers in vain "to tell you that in my humble judgment if you live to be one hundred years old . . . you will in no subsequent ten days bring more genuine joy to your people than attended the anonymous announcement at the Art Museum last night." Lovett also teased his friend: "I have the impudence to add that I would give ten of my own span to have had the privilege of listening in on some of the personal exhortations."[27]

Will's success attests to his status in the business community and to the charisma of his personality. Like his sister, Will refused to take no for an answer, but his methods tended to be brutally direct rather than charmingly persuasive. The campaign shows a thoroughly organized mind willing to work very hard. Taking the reins in late March, Will prepared lists of subscribers to any league activity, lists of those who already had given, and lists of those who had "already subscribed but not enough." When he could not meet with a prospect in person, he sent pointed letters and telegrams urging recipients to "join in this free will gift to the community without political sectarian fraternal or racial restrictions."[28]

When turned down, he turned up the heat. To John F. Dickson, nephew of the league's first benefactor, he telegraphed, "Your family name and connection with the ideals of the art museum . . . impel you to subscribe . . . You have no alibi so far as your business is concerned and I think your family interest is such that you ought to deny something else." To James A. Baker, he applied flattery, logic, and moral suasion. While "not in [his] heart to rebuke" the eminent business and social power broker, Will noted that Baker's "declination disheartened me so grievously" that he must try again for the sake of Baker's "family name and fame for several generations." Baker's position as head of Rice Institute, tied so closely to the museum's progress, and his role as lawyer, banker, and citizen impelled his participation—"you are more completely identified with the commercial, financial, educational and realty development of Houston than any other man, bar none." As someone of Baker's stature, who had made a fortune in the town, the "amount of money involved and the terms of payment are relatively so insignificant as to be ridiculous." Will closed with a plea to reconsider "if for no other reason than to encourage me and a number of other younger men" to be similarly generous. Both Baker and Dickson joined the list of resubscribers.[29]

If his requests were insistent, Will's thank-you letters assured donors of his "sincere appreciation of your cooperation in this movement for the aesthetic advancement of this beloved community."[30] His dedication to the museum's fiscal health did not stop with this one effort. After telling Watkin to "go ahead" with his original plan, Will wrote twenty-two of the original subscribers in December 1925 requesting additional funds to finish the two wings and furnish the building. In 1926 he urged the museum to establish an acquisition fund, a suggestion that took form as the Houston Friends of Art (1926–1951), a membership support group of three hundred Houstonians.[31] Through Will's efforts the museum had been launched. Leading by example, he, Ima, and Mike had made contributions "of such generous proportions that they commanded from those he solicited the extraordinary response that followed."[32]

Will also made an impact on museum effectiveness in other ways. He pressed trustees to invite all Houstonians to enjoy museum programs and stressed the importance of opening museum doors to black citizens. The board honored Will's wish to offer African Americans a museum experience, an action based on Progressive Era beliefs that fine art transcended political, social, or ethnic boundaries.[33] From October 3 to 10, 1930, Houston joined New Orleans and Los Angeles to co-host Works by American Negro Artists, a touring exhibition that made an interesting comment on segregation's complexity in the South's two largest cities.[34] With Will's support, the museum began to develop an acquisition and exhibition policy. In a letter to Florence Fall on March 2, 1925, Will promised to lend the Hogg Brothers Remington Collection for one month each year, even though Mike believed the collection should remain in the Hogg Brothers offices. Before the museum opened in April 1924, it possessed only forty-eight objects, most the legacy of George M. Dickson, and construction expenses and salaries for a part-time staff swallowed all available funds.[35] For many years only the director's ingenuity, the willingness of collectors like Hogg Brothers to lend prized possessions, and the foresight of a few discerning donors brought works of aesthetic value to museum galleries.

The Hoggs befriended James H. Chillman Jr., the museum's first director, and supported his policies enthusiastically. Chillman's wife, Dorothy, became a confidante and advisor to Ima and helped her develop the interiors and contents of Bayou Bend's period rooms in the 1950s and 1960s. Museum architect William Ward Watkin had suggested that his protégé and Rice colleague James Chillman accept the post of museum director, considered a part-time job in 1924, and Chillman often worked without salary so the museum's operating bills could be paid during the lean 1930s. This sacrifice, although substantial, was made possible because Chillman continued as professor of architecture and art history at Rice Institute. A native of Philadelphia who had received his bachelor's and master's degrees at the University of Pennsylvania, Chillman devoted thirty years to building the museum's collections.

Chillman's academic training enabled him to discern works of value and advise Houstonians who wished to form collections for themselves or for the museum, but he believed firmly that art was not "a shrine on a mountaintop or Old Masters in a museum." Instead he tried to show timid collectors or museum visitors why good art should be "closely associated with the everyday life of the people."[36] Strapped by a small budget, Chillman supported local talent and initiated the Annual Exhibition of Works by Houston Artists (1925–1960), the Annual Texas Photographers exhibits (1926–1953), and the Annual Exhibition of Works by Texas Artists (1940–1961). These innovations married necessity to community outreach by nurturing the local art scene and securing exhibits of interest to the community at relatively low cost. While Chillman encouraged regional artists to exhibit at the museum, he relied on a handful of benefactors like the Hoggs to provide a permanent legacy. He also retained the goodwill of Rice Institute and called on fellow professors to organize museum projects, serve on the board of directors, and preach the importance of high-quality art institutions to the public.

WILL AND HIS REMINGTONS

The Hoggs began the collecting careers that would provide their most lasting legacies to Houston in 1920 when Ima purchased her first New England armchair and Will his first oil painting by Frederic Remington. Although no municipal or state museum existed in Texas at that time, brother and sister knew at once that their collections would ultimately reside in a museum in their beloved home state. Ima often claimed that collecting was a disease she had acquired in childhood when pebbles and wildflowers seized her imagination. Mike sometimes teased her about her "magpie proclivities," and observers thought Will's buying sprees illustrated an impulsive personality. In fact, the Hoggs' collecting activities suggest an overarching vision and systematic approach informed by aesthetic insight and intellectual curiosity that enabled them to collect works of great distinction.

With two exceptions—Ima's collection of works on paper by contemporary European and Mexican artists and Will's collection of perfume bottles purchased as a wedding gift for sister-in-law Alice—Hogg family purchases illuminate their understanding of American history and their view that this history shaped the destiny, identity, and culture of nation, state, community, family, and individual.[37] To the Hoggs, collecting works of art was a socially valuable way to mold and define a civic identity for Houston; works of art lodged in a museum would perform the public functions of explaining the past and clarifying values shared with the wider national community. These collections would proclaim Houston a seat of culture and a haven for humanitarian understanding. The Hoggs believed superbly crafted furniture, Native American Southwestern artifacts, and paintings by American artists interpreted the mythical elements of progress, westward expansion, and individual fulfillment that bespoke a unique American heritage and formed a foundation on which to build future dreams. By housing these collections in Houston, they tied the city to an older, broader national heritage. The Hoggs were among the first collectors to teach a hesitant public that fine art did not have to originate in Europe to have lasting value.

Three characteristics marked the Hogg family's approach to collecting: the Hoggs explored uncharted territory; they studied the subject matter of their collections thoroughly; and they worked with experts and trusted dealers to discover and authenticate potential purchases. When Will decided to acquire paintings and sculpture by Frederic Remington (1861–1909), few were interested in the artist and no catalogs of his work existed. Ima bought her New England armchair before Henry Francis du Pont conceived his American period rooms at Winterthur (first purchase 1923), before the Metropolitan Museum in New York opened its American Wing (1924), and before John D. Rockefeller Jr. decided to rescue Colonial Williamsburg (1926)—indeed, long before academic art historians deemed American decorative arts worthy of serious study. Similarly, Ima helped establish widespread interest in kachina dolls, Native American pottery, and Texas furniture when she began collecting these objects. Will and Ima were among the first to recognize and affirm the still-contested idea that material culture provides historical insights not revealed by the archival record. Finally, in the 1960s Mike's widow, Alice Hogg Hanszen, procured the first important pre-Columbian collection to be exhibited permanently in Houston. Her contribution reinforced Hogg family beliefs that America's heritage predated European incursion and melded cultural traditions.

Once they decided to invest in an artist or art form, the Hoggs immersed themselves in the subject. Will unearthed old magazines and color plates from *Collier's* magazine and other sources to understand the scope of Frederic Remington's work. Will was drawn to the artist's personality and marked passages about Remington's attraction to art and to a life of action, the fact that the artist did not smoke, and Remington's need to watch his weight.[38] Ima read voraciously, traveled extensively to train her eye, and even took classes to expand her knowledge. If in doubt, she picked up the telephone and called an expert. Both siblings amassed extensive libraries of works on Americana and related visual and decorative arts, and Will ordered two subscriptions of the magazine *Antiques* when it began publication in 1922, one for the New York apartment and one for their home in Houston.[39] Like many collectors, Will and Ima were dedicated, serious, and thorough; they enjoyed the hunt for unexpected treasure, haunted galleries and antique shops, and delighted in driving a hard bargain; and they loved to share their discerning knowledge and many discoveries with others. Although they relied on trusted dealers to help them find coveted objects, they made purchases only after considered examination and thought—and a good deal of negotiating. Ima worked closely with James H. Chillman Jr. during his long tenure as Museum of Fine Arts director, and in the 1960s Alice responded personally to calls for support from museum director James Johnson Sweeney.

When the Museum of Fine Arts opened its doors in April 1924, visitors could admire ten works by Frederic Remington from the Hogg Brothers collection and *Contentment*, a painting by George Inness that Will had purchased for his home. The next year Will suggested that the museum organize the nation's first memorial exhibition of Remington's work and loaned the entire Hogg Brothers collection, at that time composed of thirty paintings and illustrations and one bronze sculpture.[40] From January 3 through 18, 1931, the museum displayed a collection of Remington works that had grown to include twenty-three oils, forty-two black-and-white "illustrations," four pen-and-ink sketches, and one sculpture. The loan memorialized "Mr. Hogg's sympathetic friendship and support of the museum, from its beginnings." Volunteers from forty-six civic, literary, and professional clubs served as hosts and hostesses for this tribute to Will Hogg and his collection. Ima, as a member of the board, greeted guests on Sunday afternoon, January 4, and the exhibit received extensive press coverage.[41] During the 1936 Texas Centennial celebration, the museum borrowed several Remington works from Hogg Brothers, and in 1939, 1940, and 1941, works from the collection were displayed in museum galleries.[42]

The Remington works comprised the first Hogg family collection to be assembled, but they were not transferred to the museum until 1943, after Mike's death and a reorganization of Hogg family business interests.[43] In January 1942 Ima hired Charles Muskovitch, conservator of art for the Dallas Museum, to study conservation and restoration needs of the Remington Collection.[44] When satisfied that the paintings were ready for the museum, she, brother Tom, and sister-in-law Alice began negotiations to make the transfer. By May 18, 1943, museum trustees and donors were ready to announce a formal gift of the collection to the museum. In press statements, Ima reiterated the "understanding and desire" of all family members that the collection "portraying an earlier period of Southwestern life, should be preserved . . . for the use of the public and for the citizens of our state." Ima requested that "within a reasonable time after the war," the collection be installed as a unit.[45] The deed of gift also stipulated that the collection be neither circulated nor loaned and that if the museum could no longer use the works for exhibit purposes, the complete collection be donated to the University of Texas or to some other museum in Texas.[46] The spring 1944 museum bulletin highlighted the Remington Collection and Will's outstanding "personal efforts in rallying citizens" that made possible a debt-free building.[47] In 1973 the collection was reinstalled in the new Brown Pavilion. With Ima's permission, some works of "inferior quality" were sold or traded so that paintings by distinguished American artists could be added to the permanent collection.[48]

Although Will himself made no specific comments about his interest in Remington, he gathered clippings in a scrapbook that suggest he was intrigued by the artist's depictions of man's confrontation with his environment, imaginative ability to capture a vanishing way of life, and empathy with Native Americans.[49] Art historian Emily Neff says Will may have been drawn to Remington's heroic view of American history and may have identified with the artist and the strong emotions his paintings excited; Remington's characters were unpretentious fighters, their stories direct, their values of individualism, self-reliance, and determination ones Will admired. Moreover, Neff hypothesizes, Will must have felt that these important works of art, like the collections of pewter, glass, Windsor furniture, and looking glasses he was also acquiring, illuminated an overarching national identity grounded in a common past. Neff concludes that Will may have believed he was preserving the reputation of an artist whose popularity seemed to be fading.[50] Her analysis, based on close reading of family papers, suggests a broader reading that links Will's collection to the family's civic activism and philanthropy in other areas of urban life. Will's interest in Remington, like his passion for city planning, sustained his vision of a great American city whose residents were bound to other regions of the country by a unifying national culture.

If Will left no written explanation for his collection, he spoke through his actions: the paintings adorned the offices of Hogg Brothers and other family enterprises headquartered in the eight-story Great Southern Building on Preston and Louisiana from the early 1920s until their removal in 1943. Hoping to inspire by example, Will wanted other businessmen to understand the importance of the nation's cultural heritage, form collections of their own, and donate them to public institutions where they could be enjoyed by everyone. The Hogg Brothers collection became famous. Visitors to the Democratic National Convention in 1928 and other collectors of Western American art like Will's crony Will Rogers or fellow Texan Amon Carter examined the Remingtons; and Houstonians understood that one day the works would reside in a museum. Will's example did inculcate a sense of civic responsibility in his associates, several of whom began to form collections of their own.

Ima urged her brother to broaden his taste, but Will must have satisfied his need for an art collection through his intense and in-depth pursuit of works by Remington and a handful of landscapes by other American artists.[51] Will had probably seen works by Remington during his prolonged stays in New York or in the collection of Joseph Cullinan, who had bought a bronze and a few watercolors by the artist in the 1910s, but he did not seriously consider a purchase until late January 1920, when he discovered some Remingtons at Levy's Galleries in New York, or early February, when he purchased *Drawings by Frederic Remington* (1897). For the next seven months he studied available examples and then plunged into a buying frenzy in September that netted one bronze and twenty-five paintings and works on paper from three galleries in a few days.[52] In early October, Will urged his sister to visit the paintings he had purchased for Hogg Brothers' offices but forbade her to ask the price![53] He also sent her a list of paintings by George Inness and other American landscape artists to purchase for their home. Ima declared that this list "took my breath away" and suggested that they "look together and decide together" because she had "a few ideas which I have gathered from having thought often and looked often and considered the great collections of Europe and this country."[54]

By 1924 when he purchased *A Cavalry Scrap* from the estate of John Jacob Astor, Will owned the largest collection of Remington works outside the artist's own museum in Ogdensburg, New York, and he had reclaimed Remington as a major American painter. Will seems to have agreed with novelist of the Old West and Remington friend Owen Wister, who declared that Remington was "not merely an artist; he is a national treasure."[55] While Will added a few objects to the collection before his death in 1930, he never again experienced the focused passion to acquire that had gripped him in the early 1920s.[56] Yet his homage to Remington remains one of the museum's prized collections. In 1933 museum trustees expressed institutional gratitude for Will's determined fund-raising and outspoken advocacy by placing a plaque near the original entrance. Citing Will's "interest in art," his "vision," and his "civic consciousness," the tribute concludes, "his many virtues endeared him to [Houston's] people."[57]

EARLY MUSEUM BENEFACTORS, 1925–1945

While Will established the precedent of enhancing museum offerings through loans and bequests, two Houston women—Emma Richardson Cherry and Annette Finnigan—tried to help the infant museum through acquisition. Emma Richardson Cherry, sixty-four-year-old doyenne of Houston's professional artists in 1924, had been lobbying for a museum since arriving in Houston in 1898. She and her "art-minded" friends had persuaded Abe Levy to allow them to sit outside Levy Brothers, tin cups in hand, to solicit funds to buy land for a building. By 1924 Cherry wanted to provide works of art for a permanent collection.[58] Her efforts tested the youthful Chillman's tact but helped him articulate an accessions policy. Without authorization, Cherry had asked friends to give their paintings to the museum, and the director was forced to explain to his "ever-enthusiastic" patron that only the Accessions Committee could undertake discussion with prospective donors, make purchases, or authorize gifts: "I know you will collaborate with us in the future . . . know[ing] of our general regulations" and "will help me in making this fact known to our many friends who might solicit gifts to the Museum and all unknowingly place us in an embarrassing position."[59] One can only imagine eager art supporters desperate to fill sparsely furnished halls, grasping gifts by little-known practitioners whose artistry failed to meet the stringent aspirations of a young academic trained in Philadelphia and Europe. Chillman mollified Cherry, who presented her portrait of Florence Fall to the museum in 1925 and participated frequently in annual exhibits of Houston and Texas artists.[60]

Happily Annette Finnigan, the museum's first major benefactress, better understood the difficulties of developing a collection of museum quality with limited funds. A graduate of Wellesley College (1889–1894), where she studied art history and drawing and joined the Campus Art Society, Finnigan was a brilliant woman whose father specified in his will that she execute his estate and run his statewide businesses.[61] Finnigan had been an active suffragist at Wellesley and in New York City. When her family moved to Houston in 1903, she and her two sisters called the first meeting of the Houston Equal Suffrage League in their home and campaigned unsuccessfully for female representation on the school board. Busy with business affairs following her father's death in 1909, Finnigan nonetheless founded the Women's Political Union the same year and became president of the Texas Woman Suffrage Association in 1914. She stayed active in the movement until 1916, when she was felled by a mysterious illness, later thought to have been a stroke. Recognizing that she had to abandon her active life, Finnigan returned to New York to be near her married sisters. To fill the void left when her business career ended, Finnigan began a lifetime of leisurely travel that carried her to Europe and the Middle East each year and to Houston for a few months every winter.[62] James Chillman described Finnigan as the "ideal Museum collector in many ways . . . because she would always ask me what I would want . . . rather than imposing her ideas on the Museum."[63]

Sometime in 1929 or 1930 Finnigan approached Chillman about forming collections for the museum. Chillman saw an opportunity to marry Finnigan's expressed interest in antiquities to his desire for a comprehensive collection featuring examples from every artistic period, genre, and culture. An avid student, Finnigan sought the advice of Sir Arthur Evans, legendary archeologist and excavator of King Minos's Palace at Knossos, Crete.[64] Each winter beginning in 1931, crates of treasures arrived at the museum to be opened and "anxiously" examined by Finnigan, Chillman, and Adaline Wellborn, the museum secretary-curator. If a fragile and aging lady accompanied by cane and companion, Finnigan nonetheless battled with patriotic customs officials who reclaimed many of her "most priceless" discoveries in 1936.[65] Seventy-three Egyptian and Roman objects entered the collection in 1931; in 1933 Finnigan shifted focus and procured more than one hundred Asian and Indian textiles. In 1934 she donated seventeen Greek vases, Byzantine ecclesiastical garments, Asian and other textiles, and old lace. More textiles and some jewelry entered the collection early in 1935, and a trip to Spain later that year provoked a shopping frenzy. More than fifty objects, including ecclesiastical furniture and textiles and dueling pistols, were unpacked in Houston in 1936.

In 1937 Finnigan purchased what remains one of the museum's great treasures—an exquisite, perfectly preserved, gold foil laurel wreath from the Hellenistic period (330–27 BCE). The extremely rare, very fragile wreath accompanied its owner in death to signify honors won in life.[66] Finnigan had been a fine athlete and considered the wreath one of her most important discoveries. In 1937 she also brought to Houston three objects that remain signature pieces in the museum's antiquities collection: a third-century BCE alabaster hydria used to carry water that was excavated in Athens in 1933; a marble cycladic figure circa 2800–2300 BCE; and a mid-fourth-century BCE grave stela for a woman. Only a serious collector of respected reputation could have secured these recently excavated works for a little-known museum in remote Texas.

In 1940 the museum produced a catalog that describes sixty-five examples of fine lace exhibited at the museum that year and praises Finnigan as "quiet and retiring" but possessed of a "sharp public spirit and fine personal taste which have" exerted "outstanding . . . influence upon public taste and knowledge."[67] At her death in 1940 contemporaries estimated that one-half to two-thirds of the objects in the museum's collection had been provided by Annette Finnigan. Her knowledge, foresight, and consideration of Director Chillman's needs secured treasures that retain their value and importance more than seventy years later.

Despite publicity surrounding Annette Finnigan's spectacular discoveries and generous gifts, the museum struggled to meet its modest budgets in the years before World War II. Artist Emma Richardson Cherry feared that this weak support meant Houstonians' appreciation of art was "only skin deep," but historian Susie Kalil believed that art flourished in Houston even as museum funding sagged, largely because museum outreach programs successfully bridged the gap between public and artist.[68] In 1923 historian and critic Stella Hope Shurtleff launched the Thursday Art Previews (1923–1935) to build the public's confidence in its ability to appreciate and enjoy works of art.[69] These lectures proved so successful that the William Claytons established the Shurtleff Foundation to underwrite free public talks by Mrs. Shurtleff at the museum, and these lectures continued until the early 1950s. In the 1930s Susan Vaughan Clayton, Ima Hogg, and other supporters formed a group to underwrite Shurtleff's research for a history of art and art museums in Texas. By November 1924 Director James Chillman was offering public talks on Saturdays, and the Art League was sponsoring special lectures "by representative artists and people of Houston who have studied the old world masters in their native haunts." Because so many league members were decorating new homes in the 1920s, Mrs. Chillman gave a series of talks about decoration and furniture in 1924.[70] The Houston Friends of Art, founded in 1926 to secure works for the permanent collection, also promoted museum membership. A museum school organized by Art League volunteers opened in the fall of 1927 and two years later offered its first free class to twenty-five talented children who, regardless of residence or financial status, "express a recognizable aptitude for color and line." For several years Art League founder Florence Fall, Will Hogg, the Claytons, Joseph Cullinan, and other museum advocates financed these free classes.[71]

Loan exhibitions from commercial gallery owners in New York City who were keen to build a clientele among the wealthy oil barons, shows of work by local artists, and museum art school displays stimulated lively discussion among patrons, while museum space devoted to "half-dollar" exhibits that displayed local collectibles helped convince viewers that "art collectors need not be rich."[72] The Hoggs, Mayor Oscar Holcombe, and Houston's civic leadership joined hands January 9 23, 1926, to sponsor a Program for Leading Living American Artists. Volunteers from more than fifty civic clubs as diverse as the Chamber of Commerce, the United Daughters of the Confederacy, the Club of Applied Psychology, and the Lumberman's Club welcomed the public and affirmed the museum's civic purpose. In January 1931 cultural critic Hubert Roussel declared the city "abloom with old masters" thanks to a "big show" (January 3–18, 1931) of works by El Greco, Franz Hals, Gainsborough, Goya, and other European luminaries of the seventeenth and eighteenth centuries, courtesy of the Reinhardt Galleries of New York. Hanging with this "glorious" show were seventy examples of "bold, vivid" works by Frederic Remington from the Hogg Brothers collection, "far and away the most representative group" by this artist.[73] During its first decades, the museum also brought works by contemporary realist Rockwell Kent, who told Houston artists in 1938 that they "must evolve their own culture," not mimic New York dictates. Although fully aware of the public's cultural conservatism, the museum introduced Houstonians to the abstract painting and sculpture of leading international contemporaries (1928, 1929) and the lithographs of Mexican artist José Clemente Orozco (1930).[74]

The museum may have struggled to build financial backing, but it was rich in volunteer friends during the Depression years. Former Art League members continued to welcome visitors, oversee educational activities, and hold fund-raising events. In 1930 they were joined by members of the Garden Club of Houston, founded in 1924, who offered to design and maintain the grounds. Estelle Sharp, a museum trustee and Garden Club member, commissioned landscape architect Ruth London to prepare a master plan for the grounds in 1931. Lack of funds precluded execution of the scheme, but a reduced plan for the point at which Montrose and Main intersected was completed in 1937 after the City Council approved $600 on August 12, 1936, to build a concrete bench.[75] In 1932 the Junior League, formed in Houston in 1924, began a volunteer tradition at the museum that continues to the present and has incorporated tours for students from public schools since 1943.

Most important for the poorly staffed museum was the organization in May 1939 of the Museum Guild, created by thirteen women who lived near the museum and wanted to "supplement the work of the Museum staff with special regard to those projects which come outside the regular Museum appropriations, either of time or money."[76] Director James Chillman and curator Adaline Wellborn Bruhl outlined how volunteers could keep the staff "in touch with practically every phase of life in this community" by cooperating with other arts groups and publicizing museum activities. Within two years, sixty volunteers were maintaining satellite exhibits at the Second National Bank, cataloguing library possessions, sponsoring summer concerts on the terrace, and serving refreshments in the lounge.[77] Nancy Tips, a founding member of the guild, approached her husband, KPRC radio station Manager Kern Tips, about a fifteen-minute public service weekly program to cover "every possible point at which art may touch the consciousness of the general public." Broadly interpreted, the project, christened *Look and Listen* in September 1939, included programs by Chillman on art, programs on slum clearance, on the San Jacinto Memorial, on the romance of gems by a Corrigan's Jewelry store manager, and on the murals and sculptures at City Hall.[78] Lacking paid staff, the museum relied on the hardworking volunteers to advertise activities and keep the doors open until after World War II. As a result citizens felt the museum was indeed built by and for them.

IMA'S COLLECTIONS OF WORKS ON PAPER
AND SOUTHWESTERN ART

As chairwoman of the Accessions Committee in 1927–1928 and member again in 1930–1932, Ima was well apprised of museum needs and monetary shortfalls. In 1927 she joined Estelle Sharp, the William Claytons, the W. S. Farishes, and Houston Friends of Art to purchase *American Motherhood* by Charles W. Hawthorne for the permanent collection.[79] During these years she formed two collections that extended museum offerings to new areas and expanded traditional definitions of fine art: works on paper by contemporary artists and Native American art of the Southwest. Ima enjoyed both collections in her home for some years, but correspondence indicates that she always intended to place them in the museum's care.

Ima first explored late-nineteenth- and early-twentieth-century paintings and sculpture on her travels abroad and during her residence in New York City. New York's establishment had not yet embraced contemporary modernist artists in the late 1920s. Dealers Valentine Dudensing and Pierre Matisse displayed Miro, Matisse, Picasso, and the cubists; Julien Levy Gallery sold surrealist works; and the J. B. Neumann Gallery featured German expressionism. But the Metropolitan Museum owned no works painted after 1900, and the Museum of Modern Art (1929) and the Whitney Museum of American Art (1930) were still on the drawing boards. Although first attracted to American antiques, Ima quickly turned to other media. In 1928 while in New York she purchased her first example of twentieth-century art, *Meditation (Portrait of Lorette)* by Henri Matisse (circa 1916). The oil painting graced a wall in the drawing room at Bayou Bend until 1948, when Ima gave it to the museum.[80]

In 1929 Ima set out on what proved to be a great art-collecting adventure—a summer trip to Russia, Norway, and Finland followed by a sojourn in Munich, Berlin, and Paris. In Russia she experienced abstract expressionism for the first time and was fascinated, confiding to friend Julia Ideson, "the Russian experience was the richest I ever had."[81] As soon as she turned back to Western Europe she began examining works on paper by giants of the contemporary art scene. While in Munich in August 1929, she purchased work by well-known French contemporaries including Henri Matisse. In Paris that September, she acquired four Picasso prints and the Picasso pastel *Three Women at the Fountain* (1921) that would be displayed in her home until the 1960s. While traveling with Will during the summer of 1930, Ima discovered works on paper by a less accepted and more daring group of modernists, Oskar Kokoschka, Lyonel Feininger, and Paul Klee. Intrigued by German expressionism, she expanded her collection in the winter of 1931 to include works by Wassily Kandinsky, Kathe Kollwitz, and several other modernists who were represented by a German dealer in New York. In the fall of 1931, while touring in Mexico City, she purchased her first watercolors by

Roberto Montenegro, an artist she continued to collect through the 1930s.[82]

Museum records indicate that many of the eighty-four prints, drawings, and watercolors Ima gave to the museum in 1939 were always intended for the museum's collection even though each work "seems to have been selected because of its unique appeal to the discriminating taste of the collector." Ima asked galleries to ship her purchases directly to the museum, and she haggled over prices and demanded special "museum" discounts because she intended to form a public collection.[83] Chillman had counseled with Ima about her purchases and must have been eager to accommodate his good friend, as the acquisitions remained in her home for nearly a decade. In the fall of 1937 Ima made a formal offer to transfer the works on paper to museum possession, pending necessary cataloguing and curatorial work. By then her collection encompassed works by European, American, and Mexican artists.[84] In June 1939 the works on paper were moved to the museum.[85] Expressing "deep personal thanks" for a gift that "enriched the collections many fold," Director Chillman relayed "delight" and told Ima that the individual items were of "high artistic value" and assembled "with a taste and sensitive discrimination for which any words of congratulation seem inadequate."[86] Ima's gift provided important additions to the museum's collection, secured Houston's first examples of works on paper by well-known late-nineteenth- and early-twentieth-century artists, and enabled the museum to begin building a department of prints and drawings. Indeed, a watercolor figure study introduced Houston to John Singer Sargent, and lithographs by George Bellows and Japanese-born Yasuo Kuniyoshi were the first examples of these artists to enter the permanent collection.

A museum summary of Ima's holdings aptly noted that the German examples reflect introspection, intellectual curiosity, and an "effort to penetrate further into the unknown," while the American group illustrated Ima's personal taste and "sympathetic and understanding regard" for the artists, most of whom were her friends or acquaintances.[87] Years later, Ima told Bayou Bend curator David Warren that she was interested in the "tonal aspect" of Kandinsky and Klee, who incorporated musical ideas in their works. She also remarked that she enjoyed the "private aspect" of works on paper, which could be stored in a drawer and easily examined as one would a book or small object. Except for the larger Picasso pastels, Ima did not frame or display any works on paper at Bayou Bend; nor were these objects listed in 1933 room inventories, further confirming both their intimate appeal and their ultimate destination at the museum.[88]

In December 1966, Ima transferred ownership of Picasso's *Three Women at the Fountain* and *Heads of Two Women* to the Varner–Bayou Bend Heritage Fund, established in 1956 to allow her to use tax benefits to acquire, hold, transfer, and manage property destined for the Museum of Fine Arts or for other philanthropic projects. The trust sold *Heads of Two Women* to the Norton Simon Foundation in 1968 with the understanding that it would be given to a museum in Texas. In August 1969 the Varner–Bayou Bend trustees voted unanimously to donate Ima's beloved *Three Women* to the museum. Museum patrons and journalists celebrated Ima's generosity with receptions and extensive press coverage. In her small but important collection of works on paper Ima had satisfied personal needs while "greatly increas[ing] the community's aesthetic wealth."[89]

The Hoggs had long been intrigued by indigenous cultures in Texas, New Mexico, Arizona, and Mexico. Their library contained several volumes on the conflict between Anglo settlers and their Mexican overlords that ended in formation of the Texas Republic; Will and Mike owned extensive ranchland in northern Mexico during the 1920s; and Tom finally settled on a ranch in Arizona, where Ima visited him during the 1930s and 1940s. Why Ima decided to form a collection of pueblo art for the museum is not clear, although her motives for acquiring the objects are suggested by her deed of gift and by a KPRC *Look and Listen* segment in July 1941. Ima believed pueblo art represented the finest craftsmanship of urban Native Americans and as such was as important an element of America's heritage as the products of eighteenth-century New England artisans. Sometime in the 1920s Ima "discovered that the American Indian possessed a rare feeling for beauty, a fine sense of design, and superior craftsmanship"—qualities that characterized all Ima's collections. She spent several years "studying and carefully collecting this indigenous American art."[90] Her collection, although not comprehensive, had "been selected with some care" for "a museum which intends to have a department of Southwest Art."[91]

With Ima Hogg it is difficult to know exactly who articulated the intention of forming this department of Southwest Art for the museum. Was Ima intrigued by kachina dolls and Southwestern pottery and jewelry on trips to Arizona and Santa Fe in the late 1920s? In a burst of enthusiasm did she tell Chillman she wanted to form a collection for the museum? Or did he suggest that Ima underwrite the cost of a lecture on American Indian art in February 1930 and encourage her to build a collection appropriate for museum display?[92] In February 1929 Buton Staplie of Coolidge, New Mexico, corresponded with "Irma" Hogg about a necklace, an exhibit, and a lecture, and in February 1930, Ima helped Director Chillman curate a Loan Exhibition of Houston-Owned Indian Handcrafts from Crafts del Navajo of Coolidge (February 2–23, 1930).[93] American Indian pottery was a subject of interest in 1930 to journalist and Hogg family friend Dorothy Hoskins, who agreed with Ima that Native American ceramics represented high-quality urban craftsmanship of the pueblo culture. Hoskins noted that these important products, which married design and function, were fashioned by women artists.[94] All her life Ima supported professional aspirations of women in the arts and social sciences, and she may have hoped to encourage these female artisans by displaying their products in a museum.

Ima made her first purchases of Southwestern art in September 1928 from Fred Harvey in Albuquerque, and she discovered several objects in Santa Fe and Zuni, New Mexico, in the fall of 1932. During a three-month stay in New Mexico in 1934, she found several pieces at the Old Santa Fe Trading Post and bought the sixty-one Hopi kachinas, four musical instruments, and one large jar that Ina Sizer Cassidy had collected between 1912 and 1933. Correspondence in June 1935 with the Spanish and Indian Trading Company reveals Ima's tough bargaining and clear intention of donating her purchases to a museum; she demanded and received a "museum" discount of nearly 20 percent on thirty-five items. Although she continued to buy items in the 1940s, she had essentially satisfied her goals by 1936 when she began lending watercolors to the museum for summer exhibits. Ima approached the purchases with her characteristic intellectual curiosity and eye for beauty. Before turning over objects permanently to the museum she corresponded with experts at the School of American Research in Santa Fe and at the Indian Department in Albuquerque regarding the ethnography of nineteenth-century examples and information about contemporary artists, particularly the important Martinez family of potters from the Pueblo San Ildefonso.[95]

Photographs of the library at Bayou Bend taken in the 1930s or early 1940s show the room furnished with several examples of North American pottery, but Ima gradually placed the entire collection on long-term loan at the museum. In 1941 she told Chillman of her intention to make the loans permanent and in August 1943 set forth the terms of her gift: the gift would be executed officially in 1944; should the collection no longer fit the museum's exhibition mission, trustees would convey it to another museum in Texas; she reserved the right to borrow items of jewelry— which she did frequently during the next three decades; the gift was made anonymously; objects were to be labeled "Bayou Bend Collection"; and

Ima provided $1,200 to construct exhibit cases. The board unanimously endorsed her generosity in November 1943 and launched what became an extensive Art of the Americas Collection.[96] With the transfer of the American Indian Collection to the museum, Ima established a pattern that would guide the subsequent transfer of her entire Bayou Bend property to museum custody. First she worked with the museum to make her gift at a time when the staff was prepared to receive a large collection; next she sought expert advice to verify the collection's value and discover whatever could be learned about each object; and finally, she provided funds to help prepare objects and exhibit space. This method of transfer through loan exhibits and subsequent gift educated the public, generated interest in the subject matter, and allowed Ima to take advantage of tax laws.

By 1944, when the museum celebrated its twentieth anniversary, the Hoggs had provided it with three major collections that greatly expanded the breadth and depth of museum offerings: Hogg Brothers Remington Collection, Works on Paper, and Southwestern Art. The family also had devoted years of service to board committees and loaned individual works of art to numerous exhibits. Ima served as museum trustee (1925–1933) and an advisory trustee (1955–1960 and 1962–1967) and was named a life trustee in January 1970. During her tenure she was chairman of the accessions committee (1927–1928, 1930–1931) and Bayou Bend advisory committee (1959, member until 1975), and served on the entertainment (1926–1927), endowment (1939), and buildings (1955–1959) committees. She served as honorary curator of Early American art from 1948 to 1956. Mike purchased furniture in the Federal and Queen Anne styles and enjoyed Chinese porcelains and Oriental rugs in his home, but he was not a major collector. Nonetheless, his interest in the museum's success never wavered, and he was elected trustee in 1939, served until his death in 1941, and participated on the finance (1939) and budget (1940) committees. Mike's widow, Alice Hogg Hanszen, became an active advisory trustee in 1963 and a life trustee ten years later. She served with Ima on the Bayou Bend advisory committee (1963–1970, 1974–1976) and was an important benefactress during these years.[97]

Although Mike was not always enthusiastic about lending objects to the museum, Ima loaned two bronzes to an exhibition in March–April 1929, a sampler to the Silhouettes and Samplers exhibition in April–May 1929, and a candle stand in March 1930. That year she participated in the José Clemente Orozco exhibition of drawings and lithographs, and in 1947 she loaned Matisse's *Girl in Green (Meditation)* to 55 Works of Modern Art Owned in Houston (January 12–February 3, 1947). In February 1957

Ima loaned a Picasso pastel, and Alice loaned a Maurice de Vlaminck still life to a museum exhibit featuring nineteenth- and twentieth-century French painters in Houston collections. From February 26 through March 4, 1957, Colonial Portraits in the Ima Hogg Collection demonstrated the importance of her newest collecting interest. Included in the brief loan were John Singleton Copley's *Mrs. Paul Richard* and *Portrait of a Boy*, Charles Willson Peale's *Portrait of a Girl* (now identified as *Boy with Toy Horse*), two portraits by John Wollaston, Joseph Badger's *Portrait of Elbridge Gerry*, and portraits by Joseph Blackburn and John Greenwood. During these years when the museum was so dependent on works from private Houston collections, curators mounted numerous small exhibitions of short duration, which enabled the museum to show a wide variety of objects to its public without depriving owners of prized possessions for too long. The exhibitions, fully insured by the museum, also encouraged Houstonians to purchase quality art for their homes or offices and share these collections with the public.[98]

MUSEUM EXPANSION, 1945–1977

During World War II, Director Chillman and board Chairman Ray L. Dudley promoted the museum as a community asset that would "strengthen public morale by providing . . . instruction, . . . recreation, and . . . a place of quiet contemplation." Dudley emphasized "the inspiration" of art and music as beneficial and soothing. Like his friend Ima, Dudley believed that cultural institutions would help ensure successful prosecution of the war and facilitate postwar rehabilitation.[99] Despite wartime pressures, the 1940s generated riches for the museum. Ima's gifts of works on paper (1939), the Remington Collection (1943), and the Southwest Collection of Native American Art (1944) and Annette Finnigan's final gift of fine old lace (1940) were overshadowed by the extraordinary generosity of two New Yorkers, Edith A. and Percy S. Straus, whose oldest son had migrated to Houston. Announced the morning Japanese planes struck Pearl Harbor, December 7, 1941, their gift of fifty-nine paintings and works on paper and twenty-eight sculptures and reliefs raised the value of museum offerings to unforeseen heights and enabled the city to take a major step toward "Great Art Center" status.[100] Percy Straus, former president and chairman of R. H. Macy and Company, and his wife sought the assistance of scholars and experts to purchase a large collection of Italian Renaissance works of art and major examples of the Flemish, German, French, and British schools as well as several Roman and medieval objects. Although residents of New York, the Strauses were friends of Jesse Jones and wanted to enrich an art center removed from New York's vast artistic treasury. Hoping to enhance their son's social position, they chose a Southwest boomtown pushing to achieve international recognition in business and the arts.[101]

In 1947 Sara Campbell Blaffer, widow of Humble Oil Company founder Robert Lee Blaffer, announced that she would donate works to the museum by building the Robert Lee Blaffer Memorial Collection of European Masters (1947). In 1952 her son, John H. Blaffer, and his wife, Camilla, donated more than $250,000 to construct the Blaffer Wing and complete William Ward Watkin's 1924 design.[102] In March 1948, heirs of Frank Prior Sterling donated the land and home at 1505 South Boulevard to the museum in his memory. Museum trustees sold the property to insurance executive and symphony supporter Gus Wortham in 1950 and used the funds to renovate interior museum space as the Sterling Galleries (open 1953). These galleries were quickly filled by a gift from the Kress Foundation, which informed museum trustees in 1949 that it wished to place thirty-three paintings on permanent loan in Houston. In 1930 Samuel H. Kress, one of the most important art collectors in the United States and a friend of Jesse Jones, had given the museum its first Italian masterpiece, *Holy Family with Donatrice* (circa 1550) by Lorenzo Lotto.[103] In 1933 part of Kress's touring collection of Renaissance, baroque, and eighteenth-century masterpieces was exhibited in Houston during an eight-month tour of the United States. The Kress treasures complemented the Straus installation and became a permanent gift in 1963.[104]

These donations expanded the quality and depth of museum holdings and spurred civic interest in all art genres. The Associated Artists of Houston exhibited and sold works by its members during these years. In 1948 volunteers chartered the Contemporary Arts Association to stimulate interest in contemporary artists of international repute, and several local artists formed the Houston Art League to support shared studio space. Local artists attuned to international trends and newcomer art patrons Dominique and John de Menil, chairman of Schlumberger Oil Field Services company, challenged the museum's focus on art of the past and demanded that more attention be paid to contemporary expression. As businessmen introduced the latest technology to Houston's cutting-edge economy, so too, they argued, should Houstonians support the latest trends in artistic development. During these years the Menils began five decades of cultural leadership that culminated in the opening of their own museum on June 7, 1987.[105] Houston's segregated art scene shattered when mural painter John Biggers and sculptor Carroll Simms arrived at Texas State University for Negroes (now Texas Southern University) in 1949 to establish a fine arts department. Stunned by the lack of artistic opportunity for minority students, Biggers nurtured self-expression and established a national reputation that could not be ignored by Houston's white art patrons.[106]

While the Menils hosted "a parade of some of the most creative people in the art world" in their home, the museum also recognized that the dynamic 1950s demanded new approaches.[107] By 1950 the museum could no longer comfortably house its collections, loan exhibits, outreach programs, staff, and volunteers. Postwar economic prosperity and its attendant population explosion prompted trustees to consider remodeling and expanding the facility. Trustee Nina Cullinan, who was keenly aware of space limitations and eager to promote better appreciation for contemporary art, donated more than $600,000 for a major addition to the museum. The gallery was to be named for her parents, Joseph S. and Lucie Halm Cullinan, and was supported by an additional gift of $100,000 for maintenance. Taking a bold step, the trustees hired internationally known architect Mies van der Rohe to develop a master plan, undertake renovations, and design the Cullinan addition. Nina Cullinan's generosity inspired substantial gifts from Olga Keith Wiess, Jesse and Mary Gibbs Jones, and Harris and Carroll Masterson to remodel existing space for galleries that continue to memorialize their donors.

Trustees recognized that physical and program expansion demanded a full-time director and enlarged professional staff. James Chillman had served valiantly as part-time director and Rice professor for thirty years. Although the board begged him to remain as full-time director, Chillman could not forgo an assured academic pension and other benefits for an experimental director's post that promised no financial security. In April 1954 he accepted well-deserved emeritus status and made way for Lee H. B. Malone, a Yale-educated specialist in Italian Renaissance art, at the time the area most extensively represented in the museum's collections. Malone oversaw a shift from volunteer to full-time professional staff, created the Permanent Endowment Fund (January 1956), opened the Wiess and Jones Memorial Galleries (January 1958), and organized the gala dedication of Cullinan Hall (October 1958).

In these years of transition, the museum attracted new friends whose generosity and imagination benefited Houston for decades after Ima Hogg's death. When wildcatter Hugh Roy Cullen's daughter Agnes

Cullen Arnold died in 1969, family members established the Agnes Cullen Arnold Accessions Endowment Fund to honor her love of painting and sculpture and to acquire masterworks for the museum in perpetuity. Alice Pratt Brown, wife of entrepreneurial builder George R. Brown, developed a love affair with art as a young girl and all her life took frequent "art trips" to visit collections, purchase treasures, and support favorite artists. In 1964 the family's Brown Foundation trustees created the Alice Pratt Brown Museum Fund in her honor to support museum operations and maintenance and to begin a tradition of family generosity that continues a half-century later.[108] Alice's sister-in-law Margaret, wife of Herman Brown, served for years on the museum's board of trustees, enlisted several important donors for the museum, and financed important purchases, often to honor family members. A woman who understood the museum's broad mission, Margaret Brown helped Ima transform Bayou Bend to a house museum as a member of the Bayou Bend advisory committee and encouraged contemporary artists as a member of the modern art committee. When the museum undertook a $15 million capital campaign in 1970–1971, the Brown Foundation provided $4 million to build the Mies van der Rohe–designed Brown Pavilion, which more than doubled exhibition space.[109] In 1973–1974 the Becks established the John A. and Audrey Jones Beck Fund to acquire impressionist works of art, and they began placing pieces from their own collection on long-term loan at the museum.

The catalog of Hogg family benevolence to the museum continued to expand as both Ima and Alice pursued new projects in the 1960s. Alice married family friend and neighbor Harry Hanszen in 1948 but was widowed again a few years later. In the 1960s she began to collect seriously and loaned works to museum exhibits. She also provided generous funds so important works like Claude Monet's *Waterlilies* (given 1968), Ferdinand Bol's *Woman at Her Dressing Table* (given 1969), Benvenuto di Giovanni's *Saint Francis* (given 1970), and Odilon Redon's charcoal *Arbres* (given 1972) could be added to museum holdings. Alice worked closely with Ima during Bayou Bend's reorganization as a member of the advisory committee and provided funds to purchase a silver tea set (circa 1783–1800) by New Jersey silversmith Henry Lupp, a sideboard (1825–1835) attributed to the workshop of New York cabinet maker Joseph Meeks, and a Philadelphia loo table (1825–1835) for the Chillman Suite.[110]

Most important, Alice developed a friendship with Director James Johnson Sweeney (1961–1968) and helped him purchase the museum's first major collection of pre-Columbian art. The public had been spellbound by a giant sixteen-ton, nine-foot Olmec head that gloomily surveyed the Bissonnet Street entrance while on loan for several months in 1965. That year Alice gave the museum clay, bone, and stone figures, vessels, and vases and jade ornaments comprising a group of more than three hundred objects from Mexico that had been collected by San Antonio residents Ralph Fabacher and Higford Griffiths and authenticated by Gordon F. Ekholm of the American Museum of Natural History. Lauded as "one more evidence of her wise and loyal help," her gift "notably" enriched the museum's ability to interpret native cultures of the Americas by reformulating Ima's "department of Southwest Art" as the Art of the Americas department. Museum patrons accepted the gift enthusiastically when the works were put on display in February 1966.[111] The exhibit's award-winning catalog cemented Alice's interest, and she continued to provide generous gifts until her death in 1977.

Houston's great Museum of Fine Arts, with its extensive campus, long roster of donors, and comprehensive collection, reflects the power of cultural philanthropy and individual imagination to enrich lives, erect institutions "for the use of the people," and create a community identity through "the collective effort of many." The Hogg family used the municipal art museum to promote Houston as a haven of humanitarian values. Through the museum's collections, Houston's citizens could become citizens of the world by connecting with traditions of culture from all historic periods and by learning to appreciate imaginative expression from all regions of the globe. The Hoggs understood that their museum formed a critical piece of the institutional infrastructure that defined a great city. They organized fund drives to build the institution and encouraged business executives to follow their example as donors to the museum itself and as framers of corporate art collections that linked fine arts to sound commercial practice. They propelled the museum forward by lending works to exhibits, by nurturing local and Texas artists, and by making the museum the final custodian of their own collections. As pacesetters, the Hoggs characterized fine art as inclusive and encouraged Houstonians to identify with a broad heritage that embraced decorative arts from the Eastern Seaboard, pottery and kachina dolls from the Old Southwest, and pre-Columbian artifacts from Mexico, as well as art of contemporary European masters. They made sure that the museum built by the people was open to all by supporting free admission, special attention to black visitors, educational programs, and an unintimidating atmosphere that suggested that anyone could become a collector or enjoy art. Through art, the Hoggs believed, Houstonians could understand their American heritage. Through art, Houstonians could move closer to the urban ideal imagined by the Hoggs, whose dream for a world-class municipal museum has been fulfilled by generations of Houston art lovers "willing to share their treasures with others."[112]

Chapter 7
The Bridges That Unite Us

March winds whipped azalea blossoms and warped graceful arches of water spraying from a fountain in Bayou Bend's Diana Garden as art collectors and dignitaries gathered in a sheltering tent to celebrate the culmination of a dream. Swathed in furs and sporting one of her signature hats, Ima Hogg looked through the tent to the sunlit gardens beyond and thanked her "many, many dear friends and visitors" who had come to help her dedicate Bayou Bend, her home of thirty-seven years, as the decorative arts wing of the Museum of Fine Arts, Houston. Now, she told them, she was "free to pursue my other projects and . . . watch the sunsets from my high-rise apartment. . . . While I shall continue to love Bayou Bend . . . in one sense I have always considered I was holding [it] in trust for this day. Now Bayou Bend is truly yours!"[1]

Every year since 1934, Ima had opened her garden to the public in March so her azaleas could be enjoyed by all. On March 5, 1966, she relinquished custody of house, garden, and treasured furnishings to Museum of Fine Arts trustees, who would preserve her gift for the people of Texas forever. Chilly weather could not cool the warmth of her generosity or the enthusiasm of orators. Museum board Chairman Edward Rotan noted, "All the beauty we see around us . . . is essentially the creation of one dedicated person. It represents the culmination of years of generous application of study, imagination, courage, knowledge and resources all pointed to this particular day." Museum Director James Johnson Sweeney spoke directly to Miss Hogg: "You have brought together history, aesthetic, sentiment and a tireless devotion to an ideal. . . . Bayou Bend, Miss Hogg, is your 'poem,' which you have turned over to us for safe keeping and enjoyment." Texas Governor John Connally, Houston Mayor Louie Welch, Winterthur Museum Senior Research Fellow Charles F. Montgomery, and University of Texas Chancellor Harry Ransom praised her generosity, devotion, foresight, and genius "in projecting the fact of times past into the imagination of the future."[2]

Saturday's formal dedication marked the main event of a weekend that "belongs to Miss Ima Hogg." Ima entertained important collectors from across the United States, Houston leaders, and current and former governors on Friday evening at a black-tie dinner at the Houston Country Club. Director Sweeney, his wife, and members of the museum board honored the "twinkling-eyed octogenarian" at a museum reception after the Saturday dedication. Sporting "an orchid rose and black print dress, a black ensemble coat, and an orchid hat," Ima received her friends and well-wishers. That evening several of Ima's close friends entertained dedication participants at small dinner parties in their homes.[3] With appropriate fanfare, Bayou Bend and its caretakers had begun the long journey to bring "Texas, an Empire in itself, . . . closer to the heart of an American heritage which unites us."[4]

IMA'S DREAM

The March 1966 celebrations crowned years of hard work that began as a dream imagined in 1920 when Ima bought her first piece of American furniture. Immediately she knew she wanted to form a collection of American decorative objects for a museum in Texas. Never mind that there was no museum in Texas; never mind that few scholars deemed American furniture worthy of attention; Ima knew what she wanted, and for a decade she and beloved brother Will were dedicated accomplices. Over the years the collection grew and grew until it filled twenty-two rooms at Bayou Bend. Encouraged by friends on the museum board and by similar projects in the Northeast, Ima concluded that she could best display her collections and transmit America's heritage if she transformed her home and gardens into a public museum and park. By the 1950s, she had decided to create period rooms similar to those at Winterthur in Delaware or at the American Wing of the Metropolitan Museum of Art in New York City. In these period settings she would entirely withdraw her personality so that each room could tell some part of America's story through presentation of decorative arts objects.

Always fascinated by history, Ima believed material culture as much as archival evidence explained the values of America's founders and illuminated America's story, but the process of transformation from house to museum was complex. Bayou Bend is an outstanding example of 1920s colonial revival architecture, worthy of preservation in its own right. Despite decades of collecting, Ima recognized that her collection was yet incomplete, and she knew that discoveries made every day changed scholarly readings of the past. Guided by Charles Montgomery and other experts, Ima developed a multifaceted approach to her period rooms. Some, like the Murphy Room, which houses seventeenth- and eighteenth-century examples, became gallery repositories for artifacts of an era. Others, like the mid-nineteenth-century Belter Parlor, re-create period settings. Still others, like the dining room with its 1928 canvas wall coverings that depict dogwoods and peonies on gold leaf, retained colonial revival influences appropriate to the house itself. Whether collecting an object or transforming a room, Ima looked for aesthetic value, historic importance, and cultural meaning. Through the objects she arranged she hoped to lead later generations back in time but forward to a clearer understanding of their cultural heritage.

Houston in the 1950s inspired public relations hyperbole. Declared number one in the value of its industrial plant and the largest city in the South by 1950 census takers, Houston also boasted the most hospital beds in the state by 1951 and was named the second-largest port in the nation in 1952. Building programs threatened gridlock at Rice Institute, the University of Houston, Baylor College of Medicine, the University of Texas Dental College, and the Texas Medical Center, whose ambitious backers lured medical personnel recently discharged from service in World War II and the Korean conflict with promises of expansion into every medical arena. Air-conditioned office buildings punched the skyline as corporations moved regional and national headquarters to the vibrant metropolis, and freeways linked suburban developments to downtown and industrial centers.[5] Volunteer groups expanded opera, ballet, and theater offerings, and Ima Hogg, as president of the Houston Symphony (1946–1956), sponsored artists and conductors of world-class status. At this moment of commercial vigor and public excitement, had Houston at last created "a climate essential to the flowering of genius"?[6] Perhaps Ima thought so, because on December 30, 1956, museum trustees announced that she would deliver Bayou Bend's house, gardens, and collections into their care.

Such generosity was unprecedented in Houston or in Texas. In 1951 Henry Francis du Pont had established his Delaware home at Winterthur as a museum of Americana, but benefactions of this magnitude continued to be exceptional cause for celebration. Ima had long insisted that her collections were intended for public enjoyment, and archival records bear witness to her sincerity and consistency of purpose. As she began to reconsider her estate after Mike's death in 1941, Ima realized that the sheer number of objects at Bayou Bend would overwhelm any extant or future Texas museum. She and Houston Museum of Fine Arts board President Ray L. Dudley (1941–1943) discussed transferring the Bayou Bend property, house, and contents to the museum's custody. At the time she quailed before "seemingly insurmountable obstacles" but, intrigued, soon "began to entertain Mr. Dudley's suggestion as a possibility."[7] As usual with Ima's projects, a long period of gestation and negotiation preceded the announcement of final provisions. Plans to transfer her home, gardens, and Americana collections took shape in the 1940s and early 1950s and were confirmed during a house party at Bayou Bend when she discussed the proposed gift with fellow collectors who were in town for the Houston Antiques Forum on March 9–11, 1956. Not surprisingly, they urged her to proceed.[8]

Ima's donations of the Remington, Southwest Art, and Works on Paper Collections tested the museum's ability to absorb, display, and appreciate her gifts while making room at Bayou Bend for new purchases. After a collecting hiatus during the 1930s Ima returned to the quest for American decorative arts objects of highest aesthetic and historical value in the 1940s, and the museum intensified its pursuit of her patronage by naming her honorary curator of Early American Art (1948–1956).[9] The Museum continued to suffer budget shortfalls, and the board agreed in the immediate postwar years to nominate amateur experts as volunteer curators, but their choice also suggests that the subtle dance of courtship was well under way.[10] Invoices and correspondence from 1943 on show the evolution of Ima's thinking as she gradually clarified her purpose to arrange her collection so its didactic message would tell America's story. For some years Ima had transferred ownership of specific objects to the museum, always with the understanding that they remain in situ at Bayou Bend until such time as she could no longer use them. In December 1953 she received assurances that these and any prospective gifts from her "rare and distinguished collection of furniture and other art treasures" would be properly preserved and displayed. In this "special exception" to the museum's policy not to give assurances about future retention or display of gifts and bequests, the museum tried to assuage Ima's fears that her wishes might be disregarded or her collections dispersed.[11] With this promise, Ima's plans to transfer her property to the museum took firm shape, and her negotiations with museum trustees intensified.

Two decades later Ima described these discussions as an "awful time." Friends remembered that people were "so ugly to her . . . she just took to her bed" with sciatica. Even Director James Johnson Sweeney seemed "indifferent."[12] Neighbors in the independent subdivision of Homewoods had to be persuaded that their tranquil enclave would not be invaded by tourists, and in 1954 Ima asked her lawyers to prepare consent forms for presentation to Homewoods residents, who did not all comply until December 1956.[13] Baker and Botts lawyer Francis G. Coates, the museum's board president from June 1953 to May 1958, was eager to accept Ima's extraordinary gift but felt he could not recommend board acceptance unless Ima promised to establish an endowment to cover operation, upkeep, and maintenance costs.[14] Ima wanted the museum to match any monetary gifts she might make. Both Ima and the museum needed the city's cooperation to develop parking on city property across the bayou from her home and to construct a footbridge for public access to Bayou Bend.[15] Despite these hurdles, Ima was sufficiently satisfied with preliminary discussions by July 1956 to draw up a detailed four-page plan for converting her home into a decorative arts center. On September 4 she asked Coates to seek board approval for the plans, which included her promise to establish a trust fund to cover operating costs—a gift that would be matched by museum fund-raising. Board members accepted her terms at their September 17, 1956, meeting.[16]

Then began a decade of preparation during which it became clear that Ima had thought about every aspect of Bayou Bend's future, including funding, governance, preparation of the collection, docent instructors, and care of the gardens. On November 14, 1956, Ima, Alice Hogg Hanszen, and Dixon H. Cain became trustees of the Varner–Bayou Bend Heritage Fund, an estate-planning instrument that allowed Ima to disperse her estate through a complex series of property and stock transfers to a Bayou Bend endowment trust and to her other eleemosynary projects.[17] When the museum announced Ima's gift on Sunday, December 30, 1956, it described Bayou Bend as "one of three leading collections of Americana anywhere in the world" and explained that Ima would continue to reside at Bayou Bend and supervise arrangement of her collections "for the purpose of opening the house and grounds to the public."[18] In May 1957 the board resolved to accept conveyance of Bayou Bend to the museum and promised to defend the gift against any legal action taken to prevent Ima's wishes from being carried out. By December 1959 legal and funding issues were resolved, and Bayou Bend officially became the property of the museum.[19]

At the January 26, 1960, board meeting, trustees honored Ima's wish that a Bayou Bend advisory committee be established to act as liaison between herself and the museum and to oversee operations and possible changes to the house's structure or the collection's contents. Trustees named her curator of Bayou Bend and unanimously approved a testimonial of "deep admiration for her lofty purpose in presenting to the citizens of Houston and the generations to follow, a rich example of their heritage."[20] The advisory committee, which held its first meeting on February 24 at Bayou Bend, developed a Friends group to raise funds that would match Ima's endowment pledge of $750,000. The committee helped establish a docent volunteer organization to explain the collection to guests and provided oversight and suggestions for the conversion process and for future development of the collection. On May 23, 1962, Ima presented a deed of gift to the museum that covered contents of the house, pending authentication by experts, and in January 1965 she announced that it was time to make final plans to complete the transfer and hire a curator.[21] David Warren, a youthful graduate of Princeton University and the Winterthur–University of Delaware program in decorative arts, began his long career as the collection's caretaker (July 1965–December 2003). Her transitional plans in place, Ima moved to a high-rise apartment, and friends helped her organize the gala dedication on March 4 and 5, 1966.

Journalists, friends, politicians, fellow collectors, oral historians— repeatedly people asked Ima Hogg why she had formed her collection and why she had given it to the people of Houston. She would reply playfully that she must have been born "with a fever for collecting" and could only "blame" her family for introducing her to beautiful relics of the past that sent her on a "mad career." She also recalled "haunting" museums in Europe and comparing "indigenous American architecture with European buildings"—a "fascinating pastime." Seriously and consistently for fifty-five years, Ima would recall an Early American chair of New England origin that she had seen in artist Wayman Adams's studio in 1920; from the moment her curiosity was aroused and her aesthetic sense excited, she knew she wanted to form a collection of American objects for a museum in Texas.[22] Although there was no museum in Texas in 1920, Ima began her quest with the enthusiastic approbation of her brothers. Indeed, in the 1920s Will and Ima often seemed engaged in a synergistic contest to see who would collect more fine objects for their homes and offices. In later years, Ima explained that she was attracted to Early American decorative arts because of their intrinsic aesthetic value, because these objects revealed the "circumstances and events surrounding the lives of our Founding Fathers," and because she hoped to inculcate in others "a greater respect for the cultural life of our early American forefathers." She herself had "learned to respect the heritage of our country more through furniture and art than anything else."[23] Without her inspired collecting, claims Founding Director Emeritus David B. Warren, there would be "virtually" no material culture from the colonial and early national periods in Texas today.[24]

Governor Hogg's children remembered their father's reverence for America's heritage. Like him, they believed that only by understanding how their forebears had lived could Americans grasp the meaning of democracy, appreciate the values incorporated in the constitutional system, and plan for the future. In forming their art collections, the Hoggs did not look to Europe for affirmation but rather to American artists and artisans whose work proclaimed the values of their times and provided lessons for the present day. Ima and Will realized that these objects best expressed the subtle transformation that occurred when Europeans encountered the open spaces and natural bounty that was the New World. "There's something peculiarly American about the work Englishmen did when they got here," Ima noted in 1966. "American furniture is not as pretentious; the proportions, carving and veneering are more pleasing to the eye. . . . American portrait painters painted for character."[25] As Southerners who traveled widely and enjoyed long sojourns in New England, residence in New York, and frequent visits to the West, Ima and Will were acutely aware of the regional differences that continued to separate Americans. By bringing examples of colonial and Early American production from the Atlantic Seaboard to a museum in the Southwest, Ima hoped in her "modest" way to erase regional misunderstandings. Texans and all Americans, she explained, shared strong reverence for personal freedom, individual action, self-sufficient survival, and plain hard work. Workshop practices of colonial cabinetmakers combined group cooperation with individual initiative and suggested to Ima a model for resolving community differences.

When Ima decided to transfer Bayou Bend and its collections to the museum, she reinforced long-held family beliefs that citizens of the United States had melded many traditions into something distinctly American. By entrusting her treasures to the people of Houston, she affirmed the family's faith that the community shared a curiosity about its heritage. In forming her collection and presenting it to the public, Ima had, in the words of museum Director James Johnson Sweeney, "given, not only a work of art, but an example of fuller living and an incentive to a fuller life."[26] No praise could have more aptly summarized Ima's progressive purpose: for her, collecting was both a pleasurable personal joy and a virtuous civic duty. Through good husbandry of her fortune and reverence for her family's values, she had found objects of beauty and historical significance "to stimulate a keener interest in the social and economic history of our country" so visitors could "delve more deeply into the roots of our American heritage."[27]

THE HOUSE

The Hoggs shaped their vision of America and its values through the structure of Bayou Bend itself as well as through the collections they amassed and the gardens Ima created. Like so many of the Hoggs' interests, the genesis and development of Bayou Bend served several goals. Will, Ima, and Mike spoke of Bayou Bend as the culmination of a dream to create the long-sought home that seemed to elude the family after its losses in the Civil War. Emily Neff, in her chronicle of the Hogg Brothers collection, suggests that Will was searching for the ideal "home" when he remodeled Varner in the 1920s. Home does seem to have had special meaning for Will in his role as paterfamilias, but Ima's relationship to the property was ambiguous.[28] Although she poured heart and soul into the planning, decoration, and care of the structure her brothers began to call "Miss Ima's house" even before it was ready for occupancy, she expressed no regrets when she left Bayou Bend. She often said the house was built only as a residence, its contents to form a "nucleus for other accessions in the decorative arts" at some museum in Texas, but she also reiterated that she had long felt she was only "holding Bayou Bend . . . in trust" until it could be dedicated to the public.[29]

Architectural historian Stephen Fox suggests a commercial purpose for the home. Developers of subdivisions often built grand dream houses, which they occupied, to advertise the ideal to which potential buyers might aspire, and over the years, Bayou Bend did serve as a model of inspired planning and high-quality construction for elite residential neighborhoods. Fox also posits the intriguing idea that Bayou Bend's placement on its site tempers crass commercialism with familial reticence. Usually developers' imposing houses faced a public thoroughfare and commanded attention through scale, placement, and landscaping. Bayou Bend, in contrast, is hidden from public view at the end of a long, winding driveway. While this seclusion could serve as a particularly enticing advertisement for the charms of protected "country" life, Fox argues that placement of the house makes concrete the Hoggs' love-hate relationship with public recognition. Although compelled by strong moral tenets to take leadership positions in the civic arena, these children of a famous

Texas politician shunned publicity. Fox suggests that their rhetoric of disinterest, like their hidden house, expressed a desire "to escape notoriety, suspicious criticism, and opposition."[30]

The scale and arrangement of the interiors at Bayou Bend indicate that the Hoggs envisioned a civic purpose for their home. If they did not at first see its potential as a house museum, they certainly understood its value as a gracious setting for civil discourse. Although welcoming and human in scale, the commodious and elegant downstairs reception rooms—a central hall, dining salon, and drawing room—could accommodate the musicales, meetings, and receptions that were frequently held there. The large, sunny library crammed with books bespoke the family's intellectual fervor and progressive conscience, and the comfortable bed-bath guest suites upstairs anticipated the stream of conductors, dignitaries, and friends who would visit the estate. Even Ima's large upstairs sitting room could easily accommodate visitors. By contrast, the home next door to Bayou Bend that Mike and Alice Hogg purchased from Judge F. C. Proctor clearly served a domestic purpose. Placed far from the road on a large wooded lot, the Norman-style house, while boasting elegant and sophisticated drawing and dining rooms, had a modest entrance and charmed visitors with its intimate book room and sun room that suggested family activity.[31]

Bayou Bend's house, outbuilding, and gardens, listed on the National Register of Historic Places and as a Recorded Texas Historical Landmark, distill most vividly a sophisticated taste refined by years of observation and study to provide an example of elegant domestic life as well as a narrative of American history. Visitors leave a winding lane in the heart of America's fourth-largest city, and like pioneer settlers before them, traverse woodland, now carefully sculpted but still retaining a natural appearance. The woods open onto a generous clearing before a handsome stucco structure built by Houston's finest craftsmen to announce man's conquest of the wild. Designed to recall Southern colonial adaptations of the Palladian English country house, the central block is joined to two wings that embrace travelers and guide their eyes back toward the central door and welcoming hall. Hidden behind the west wing and down a sloping service drive is a multipurpose two-story outbuilding that originally housed a gardener's cottage, three-car garage, servants' apartments, and storage.

Once inside the 12,000-square-foot main house, visitors are quickly drawn through the central entrance hall to a doorway opposite the entrance that opens onto a broad terrace and vast expanse of lawn, garden, and barrier woods. Interiors are organized to complement period furniture and to define public, private, and domestic functions. The curving staircase in the entrance hall bears witness to Ima's affection for the Greek Revival Texas Governor's Mansion where she had lived as a young girl. To the left of the entrance lies a symmetrical dining salon that reflects the neoclassical taste of the early republic, and to the right an elegant drawing room replicates the colonial saloon at Shirley Plantation in Virginia.[32] Long windows in these public spaces recall Charleston and New Orleans and attempt to catch whatever breezes might blow inland from the Gulf of Mexico, while high ceilings emphasize the lofty purpose of Hogg family civic discourse. The library, placed in the connecting section between the main block and the brothers' wing, uses paneling that recalls a 1740s room in the Portsmouth, Rhode Island, Metcalf Bowler House and suggests the coziness of a family gathering place with its lower ceiling and huge fireplace.[33] In their original configuration, the sitting room, tap room, and kitchen that comprised the brothers' downstairs rooms also had lower ceilings, dark wood paneling, and an intimate scale in harmony with New England traditions and domestic pleasures. In her upstairs sitting room and bedroom, Ima incorporated old floorboards and a mantel rescued from demolished buildings in Salem and Ipswich, Massachusetts, to transfer New England values to Houston and complete her personal sanctuary. Guest bedrooms feature architectural details in keeping with the colonial revival taste so popular in the 1920s.

Scholars have emphasized Bayou Bend's relationship to the "country house" and colonial revival traditions first made popular by elite families in the late nineteenth century.[34] While the country house was often set on one hundred acres or considerably more, its purpose was residential and recreational, not commercial. Experimental farms or orchards and extensive outbuildings announced the owner's hobbies, not the sources of his wealth. If quasi-public because owners invited strangers to examine specimen plants and animals or stroll through manicured gardens, these country estates still were domains of privacy. Bayou Bend, with its sole outbuilding, suggests this tradition on a suburban scale.

Because of its unique and eclectic synthesis of styles and technologies, Bayou Bend represents an important regional expression of the handsome colonial revival houses popular throughout the United States in the 1920s. Although constructed with the most up-to-date building practices and domestic amenities, Bayou Bend created a Houston style by fusing Georgian elements associated with English settlers of the Atlantic Seaboard (the Palladian five-part floor plan), Spanish elements associated with colonists of Louisiana and the Southwest (the stucco exterior and grillwork details), Greek Revival elements associated with citizens of a liberated republic (the central portico and symmetrical elevations), and Southern elements associated with Texas's antebellum past (architectural details and façades). This "Latin Colonial" fusion style accommodated a warm, humid climate as well as the owners' wish to continue nationally acclaimed residential preferences in a consistent scheme that emphasized the stability and security advertised to prospective buyers in the River Oaks and Homewoods subdivisions.[35]

John F. Staub (1892–1981) is traditionally listed as Bayou Bend's architect of record. A native of Knoxville, Tennessee, Staub graduated from the Massachusetts Institute of Technology and began his architectural practice in the offices of New Yorker Harrie T. Lindeberg, a respected and popular builder of elaborate country houses. Sent to Houston in 1921 to supervise Lindeberg commissions there, Staub remained for sixty years and became the city's most popular and enduring advocate of eclectic domestic architecture. Staub's handsome, well-built structures remain prized residences in a city whose citizens more typically destroy the old and worship the new. Staub's houses, "simple yet elegant, expensive but never vulgar," suited the aspirations of new corporate oil money as well as the taste of established Houston families.[36] According to legend, Staub met the Hogg brothers in July 1924 at a dinner on the Rice Roof at which Will introduced Hugh Potter to potential investors and explained his visionary dream of a new planned community to be called River Oaks. Staub quickly agreed to design model homes for the Hogg-Potter development and began a lifelong family friendship that led to collaboration on numerous civic projects. Staub and Ima developed their first Latin colonial design for a speculative home on Chevy Chase, and Staub adapted the floor plan of that house for his second model home, although he gave its exterior a Federal-style finish.[37] In 1926, after the Hoggs selected lot C for their future home, they invited Staub and Birdsall P. Briscoe (1876–1971) to collaborate on a site plan and house design.[38]

Staub claimed Bayou Bend as his great triumph of domestic architecture and said he and Briscoe agreed to a division of design responsibilities that allowed Staub to take the lead in building the Hoggs' home while Briscoe devoted his energies to the house being built for Judge F. C. Proctor and his wife on property adjacent to Bayou Bend.[39] Correspondence with "Mssrs. Briscoe and Staub" and equal payments to each man throughout the design and construction phases suggest that Briscoe may have had more impact on the Hoggs' home than Staub later acknowledged.[40] Briscoe, an old friend of Will Hogg's from university days, had worked closely with Will to transform Varner from a modest antebellum farmhouse to a grand colonial revival plantation. Varner's pillared façade, grafted onto the original building, purposefully recalls Mount Vernon and memorializes Will's father by making a "visual connection between [George] Washington and [Governor Hogg's] retirement to a 'simpler' life after [long years] devoted to public service," thereby linking a Texas hero to an overarching national heritage.[41] Similarly the north front of Bayou Bend boasts stately pillars and a porch overlooking the bayou in the style of colonial Virginia river homes. Briscoe and the Hoggs had discussed developing other residential neighborhoods before the River Oaks project began, and Briscoe was one of four architects hired to provide model plans for the corporation. In February 1926 Ima confided to Will that "Mr. Briscoe and Mr. Staub are working very congenially together, and I am delighted over having made this double choice."[42]

Whether it was Staub alone or Staub and Briscoe working as partners to design Bayou Bend may be a moot point because there is no question that Bayou Bend was the dream of Will and Ima Hogg. Hogg family housekeeper Gertrude Vaughn recalled that the two fought (or debated) over every issue to the bitter end while Mike watched the struggle without much comment. Ima usually won the arguments, but Will demanded weekly written reports of progress and scrutinized every detail even when out of town on his frequent business and pleasure trips. Ima sent Will a copy of the "working" plans in February 1926, explaining that she and the architects are trying to get "maximum comfort" in "minimum space" and "exterior balance in proportion." Proud of the work to date, she described the "stunning" elevations, which have "a great deal of character of old Charleston southern houses, which has always been much my idea." The south façade door closely resembles the 1803 Nathaniel Russell House in Charleston, while the outline of the north façade suggests the shape of Charles Carroll's Homewood built near Baltimore in 1801.[43] Ima recalled that she had requested the five-part Palladian floor plan and had suggested the Latin colonial stucco, cast-iron grillwork, and pink color as most appropriate for Houston's climate. Plans were progressing well by November 22, 1926, when Will returned a scheme with suggestions for improvement: location of an ironing board and maid's closet; reduction of the moth room but enlargement by two feet of the men's wing; French doors; and gun storage in the moth room instead of the trunk room.[44] Only a few days earlier the house's footprint and location had been approved.[45] On March 22, 1927, Will specified instructions about tile and color schemes for Ima's bath and for the bath and dressing rooms in the "Fat Men's Wing."[46] If possessed with expansive vision, Will was also passionate about small details.

By June 1927 Will exclaimed, "The more I look at the plans of that house and visualize that house, the more I am entranced by the simplicity and practicality and what, I think, will be the comforting loveliness of it."[47] By the summer of 1927 plans were approved and contracts drawn up with general contractor Christian J. Miller (1872–1954). Construction began and continued through most of 1928. Miller and his talented craftsmen built a magnificent residence worthy of the collections it contained and the national acclaim that quickly followed. The home incorporated period details when available. Ima had traveled about New England in the summer of 1927 hunting down woodwork, paneling, beams, bricks for the fireplaces, and old floorboards, but most of the millwork and flooring were carefully crafted onsite. By 1931 the house had been reviewed in two national publications, the first of many published references to the handsome home.[48]

After years of planning and discussion, the family finally sat down to its first meal, a breakfast on November 6, 1928, attended by Ima, Mike, Will, and their close friend and business partner Raymond Dickson. Also noted in the embossed guest book labeled "Bayou Banks" were those who served the repast, Gertrude Anderson (later Vaughn), Ben Mouton, Della Jones, and Charles Rhodes Jr. On Friday, November 9, Will and Ima hosted their first informal dinner, and on November 13, Tom and Marie Hogg, en route to New York, joined their three siblings for "Our *First* Family Dinner."[49] Ima had confided to close friend Julia Ideson that she wanted a house name that would suggest rural contentment, and by 1929 "Bayou Bend" had supplanted "Bayou Banks" to reflect the property's location on a bend in Buffalo Bayou.[50] Unfortunately, Will did not enjoy many months in the "Fat Men's Wing" because he departed for Europe on November 1, 1929, never to return. After Mike married Alice Nicholson in 1929, the newlyweds lived briefly at Bayou Bend but soon found their own house and within two years had settled next door. Bayou Bend was indeed Ima's house.

THE COLLECTION

If Bayou Bend's owners and architects imagined a Latin colonial exterior that tied the building to traditions of the region, Ima insisted that her "authentic" interiors be related closely to America's colonial and early national heritage.[51] At first this "authenticity" lay primarily in architectural features inspired by colonial and early Federal homes in New England, Philadelphia, Virginia, and Tennessee. Photographs and inventory lists reveal that Bayou Bend was originally furnished as a comfortable family home with a delightful mix of objects. In the 1930s Ima's sitting room housed an antique Mexican chest, a Hopi Indian bowl, a Picasso gouache, a Russian silver cigarette case, and American furniture and glasswares.[52] In the 1910s Ima had purchased English antiques for the family's apartments and house on Rossmoyne, and only gradually were these pieces replaced by American examples. When Ima and Will began collecting in 1920, with Mike's good-natured acquiescence, they were furnishing two apartments and an office in New York, the plantation house at Varner, and new offices for Hogg Brothers Inc. in Houston, as well as embellishing their home on Rossmoyne. For a decade brothers and sister teased each other about extravagant "antiquing around." "Mike says save a little money for next year," admonished Will in 1927, "and remember we are going to play along with you in the antique line the rest of your life, so don't do like I do—get het up all of a sudden and buy without looking back and then probably be sorry for it the next day."[53]

Ima was recuperating from a long illness when she saw the chair in Wayman Adams's studio that inspired her to suggest that the family form a collection of American furniture and other objects for a museum in Texas. Hoping to help her recover and genuinely intrigued, Will quickly got "het up" and took the lead, advising his sister, negotiating purchases, and making several major decorative arts acquisitions that remain in the Bayou Bend collection. In January 1920 Will bought a Massachusetts gaming table (circa 1800–1820) from Collings and Collings for the Hogg Brothers office, and a few months later Ima bought her "first chair" from the same dealer.[54] In January 1921 Will told Ima he was looking for a "Duncan Fyffe [sic] American table" and then splurged at the Louis Guerineau Myers sale held at the American Art Galleries in February, at which he purchased sixteen Windsor chairs and several other pieces of furniture. A year later at the January 1922 sale of the Jacob Paxson Temple Collection, Will bought several lots of furniture, ceramics, and glass and the exceptional oil on canvas by Edward Hicks (1780–1849), *Penn's Treaty with the Indians* (circa 1830–1840). Ima also purchased ceramics, glass, and furniture at the 1922 and 1923 Temple sales, but instead of confronting the auctioneer herself, she asked portraitist Wayman Adams to act as agent for her. In 1922 on a visit to the Norristown, Pennsylvania, shop of William B. Montague, Ima discovered important porcelain pitchers produced in Philadelphia in the 1830s by William Ellis Tucker and his partners.[55] Collings and Collings, New York, presented several museum-quality objects to the Hoggs during the decade, including a rare set of eight side chairs with accompanying settee (1927) that was used in the dining room at Bayou Bend for many years, a desk with burl veneer (1927), and a fine tambour lady's writing desk (1928) that remains one of the collection's star attractions.[56]

By July 1926, Ima had discovered twenty dealers in New England who enjoyed her patronage, and the Hoggs had joined the "1920s craze" to find American antiques.[57] Antiquarians had been interested in Americana since the mid-nineteenth century, spurred by patriotic or romantic sentimentality, curiosity about the possessions of famous figures, or a desire to understand family and national history. The confusion of late-nineteenth-century urban sprawl and the clangor of industrial growth repelled many early collectors, who prized the patina of old furniture and pewter and admired the craftsmanship of beaten silver, homespun textiles, and handmade goods. By the early 1900s a few museums and publications had begun to extol American antiques for both historic and aesthetic qualities. Ima and her brothers were not alone in believing that these objects reflected American character and values. The Roaring Twenties attracted major collectors who sponsored shows, made collecting socially acceptable, and battled to outspend each other at blockbuster auctions.

When Louis Guerineau Myers (1874–1932) decided to auction seven hundred objects (including forty-five Windsor chairs) in 1921, he caused a sensation. Crowds squeezed into the American Art Galleries in New York, and bidders set record prices. During the 1920s the Metropolitan Museum of Art popularized the concept of colonial and Federal period rooms when it opened its American Wing in 1924. and the Hoggs quickly befriended Charles Cornelius, scholarly associate curator of American art responsible for Americana collections. Myers began the quest to identify regional characteristics when he grouped furniture by place of origin at the popular 1929 Girl Scouts Loan Exhibition in New York, and George McKearin awakened collectors to the beauties of American glass when he sorted his five hundred loan exhibition objects by type in his scholarly exhibit-catalog entries. Henry Francis du Pont (1880–1969) sought the finest high-style objects with a connoisseur's eye, while Henry Ford (1863–1947) was the first to document the hardships of pioneer life in his collections of rural artifacts. In 1930 Francis Patrick Garvan (1875–1937) celebrated his twentieth wedding anniversary by giving several superb pieces of furniture to Yale University to begin a "circulating library" of antiques that could be shared with institutions around the country to teach Americans about their patrimony. Ima did not forget these approaches to collecting when she decided to transform her home into a house museum; the finest examples of urban craftsmanship, the humble pots of frontier farmers, period rooms, and an overarching didactic purpose all played important roles at Bayou Bend.[58]

Even as neophyte collectors, Will and Ima established patterns that foretold success, and their mutual enthusiasm and friendly competition fueled their avid pursuit of new treasures. If Will enjoyed the exhilaration and uncertainty of auction bidding, Ima preferred to establish relationships with trusted dealers. She bought objects she had examined on trips to the East, and she carried on extensive correspondence to learn about the provenance of each piece and its possible maker. Both Hoggs knew about other major collectors, and both were attracted to objects that were aesthetically pleasing, unusual, and of historic importance. The tambour writing desk purchased in 1928 exemplifies the Hoggs' astute perception and Ima's keen interest in the lives of American women. Of handsome mahogany with intricate inlay, the desk still garners acclaim as one of the most beautiful examples produced by the well-regarded Seymour brothers of Boston (1794–1820); a new form at the time, this desk also suggests new expectations for women of the new Republic, who were assumed to be educated, outward-looking correspondents in need of storage space for their papers and a permanent surface for writing. This desk enabled Ima and the docents who followed her to explain how women like Abigail Adams constructed their brilliant correspondence with family members who were pursuing public service far from home, and it subtly tied the Hoggs and other Houston families to a wider national heritage.[59]

THE GARDENS

When Ima lost her collecting partner in 1930, she turned instead to other pursuits. During the Depression decade her days were filled with efforts to sustain the Houston Child Guidance Center and rebuild the Houston Symphony Orchestra, and she worked closely with Mike to establish the Hogg Foundation for Mental Health. She also discovered shared gardening interests with sister-in-law Alice, who specialized in growing dahlias and lilies and was an active participant in River Oaks Garden Club projects after she married Mike.[60] Now next-door neighbors, both women spent hours designing and building their gardens and planted their shared driveway with "unlimited" dogwood and redbud trees, azaleas, and "thousands" of daffodils.[61] Alice's Dogwood and Clock Gardens were well known to Houstonians who visited them on annual garden pilgrimages and azalea trails from the 1930s through the 1950s. Bayou Bend has been featured in every Azalea Trail since the fund-raising event was inaugurated in 1936.[62]

To the Hoggs, gardens were as important as the houses that sat within them because they provided the refuge from commerce and industry considered beneficial to all citizens and because they signaled the city of trees and plants that River Oaks was intended to inspire. Bayou Bend was always imagined as a house within a garden. When placing the structures, Ima, Will, and the architects were careful to preserve plants and trees when possible.[63] Governor Hogg had instilled a love of nature in his children, who had vivid memories of their parents' and grandparents' gardens. Ima recalled her Grandfather Stinson's brick-edged flowerbeds filled with bulbs, jonquils, roses, and dogwoods, all favorites used in Bayou Bend gardens. Like her father, Ima enjoyed the challenge of experiment and used several species that had not been tried in Houston's difficult climate and clay soils.[64] Indeed, to Ima goes credit for popularizing the azaleas and camellias that now predominate in Houston's gardens but had first been used in antebellum gardens of the Southeast and Louisiana. Challenged by Houston's recalcitrant clay, Ima corresponded with soil experts and requested numerous soil tests so she could discover the proper mix and transform nature to suit her idea of beauty.[65] As the gardens at Bayou Bend developed, they became models for horticultural aspiration, a part of the Southern Garden Renaissance that included major embellishments at Shadows on the Teche in New Iberia, Louisiana (1922); Bellingrath Gardens in Mobile (1927), and Longue Vue in New Orleans (1939).[66]

Horticulture in the late nineteenth and early twentieth centuries was an important occupation for women, both as professionals and as family custodians of the domestic domain. Like so many female pursuits in those years, gardening had both a personal and a civic dimension, and it was considered a respectable occupation for women who were forced, or eager, to earn a living. Garden lovers advocated public parks and tree-lined parkways; they fought billboards and coordinated trash pick-up days; and they organized garden clubs, which sponsored conservation projects, landscaped public institutions, and educated their members through trips and lectures. Residents had barely settled in River Oaks when Will urged his female friends to form the River Oaks Garden Club in 1927. Ima and Alice, who joined as soon as they moved to River Oaks, were active club members. Alice served as president (1931–1932, 1938–1939), and club records show that both women opened their homes for meetings and tours and held committee posts into the 1950s. Ima welcomed Garden Club of America annual meeting attendees in 1939, when she produced an innovative, and experimental, night lighting scheme for an evening garden party, and again in 1955, when she served as hospitality chairwoman.[67] During the years Ima and Alice were most active, the club sponsored an annual pilgrimage (from 1934 to 1938?) and the Azalea Trail (1936 to present).[68] These garden tours and other fund-raising activities supported landscaping at Faith Home (DePelchin Children's Center), River Oaks Elementary School, the Forum of Civics, and, after 1961, Bayou Bend.

Just as John Staub recalled Bayou Bend as his masterpiece, so C. C. (Pat) Fleming and his partner, Albert Sheppard, claimed Bayou Bend Gardens as their primary creation. Records make clear, however, that Ima consulted a number of experts and that the basic plan for the gardens was in place long before Fleming and Sheppard began to practice in Houston in the late 1930s. In reality Ima was the mastermind behind her gardens. A work in progress, the gardens were nonetheless an integral part of the house-building project. By 1927 River Oaks engineer Herbert Kipp had prepared a topographical survey, treated extant trees, and planned the driveway and sprinkler systems. That year the Blume System landscape gardeners surveyed trees and suggested plantings, and Teas Nurseries was paid for plant materials. In 1928 Hare and Hare, who had provided ideas for River Oaks Corporation and would produce Houston's 1929 master plan for Will, submitted an elaborate formal scheme whose grand architectural elements included a teahouse and vied with the main house as constructed space. Perhaps because of the grandiose scale, or the projected expense, the plan was never executed, although three ideas were incorporated in Ima's garden plans: trails through woodsy terrain, a garden on the east side of the house, and terracing to the north of the house.[69] William Caldwell of Houston Landscape Company planted the East ("upper") Garden adjacent to the brothers' living rooms in 1928, and in 1929 the brickwork for Ima's ornamental "lower" garden, which recalled Stinson family designs, was laid out on the west side of the property near the bayou and planted with roses and perennials. In May 1929 Ima finally hired her first team of three gardeners and invited her friends to a garden party.[70]

In the 1930s Ima consulted several experts. After a major flood on May 31, 1929, she called Blume System to repair damage to seventy-five trees. Ruth London, a graduate of the Lowthorpe School of Landscape Architecture and Horticulture for Women established in Groton, Massachusetts, in 1901, practiced for forty years in Houston and took space in Studio Gardens, the haven for horticulturists and artists sponsored by Estelle Sharp before World War II (1930–1937). She designed a green garden for Ima (1932) and worked on plans for a peach garden before turning her attention to the reorganization of Ima's East Garden and development of an azalea garden in 1934.[71] Undoubtedly Ima knew about the lecture given in Houston on March 25, 1934, by Ellen Biddle Shipman (1869–1950), doyenne of female landscape architects. A participant in the artist colony at Cornish, New Hampshire, Shipman opened her all-woman office in New York in 1920 and traveled the country lecturing and consulting well-heeled clients. Many Garden Club of America members requested her services, and her gardens were published in the popular gardening magazines. Shipman's gardens, like Ima's, reduced the formal architectural elements popular in earlier gardens and enticed visitors into small-scale "secret garden" refuges from modern city sprawl and industrial harshness.[72] Shipman had several clients in Houston, and in January 1938 she consulted with Ima about placement of a statue in the large formal space that became the Diana Garden. However, years later Ima confided to architect and Staub biographer Howard Barnstone that she was dissatisfied with Shipman's plan because its scale was too small for the site.[73] In late January 1938 Ima began her association with Fleming and Sheppard, who reworked the Lower Garden, finished the Diana Garden installation, and placed Clio and Euterpe in their bowers (1939).

These consultations notwithstanding, Ima wanted to express her own personality in her landscape plans. Her scrupulously maintained garden books include her own sketches for garden layouts and meticulous records of all the seeds and plants she ordered, where they were placed, and how they grew. She recorded many experiments in the 1930s and even then was using her favorite blue, pink, and white color scheme. While away from Bayou Bend on frequent trips for pleasure or health, Ima kept close control of her gardens through correspondence with Hogg Brothers business manager H. E. Brigham. Brigham carried out Ima's orders, hired gardeners, and reported storms, problems with dead trees and nut grass, and efforts to acclimate azaleas, camellias, and roses to Houston's clay soils.[74] In 1930 Ima planted her first, experimental azalea, and in 1932 the first camellias were placed in the garden to the east of the house. By 1936 hundreds of azaleas had adapted to Houston's soil, and in 1937 Ima ordered hundreds of camellias from Edward Avery McIlhenny of

Louisiana. She also tried growers in California and Alabama and kept replacing plants throughout the years, always intrigued by new varieties.[75] She developed an extensive library of garden books and saved back issues of several horticulture magazines.[76] If the gardens benefited from expert advice, they are, in reality, the embodiment of Ima's imagination and interests.

Fourteen acres of gardens and protective woodland define the Bayou Bend property boundaries. Bordered on three sides by bayou fingers and on the fourth by the driveway that was originally shared with Mike and Alice, the gardens express Ima's love of natural beauty and her view that art and nature were inseparable necessities for a happy, productive life. These magical garden spaces, whether formal, whimsical, or contemplative, open and inviting or secret and surprising, harmonize Ima's interests and tell stories that anticipate the room narratives inside the house.[77]

Visitors who approach the house from Lazy Lane, as Ima's friends would have done, encounter the quiet, contemplative White Garden, first mentioned by that name in 1934–1935. Perpetually in bloom, this private oasis hidden in the woods features Ima's favorite dogwood in March. Alvin Wheeler, Ima's gardener for thirty years, loved this spot, which was dedicated to his memory in 1971. Guests who walk through the Deer Park of woods, dogwood, and redbud or along the driveway next encounter Ima's joyful Butterfly Garden, designed in 1940–1941 by Ima and Albert Sheppard in a butterfly brickwork pattern of pathways and beds, planted since World War II with boxwood hedges and pink Kurume azaleas to emphasize her love of pink and delight in ephemeral nature. The charming scale is feminine and welcoming, and the butterfly became the talisman of the Bayou Bend collections. Across the driveway from Ima's butterfly lies a circular topiary Bicentennial Garden conceived with landscape architect A. Gregory Catlow at the end of her life to celebrate the United States' birth. Topiary animals, including the emblematic American eagle and wildlife believed to have inhabited East Texas woodlands in 1776, were installed shortly after her death.[78]

Like many colonial revival homes built in the 1920s, Bayou Bend has a formal outdoor room that unites constructed and natural space as well as a broad sweep of lawn that draws the eye to an important distant focal point. Walled by a hedge that protects the East Garden from driveway and woods, the large outdoor room adjacent to the brothers' wing features a fountain in a small octagonal pool, a wrought-iron fence, and furniture decorated with a lyre motif that recalls Ima's musical interest. Designed as an open garden in 1927–1928 by Ima and William Caldwell of Houston

Landscaping Company, the area was reworked by Ruth London in 1934 as a formal garden room with beds of pink azaleas and blue pansies. When the pool leaked in 1935, Ima turned the slope behind the East Garden into a Waterfall Garden of ferns and greenery that terminates in a rocky tarn and demonstrates the beauty of natural drainage techniques.[79] The visitor leaves the East Garden room and enters the north terrace that runs along Bayou Bend's north front.

A broad greensward slopes gently toward the bayou and terminates in the formal Diana Garden, named for a statue of the huntress Diana, goddess of maidens and the moon, that stands there. The house and Diana Garden form a vertical axis, which is balanced by a horizontal axis that terminates in the Euterpe Garden on the east and the Clio Garden on the west, again named for the statues that dominate them.[80] Garden statuary was a staple of elegant landscaping in the United States by the time Ima began planning her formal garden.[81] Floods invaded the low north garden in 1932, 1933, and 1936, but by 1937 Ima turned her attention to this large area and began to clear small trees (under twelve inches in diameter) and grade the terraces that visitors encounter today. While on a trip to Italy that summer, she purchased a reproduction of the Versailles Diana, benches, and urns from Florentine sculptor Antonio Frilli. She also commissioned Frilli to make replicas of Clio and Euterpe to complete her plan. In choosing these classical figures, Ima gave visual form to core beliefs: Diana, the huntress, represented action in the present; Clio, muse of history, reflects quietly on the past, while Euterpe, the muse of music, supports eternal delight and a future of inspiration.

In 1938 Houston gardeners accelerated their landscape improvements to prepare for the Garden Club of America annual meeting announced for March 1939. Ima was anxious that her statues arrive to grace this grand event, but only Diana was in place (spring 1938), and the muses arrived a month after the meeting ended. Clio was placed in the brick ornamental garden abutting the service building. In 1939 Euterpe took her place between two old trees, a loblolly pine and an American sycamore, in a shaded, natural grove appropriate for quiet reflection.[82]

In 1961 Ima nestled a surprise garden into space cleared by Hurricane Carla's violent winds. Again she used her favorite brick border and paving, but she also constructed a retaining wall to control erosion caused by Houston's torrential storms. The circular shape and belts of colorful azaleas in the Carla Garden remind visitors that Ima loved the circus. Redesigned in 1971, the garden's intimate solitude provides space to consider nature's transformation. Although her gardens were essentially complete by 1941, Ima continued to struggle with stubborn soil, special azalea feeding formulas, and constant maintenance. Every year she ordered thousands of bedding plants (blue pansies especially) and bulbs so her gardens would shine for Azalea Trail in the spring.[83]

When the River Oaks Garden Club asked her to open Bayou Bend for the 1957 Azalea Trail as she had done every year since the club's first pilgrimage tour, she demurred; too much work needed to be done to correct years of indifferent care, she said. For the first time, she requested club help to prepare for the trail and offered $2,000 for plantings and labor if the club would appoint assistants. Honored to comply, the club named a committee, undertook the work, and set in motion an idea that matured four years later when the club assumed full management of the gardens.[84] In May 1961 Ima received gratifying word that the River Oaks Garden Club wished to assume permanent supervision of the gardens and pay for a "skilled gardener at least one day a week."[85] In 1966 the club announced it would place fresh flowers in the house each week, an embellishment particularly appreciated by touring guests. In 1967 club members established a Garden Endowment Fund to attract donations and memorial gifts, manage receipts from fund-raising events, and provide income for garden maintenance.[86] Until her death in 1975 Ima continued to support garden development by purchasing plant materials each year, and at the end of her life she provided funds to build a greenhouse in Bayou Bend's service area.[87]

THE TRANSFORMATION

In the 1940s, when Ima and Ray Dudley began to discuss the future of Bayou Bend, Ima returned to collecting with renewed purpose and focus. The marriage of aesthetic excellence and historic significance that had characterized her first purchases continued to inform Ima's acquisitions, but at first she felt "rusty" and isolated from the rapidly developing postwar antiques market. In 1946 she wrote to Joseph Downs, curator of the American Wing at the Metropolitan Museum, New York, for advice. Houston museum Director James H. Chillman Jr. also corresponded with Downs about furniture and pewter, seeking details and authentication for objects being considered for "a museum collection."[88] This close association between the Metropolitan Museum and Ima continued in the 1950s when Vincent D. Andrus, Downs's successor as American Wing curator, accepted a retainer from the Museum of Fine Arts to serve as Ima's advisor—a rare inter-museum exchange. In 1953 Ima entered a new, more intense phase of interaction with other collectors when she attended her first Antiques Forum at Williamsburg. The forum became a much-anticipated annual event where she met colleagues and developed a circle of dear friends who shared her passion for preserving America's cultural heritage. Many were working on museum projects of their own.[89]

The "antiquees," as Maxim Karolik dubbed the group, included Henry Francis du Pont, who was developing Winterthur; Electra Havemayer Webb, patron of Shelburne, Vermont, installations; Henry and Helen Flynt, who were restoring Historic Deerfield, Massachusetts; and the redoubtable Katharine Prentis Murphy, whose expertise dominated the fields of seventeenth- and early-eighteenth-century collecting.[90] Despite great confusion that attended their first meeting in 1951, Katharine Murphy and Ima Hogg became inseparable long-distance friends who chatted on the telephone every Sunday morning when apart and who met often at house parties and on Ima's frequent scouting trips in New England.[91] Ima's interaction with these brilliant and well-informed collectors and with dealers Israel Sack, Bernard Levy, and John Walton greatly expanded her expertise about American decorative arts and her aspirations for Bayou Bend. Friends recalled that Ima was shrewd and tough when she bargained and "relished the chase," especially when her rival was Henry Ford, Henry Francis du Pont, or some other formidable huntsman.[92] Dealers wrote her frequently, even sent occasional Christmas gifts, and knew how to whet her appetite by comparing their offerings to works in another famous collection, by emphasizing the quest's difficulty, or by suggesting that a rival was pursuing the same object.[93]

The Bayou Bend collection is really many collections that allowed Ima to interpret America's story through the artifacts of material culture. Fascinated by the high quality of American craftsmanship and the ability of artisans to marry beauty and function, Ima often made daring aesthetic choices. In 1944 she extended the meaning of "antique" beyond its then-current 1830 terminus to include rococo revival furniture made by John Henry Belter, a German immigrant who worked in New York (circa 1845–1865) and combined new lamination technologies with traditional hand-carved decoration to produce suites of furniture synonymous with mid-Victorian domestic taste.[94] Visitors often note the scale of Ima's purchases: feminine, straightforward, welcoming, domestic, her pieces do not dominate the room or the people within it. Nor were the rooms ever cluttered; rather each object is allowed its space for the reflection, comprehension, and enjoyment of user or viewer.[95] Ima's eye for beauty and sensitivity to scale were informed by methodical purpose. In the 1930s

Hogg Brothers made inventories of objects and books in the collection, and in the 1940s Ima began making lists of the many paintings, ceramics, glasswares, textiles, and metal objects she needed to complement the furniture and complete the room settings that would recreate America's birth as a nation. These lists guided transformation of the house to a museum in the 1950s and 1960s and continue to influence purchases for the collection.[96] Indeed, Ima foresaw Bayou Bend as a living museum and was unusual among collectors in urging Museum of Fine Arts curators to add objects or make replacements if superior examples were found after her death.

Ima never lost her zeal for bargaining, as her numerous letters "arguing" with dealers about discounts testify. By the 1950s her intensive buying was having an impact on the antiques market, and she often used agents to scout for objects and buy for her. She developed a strategy of collecting, often expressing horror at suggested prices, demurring that decisions could not be made without consulting her advisory committee formed in 1960, or pretending indifference to drive a hard bargain. Whether these strategies actually worked is hard to say; evidence suggests that on several occasions she just could not bear the suspense of a waiting game and succumbed to the passion to possess that lurks in the heart of every collector.[97] Like her peers, she never forgot an object. In the 1960s, after Wayman Adams's death, Ima pursued the Queen Anne–style chair she had seen in his studio in 1920. Wishing to obtain the chair that had inspired her first purchase, she wrote the artist's widow to say she would be "happy to have [the chair] any time that you feel like disposing of it" for "sentiment's sake."[98] In 1968 the chair finally came to Bayou Bend when Adams's son relinquished it.

Ima enjoyed the intellectual challenge of reorganizing Bayou Bend as a series of period rooms that would explain the heritage of Anglo America and the Founding Fathers. Extensive correspondence with dealers and former owners reveals that she wanted to learn about every object's history. She actively scoured shops for items, made the purchases, authenticated her discoveries, and ultimately placed each object in its room setting. Ima felt "remote in every way" from antique sources, but because of her personal attention to every detail and her profound knowledge of American culture, prominent dealers like Israel Sack came to recognize a connoisseur who "should have the best antiques that money can buy, because I know you enjoy fine things."[99] Ima would not reveal her favorite object or room to public questioners, but she was first attracted to seventeenth- and early-eighteenth-century New England furniture, and her first room installation, the Murphy Room, showcased this period. Overall, however, the collection is strongest in rococo examples made in the years during the Revolutionary period (1760–1785) and in neoclassical examples made immediately after independence (1785–1810), five decades when Americans were defining a national identity. In these examples of the nascent urban culture, transplanted craftsmen interpreted European traditions in a uniquely American way that intrigued Ima. In these years was born that new entity, the American.

Once the museum officially accepted her gift in 1957, Ima consulted experts and her advisory committee and developed extensive, meticulous plans to convert her home to "a harmonious setting" for her collection.[100] Charles Montgomery, director of Winterthur, urged Ima to develop a story she wanted to tell in each room. He reviewed the collections, made invaluable suggestions, and helped Ima organize detailed worksheets for each room with inventories of objects to be displayed.[101] Montgomery persuaded Ima to chronicle the story of her collecting career, which she set down "with real temerity."[102] "Antiquee" friends Henry Francis du Pont, the Flynts, John Graham II, Maxim Karolik, Katharine Prentis Murphy, and others formed an honorary advisory committee. They took seriously her request for help and responded to a detailed questionnaire with many thoughtful suggestions and treasured gifts.[103] Other authorities studied the collection, authenticated objects, and suggested placement of treasures in the period rooms, but, once again, the vision behind every decision was Ima's own.[104] In some rooms only the narrative had to be decided and the objects selected; other rooms required removal of built-in bookshelves, inappropriate in American homes before the twentieth century. Still other rooms needed extensive remodeling, including the removal of walls and the installation of appropriate woodwork and fireplace details. Purchases trace the progress of her renovation as she moved from room to room, but clearly the overall concept for the collection's mission was in place before serious work began in 1959, as Ima bought important objects in all media and styles each year, whenever appropriate examples from her wish lists became available.

Most poignant, perhaps, was Ima's struggle to create her first installation, the Murphy Room, named to honor her dear friend Katharine Prentis Murphy (1884–1967). Ima and Katharine collaborated on the room, which is similar to installations Katharine completed for several other museums, including Prentis House at Electra Havemayer Webb's Shelburne Museum, finished in 1957. Katharine gave Ima at least thirty objects, and John Graham, director and curator of collections at Colonial

Williamsburg, chose the room's colors and helped arrange the furniture. According to Ima, he and Katharine Murphy "performed miracles" and guided her through the treacherous pitfalls of room transformation.[105] Several small rooms in the brothers' wing were remodeled to create a gallery for seventeenth- and early-eighteenth-century objects. Katharine and Ima began planning in 1958, and by April 1959 Ima was "so anxious to get things going, but it seems everything is delayed" as she waited for architect John Staub to complete drawings. Laid low by illness through the spring and summer months, Ima wrote often to Katharine exclaiming over slow progress and messy plaster but thrilled by Katharine's gifts, despite Ima's vehement pleas that her "more than generous" friend must stop buying objects for the room. Still bedridden on July 3, 1959, Ima wrote eagerly, "I can hear the hammering going on in your room downstairs and I am very excited!" In August she exclaimed over "six beautiful wine glasses" and decided that "from now on I shall keep the room closed because I don't want anyone to see it now until it is complete." As the project ended, Ima's good health returned. A safe birth and happy christening of the room with Katharine and many friends in attendance brought Ima a glorious thanksgiving in 1959. To Katharine Ima exclaimed that the room "is a great joy to me and to everyone who sees it. . . . I . . . am deeply grateful!"[106] Buoyed by the enthusiastic welcome that greeted the experimental Murphy Room, Ima proceeded methodically to complete the transformation, reporting progress at regular intervals to the museum's board.[107]

The decision to develop period room settings caused Ima to build new collections of metal wares and paintings and greatly expand holdings in furniture and ceramics. In the 1950s Ima concentrated on completing her furniture purchases in the mannerist, baroque, and rococo styles and began serious collecting of period-appropriate paintings, including four major works and several drawings by premier colonial portraitist John Singleton Copley (1738–1815). In 1954 she purchased two Copley oil portraits from galleries and plotted with dealer Bernard Levy to acquire treasures from the famous collection of Mr. and Mrs. Luke Vincent Lockwood. In a triumph of auction finesse, Levy purchased two Copley pastels, *Portrait of Mrs. Gawen Brown* (1763) and *Portrait of Mrs. Joseph Henshaw* (circa 1770), for his delighted client.[108] During this decade Ima also purchased several outstanding silver tankards, porringers, and teapots as well as a number of rare pewter examples. The silver collection, although small, includes exceptional examples of popular period forms by most of America's prominent silversmiths working from 1650 to 1850.[109]

In the 1960s Ima focused on the neoclassical and Grecian periods (1785–1835) and expanded her silver, pewter, and ceramics holdings while adding important paintings by period luminaries Charles Willson Peale (1741–1827), James Peale (1749–1831), and Gilbert Stuart (1755–1828). The help of dealers and lookout scouts notwithstanding, Ima's extensive buying sprees are impressive. Even if cost had been no object, simply finding hundreds of museum-quality works when far removed from the antiques market demanded energy and persistence as well as luck and good friends. By the 1950s "antiquing" had become a sport enjoyed by growing numbers of Americans with capacious pocketbooks, and Ima faced increasingly stiff competition for a finite number of period objects.

Nor did Ima rest after she moved from the house in late 1965. Instead she and curator David Warren began remodeling the servants wing as the Chillman Suite to honor her friend and consultant Dorothy Dawes Chillman and to display Grecian decorative arts (1810–1835). As was so often the case with Ima's projects, she had been intrigued by a 1963 exhibition catalog, *Classical Style in America*, the first museum project that examined the style professionally. Careful study of the catalog and curator Warren's "reasoned" enthusiasm led to an innovative installation, opened to the public in 1969.[110] In 1970–1971, Ima and her youthful curator reworked space between the front hall and kitchen wing to create the Victorian Belter Parlor (1850–1860), and during the last years of Ima's life they redecorated the Maple Bedroom by adding a fireplace and paneling to depict a country home lived in by many generations of one family. Although she had passed her ninetieth birthday, Ima frequently visited the bedroom during its remodeling and insisted that the three-color fireplace wall be repainted until the colors satisfied the scheme she had imagined. Ima and her companion also developed curtains and bed hangings for the room. Ima viewed Bayou Bend as an evolving work and was negotiating for a portrait and other objects at the time of her death in 1975. To commemorate this brilliant career of civic activism and memorialize her sister-in-law, Alice Hogg Hanszen provided funds to transform Ima's dressing room and bathroom into a memorial room to house artifacts that explain the Hogg family's many interests and wide-ranging philanthropy.

INTERPRETING THE COLLECTION

Volunteers were essential to all Ima's philanthropies. She well knew that her wealth could not sustain her vision; she recognized that this vision would live and succeed only if others adopted it as their own. Most important, she believed that in the civil society of a thriving democracy, empowered citizens would bring spiritual and emotional strength to their communities only through active participation in municipal institutions. As Ima prepared in 1961 to turn over management of her gardens to volunteer members of the River Oaks Garden Club, she also devised a plan to train volunteers to interpret the collection. If the Bayou Bend Collection and Gardens proclaim the Hoggs' faith in the power of a unifying national heritage to shape individual lives, the Bayou Bend Docent Organization affirms the family's belief that citizen involvement in civic institutions will make dreams manifest and transmit hopes to future generations through education.

In 1961 Ima invited younger friend Eugenia (Mrs. Borden) Tennant to lead a group of women who would be trained to serve as docent interpreters of the objects in the collection. Members of the early classes included schoolteachers Ima had met while serving on the school board, young women who worked with her on symphony committees, daughters of friends, and colleagues from the River Oaks Garden Club. Virginia Elverson, a young member of the second docent class, says women often did not know they loved antiques until Miss Hogg told them they did.[111] By carefully selecting members of the early classes, by transmitting her enthusiasm to them, by instilling in them her passion for excellence, and by making the experience one of joyful friendship, Ima ensured that her legacy would be admired and transmitted even as it was adapted to accommodate changing times. Over the years, some docents have become recognized scholars in the fields of decorative arts and American history; others have acquired museum-quality collections and become major donors to the Museum of Fine Arts; several have remained active volunteers within the organization for more than thirty years; and the ranks have been expanded to include a lively cadre of male docents.

In July 1961, at Ima's request, a recent University of Delaware and Winterthur Museum graduate named Jonathan Fairbanks journeyed to Houston to teach the first, carefully selected, class of twenty-two "charming ladies who will serve as volunteer docents."[112] Fairbanks went on to become the legendary curator of decorative arts at the Boston Museum of Fine Arts (1970–1999), prolific author, painter, and professor at Wellesley College, Boston University, and Harvard; but at Bayou Bend he and his determined mentor had to conjure an "ideal" house tour and training program from their imaginations. Years later Fairbanks described Ima as the "Grand Master" of Americana collectors, a "pioneer" and artist who used "real objects from the historical past as her palette" to "reconfigure her collected items into imagined human habitats."[113] He has also noted that the search for objects to furnish a period room, the most complex type of museum installation, becomes "a seemingly endless pursuit requiring knowledge, patience, means, and longevity," blessings enjoyed in abundance by Ima Hogg.[114] From 1962 until David Warren's advent in 1965, aspiring docents used Fairbanks's remarks as their guide for continued research and self-training. Ima's "dearest friend," Eloise Chalmers, provided "noteworthy" research and "worked days upon days" to catalog books and papers for an infant docent library.[115]

Director Warren and the educational curators who served under him formalized the teaching process and worked with docents to establish a touring schedule and numerous outreach programs to extend docent education into the community and provide special instruction for students at the elementary through high school and college levels. Provisional docents, who pledge to serve for five years, take a three-month course that includes lectures and onsite discussion and is completed only when the trainee has passed a final exam, prepared a research paper, given a practice tour, and completed a semester of touring. Active docents attend monthly meetings at which docent colleagues, museum curators, and guest lecturers detail the latest discoveries in the ever-evolving fields of material culture and American history. In the tradition established by Ima and her first classes, docents combine camaraderie with lifetime educational goals while they perform the civic duty of interpreting America's past to the public.[116]

Guests began to tour the house while Ima was still in residence. Sometimes these early visitors received a bonus—and nervous docent guides a shock—when Ima popped out of her sitting room and joined the group. Other volunteers also wanted to help Ima share her legacy. In 1968 the Houston Junior Women's Club began its long relationship with the collection. Today club volunteers welcome visitors one Sunday afternoon every month at family days that provide children of all ages a glimpse of downstairs rooms, extended rambling in the gardens, and hands-on activities that bring the past to life with music, costume, and crafts. Club fund-raisers benefit Bayou Bend collections. Houston's Theta Charity Antiques Show, one of the nation's outstanding gatherings of art and antiques dealers since its founding in 1952, has included Bayou Bend as a beneficiary since 1969. Ima had been an early supporter, and Theta funds are used to purchase items from her wish lists. Bayou Bend has shared its treasures with thousands of shoppers in "petit museum" displays.

IMA'S LAST CAREER, HISTORIC PRESERVATIONIST

As if transforming Bayou Bend into the decorative arts wing of the Museum of Fine Arts, Houston, did not consume enough imagination and time, during the last three decades of her life Ima also supported the Harris County Heritage and Conservation Society, organized in May 1954, and undertook several major historic preservation projects in Texas to honor her family and to illuminate important elements of the state's complex history.[117] Throughout their adult lives, Will, Ima, and Mike nurtured family ties, cared for widowed or orphaned relatives, and memorialized their father's accomplishments. While proud of their own family's contributions, the Hoggs emphasized that all families built the nation, and they presented the Hogg family as but one example of how Americans had built their communities. Love of history, a desire to explain the American experiment, a wish to link the Hogg family's experience and all Texans to the nation's drama—these motives inspired Ima and Will to collect. They also caused Will and Ima to furnish Hogg Brothers offices with antique furniture, hooked rugs, Remington paintings, early glass, and homey objects that masked commercial crassness and proclaimed an "American" image of ethical business practice infused with strong family values.[118] Will and Mike frequently corresponded with each other and with Confederate history buffs about transferring their Grandfather Hogg's remains from a battlefield site near Corinth, Mississippi, to a family resting place. All the children worried about maintaining the trees at their father's grave and made sure pecans harvested at the site were distributed to the people of Texas, in compliance with their father's wishes. Memorials to their father, and after 1931 to brother Will, were a consuming concern for Mike and Ima. For Christmas gifts to Mike and Tom in 1935, Ima compiled "Family Letters" written by the four Hogg children, their parents, and their Aunt Fanny; in the last two years of her life Ima began reorganizing these letters for publication.[119]

In 1939 Mike was named to a state commission charged with securing property in Quitman, Wood County, as a memorial to Governor Hogg. Battling the cancer that killed him in 1941, he asked Ima to take over his work and thereby launched her final career as historic preservationist. The Quitman project evolved slowly and was not completed until November

1974.[120] Ima worked with state officials and Texas Parks and Wildlife Department personnel to complete Mike's efforts to buy 26.7 acres in Quitman for the park that would commemorate their father's life; the purchase was completed in 1945 and deeded to the state in 1946.[121] Ima used family money to restore her parents' first home, the Honeymoon Cottage, built on the land in 1876. In the cottage she conceived a museum-shrine to tell the story of her family and other pioneering settlers in East Texas. Opened to much fanfare in March 1952, the cottage housed family heirlooms and pictures, her father's desk, and a family Bible. Working closely with E. A. (Eddie) Spacek, Ima oversaw refurbishing and installations, including recreation of the bedroom in which brother Will was born.[122]

To further explain the Hogg family's East Texas roots, Ima acquired the old Stinson House she had remembered so fondly from her childhood and had it moved thirteen miles to the park. She collaborated with architect Wayne Bell on the building's restoration from 1968 until its completion in November 1974. During the process Ima helped organize the Ima Hogg Museum as a research and display center for the study of East Texas heritage. At the May 25, 1969, museum dedication, Ima thanked a crowd of well-wishers for the "beautiful museum" and told of her happy childhood summers in Wood County and her present joy that her parents' cottage and her grandparents' home would forever be "all nestled together around this museum." She felt she was "coming home" at last to the place in East Texas where her family and hundreds of other settlers "turned . . . wilderness into productive farms and graceful homes."[123] In 1941 Mike, Ima, and Tom purchased another East Texas tract of nearly 178 acres near Rusk as a park memorial to their father. Now the Jim Hogg Historic Site administered by the city of Rusk, the park includes the land surrounding Jim Hogg's birthplace and a family gravesite at Mountain Home. During the last years of her life, Ima conducted Arbor Day tree plantings at the park to fulfill her father's command that his children make Texas a domain of trees.[124]

Retelling the story of her family and pioneering settlement at Quitman and Rusk made Ima see how Varner could be restored to continue the family saga and explore Texas's economic expansion in the later nineteenth and early twentieth centuries. Ima first considered making the property a park and museum in 1942, not long after Mike's death. Mike, Ima, and Tom had often discussed Varner's ultimate fate. In his September 1941 will, Mike laid out a strategy his sister followed after Tom died in 1949. Mike's will stipulated that 52.67 acres of the Varner estate be reserved for the state as a museum and park in the names of Jim and Sallie Stinson Hogg's four children "in tribute to the memory of their beloved father and mother."[125]

Varner presented a dilemma for Ima. At Quitman, Ima was able to preserve two structures that had fallen into disrepair but had not undergone changes that compromised their historical integrity. Varner was a different matter. The house and property had been dramatically altered during the years since 1826, when Martin Varner received his land grant from the Mexican government as part of the Stephen F. Austin colony. Sugar, cotton, and oil had sustained the families who lived there, a trajectory of the state's economic development. Varner as a home place and experimental farm was Governor Hogg's pride and great joy. To the children Varner had been a "holy place," and Will, with his usual expansive enthusiasm, had "tried to fix up the old place as George Washington would do if he had a bankroll."[126]

In 1916, Will asked architect and friend Birdsall Briscoe to link what had been a simple family farm to grand colonial revival design schemes. To Ima's subsequent dismay, during the 1919–1920 remodeling, Will removed porches and added porticoes, pergolas, and satellite wings that dramatically changed the house's original appearance.[127] Furnished with family possessions from childhood homes in Austin, antique "copper and pewter stuff" found by Will as early as 1916, and period furniture, Varner revealed the evolving ambition of increasingly wealthy Texans. When Ima decided to create Varner-Hogg Plantation State Historical Park, named for its first and last owners, she chose to retain Will's transformations because they showed Varner's history and development. The alterations she made explained the economic expansion of the Gulf Coast from an 1830s economy based on slave labor, sugar, and cotton to a 1920s economy of boomtown oil discovery and exploration.

Ima worked in partnership with the Texas State Historical Survey Committee, the Texas Historical Foundation, and a local advisory committee. She interviewed residents, rediscovered much Brazoria County history, and preserved the property's plantation past, thereby encouraging scholars to explore plantation roots of black and white Texans.[128] Always a hands-on benefactress, Ima made frequent trips to the worksite, stayed in Miss Ima's Cottage while supervising activities, and purchased numerous objects for the interiors. She dedicated the park on March 24, 1958, her father's one-hundred-and-seventh birthday, and realized another dream by uniting family and state history in the interior displays. Family and period furniture, Texian campaign commemorative ceramics, George

Washington memorabilia, portraits, and photographs tell Ima's story of Texas, link that story to America's past, and fulfill family wishes to share its own good fortune with all the people of the state.[129]

For Ima these reconstructions of earlier lifestyles stimulated self-understanding and "advancement through knowledge of the past."[130] She undertook the work at Winedale after she turned eighty, vigorously pursued projects there until the last months of her life, and redefined the open-air museum concept. No longer merely a repository of artifacts for contemplation and instruction, Winedale became a "laboratory for the revival and restoration of a way of life" where students and public could rediscover the immigrant journey and examine the "transmission of craftsmanship" from Germany and Bohemia to the New World. At Winedale, a rural hamlet in Fayette County about eighty miles west of Houston, Ima gathered period houses, nurtured Shakespearean drama in an old barn converted to theater use, and sponsored classical music festivals to provide an adventure that blurred the distinction between "high art" and "folk" expression.[131]

Introduced to the German American culture of the area by Houston friend and antique dealer Hazel Ledbetter, Ima visited several properties in July 1962 with Harris County Heritage Society Director James A. Nonemaker. She purchased the Lewis-Wagner house and 130 acres in late 1962 and asked Houston architects Langwith, Wilson, and King to prepare plans for restoration work. Her team began preservation work in 1964. In 1965 Ima promised the project to the University of Texas, and it became a center for research, teaching, and public outreach.[132] What had begun as the restoration of an old inn along the stagecoach route from San Felipe to Bastrop became a complex project that involved faculty advisors from the university's art, architecture, music, history, drama, botany, archeology, and biology departments—a holistic effort to examine the flora, fauna, and people of a region and "to collect, preserve, and interpret to the public artifacts and processes of life in the past."[133] Guests at the University of Texas dedication ceremonies on April 8, 1966, participated in "an old-fashioned German Barbecue" and band concert, heard Charles van Ravenswaay, director of Winterthur, and watched theater and folk dancing presented by the university drama department.[134]

Ima loved German music and culture. Her time as a student in Berlin had been happy, and she admired German industriousness and passion for freedom. To her it was significant that German immigrants did not own slaves but had wrested prosperity from the harsh Texas climate through communal and family effort.[135] Ima began restoring the Lewis-Wagner house and Four-Square Barn on their original sites and moved a Texas dog-run house (Hazel's Lone Oak Cottage), the McGregor Greek Revival–style planter's home, and a classic revival farmhouse (destroyed by fire in 1981) to the site for restoration. The beautifully painted ceilings and other decorative work in the Lewis-Wagner and McGregor houses particularly delighted Ima because the decoration typified German craftsmanship. She studied preservation techniques, hired youthful architectural overseers, and began to collect furniture made in the surrounding counties.

Ima did not leave execution of the Winedale project to others. Most Saturdays found the octogenarian and her treasure-laden station wagon in Winedale on inspection tours. She climbed through rubble, chose wallpaper and colors herself, and insisted on detailed weekly reports.[136] In the last years of her life, Winedale became a retreat where she celebrated her birthdays, enjoyed music, and played a cat-and-mouse collecting game with competitor Faith Bybee, who was restoring Texas pioneer structures at nearby Round Top. Amusing correspondence among the curators of Bayou Bend, Varner-Hogg, and Winedale reveals Ima's intimate interest in all her projects. Although she had deeded property and contents to various public entities, she still viewed them as "hers," and she would frequently remove objects from one museum and take them to another where she felt they might be more effectively used.[137] Ima's determination to preserve America's multifaceted heritage ceased only with her death in August 1975.

Houstonians, and indeed all Texans, had become Ima's family. As she carefully arranged her collections to explain the story of America's past, she thought of future generations and the communities they would build because they appreciated the legacy of those who had gone before. The past—its hold on the present and its role in shaping the future—was a constant theme in Hogg family debates. Governor Hogg and his children believed that democracy's survival depended on a citizenry well versed in its heritage and values. This credo shaped the Hoggs' educational philanthropy, inspired their art and Americana collections, and propelled them to lives of civic activism. Proud of their family's contributions to America's story and aware that they, too, were public actors, they memorialized their parents and preserved papers pertaining to the institutions they supported. Yet they also built a wall of privacy. Will made hundreds of anonymous gifts and shunned recognition; Ima withdrew her personality from Bayou Bend to create period rooms that reflect a national heritage, not her story; and Mike left a modest paper trail that barely outlines the parameters of a busy civic life. As protector of the family's legacy, Ima may have felt history could be controlled by the actors themselves. She kept careful watch over biographers who wanted to study her father or her older brother. Although she preserved papers that illuminated family ties to important community institutions, the personal is sometimes missing from this extensive record. As the artisans of old are known to us by the furniture they made, so the Hoggs are remembered by the institutions they built.

Epilogue

In 1905 Governor James Stephen Hogg moved his business interests to Houston, a sleepy Southern town awakening to the promise of modern life. Some citizens dreamed of cultural amenities that would balance business expansion, but most were content to picnic on the bayous, browse in the lending lyceum, shoot birds on the flat prairie, or join friends for musical or literary afternoons. Residents walked to work along dusty (or muddy) streets; chickens and cows foraged in backyards; church steeples defined the skyline; and wooden opera houses welcomed traveling entertainment. Trolley cars clanged along Main Street, which was criss-crossed by telephone wires, but the urbanizing challenges of New York, Chicago, or St. Louis had not yet reached the Gulf Coast port.

In 1975 the governor's only daughter, Ima, died at age ninety-three. Still an active participant in civic life, she left behind the fourth-largest city in North America, a megametropolis and major shipping center traversed by multilane freeways. The car was everyone's chariot of choice; skyscrapers dominated multiple "downtowns"; oil refineries and chemical plants pumped millions into the economy each week; residents cheered homegrown professional sports teams or attended nationally acclaimed symphony, ballet, opera, and theater performances; and the region's great civic art museum had expanded its campus several times. Major universities, a renowned medical center, and a space center drew a highly educated workforce to the city and its satellite suburbs, but Houstonians struggled daily with the consequences of modernization.

Will, Ima, and Mike Hogg and their circle of progressive friends nurtured a legacy of civic responsibility. They recognized that citizens must temper unhampered economic expansion with concern for the quality of life their city provided everyone. Contemporary life brought sprawl, confusion, congestion, and pollution as well as lifesaving medicines, rockets to the moon, and unimagined domestic comfort and leisure. Houston in the new millennium is a metropolis transformed by changes of the past century. No longer a somnolent biracial town controlled by white men, Houston is a dynamic international beacon inspiring residents of several surrounding counties. Within city limits reside nearly two million citizens whose fastest-growing ethnic groups are Hispanic and Asian. Without a majority voice, Houston is poised to become a premier multicultural melting pot if it can build on its historic foundation of boundless optimism, energetic activism, and welcoming hospitality.

The Hoggs' civic activism provides a model for Houstonians who hope to capitalize on their city's diversity. The Hoggs believed that the oil fueling their beneficence was a natural resource, not the product of their labor, and as such must be held in trust by them for the people of Texas. Earnest children of a serious family, Will, Ima, and Mike also believed citizens of a democracy must nurture the communities that had nurtured them. They became philanthropic entrepreneurs who created institutions that empowered others to address the complexity of modern life. They provided tools, not hand-outs, so others could create the wealth found in satisfactory lives. They leveraged the power of their family's reputation to gain widespread support for civic causes. The Hoggs revered personal freedom and the tenets of constitutional democratic governance, so they fought for ideas they believed supported the individual and the democracy that was every American citizen's unquestioned birthright: a beautiful, safe physical environment; a well-ordered home; and a milieu enriched by lively cultural opportunities.

Ima thought her Bayou Bend collections built bridges from the empire that was Texas to the Atlantic Seaboard of America's founders. In fact, all the Hogg philanthropies attempted to unite citizens in the community and tie community to state and nation. As practical idealists, the Hoggs advocated cooperation and tried to bring diverse groups together to confront common problems and find community solutions. This model of collaboration was best articulated in convening conferences institutionalized by the Hogg Foundation. By engaging business leaders, government officials, and volunteers, the Hoggs tried to show how the conflicting motives of profit, power, and philanthropy could be fused to achieve community goals. For the Hoggs, philanthropy was a creative art; they visualized the components of an ideal urban environment, and they communicated this vision to others. Stewards of a family fortune and a family value system, Will, Ima, and Mike led by example as volunteers, activists, and donors in philanthropic careers marked by their breadth, persistence, and duration. Their successes and failures suggest that all citizens, however fallible, have critical roles to play in their communities.

Nearly a century after their civic activism first influenced the quality of life in Houston and in Texas, the institutions they built continue to thrive and define community life. The Houston Symphony Orchestra and the Museum of Fine Arts, Houston, and its decorative arts wing at Bayou Bend have attained international status and continue to "affirm the core values of our democratic society . . . freedom of expression, the pursuit of happiness, and the inherent dignity of each individual," as the Hoggs hoped they would.[1] The Texas Medical Center is the city's largest employer, and the Child Guidance Center, now blended with the DePelchin Children's Center, has enlarged its campus and become the premiere guide for child-caring services in the city. Memorial Park is a favored green space for thousands of daily visitors, and River Oaks still shelters its upscale residents from urban tumult on tree-lined streets. The Hoggs' gifts to higher education set a course followed by thousands of devoted alumni and supporters who have created internationally acclaimed institutions. It is hard to imagine Houston without the many organizations touched by the Hoggs and their farsighted friends.

Today as in the Hoggs' day, Houstonians struggle to protect their heritage, to identify a common community good, and to preserve diverse and often divergent values. Just as Houston idealists were challenged a century ago to husband their resources carefully and build a great city, so in the new millennium are Houstonians called to distribute the city's wealth and engage fellow citizens in ways that foster "the participatory, egalitarian and open character of public life at the heart of democratic movements."[2] Through the collective effort of many, Houston can continue along its trajectory of promise.

Today when crowds gather at Bayou Bend, they come not to mourn the passing of Texas's "First Lady" but to celebrate the legacy of a family's vision. As parents pose before the pink azaleas and children race about the garden, they pay homage to the Hoggs' wish that all Houstonians could enjoy the natural beauty of their environment and the cultural heritage of their past to fortify them for daily struggles that lie ahead. Today as in the Hoggs' time, thousands of Houstonians give generously to build a better city. Today as then they recognize their city's many flaws and problems, band together in coalitions, and work—to improve their library system, to reform their schools, to clean up their environment, to save their parks, to plant more trees, to preserve their cultural institutions, and to demand responsive action from city officials. Today, as always, greed and limited vision mar the great city Houston might become, but many Houstonians still envision a metropolis of destiny and appreciate a heritage of hope and civic engagement.

Notes

ABBREVIATIONS

The following list is a key to abbreviations used in endnotes.

BE Board of Education, Houston Independent School District
CAH Center for American History, University of Texas at Austin
DCC DePelchin Children's Center (including Houston Child Guidance
    Center material)
HFR Hogg Foundation Records
HMRC Houston Metropolitan Research Center
HPL Houston Public Library
IHP Ima Hogg Papers
IHPC Ima Hogg Program Collection, University of Houston Archives
JSH James Stephen Hogg Papers
MFAH Museum of Fine Arts, Houston
RU Rice University
UH University of Houston
WHP Will Hogg Papers
WRC Woodson Research Center, Rice University

NOTES

The four epigraphs after the book's dedication that quote James, Will, Ima, and Mike Hogg, respectively, are taken from the following materials. James Stephen Hogg, First Message to the Twenty-second Legislature, January 21, 1891, in *Addresses and State Papers of James Stephen Hogg*, Centennial Edition, ed. Robert C. Cotner. With biographical sketch (Austin: University of Texas Press, 1951), 122–123. William Clifford Hogg to Herbert Hare, Kansas City, letter, July 14, 1925, Box 2J299, City Planning folder 1924–1926, WHP, CAH. Ima Hogg, November 1952, Speech, 3B168, folder 5, IHP, CAH. Michael Hogg, Speech, Box 2, folder 7, Mike and Alice Hogg Papers, Archives, MFAH.

PREFACE

1. The youngest child, Thomas Elisha (August 10, 1887–March 9, 1949), did not join his siblings in Houston.

2. Ima Hogg, November 1952, 3B168, folder 5, IHP, CAH.
3. Lawrence J. Friedman, "Philanthropy in America: Historicism and Its Discontents," in *Charity, Philanthropy, and Civility in American History*, ed. Lawrence J. Friedman and Mark D. McGarvie (Cambridge, England: Cambridge University Press, 2003), 9, 10.
4. Ima Hogg, remarks, "Bayou Bend Dedication," March 5, 1966. Pamphlet privately printed by Ima Hogg, 11. IHP, Archives, MFAH.
5. Robert L. Payton, "Philanthropy as a Right," in *The Citizen and His Government*, ed W. Lawson Taitte (Dallas: University of Texas at Dallas, 1984), 126.

PROLOGUE

1. Personal recollection of the author; clippings, *New York Times, Houston Chronicle, Houston Post*, Miss Ima Hogg, Vertical File, Archives, MFAH.
2. *Chronicle*, Aug. 21, 1975, editorial, sec. 4, p. 4; *Chronicle*, Aug. 20, 1975, sec. 4, p. 26; Lonn Taylor, "Miss Ima Hogg," *Texas Observer*, Sept. 5, 1975, 11.
3. *Post*, Aug. 23, 1975, 3A; *Chronicle*, Aug. 23, 1975, 1.

CHAPTER 1

1. Houston Telephone Directory, December 1905; City Directory, 1905–1906. Will Hogg ("father has decided on Houston" as the family's future home) to Mike Hogg, March 7, 1905, 3B124, folder 1, IHP, CAH; engraved announcement of the governor's withdrawal from Hogg and Robertson in Austin and his admittance to the firm of Hogg, Watkins, and Jones in Houston, Feb. 1, 1905, 2J215, JSH, CAH.
2. W. G. Jameson, Chief Surgeon International and Great Northern Railroad, to Dr. J. R. Moore, Galveston, Dec. 4, 1905, W. G. Jameson Letter File 197, WRC, RU.
3. *Telegraph and Texas Register*, front-page advertisement, Aug. 30, 1836, and for several months thereafter. On Dec. 30, 1836, the brothers added "The Present Seat of Government/Of the State of Texas" to their header.
4. The Long Row is preserved today as part of the Harris County Heritage Society exhibit at Sam Houston Park in downtown Houston.
5. Judy King, *Except the Lord Build . . . : The Sesquicentennial History of First Presbyterian Church, Houston, Texas, 1839–1989* (Houston: The Church, 1989), 6; *Telegraph and Texas Register*, April 4, 1837.
6. Advertisement, *Telegraph and Texas Register*, Dec. 30, 1841. Their store is said to have been the first frame house built in Houston. A pair of silver tablespoons marked "Torrey & Bro" was acquired in Nov. 2003 for the Bayou Bend Collection and may be the "earliest silver bearing marks of a Texas maker or retailer." Agenda item, Bayou Bend and Collections Committees, MFAH; Sally Anne S. Gutting, Jameson Fellow at Rice University and Bayou Bend Collection and Gardens, paper, in author's possession.

7.   Original plat in David G. McComb, *Houston: The Bayou City* (Austin: University of Texas Press, 1969), 16; James L. Glass, "The Original Book of Sales of Lots of the Houston Town Company from 1836 Forward," *Houston Review: History and Culture of the Gulf Coast* (hereinafter cited as *Houston Review*) 16 (1994): 176; Stanley E. Siegel, *Houston: A Chronicle of the Supercity on Buffalo Bayou* (Woodland Hills, CA: Windsor Publications for Harris County Historical Society, 1983), 24. See Map Collection, Texas Room, HPL.

8.   In 1842 Sam Houston returned the capital to his namesake city for a few months before moving it to Washington-on-the-Brazos in September 1842. In 1845 Austin was made temporary capital and became the permanent capital in 1850 after an election choice among Austin, Houston, and Waco.

9.   Population figures from the U.S. Bureau of the Census are as follows—1850: 2,396; 1860: 4,845; 1870: 10,382; 1880: 16,513; 1890: 27,557; 1900: 44,633. Statistics on the town's black population during this time come from Arthur C. Comey's 1913 draft of City Plan for Houston—1850: 533; 1870: 3,691; 1880: 6,479; 1890: 10,370; 1900: 14,608 (MSS 69, Box 10, folder 5, Joseph Cullinan Papers, HMRC, HPL). Other ethnic groups, including a growing Mexican population, were grouped with "white" data during this period. F. Arturo Rosales estimates that about 2,000 Mexicans lived in Houston by 1908; "Mexicans in Houston: The Struggle to Survive, 1908–1975," *Houston Review* 3 (Summer 1981): 224.

10.   Judy King (*Except the Lord Build*, 71) credits Reverend William States Jacobs, pastor of the First Presbyterian Church, with coining the slogan "Where 17 railroads meet the sea, there will arise a great city even if it were in the Sahara Desert."

11.   Photo, October 1894, in J. H. Freeman, *The People of Baker Botts* (Houston: Champagne Fine Printing and Lithographing, 1992), 35; McComb, *Houston*, 111.

12.   His son Edward Mandell House, a major supporter of Governor Hogg and Hogg's political heirs from 1899 to 1907 and a principal advisor to Woodrow Wilson, secured federal government posts for many Texans during the Wilson presidency.

13.   Andrew Forest Muir, *William Marsh Rice and His Institute: A Biographical Study*, ed. Sylvia Stallings Morris (Houston: William Marsh Rice University, 1972), 151, charter of incorporation, May 1891.

14.   See Joe R. Feagin, *Free Enterprise City: Houston in Political-Economic Perspective* (New Brunswick, NJ: Rutgers University Press, 1988), 51–56; Francisco Arturo Rosales and Barry J. Kaplan, eds., *Houston: A Twentieth Century Urban Frontier* (Port Washington, NY: Associated Faculty Press, 1983), 13–19.

15.   Elisabeth O'Kane, "To Lift the City Out of the Mud: Health, Sanitation, and Sewerage in Houston, 1840–1920," *Houston Review* 17 (1995): 3–27.

16.   Freeman, *People of Baker Botts*, photo, 29; Siegel, *Houston*, photo, 98.

17.   I. J. Isaacs, ed., *The Industrial Advantages of Houston, Texas, and Environs, also a Series of Comprehensive Sketches of the City's Representative Business*

Enterprises (Houston: Akehurst, 1894), 7–36; quotes from title, 7, 23, 32. Census figures show an 1890 population of 27,557 and a 1900 population of 44,633. The 1916 *Illustrated City Book of Houston, Containing the Annual Message of Ben Campbell, Mayor of the City of Houston* (Houston: Cumming and Sons, Art Printers, 1916), 12, 27, lists Houston as the largest inland cotton port, handling more than 3 million bales a year, and by 1916, eighty-one lumber companies were headquartered in the city.

18. Elizabeth Hayes Turner, *Women, Culture, and Community: Religion and Reform in Galveston, 1880–1920* (New York: Oxford University Press, 1997), 34.

19. Caldwell Reines, *Year Book for Texas, 1901*, quoted in Siegel, *Houston*, 121, and in John S. Spratt, *The Road to Spindletop: Economic Change in Texas, 1875–1901* (Dallas: Southern Methodist University Press, 1955), 274.

20. Marilyn McAdams Sibley, *The Port of Houston: A History* (Austin: University of Texas Press, 1968); Walter L. Buenger and Joseph A. Pratt, *But Also Good Business: Texas Commerce Banks and the Financing of Houston and Texas, 1886–1986* (College Station: Texas A&M University Press, 1986), 22–25; McComb, *Houston*, 94–96.

21. "Joseph C. Hutcheson," *Handbook of Texas Online*, www.tsha.utexas.edu/handbook/online, accessed March 1, 2004; Hutcheson Family Papers, WRC.

22. Ethel Ransom Art and Literary Club Collection, HMRC, HPL; The Married Ladies Social, Art, and Charity Club Papers, HMRC, HPL; Audrey Y. Crawford, "'To protect, to feed, and to give momentum to every effort': African American Clubwomen in Houston, 1880–1910," *Houston Review* 1 (Fall 2003): 15–23.

23. Bylaws of the Houston Foundation, 2J371, folder 1, WHP, CAH; *The Community: A Review of Philanthropic Thought and Social Effort* I (May 1919): 1, in WRC.

24. Julia Cameron Montgomery, *Houston as a Setting of the Jewel: The Rice Institute, 1913*, reprint (Houston: Rice Historical Society, 2002), 44; first published in 1913 by Julia Cameron Montgomery.

25. Editorial, *Chronicle*, Dec. 19, 1913, 4; "Tag Day Was Great Success," *Post*, Dec. 19, 1913, 12.

26. Karen J. Blair, *The Torchbearers: Women and Their Amateur Arts Associations in America, 1890–1930* (Bloomington: Indiana University Press, 1994), estimates that by 1895 more than 100,000 women participated in club activities nationwide.

27. Dorothy Knox Howe Houghton, *The Houston Club and Its City: One Hundred Years* (Houston: Gulf Printing, 1994), 7, 10, 13 (early members).

28. Quotes from Thalian Club articles of incorporation (1901) and Margaret Halsey Foster (1908) in Houghton, *Houston Club*, 20.

29. Andrew Carnegie, "Wealth," *North American Review* 148 (June 1889): 653–664.

30. Montgomery, *Houston as a Setting*, 5.

31. Joseph Lewis and Lucanda McMath Hogg had seven children: Martha Frances Hogg Davis (1834–1920), Julia Hogg McDugald Ferguson (1839–

1896), Thomas Elisha (1842–1880), John (1848–1912), James Stephen (1851–1906), Joseph Lewis Jr. (1854–1873), and Richard (1856–1863).

32. Kathleen Sproul, "James Stephen Hogg: March 24, 1851–March 3, 1906," pamphlet printed on the occasion of the dedication of the Varner-Hogg State Park, West Columbia, TX, March 24, 1958, 9.

33. I am indebted to Lonn Taylor for the insight that Ima seemed typical of the generation that grew up in the aftermath of the Civil War and developed a "fierce desire" to see Texas "recover from defeat" and "take its place as a leader among states." Lonn Taylor to author, email, Dec. 12, 2002. Information about the Hogg family comes from Ima Hogg, "Reminiscences of Life in the Texas Governor's Mansion," in IHP, Archives, MFAH, and in 3B168, folder 4, IHP, CAH; Virginia Bernhard, *Ima Hogg: The Governor's Daughter* (St. James, NY: Brandywine Press, 1984), 17–32; William Lee Pryor, "'The Fate of Marvin': An Epic Poem of the Civil War by a Texas Soldier," *Texas Quarterly* (Summer 1977), 8–9; Bruce J. Weber, "Will Hogg and the Business of Reform" (Ph.D. diss., University of Houston, 1979), 3–4; Robert C. Cotner, *James Stephen Hogg: A Biography* (Austin: University of Texas Press, 1959), vii, 63, 447–454; Varner-Hogg dedication pamphlet; other reminiscences, 3B130, folder 3, IHP, CAH.

34. 2J418, JSH, CAH; information about Jim Hogg's youth is found in Cotner, *James Stephen Hogg*; Bernhard, *Ima Hogg*, 22–24; Varner-Hogg dedication pamphlet; Louise Kosches Iscoe, *Ima Hogg, First Lady of Texas: Reminiscences and Recollections of Family and Friends* (Austin: Hogg Foundation for Mental Health, 1976), 19.

35. James Stephen Hogg (1851–1906) and Sarah Ann "Sallie" Stinson Hogg (1854–1895) were the parents of four children: William Clifford (Jan. 31, 1875–Sept. 12, 1930), Ima (July 10, 1882–Aug. 19, 1975), Michael (Oct. 28, 1885–Oct. 10, 1941), and Thomas Elisha (Aug. 10, 1887–March 9, 1949).

36. Edward M. House claims Texas under Jim Hogg was the "first in the field" to enact progressive legislation and was followed by Wisconsin, California, and other touted "progressive" states. Charles Seymour, ed., *The Intimate Papers of Colonel House*, vol. 1, *Behind the Political Curtain* (Boston: Houghton Mifflin, 1926), 35.

37. *Chronicle*, Aug. 18, 1934, letter to the editor; Bernhard, *Ima Hogg*, 38–41. In Seymour, *Intimate Papers*, 28, Edward M. House assessed Governor Hogg's reforms at "the centre of the storm" between progressive and conservative Democrats.

38. Ima Hogg, draft of comments made to the Board of Regents, University of Texas, March 8, 1962, MAI9/Ul, folder 4, HFR, CAH.

39. See Leonore Davidoff and Catherine Hall, *Family Fortunes: Men and Women of the English Middle Class, 1780–1850* (Chicago: University of Chicago Press, 1987); and Stanley Coben, *Rebellion Against Victorianism: The Impetus for Cultural Change in 1920s America* (New York: Oxford University Press, 1991).

40. Elizabeth Brooks, *Prominent Women of Texas* (Akron, Ohio: Werner, 1896), 163.

41. Ima Hogg, "Reminiscences of Life in the Texas Governor's Mansion," 7 (description), 10 (partner), 2 (gum), 6 (inventories), 3B168, folder 4, and Ima Hogg to Mary Koock, April 16, 1964, 3B163, IHP, CAH.

42. James Stephen Hogg to Ima Hogg, March 1, 1902, IHP, Memorabilia Series 11 and 13, Box 15, folder 2, correspondence 1888–1909, Archives, MFAH.

43. Ima Hogg to Gordon K. Shearer, director, Texas State Parks Board, Jan. 19, 1951, 4W263, folder 7, IHP, CAH.

44. "Reminiscences," 24, 25, 3B168, folder 4, IHP, CAH.

45. "Reminiscences," 18, 19, 3B168, folder 4, IHP, CAH; clipping, Winnsboro *News*, Wood County, Feb. 16, 1967, Series 14, Scrapbook I, 6, IHP, Archives, MFAH; Ima Hogg, oral history, HMRC, HPL.

46. Correspondence, series 1, box 4, folder 2, IHP, Archives, MFAH; correspondence between Ima Hogg and H. E. Brigham, 3B151, folder 1, IHP, CAH.

47. James Stephen Hogg to sister [Martha Frances Davis], Oct. 14, 1895, 3B111, IHP, CAH.

48. William C. Hogg to Sallie Stinson Hogg, May 16, 1895, 3B118, IHP, CAH. See Emily Ballew Neff with Wynne H. Phelan, *Frederic Remington: The Hogg Brothers Collection of the Museum of Fine Arts, Houston* (Princeton, NJ: Princeton University Press, 2000), 10–11, for an excellent analysis of Will's feelings about his mother.

49. "Reminiscences," 3B130, folder 10, IHP, CAH.

50. Ima Hogg to Robert Sutherland, Aug. 24, 1970, interview, Round Top, MAI9/U1, folder 12, HFR, CAH; Ima Hogg to Anson Phelps Stokes, Aug. 22, 1903, 3B131, folder 1, IHP, CAH; letters, Oct. 17, 1910, and March 28, 1911, 2J343, folders 2 and 3, WHP, CAH.

51. Ima Hogg to author, conversations in 1974, 1975; Bernhard, *Ima Hogg*, 31, based on Ima's reminiscences.

52. Coben, *Rebellion Against Victorianism*, 4, outlines a "configuration of virtues" based on hundreds of contemporary statements about character.

53. James Stephen Hogg to Ima, Michael, Thomas Hogg, in South Egremont, Mass., July 18, 1904, 2J215, folder June 3, 1904–Dec. 19, 1905, JSH, CAH.

54. James Stephen Hogg to William C. Hogg, April 19, 1892, 2J327, folder 1, WHP, CAH; and volume of letters to William C. Hogg, April 19, 1892–Oct. 7, 1899, 2J418, JSH, CAH, on official governor's stationery.

55. James Stephen Hogg to William C. Hogg, from Fifth Avenue Hotel, April 26, 1895, letterbook, 2J418, JSH, CAH.

56. James Stephen Hogg to William C. Hogg, from Waldorf-Astoria, June 26, 1899, letterbook, 2J418, JSH, CAH.

57. Letters to Ima Hogg on following dates: April 29, 1902 (aboard Southwestern Limited), June 12, 1904 (Ima in Holyoke, Mass.), Oct. 9, 1902 (Beaumont), Nov. 24, 1902 (James S. Hogg at Rice Hotel), Nov. 7, 1902 (Ima in New York), May 29, 1902, 2J215, folders 2, 3, 6, JSH, CAH.

58. Jane Addams, *Democracy and Social Ethics* (New York: Macmillan, 1916), 83.

59. James Stephen Hogg to Ima Hogg, July 10, 1899, 3B111, IHP, CAH.

60. James Stephen Hogg to Ima Hogg, Nov. 16, 1902, May 6, 1903, 2J215, JSH, CAH.

61. On Ima's thirteenth birthday her father wrote, "My confidence in the purity of your nature, in your deep regard for the rectitude and refinement of your sex . . . firmly . . . justifies my hope that in no act of your life shall I ever find cause for disappointment or regret. God bless you my worthy daughter." James Stephen Hogg to Ima Hogg, July 10, 1895, 3B166, folder 1, IHP, CAH.

62. W. S. Sutton, Dean of Education, University of Texas, to William C. Hogg, Oct. 12, 1915, 2J311, folder "Educational Work in Texas, June 19, 1915–Dec. 17, 1919," WHP, CAH.

63. Sproul, "James Stephen Hogg"; and 2J296, WHP, CAH, statement regarding his father's death at the home of Frank C. Jones, Houston.

64. Draft to the Board of Regents, March 8, 1962, MAI9/U1, folder 2, HFR, CAH.

65. William C. Hogg to Colonel James A. Stinson, Winnsboro, July 6, 1906, 2J327, folder 1, WHP, CAH.

66. In 1905 there was talk of suing the International and Great Northern Railroad Company, although witnesses stated that the governor had not complained when the train jolted in a coupling. The railroad's chief surgeon suggested obesity or a bad cold as reasons for the governor's subsequent heart trouble. W. G. Jameson, chief surgeon, International and Great Northern Railroad, to Dr. J. R. Moore, Galveston, Dec. 4, 1905, W G Jameson Letter File 197, WRC.

67. Jacqueline Haun, archivist, Bunn Library, Lawrenceville School, email and letter to author, June 29, 2007, states that Lawrenceville records show Tom completed grades 8 and 9 and attended Lawrenceville from Sept. 26, 1903, to June 1905. Letters in the Lawrenceville archives reveal that Will supervised the younger boys' education for his father, doled out allowances, and corresponded with the headmaster about Tom's poor study habits. Also in letters, 3B126, folders 1, 2, IHP, CAH; Deposition of Thomas Hogg, 3F389, Hogg Family Papers, CAH.

68. William C. Hogg to Judge James H. Robertson, Austin, March 16, 1906, 2J327, folder 1, WHP, CAH. "Memo of absences from the state of Miss Ima Hogg" records travel and study in Europe from July 1907 through October 1908, 2J328, WHP, CAH; 3B118, folder 3, IHP, CAH, confirms the dates.

69. Houston City Directories, 1906, 1907, 1908.

70. William C. Hogg to Michael and Thomas Hogg, March 1, 1909, letters about allowances, travel, career, Box 15, folder 2, IHP, Archives, MFAH.

71. Diary, March 26, 1917 ("Sup at 4410 Rossmoyne for first time"), 2J399, WHP, CAH. At first the Hoggs rented from developer Ross Sterling. William C. Hogg to R. S. Sterling, Aug. 26, 1916, 2J328, WHP, CAH; diary Feb. 24, 1919, 2J299, WHP, CAH, notes purchase. The Hoggs later sold this house to Ima's close friend Estelle Sharp.

72. Houston City Directories, 1908–1912.

73. Hugh L. Stone, vice president and general council, Gulf Oil Corporation, Pittsburgh, Jan. 20, 1933, Box 1, folder 7, Mike and Alice Hogg Papers, Archives, MFAH.

74. William C. Hogg to David M. Pickens, April 13, 1923, 4W271, IHP, CAH; William C. Hogg to Ima Hogg, May 3, 1918, 3B119, IHP, CAH.

75. Scrapbook 1, p. 15, series 14, IHP, Archives, MFAH.

76. See the Girls' Musical Club, Houston, program for 1914–1915, Texas Room, HPL.

77. William C. Hogg to E. C. Lufkin, Dec. 30, 1913, Box 16, folder 1, James L. Autry Papers, WRC.

78. William C. Hogg to the Chamber of Commerce, Houston, Sept. 21, 1914, Lovett Papers, Box 43, folder 10 (Hogg Family), WRC; William C. Hogg to various, September–November 1914, Cullinan Papers, Box 59, folder 1, HMRC, HPL.

79. The Hoggs began exploring for oil at Varner, West Columbia, during the governor's lifetime. By 1917, when the well W. C. Hogg 1 blew in on May 13, it was clear that West Columbia would be a major producer, and on January 15, 1918, Tyndall-Hogg No. 2 heralded a rich discovery. In 1921 West Columbia wells produced more than 12 million barrels; twenty-six years later, they continued to pump more than 2 million barrels a year. William Booker Ferguson, longtime financial advisor to the Hogg family, said Jim Hogg chose the West Columbia property on the advice of Anthony F. Lucas, an expert in salt-dome topography who brought in the discovery well at Spindletop in 1901. The Patton property abutted the Kaiser Mound area, which displayed gas seeps and a central, swampy basin indicating a salt dome near the surface. Subsequent purchases increased the governor's Kaiser Mound holdings. Ferguson, "Hogg Family Financial History," Vertical File, Archives, MFAH.

80. William C. Hogg to Ima Hogg, April 1, 1918, sale to Garrow, MacClain, and Co., 3B119, folder 1, IHP, CAH.

81. William C. Hogg to Edward M. House, March 19, 1917, Dec. 22, 1917, and William C. Hogg to R. G. Hutchins Jr., National Bank of Commerce of New York City, March 25, 1918, telegram, in 2J336, folder 6, WHP, CAH; letters to William Jennings Bryan in WHP, CAH, passim.

82. Diary, July 20–22, Aug. 1, 8, 1918, 2J399, WHP, CAH, records visits to or consultation with doctors. Edward Prather to William C. Hogg, July 29, 1918, 3B119, folder 1, IHP, CAH, regarding bed rest.

83. William C. Hogg to EEC, Aug. 27, 1918, 3B119, folder 1, IHP, CAH; diary, Aug. 13, 31, Sept. 27, 2J399, WHP, CAH; William C. Hogg to D. Clark, Oct. 1, 1918, 3B119, folder 1, IHP, CAH. Diary, Sept. 30, shows a brief stay at a "rest cure" on Park Avenue and departure for Dr. Ford's Sanitarium on Oct. 7, 1918. Diary, Sept. 30, Dec. 4 and 24, 1918, 2J399, WHP, CAH; Ima Hogg to William C. Hogg, Oct. 18, Nov. 2, 1918, 3B119, folder 1, IHP, CAH.

84. Ima Hogg to Robert Sutherland, interviews, MAI9/U1, folder 2, HFR, CAH; correspondence between Francis X. Dercum and William C. Hogg, June 13, 14, 19, and 26, 1919, 3B119, folder 2, IHP, CAH; diary,

June 6 and July 7–9, 1919, 2J399, WHP, CAH; memo in 2J328, WHP, CAH; Francis Dercum to William C. Hogg, March 26, 1920, 3B119, folder 3, IHP, CAH.

85. Ima Hogg to William C. Hogg, Sept. 20, 1920, letter (Inness painting), January 1921, several letters (Duncan Phyfe table), Feb. 16, 1921, cable (antiques), 3B119, folder 3, IHP, CAH; diary references, Sept. 19, 20, 1920, Feb. 27, 1922, 2J399, WHP, CAH.

86. Madeleine McDermott, *Chronicle*, July 23, 1972, sec. 6, p. 8. The building was given by the Hoggs to the University of Texas in 1952 and sold to investors later that year.

87. Operation on June 24, 1921, in Jefferson Hospital, Thomas E. Hogg to Ima Hogg, telegram, 3B126, IHP, CAH; Christmas in New York, telegram, 2J328, WHP, CAH; diary entries, 1922, 2J399, WHP, CAH; Michael Hogg to Ima Hogg, Nov. 28, 1922, 3B124, folder 3, IHP, CAH.

88. Riggs (1876–1940), an internist self-taught in psychiatry, founded the Austen Riggs Center (1917) and the Austen Riggs Foundation (1919) in Stockbridge and the Riggs Clinic in Pittsfield (1920). Robert P. Knight and Cyrus R. Friedman, *Psychoanalytic Psychiatry and Psychology: Clinical and Theoretical Papers* (New York: International Universities Press, 1954), 2–3.

89. Ima Hogg to Robert Sutherland, Nov. 21, 1961, Aug. 24, 1970, interviews, MAI9/U1, folder 12, HFR, CAH; Michael Hogg to Ima Hogg, Dec. 24, 1923, Stockbridge, Mass., Christmas greetings, 3B124, folder 3, IHP, CAH. Diary, Feb. 2, 1924, 2B399, WHP, CAH, notes Ima was in Stockbridge from Armistice Day (Nov. 11, 1923) until Feb. 2, 1924. She also spent a few days in Stockbridge in November 1924.

90. Austen Fox Riggs, *Intelligent Living* (Garden City, NY: Doubleday, Doran, 1934), xvi. Riggs stated, "Work is . . . the first essential of a satisfactory life because it . . . is purposive effort" (181). Austen Fox Riggs, *Play: Recreation in a Balanced Life* (Garden City, NY: Doubleday, Doran, 1935), 6.

91. Ima Hogg, draft statement to the regents, March 8, 1962, MAI9/U1, folder 4, HFR, CAH.

92. Between 1882 and 1916 Andrew Carnegie wrote sixty-three articles, eight books, and ten pamphlets containing public addresses. Joseph Frazier Wall, ed., *The Andrew Carnegie Reader* (Pittsburgh, PA: University of Pittsburgh Press, 1992), x. Jane Addams wrote *Twenty Years at Hull-House*, *The Second Twenty Years at Hull-House*, *Democracy and Social Ethics*, and several other books during her long career.

93. Thomas Ward Gregory on William C. Hogg in *Alcalde*, October 1930, 10.

94. Ima Hogg to Robert Sutherland, Nov. 21, 1961, and May 10, 13, 1967, interviews, MAI9/U1, folder 12, HFR, CAH; memorandum on Ima's mental hygiene activities, 1948, MAI9/U1, folder 14, HFR, CAH; Ima Hogg to Robert Sutherland, April 27, 1967, MAI9/U1, folder 4, HFR, CAH. Ima Hogg, draft statement to the regents ("principles"), March 8, 1962, MAI9/U1, folder 4, HFR, CAH; phrases underlined in "A Modern Approach to Mental Hygiene Work" ("utilize"), memorandum, MAI9/U25, HFR, CAH.

95. Ima Hogg, "Bayou Bend Dedication," March 5, 1966, pamphlet (privately printed by Ima Hogg, 1966), 11, IHP, Archives, MFAH.
96. Ima Hogg, penciled memo, 1940, MAI9/U1, HFR, CAH.
97. The Hoggs owned two Park Avenue apartments from the mid-1920s through the mid-1930s.
98. John Avery Lomax, 3D205, folder 2, John Avery Lomax Family Papers, CAH.
99. Most Hogg family papers are in the Center for American History, University of Texas, Austin. The Museum of Fine Arts, Houston, and the special collections of the University of Houston also house important collections. Rice University received the family's transcribed copy of Governor James Stephen Hogg's state papers.
100. Mike and Alice Hogg Papers, MS 19, Archives, MFAH; 2J329, folder 1924–1928, WHP, CAH.
101. John Avery Lomax, *Will Hogg, Texan* (reprint, Austin: University of Texas Press, 1956), 10; first published in *Atlantic Monthly*, May 1940.
102. Ferguson, "Hogg Family Financial History," 106, MFAH.
103. *Houston Gargoyle*, Oct. 2, 1928, 8.
104. Letters, 2J345, National Democratic Convention, WHP, CAH.
105. Correspondence and clippings, Box 2, folder 2 (Prohibition Correspondence 1932–1935), Mike and Alice Hogg Papers, Archives, MFAH.
106. Mike quotes in box 2, folders 3, 7, Mike and Alice Hogg Papers, Archives, MFAH; Ima address in clipping, Aug. 28, Oct. 12, scrapbook 1, p. 27, series 14, IHP, Archives, MFAH.
107. Memorial to William Clifford Hogg, Rice Institute, Presidential Papers, President E. O. Lovett Papers 1912–1945, AR 1, box 35, folder 3, WRC.
108. Box 2J322, folders 3, 4, 5, WHP, CAH; interview Mary Cravens, Box 1, folder 21, Marguerite Johnston Papers, WRC.
109. Lomax, 3D205, folder 2, John Avery Lomax Family Papers, CAH.
110. O. D. D. McIntyre in 2J342, WHP, CAH; Nina Cullinan, interview, WRC.
111. Thomas Watt Gregory in *Alcalde*, October 1930, 10.
112. Ima Hogg, remarks at dedication in June 1968 of the Hogg Building, University of Texas, clipping in IHP, scrapbook 3, p. 57, Archives, MFAH.
113. March 26 and Nov. 1, 1929, and passim, diary, 2J399, WHP, CAH.
114. "Dirt-dauber" and other colorful language in remarks, William C. Hogg, City Auditorium, Houston, June 8, 1926, speeches in 2J352, WHP, CAH.
115. William C. Hogg to Governor Dan Moody, Austin, June 19, 1928, Cullinan Papers, Box 12, folder 2, HMRC, HPL. This widely disseminated letter is also found in the Sharp, Lovett, and Hogg papers. Will contended that Jones pushed the bounds of business ethics. Archival sources show that many Houstonians supported the convention center. Entries in Will Hogg's diary Jan. 13, 16, and 17 (met "bunch" at mayor's office to finance convention), Jan. 21 (Will and Mike agree to help finance convention), March 17 (lunch with Jones to review convention plans), March 20 and June 5 (lunch

with FDR), 2J399, WHP, CAH. For information on Jesse Jones see Bascom N. Timmons, *Jesse H. Jones: The Man and the Statesman* (New York: Henry Holt, 1956).

116. Roscoe Wright, "Tender Tempest—A Tardy Tribute to Will C. Hogg," *Gargoyle*, Sept. 21, 1930, 6, and "Millions for Learning: Will Hogg's Will Materializes His Dream," *Gargoyle*, Oct. 5, 1930, 14; "leavening influence" in Lomax, *Will Hogg, Texan*, 26; "spiritual heritage" in *Houston*, editorial, October 1930, 20.

117. *New Encyclopedia of Texas*, 2:1258, in James Chillman Papers, RG 2:1, series 2, box 3, folder 8, Archives, MFAH (Ima Hogg, Mrs. Henry B. Fall, Mrs. H. F. Ring, and Mrs. Edgar Odell Lovett are the four Houston women listed).

118. Wayne Bell, remarks to Bayou Bend Docent Organization, March 17, 2003; Lonn Taylor, interview with Martha Norkunas, Feb. 28, 1996, Winedale Oral History Collection, CAH; "Miss Ima Hogg," Sept. 5, 1975, Box 11, folder 15, Marguerite Johnston Papers, WRC; David B. Warren, "David Warren Looks Back," *The Intelligencer: Bayou Bend Collection and Gardens*, Winter 2003–2004, 5.

119. Booklet, "Miss Ima: 1882–1982 Centennial Celebration," n.p., n.d., in Miss Ima Hogg Vertical File, Archives, MFAH.

120. Iscoe, *Ima Hogg*, 21.

121. Mrs. Albert P. Jones, interview, July 31, 1985, p. 2, Box 12, folder 13, Marguerite Johnston Papers, WRC.

122. Awards include: the Amy Angell Collier Montague Award for Civic Achievement from the Garden Club of America (1959); Texan Woman of the Year (1963); the Louise du Pont Crowninshield Award from the National Trust for Historic Preservation (1966); the American Association for State and Local History Award (1969); and the Thomas Jefferson Award for Outstanding Contribution to America's Cultural Heritage by the National Society of Interior Designers (1972). She was the first recipient of the Santa Rita Award for outstanding service to the University of Texas (1968) and was given an honorary doctorate of fine arts by Southwestern University at Georgetown in May 1971.

123. Michael Hogg to Ima Hogg, Sept. 16, 1936, 3B124, folder 3, IHP, CAH.

124. Michael Hogg, speech, 1940, box 2, folder 7, Mike and Alice Hogg Papers, Archives, MFAH.

125. Palmer Hutcheson in *Alcalde*, November 1941, 30.

126. Mike prepped for the Naval Academy in Annapolis, September 1903 to February 1904, but switched to Lawrenceville, where he was placed in tenth grade. He did not graduate from Lawrenceville and went on to the University of Texas after further tutoring in Austin; Haun, Bunn Library, Lawrenceville.

127. Ferguson, "Hogg Family Financial History," 55, 83, MFAH.

128. Irvin S. Cobb to William C. Hogg, summer 1929, box 4, folder 1; O. O. McIntyre to Michael Hogg, n.d., box 4, O. O. McIntyre folder, Mike and Alice Hogg Papers, Archives, MFAH.

129. Ima Hogg, oral history, HMRC, HPL; Irvin Cobb to William C. Hogg, summer 1929, box 4, folder 1, Mike and Alice Hogg Papers, MFAH.
130. House Journal 40th Legislature, 41st Legislature. Mike supported prison reform, permanent school funding, the University of Texas, aircraft development, and Texas A&M appropriations.
131. Moody, clippings, box 1, folder 16, Mike and Alice Hogg Papers, Archives, MFAH; Michael Hogg to Ralph Yarborough, April 30, 1938, box 2, folder 1, ibid.
132. Irvin Cobb to Raymond Dickson, Oct. 11, 1941, letter, box 4, folder 6, ibid.

CHAPTER 2

The title of this chapter is taken from the name of a promotional pamphlet in River Oaks Collection, vol. 7, HMRC, HPL.

1. Elizabeth Fitzsimmons Ring File, typescript, HMRC, HPL.
2. *Gargoyle*, July 14, 1929, 15. The house was built by Nathaniel Kellum in 1847. From the 1850s into the 1870s, Mrs. Zerviah M. Noble ran a school in the building.
3. William C. Hogg to M. E. Foster, *Houston Press*, April 16, 1927, 2J299, folder 3, WHP, CAH. By 1929 the park covered 20.43 acres. Sam Houston Park now has a collection of historic houses moved there from Harris County sites and managed by the Harris County Heritage Society. The Kellum-Noble house is the only structure still on its original site.
4. Dorothy Knox Howe Houghton, Barrie M. Scardino, Sadie Gwin Blackburn, and Katherine S. Howe, *Houston's Forgotten Heritage: Landscape, Houses, Interiors, 1824–1914* (Houston: Rice University Press, 1991), 229.
5. Ring File, HMRC, HPL.
6. Elizabeth Barlow Rogers, *Landscape Design: A Cultural and Architectural History* (New York: Harry N. Abrams, 2001), 330–337; Stephen Fox, *Houston Architectural Guide*, 2d ed. (Houston: American Institute of Architects, Houston Chapter, and Herring Press, 1999), 181; David Schuyler, *The New Urban Landscape: The Redefinition of City Form in Nineteenth-Century America* (Baltimore: Johns Hopkins University Press, 1986), 41; Houghton et al., *Houston's Forgotten Heritage*, 29.
7. "A Forum of Civics for Houston," pamphlet, May 15, 1926, River Oaks Garden Club Records, Archives, MFAH.
8. *Houston Architectural Survey*, Southwest Center for Urban Research and Rice University School of Architecture (Houston, 1980, 1981), 1272; Houston Subdivision Collection, MSS 118, box 1, folder 2, HMRC, HPL; Houghton et al., *Houston's Forgotten Heritage*, 159; Fox, *Houston Architectural Guide*, 141.
9. Federation of Women's Clubs, *The Key to the City of Houston* (Houston: State Printing Company, 1908), 165, in Estelle Sharp Papers, Box 7, folder 2, WRC, RU.

10. *Daily Post*, Jan. 14, 1903, quote in McComb, *Houston*, 101; Freeman, *People of Baker Botts*, 29 (brick and block streets).

11. Houghton et al., *Houston's Forgotten Heritage*, 49, 317, pl. 106.

12. *Post*, "The Past Year in Houston," Jan. 1, 1909, 1.

13. William Ward Watkin Papers, box 2, folder 18, WRC.

14. Houston Subdivision Collection, box 1, folder 3, Woodland Heights, HMRC, HPL.

15. Houston Subdivision Collection, box 1, folder 2, Magnolia Park, HMRC, HPL.

16. Beth Anne Shelton, Nestor P. Rodriguez, Joe R. Feagin, Robert D. Bullard, and Robert D. Thomas, *Houston: Growth and Decline in a Sunbelt Boomtown* (Philadelphia: Temple University Press, 1989), 10.

17. William Ward Watkin Papers, box 2, folder 28, "Notes on Houston, 1927," WRC.

18. George Ehrlich, *Kansas City, Missouri: An Architectural History, 1826–1990*, rev. ed. (Columbia: University of Missouri Press, 1992).

19. Dec. 10, 1904, vote to form commission government; March 18, 1905, charter defining commission government approved; April 1, 1906, first commission government in office. Unlike Galveston and other cities with weak mayors, Houston retained a strong mayor with veto power over ordinances, authority to appoint all department heads with approval of the other aldermen, and ability to remove any official on his own recognizance. The mayor served as "general manager" supported by four committees, each chaired by a commissioner. Ernest S. Bradford, *Commission Government in American Cities* (New York: Macmillan, 1919), 23–32, quote on p. 6; Bradley Robert Rice, *Progressive Cities: The Commission Government Movement in America, 1901–1920* (Austin: University of Texas Press, 1977), 19–25, 86, 109.

20. Schuyler, *New Urban Landscape*, 5, 6, 85–95, 101, 120, 149, 171–172, passim; Stanley K. Schultz, *Constructing Urban Culture: American Cities and City Planning, 1800–1920* (Philadelphia: Temple University Press, 1989), 19, 87; Rogers, *Landscape Design*, 339–340; Witold Rybczynski, *A Clearing in the Distance: Frederick Law Olmsted and America in the Nineteenth Century* (New York: Scribner, 1999), 21, 131–399.

21. Schuyler, *New Urban Landscape*, 23.

22. Houston Subdivision Collection, box 1, folder 3, HMRC, HPL; *Houston Architectural Survey*, 6:1276.

23. Steven M. Baron, *Houston Electric: The Street Railways of Houston, Texas* (Lexington, KY: Steven M. Baron, 1996), 117–119.

24. Arthur Coleman Comey, *Houston: Tentative Plans for its Development; Report to the Houston Park Commission* (Boston: Press of Geo. H. Ellis, 1913). All information about Comey's work is taken from this plan, found in WRC and in Joseph Cullinan Papers, Box 10, folder 5, HMRC, HPL.

25. Comey, *Houston: Tentative Plans*, 6.

26. Paraphrase of Stephen Fox, "Public Art and Private Places: Shadyside," *Houston Review* 2 (Winter 1980): 37. See also Paul Boyer, "The Ideology

of the Civic Arts Movement in America, 1890–1920," *Houston Review* 2 (Winter 1980): 5–8.

27. Mayor's Report, 1913, HMRC, HPL.

28. Chamber of Commerce, City of Houston, *Illustrated City Book* (1916), 39–40. Data about George Hermann from *Handbook of Texas Online*, www.tsha.utexas.edu/handbook/online.

29. Mayor Ben Campbell to James A. Autry, July 15, 1915, box 20, folder 1, Autry Papers. Stephen Fox, "Big Park, Little Plans: A History of Hermann Park," in *Ephemeral City: Cite Looks at Houston*, ed. Barrie Scardino, William F. Stern, and Bruce C. Webb (Austin: University of Texas Press, 2003), 118.

30. *Houston Architectural Survey*, 5:992; William H. Wilson, *The City Beautiful Movement in Kansas City* (Columbia: University of Missouri Press, 1964), 41–54; Houghton et al., *Houston's Forgotten Heritage*, 57–58.

31. William S. Worley, *J. C. Nichols and the Shaping of Kansas City: Innovation in Planned Residential Communities* (Columbia: University of Missouri Press, 1990), 56.

32. *Houston Architectural Survey*, 6:1278–1280. Hermann Park plan in Houghton et al., *Houston's Forgotten Heritage*, 191, plate 147.

33. John O. King, *Joseph Stephen Cullinan: A Study of Leadership in the Texas Petroleum Industry, 1897–1937* (Nashville, TN: Vanderbilt University Press, 1970). Hogg-Swayne was comprised of Fort Worth politician James W. Swayne, Lampasas newspaper man William T. Campbell, and Georgetown District Judge R. E. Brooks in partnership with former Governor Hogg.

34. Joseph S. Cullinan to William C. Hogg, n.d., William C. Hogg to Ben Campbell, June 4, 1913, Joseph Cullinan Papers, box 10, folder 5, HMRC, HPL. Copies of the report are retained in the Cullinan and Hogg Papers. In May 1914 Ben Campbell sent a copy of Comey's report to Cullinan to "look over." Ben Campbell to Joseph S. Cullinan, May 29, 1914, box 66, folder 4, Cullinan Papers, HMRC, HPL.

35. Joseph Cullinan to George Kessler, May 23, 1914, Joseph Cullinan to Mayor Ben Campbell, May 27, 1914, June 30, 1914, 2J307, letter box 17–A, WHP, CAH; Joseph S. Cullinan to George Kessler, Nov. 12, 1914, box 66, folder 4, Cullinan Papers, HMRC, HPL. Family members note that Cullinan paid Kessler's consulting fees. Conversation with author, Jan. 19, 2005.

36. Joseph S. Cullinan to James L. Autry, Box 20, folder 1, James L. Autry Papers, WRC.

37. Rogers, *Landscape Design*, 423.

38. Clipping, *Post-Dispatch*, April 13, 1927, 2J301, folder 3; William Clifford Hogg to Ima Hogg, March 9, 1927, 2J301, folder 2; clipping, HECK, *Houston Labor Journal*, April 16, 1926, 2J299, folder 2, WHP, CAH.

39. Bill Pannill, "Does Houston Have a 'Character' . . . Like Paris or Rome Do?" in *Press*, 1961, reprinted in *The Bridge*, June/July 2004, 1, 2.

40. *A Garden Book for Houston* (Houston: Forum of Civics, 1929), motto in foreword. Used in every subsequent edition.

41. 1928 Map of Houston, based on data from City Engineering Department, City Planning Commission, and River Oaks Corporation, published

by the Forum of Civics, map drawer, HMRC, HPL. Ferguson, "Hogg
Family Financial History," 59, 60; *Houston Architectural Survey*, 6:1282;
list, 2J299, folder 4, WHP, CAH, records eight properties purchased
or sale pending between July 30, 1925, and April 2, 1926, for a total
$259,328.52 in cash and notes.

42. Correspondence and clippings, 2J301, WHP, CAH.
43. *Houston*, April 1921, 3.
44. *Houston*, April 1921, 17.
45. Burt Rule, in *Houston*, November 1920, 4.
46. Rule, in *Houston*, August 1920, 10.
47. George Dixon in *Houston*, April 1920, 1; November 1919.
48. *Houston*, December 1919, 1; February 1920; March 1920, 8, 26; May
1920, 7.
49. *Houston*, July 1920, 28; October 1920, 22.
50. *Houston*, January 1920, 15; December 1919, 8, 18; December 1920, 8, 14;
February 1920, 8.
51. Rule, in *Houston*, February 1921. For an excellent study of city planning
issues in 1920s Houston see Archie Henderson, "City Planning in
Houston, 1920–1930," *Houston Review* 9 (1987): 107–136.
52. Planning Commission Correspondence, City of Houston, Department of
Planning Collection, box 6, folder 1, HMRC, HPL.
53. John Willis Slaughter, secretary, Houston City Planning Commission,
to Mayor Oscar Holcombe, City of Houston, Department of Planning
Collection, box 6, folder 1, HMRC, HPL.
54. Hare and Hare platted the city of Bellaire and Forest Hill, the first
Houston suburb to feature curving streets. Roscoe E. Wright, "Hare
Tonic," *Gargoyle*, Dec. 18, 1928, 5.
55. Henry Stude, *Chronicle*, Nov. 30, 1926, 10. Terry Hershey remembers that
Ima convinced her brothers not to develop the property but to preserve it
as a forest park instead. Comment to author, May 28, 2004.
56. Ferguson, "Hogg Family Financial History," 59. Sarah H. Emmott,
Memorial Park: A Priceless Legacy (Houston: Herring Press, 1992), 23–27;
Houston Architectural Survey, 6:1281. Ownership issues are confusing
because Will Hogg listed 1,503 acres of Memorial Forest Park in a list
of "Parks Owned by the City of Houston, 1927" in *Civics for Houston*,
November 1928, 22. In fact, in 1928 half the land was still technically
owned by the Hogg family. Ima Hogg's continued vigilance found in box
7A, folder 15, Daughters of the Republic of Texas correspondence (DRT),
IHP, Archives, MFAH.
57. Presbyterian University plan in River Oaks Resume, March 1929,
2J363, folder 1, WHP, CAH. Sadie Gwin Blackburn, interview with the
author; Terry Hershey, interview with the author, May 28, 2004; DRT,
IHP, Archives, MFAH. Hershey noted that she did not know Ima Hogg
well but was invited to work with Blackburn because she had fought
to preserve Buffalo Bayou in its natural state. Hershey has worked at
local, regional, and national levels on bayou preservation, flood control,
and parks and wildlife initiatives. Blackburn, former chairwoman of
the Memorial Park Advisory Committee (1974–1998), is a nationally

respected horticulturist and conservationist, served as a docent at Bayou Bend (1961–1968), worked with Ima on the boards of the Houston Mental Health Association and Child Guidance Clinic, and was president of the River Oaks Garden Club (1975–1976), the Garden Club of America (1989–1991), and the San Jacinto Museum of History.

58. William C. Hogg to James Cravens, July 18, 1925, 2J301, folder 2, WHP, CAH. William C. Hogg to Herbert Hare, Kansas City, May 30, 1925, letter enclosing clippings showing press support for a civic center and noting the Hoggs had recently purchased at a low price and on very "reasonable terms" six acres of an estimated one hundred needed for proper park and building space (copies to J. C. Nichols, Captain James A. Baker, and Hugh Potter), 2J299, folder 2, WHP, CAH.

59. Herbert Hare to City Planning Commission, July 8, 1925, City of Houston Department of Planning Collection, folder 7, HMRC, HPL.

60. James A. Baker to William C. Hogg, June 1, 1925, 2J299, folder 2, WHP, CAH.

61. William C. Hogg to Oscar Holcombe, March 9, 1927, 2J301, folder 2 (quotes); other civic center correspondence in 2J3ol, WHP, CAH.

62. October 1926–February 1927, articles on highway funding, city streets, residential development, city planning, zoning, and parks, *Chronicle*, *Post*, and *Press*.

63. Oscar Holcombe Papers, microfiche, box 2, folder 1, December 1925–August 1928, HMRC, HPL. Also *Civics for Houston*, November 1928, 22, 34; *Chronicle*, April 4, 1926, 1, 38; Baron, *Houston Electric*, 10.

64. Fox, "Big Park," 123.

65. L. B. Ryon Jr., "The Importance of a Major Street Plan," *Civics for Houston*, April 1928, 5, 22.

66. Ryon article and map, *Chronicle*, Oct. 19, 1924, 20.

67. Hugh Potter in *Houston*, May 1926, 25, based on a zoning talk to the Rotary Club, March 19, 1926, and published in the *Chronicle*, March 10, 1926; talk praised by Mefo, March 31, 1926, 1.

68. Henderson ("City Planning," 115–117) speculates that Houston shied away from zoning because of Dallas's problems. In *Spann v. City of Dallas* (1921), the Texas Supreme Court declared the Dallas zoning ordinance unconstitutional, in part because it favored residential over other real property.

69. Clipping, Jan. 19, 1924; William C. Hogg to J. C. Nichols, Kansas City, Feb. 5, 1925, 2J299, WHP, CAH.

70. Minutes, April 14, 1925, founders meeting, May 2, 1925, 2J395, folder 1 (West-End Improvement Association), WHP, CAH.

71. *Chronicle*, Oct. 3, 1926, 28. Four Houstonians were Highway Association officers: R. H. Spencer, W. C. Hogg, W. G. Jones, and L. W. Kemp.

72. Letters to William C. Hogg from: M. E. Foster, president, *Chronicle*, June 23, 1926; John A. Embry, June 26, 1926; P. B. Timpson, Houston Land and Trust Company, Aug. 11, 1926, 2J299, folder 2, WHP, CAH.

73. Correspondence, 2J299, folders 3, 4, WHP, CAH.

74. *Chronicle*, Feb. 4, 1927, 1.

75. *Chronicle*, Feb. 20, 1927, 1, headline.

76. *Post-Dispatch*, "$6,975,000 Bonds Carry 5 to 1," April 12, 1927.
77. "Chief credit" in *Post-Dispatch*, April 13, 1927; "onslaught" in *Post-Dispatch*, April 6, 1927, clippings, 2J301, folder 3; *Press*, April 11, 1927, clipping, 2J299, folder 4; Robert Levy to William C. Hogg, April 12, 1927, 2J299, folder 4, WHP, CAH.
78. *Press*, April 14, 1927; *Chronicle*, April 11, 15, 1927, clippings in 2J299, folder 4, WHP, CAH.
79. The commission included former mayor A. Earl Amerman, W. E. Carroll, Hugh Potter, J. A. Embry, J. F. Staub, Dr. J. A. Kyle, E. R. Spotts, ex-officio chairman of the Board of Park Commissioners, S. Herbert Hare of Hare and Hare, and L. B. Ryon Jr., city planning engineer and secretary of the commission. Others who participated in the plan included former chairman M. E. Tracy, J. C. McVea, Robert L. Cole, J. W. Slaughter, Paul B. Timpson, Mrs. E. C. Murray, Herbert Godwin, and former chairman of the Board of Park Commissioners J. S. Pyeatt.
80. *Chronicle*, July 2, 1927; *Press*, July 7, 8, 9, 11, 1927, clippings in 2J299, folder 5, WHP, CAH.
81. City ordinances establishing a Department of Public Parks under the Board of Park Commissioners and a Department of Public Planning under the Houston City Planning Commission, 2J300, folder 2, WHP, CAH. See also *Houston Chronicle*, Feb. 16, 1927, 1, for an explanation of city planning bills that had been approved for submission to the public once state authorizing legislation had been passed.
82. Henderson, "City Planning," 119.
83. *Press* articles critical of secrecy, 2J300, WHP, CAH.
84. Diary 2J399, WHP, CAH, shows that Will was absent from Houston Feb. 3–26, March 19–28, May 17–June 16, July 9–Nov. 3, Dec. 14, 1928–May 3, 1929, and May 11–13, June 27–Oct. 14, and from Nov. 1, 1929 until his death in September 1930. Diary entries at the end of October 1929 show several late-night sessions held to discuss the final plan. Hugh Potter to William C. Hogg, Jan. 13, 1929 (Will in Brazil), March 2, 1929 (Will in Paris), 2J300, folder 3, WHP, CAH.
85. Meeting notes, July 5, 1927, with Will and associates D. M. Picton (his lawyer), S. L. Pinckney, H. E. Brigham, three other white and twenty-two "colored" Houstonians; minutes November 10, 1927; correspondence Dec. 7, 1927, Sept. 26, 27, 1929; all in 2J339, folder 8 (Inter-Racial Committee), WCH, CAH. C. H. McGruder to William C. Hogg, Jan. 6, 1928, 2J300, folder 2, WHP, CAH, about "disappointing progress" of the survey.
86. William C. Hogg to Herbert Hare, May 25, 1929, 2J300, folder 3.
87. Ibid.
88. Memos, 2J379, 2J318, WHP, CAH.
89. Foreword to *Garden Book*, River Oaks Garden Club rev. ed., 1950, n.p.; Ruth West, "Delphinium and Dirt," *Gargoyle*, Feb. 23, 1930, 19. The 1929 edition of *A Garden Book for Houston* was published by the Forum of Civics, supported by the Hoggs, and in 1944 Ima and other family members gave the book's copyright to the River Oaks Garden Club. This popular garden guide has never been out of print since 1929.

90.   *Civics for Houston,* January 1928, 18. J. M. Heiser Jr. Environmental Collection, box 17, folder 7, HMRC, HPL, has correspondence about joining the forum.

91.   "A Forum of Civics for Houston," pamphlet, May 15, 1926, in River Oaks Garden Club Records, Archives, MFAH.

92.   *Civics for Houston,* January 1928, 5. Architects for the renovation—John F. Staub, B. P. Briscoe, and J. W. Northrup—built houses in River Oaks. Will and Mike published their pamphlet announcing the forum in May 1926, but travel, Mike's political campaign, and other activities sidetracked development of the idea until fall of 1927 and the first meeting in early December 1927. The building was conveyed from Varner Realty to Mike, Ima, and Tom in 1932, given by them to the University of Texas, and purchased by the River Oaks Garden Club for a headquarters in 1942. Box 1, Yearly Reports, box Newspaper Articles 1927–1947, River Oaks Garden Club Records, Archives, MFAH.

93.   *Civics for Houston,* January 1928, 1.

94.   *Civics for Houston,* September 1928, 5 (quote) and lead story.

95.   Hogg-Scott correspondence, 2J318, WHP, CAH.

96.   Memo, Nov. 11, 1928, 2J301, folder 4, William C. Hogg to W. L. Clayton, Nov. 24, 1928, 2J301, folder 5, WHP, CAH. See exchange of letters, Nov. 16, 17, 1927, 2J299, folder 6, WHP, CAH. Holcombe claimed he had "no record" that he had agreed to have the city pay Hare and Hare as Planning Commission consultant or establish a commission budget. Hogg countered with two and one-half pages detailing a luncheon with the mayor at which those assurances were given.

97.   *Post-Dispatch,* June 23, 1929, clipping, 2J299, folder 1, WHP, CAH.

98.   Henderson, "City Planning," 131.

99.   John Ruskin, quoted in *Report of the City Planning Commission, Houston, Texas* (Houston: Forum of Civics, 1929), hereinafter cited as *Report,* inside cover. Will Hogg used this quote from Ruskin in River Oaks advertising materials also.

100. Hare and Hare and L. B. Ryon Jr., *Report,* 13.

101. *Report,* 9.

102. Ibid., 25. Nathan William MacChesney to Hugh Potter, May 20, 1929, 2J300, folder 3, WHP, CAH, says legislative enactment of segregation is declared void because it violates the Fifth, Thirteenth, Fourteenth Amendments. Restrictions at the time of sale of property are not violations of these amendments.

103. *Report,* 99.

104. Ibid., 91.

105. Ibid., 93.

106. William C. Hogg to Herbert Hare, Kansas City, July 14, 1925, quoting his statement to the press, 2J299, folder 2, WHP, CAH. *Houston Labor Journal,* April 16, 1926, clipping, 2J299, folder 2; William C. Hogg to Oscar Holcombe, 2J301, folder 2, WHP, CAH.

107. William C. Hogg to R. S. Sterling, April 23, 1926, 2J299, folder 2, WHP, CAH, in which Will complains about unsympathetic *Post-Dispatch* coverage of planning and tries to explain the movement's purpose. The

Post continued to express skepticism about the civic center. Clipping, April 3, 1927, 2J299, folder 4, WHP, CAH. Finally, with Works Progress Administration federal funds in the 1930s, a city center took shape downtown with a City Hall, Coliseum, and Music Hall as anchors. *Houston Architectural Survey*, 6:1285–1287.

108. Hare and Hare to City Planning Commission, July 8, 1925, City of Houston, Department of Planning Collection, box 6, folder 7, HMRC, HPL; *Houston Architectural Survey*, 6:1282.

109. Stephen Fox, "Spanish-Mediterranean Houses in Houston," pamphlet (Houston: Rice Design Alliance, 1992), 6–9.

110. Allen Peden, "Ah, the Plan!" *Gargoyle*, Dec. 15, 1929, 38.

111. J. G. Miller, "A Plea Against Zoning," *Gargoyle*, Jan. 26, 1930, 15.

112. A. L. Hemphill, "Why Fight Zoning?" *Gargoyle*, March 9, 1930, 16, 29.

113. Letter to the editor from the Houston City Planning and Zoning Commission, May 21, 1938, signed by Jesse Andrews, John Embry, C. C. Fleming, J. Frank Jungman, Dr. J. Allen Kyle, J. Robert Neal, Hugh Potter, and John F. Staub, City of Houston, Department of Planning Collection, Box 6, Folder 13, HMRC, HPL. Voters defeated zoning in 1948 and 1962. Stephen Fox, "Planning in Houston: A Historic Overview," in Scardino et al., *Ephemeral City*, 38.

114. *Report*, 100, 102, 111.

115. Scardino et al., *Ephemeral City*, ix.

116. *Press*, Jan. 9, 1930, clipping in 2J299, City Hall folder, WHP, CAH.

117. Address to City Planning Commission, undated, probably 1925, City of Houston Department of Planning Collection, Box 6, folder 6, HMRC, HPL.

118. Fox ("Planning in Houston," 34) attributes 1920s failure to three problems: "exclusive dependence" on zealous individuals; the "apathy, if not hostility," of the public; and the "ambivalence" of public officials who talked a "progressive" line but failed to accord statutory or financial support.

119. Hugh Potter, "Modern Residential Development—Its Relation to City Planning," *Houston*, May 1926, 25, 27.

120. "Our Story of River Oaks," 1925, in 2J303, folder 2, WHP, CAH.

121. Robert A. M. Stern and John Montague Massengale, eds., *The Anglo American Suburb* (London: Architectural Design, 1981), 35; Charles C. Savage, *Architecture of the Private Streets of St. Louis: The Architects and the Houses They Designed* (Columbia: University of Missouri Press, 1987), 3.

122. *Houston Architectural Survey*, 4:819–820. Rossmoyne was renamed Yoakum. Garden in Ima Hogg to William C. Hogg, April 30, 1918, 3B119, folder 1, IHP, CAH.

123. Worley, *J. C. Nichols*; Richard Longstreth, "J. C. Nichols, the Country Club Plaza, and Notions of Modernity," *Harvard Architecture Review* 5 (1896): 120–135.

124. River Oaks Corporation advertising material specifically mentions Kansas City's Country Club District, Dallas's Highland Park, Baltimore's Roland Park, Birmingham's Jemison Properties, Los Angeles's Beverly Hills, and San Francisco's St. Francis Wood as models "sifted and adapted" for River Oaks. "Living in River Oaks," 1941, n.p.

125. Ferguson, "Hogg Family Financial History," 56–62. Original directors of Varner Realty Inc. were Henry W. Stude, David M. Picton Jr., W. H. Mead, W. B. Ferguson, and J. E. Key. In January 1923 Will and Mike Hogg were elected to the board, and Will replaced Stude as president; Stude and Mike became vice presidents.

126. Stephen Fox, remarks to the Bayou Bend Docent Organization, March 18, 2002. I am greatly indebted to Mr. Fox for his insights and his willingness to share his understanding of Houston's urban scene. Notes and manuscripts in author's possession. The school gift is discussed in A. B. Cohn, assistant secretary, Rice Institute, to Henry Stude, President, Varner Realty, circa 1922, 2J367, WHP, CAH. Had the land not been used for a school it might have reverted to Rice Institute.

127. Ferguson ("Hogg Family Financial History," 62) describes easy terms for this transaction and says the note was paid "in due course."

128. "Living in River Oaks," 11, pamphlet, 1941, anniversary edition presented to Julia Ideson, River Oaks Collection, HMRC, HPL; Allen V. Peden, "Presentations," *Gargoyle*, April 10, 1928, 11 (regarding Hugh Potter).

129. Memo, April 8, 1924, 2J304, folder 1, WHP,CAH, describing acquisition of Country Club Estates Inc. Directors of the new company included Will, Mike, Hugh Potter, River Oaks Country Club founding President Kenneth E. Womack, River Oaks Country Club Vice President Walter Monteith, Will Clayton, and cotton exporter Edwin L. Neville, all friends of the Hoggs.

130. Ferguson, "Hogg Family Financial History," 63, 64; Hare and Hare Collection, HMRC, HPL.

131. Ferguson states that between 1924 and 1928 Hogg Brothers loaned $479,500 to Country Club Estates and $1,003,750 to Widee. The two companies merged in 1928, and in 1928–1930 Hogg Brothers loaned $219,300 to River Oaks Corporation. When Will died in September 1930, Hogg Brothers held notes totaling $1,822,550. The Hoggs had received only a few interest payments in May 1929 and September 1930. Potter bought the Hogg family interest for about $1,500,000 in 1936, and in 1955 River Oaks Property Owners Association assumed management. Ferguson, "Hogg Family Financial History," 64–65.

132. Hugh Potter, Report, March 1929; William C. Hogg to Hugh Potter, April 15, 1925, 2J363, River Oaks folder, WHP, CAH.

133. William C. Hogg to Ima Hogg, Jan. 10, 1926, telegram, indicates Ima had chosen the homesite by that date, 3B119, folder 4, IHP, CAH.

134. Letters, July 25, 1925; memo William C. Hogg to Hugh Potter, May 18, 1926, 2J363, Homewoods folder, WHP, CAH; Hare and Hare Collection, RGO26, folder 16, HMRC, HPL.

135. Howard Barnstone, *The Architecture of John F. Staub: Houston and the South*, foreword by Vincent Scully (Austin: University of Texas Press, 1979), 28.

136. Correspondence, 2J303, folder 1, WHP, CAH.

137. "Living in River Oaks," pamphlet, for history of the development, HMRC, HPL. In 1928, 100 families; by 1930, 300 families; in 1936, 600 families; and in 1941, almost 2,000 families for a value of more than $30 million.

138. "Panorama," flyer, 2J303, folder 1, WHP, CAH; "major work," Hogg Brothers, "Our Story of River Oaks, Chapter II, 1926," in River Oaks Collection, box 1, HMRC, HPL, and in 2J303, folder 1, WHP, CAH.

139. Brochures, 2J303, folder 1, WHP, CAH. River Oaks pamphlets in 4W201, IHP, CAH.

140. Memo from H. Lyman Armes, marketing expert from Boston, May 5, 1925, and five-page confidential memo from Hugh Potter to William C. Hogg, Oct. 23, 1925, reviewing advertising strategies and critiquing Armes's work.

141. Advertisement on the inside cover (3) of Edna Saunders's program proclaimed River Oaks "Ten Minutes to the Theatre District," *Aida* program, 1927, Scrapbook 6, IHPC, UH.

142. Don Riddle, "River Oaks: A Pictorial Presentation of Houston's Residential Park," pamphlet (Houston: River Oaks Corporation, n.d.), n.p., River Oaks Collection, HMRC, HPL.

143. March issue shows the "Laura" landing at the foot of Main Street; April issue ties the River Oaks civic mission to frontier settlement; October issue claims Houston of 1928 is as lovely and natural as but "much more comfortable" than Houston of Indian legend and Spanish romance.

144. *Gargoyle*, back covers of Jan. 26, June 1, 1930, and Feb. 8, June 14, and Oct. 4 and 21, 1931.

145. William C. Hogg to Oscar Holcombe, Oct. 27, 1927, Oscar Holcombe Papers, microfiche, Box 2, folder 5, Kirby Drive Improvements, May 1, 1924–Aug. 1, 1928, HMRC, HPL. Protest about bus traffic in William C. Hogg to Oscar Holcombe, Jan. 22, 1928, 2J301, folder 1, WHP, CAH.

146. Reservations, Covenants, and Restrictions in River Oaks Addition, Dec. 31, 1937, ed., No. 9, p. 4, in author's possession.

147. It should be noted that exceptions to this "agreement" were made almost at once for prominent Jewish families whose civic activism and wealth placed them in the upper echelon of Houston society.

148. Will became mired in misunderstanding when he tried to get the tuberculosis hospital relocated away from Buffalo Bayou and the route to River Oaks. Although he cited health and convenience arguments, critics claimed his motives were self-serving. Correspondence with Mrs. James L. Autry and clippings from *Chronicle* Nov. 23 and Dec. 28, 1927, in 2J299, City Hall folder, WHP, CAH.

CHAPTER 3

Parts of this chapter first appeared as Kate S. Kirkland, "A Wholesome Life: Ima Hogg's Vision for Mental Health Care," *Southwestern Historical Quarterly* 104 (January 2001): 416–447.

1. Founded to house children of Confederate veterans, forty years later the home served "all destitute white orphan children" of the area. Bylaws in recital program, Bayland Orphans Home Furniture Fund, Jan. 29, 1916, scrapbook 3, Ima Hogg Symphony Programs Collection, 1900–1978, IHPC.

2. Harold J. Matthews, in *Candle by Night: The Story of the Life and Times of Kezia Payne DePelchin: Texas Pioneer Teacher, Social Worker, and Nurse* (Boston: Bruce Humphries, 1942, 224–227), says she found three children. Federation of Women's Clubs in *Key to the City* (55) records two waifs deposited on the doorstep; in box 7, folder 2, Estelle Sharp Papers (1883–1965), WRC.

3. Matthews, *Candle by Night*, 226.

4. Ibid., 231; Monit Cheung, Jennifer Levit, and Carole R. Linseisen, "Children's Services in Houston: The First One Hundred Years of DePelchin Children's Center" (Feb. 20, 1996, 10), pamphlet provided to author by DePelchin Children's Center.

5. C. W. Areson, "Child-Saving for a Changing World," *Gargoyle*, Nov. 23, 1930, 11, 38–39; *Houston Architectural Survey*, 2:308; Cheung, Levit, and Linseisen, "Children's Services," 11; Matthews, *Candle by Night*, 248. In 1926 the Faith Home board purchased 14.22 acres at Brunner and Memorial Drive, but relocation did not occur until the late 1930s.

6. Clarence R. Wharton to James L. Autry, Oct. 5, 1915, James L. Autry Papers, WRC. The solicitation letter reviews Faith Home's financial struggles and asks for $250. A thank-you letter dated Oct. 18, 1915, indicates that Autry subscribed $100.

7. Cheung, Levit, and Linseisen, "Children's Services," 18–19.

8. *Gargoyle*, Oct. 16, 1928, 12.

9. Marguerite S. Johnston, *Houston: The Unknown City, 1836–1946* (College Station: Texas A&M University Press, 1991), xi; Marguerite S. Johnston, *A Happy Worldly Abode: Christ Church Cathedral, 1839–1964* (Houston: Cathedral Press, 1964), 198.

10. Ima Hogg to Robert Sutherland, Jan. 5, 1956, MAI 9/U1, folder 3, HFR, CAH.

11. Crawford, "'To protect, to feed,'" 16. Mrs. Covington lived in the Third Ward, was married to leading African-American physician Benjamin Covington, and was a prominent club woman (1903–1950s).

12. Corrine Fonde (Houston's first municipal social worker), "Rusk School, First Social Center," *Daily Post*, Aug. 6, 1916, 27. Bethlehem Settlement is often called Colored Settlement in contemporary reports. In 1934 Edith Ripley left $1 million in trust to establish Ripley House, a community center in Houston's East End. *Houston Architectural Survey*, 2:428. In May 1943, the Committee of the Houston Negro Community Center, later Hester House, organized a settlement and community center to serve the black community; it opened in August 1943. Howard Jones, *The Red Diary: A Chronological History of Black Americans in Houston and Some Neighboring Harris County Communities* (Austin: Nortex Press, 1991), 146.

13. Federation of Women's Clubs, *Key to the City*, 63.

14. James L. Autry to Estelle Sharp, Dec. 24, 1910, Estelle Sharp Papers, box 5, folder 3, WRC.

15. Federation of Women's Clubs, *Key to the City*, 63.

16. "Gracious lady" in "A Resolution," Jan. 18, 1957, box 6, folder 6, Sharp Papers, WRC; *Chronicle*, July 13, 1912, clipping, in box 5, folder 14, Sharp Papers, WRC. United Charities was reorganized into four departments: Constructive Relief, Health and Hygiene, Children's, and the Employment Bureau. Houston Social Service Bureau box RC A-28, HMRC, HPL.

17. "Negro fund" in unsigned (Estate of W. B. Sharp stationery) to Joseph L. Zanefsky, executive secretary, Community Council, undated draft, box 6, folder 7; other quotes and adjectives taken from "A Resolution," Jan. 18, 1957, box 6, folder 6, Sharp Papers, WRC.

18. Nina Cullinan, interview with Walter L. Buenger and Ruth Winterside, May 11, 1978, WRC.

19. Accounts of Will's social service donations are incomplete. A list of donations made in 1921 specifies $19,370 given to fourteen social service agencies, 2J331, WHP, CAH.

20. Will also served as first vice president of the local Boy Scouts of America, as finance chairman, and in other capacities (1914–1917). 2J296, Boy Scouts of America file, WHP, CAH.

21. William C. Hogg to Estelle Sharp, March 28, 1916, Box 22, folder 5, James L. Autry Papers, WRC.

22. Letter to William C. Hogg, Feb. 1, 1915, box 2, folder 1, James L. Autry Papers, WRC.

23. Blue book inscription in 3D205, folder 2, John Avery Lomax Family Papers, CAH. Records indicate that Ima Hogg, Will Hogg, James Baker, James Autry, Mrs. Autry, Estelle Sharp, Cora and E. A. Peden, the Sterlings, the Womacks, the Mastersons, the Espersons, and the Claytons subscribed $5,000 apiece in 1919. Correspondence, October 1919, box 25, folder 10, James L. Autry Papers, WRC.

24. William C. Hogg to E. A. Peden and Chester Bryan, April 2, 1920, box 25, folder 10, James L. Autry Papers, WRC; correspondence, box 1, folders 2–7, YWCA Collection, HMRC, HPL; letters, 1919–1920, 2J396, WHP, CAH.

25. In 2J346, folder 4, WHP, CAH; box 18, Joseph Cullinan Papers, HMRC, HPL.

26. Chamber of Commerce, City of Houston, *Illustrated City Book* (1916), 73–74; Houghton et al., *Houston's Forgotten Heritage*, 259, plate 267; Montgomery, *Houston as a Setting*, 47.

27. Joseph Cullinan to Ferdinand Trichelle, Oct. 11, 1915, box 20, folder 5, James L. Autry Papers, WRC.

28. Letters, Emma R. Newsboys Association, Jan. 15, 1916, box 18, folder 2, Cullinan Papers, HMRC, HPL.

29. Lomax, *Will Hogg, Texan*, 41–42; notes in 3D205, folder 2, John Avery Lomax Family Papers, CAH.

30. John Ross to William C. Hogg, William C. Hogg to John Ross, March 29, 1917, 2J346, folder 2, WHP, CAH.

31. Houston Foundation, minutes, Dec. 10, 1918, box 5, folder 13, Sharp Papers, WRC; William C. Hogg to Joseph S. Cullinan, March 5,

1919, 2J346, folder 2, WHP, CAH. After 1919 the Houston Street and Newsboys Club Inc. was reorganized as an independent nonprofit agency to help underprivileged boys and young men graduate from high school and become productive citizens; box 20, folder 6, SC 213, Houston Street and Newsboys Club Papers, HMRC, HPL. In 1930 Ima contributed $15.00 to the YMCA Newsboys Club; 4W271, IHP, CAH.

32. Bylaws of the Houston Foundation, 2J371, folder 1, WHP, CAH.

33. Chamber of Commerce, City of Houston, *Illustrated City Book* (1916), 541; *The Community: A Review of Philanthropic Thought and Social Effort*, May 1919, 1, in box 5, folder 26, Sharp Papers, WRC. Thomas Kelly, "Free Enterprise, Costly Relief: Charity in Houston, Texas, 1915–1937," *Houston Review* 18 (1996): 29.

34. Missions endorsed in 1916: Star of Hope, Bayland Orphans Home, Young Woman's Co-Operative Home, YMCA, Baptist Sanitarium and Women's Auxiliary, Industrial Home and Day Nursery, Houston College, Colorado Western Home for Orphans and Ex-Slaves, and Houston Settlement Association (box 5, folder 16, Sharp Papers, WRC).

35. Crawford, "'To protect, to feed,'" 15–23.

36. Box 5, folder 22, Sharp Papers, WRC. The two-year course of lectures and lab work covered local government, casework, infant and child welfare, settlements, leisure and library study, housing, sanitation and public health, delinquency and sex problems, immigrants, minorities, and legal problems.

37. William C. Hogg to Mayor Ben Campbell, Feb. 15, 1917, County Judge Chester Bryan to William C. Hogg, March 10, 1917, William C. Hogg to Mayor Joseph Jay Pastoriza and Judge Chester Bryan, May 8, 1917, 2J338, folder 3, WHP, CAH. Ironically, Will later regretted this endorsement when he tried to prevent hospital and commercial construction at the site in the 1920s after he had begun to develop River Oaks just west of Shepherd's Dam.

38. William C. Hogg to Abe Levy, May 16, 1917, 2J338, folder 3, WHP, CAH. Several other letters in May and June record his deliberations.

39. Solicitation letter; Martha Gano to Ben Campbell, president, Houston Foundation, July 13, 1918, box 5, folder 23; Social Service Bureau, report, 1917, Box 5, folder 18, Sharp Papers, WRC.

40. Casey Greene, "Guardians Against Change: The Ku Klux Klan in Houston and Harris County, 1920–1925, *Houston Review* 10 (1988): 11.

41. "Reformers," *Woman's Viewpoint*, Jan. 30, 1924, 10.

42. "New Morality," editorial, *Gargoyle*, June 30, 1929, 9; Nov. 1, 1931, 8 (Sanger, "stormy"); Feb. 12, 1929, 7 (drug abuse).

43. *Civics for Houston*, August and September 1928; *Gargoyle*, Jan. 22, 1929, 13; April 27, 1930, 6; March 15, 1931, 15; May 18, 1930, 19; March 24, 1929, 9; May 19, 1929, 15; May 4, 1930, 15.

44. Hogg in *Gargoyle*, April 27, 1930, 12; "Plea to Liberal Voters!," in *Gargoyle*, May 1, 1932, inside back cover; other exhortations, *Gargoyle*, March 23, 1930, 6; Sept. 7, 1930, 12; March 22, 1931, 12; April 12, 1931, 8; Aug. 16, 1931, 10; May 8, 1932, 11.

45. *Chronicle*, Nov. 17, 1922, 9, detailed review of the Social Service Bureau, "Houston's clearing house for charity," and its five departments staffed by twenty-five workers: relief and service, public health nursing, child welfare, women's and girl's protective, and settlement.

46. *Houston*, November 1919, 14, 20; March 1920, 10; December 1920, 25.

47. Information on Autry Memorial School and Hospital in box 13, folder 6, Cullinan Papers, HMRC, HPL.

48. Tablet, box 22, folder 1, Cullinan Papers, HMRC, HPL. All information on Cullinan gift in this box.

49. *Informer*, Jan. 26, 1929; *Gargoyle*, Aug. 11, 1929, 6, 25.

50. Summary in *Houston News: The Junior League of Houston* 4 (Fall, Winter 1999 and Spring, Summer 2000). Biographical information on Adelaide Lovett Baker in Spring 2000, 16–17; on Mary Cullinan Cravens, Summer 2000, 26–27.

51. Community Chest, Annual Report, 1930, foreword, Community Chest Files, HMRC, HPL.

52. Leopold L. Meyer, *The Days of My Years: Autobiographical Reflections* (Houston: Universal Printers, 1975), 65–67.

53. *Gargoyle*, Nov. 30, 1930, 11.

54. Annual reports, 1923–1931, Community Chest Files, HMRC, HPL; 2J306, WHP, CAH; *Chronicle*, Nov. 17, 1922, 9. A 1926 pamphlet lists Anderson Clayton at $10,000, First National Bank and the Hogg family at $6,000, and Humble Oil and Refining, Kirby Lumber, and Texas Company at $5,000 each.

55. John Davidson and Robert Fisher, "Social Planning in Houston: The Council of Social Agencies, 1928–1976," *Houston Review* 18 (1996): 21.

56. Ima Hogg, memo, May 30, 1968, MA19/U1, folder 15, HFR, CAH.

57. Theresa Richardson, *The Century of the Child: The Mental Hygiene Movement and Social Policy in the United States and Canada* (New York: State University of New York Press, 1989), 1, 1–2 (first quote), 45–48; Modern Approach to Mental Hygiene Work, MA19/U25, planning folder, HFR, CAH (second quote). For additional views of mental health care see Gerald Grob, *Mental Illness and American Society, 1875–1940* (Princeton, NJ: Princeton University Press, 1983); David J. Rothman, *The Discovery of the Asylum: Social Order and Disorder in the New Republic*, rev. ed. (Boston: Little, Brown, 1990).

58. William White, *The Mental Hygiene of Childhood* (Boston: Little, Brown, 1923), vii, xiv, 174; and Jane Addams, ed., *The Child, the Clinic, and the Court* (New York: New Republic, 1927), 19, 22, 41, 78, 93, 193–196. Undated inventory lists (Archives, MFAH) and books given to the University of Texas at Austin (CAH) reveal that the Hoggs owned works by Jane Addams, John Dewey, and dozens of volumes on mental hygiene and self-awareness.

59. Mrs. Anderson's fortune derived from the partnership of her father, Jeremiah Milbank, with Texan Gail Borden to produce condensed milk. See Clyde V. Kiser, *The Milbank Memorial Fund: Its Leaders and Its Work, 1905–1974* (New York: Milbank Memorial Fund, 1975), vii, 4, 13.

60.	*The Josiah Macy, Jr. Foundation, 1930–1955: A Review of Activities* (New York: Josiah Macy Jr. Foundation, 1955), 2, 5, 6; Ima Hogg to Dr. L. Kast, president, Josiah Macy, Jr. Foundation, Jan. 23, 1940, MAI9/U25, HFR, CAH.

61.	Margo Horn, *Before It's Too Late: The Child Guidance Movement in the United States, 1922–1945* (Philadelphia: Temple University Press, 1989), 9, 4. For a contemporary view of children's institutes see Joel D. Hunter, "The History and Development of Institutes for the Study of Children," in Addams, *Child, Clinic,* 204–214. The first Juvenile Psychopathic Institute was founded in Chicago in 1909.

62.	Richardson, *Century of the Child,* 87; Judith Sealander, *Private Wealth and Public Life: Foundation Philanthropy and the Reshaping of American Social Policy from the Progressive Era to the New Deal* (Baltimore: Johns Hopkins University Press, 1997), 138–146.

63.	Richardson, *Century of the Child,* 190; Horn, *Before It's Too Late,* 186.

64.	Frederick Lewis Allen, *Only Yesterday: An Informal History of the Nineteen-Twenties* (New York: Harper and Brothers, 1931), chapter 5.

65.	Horn, *Before It's Too Late,* 39, 37.

66.	Draft of Ima Hogg, comments to the regents, March 3, 1962, MAI9/U1, folder 3, HFR, CAH; Ima Hogg to Robert Sutherland, May 10, 13, 1967, interview, MAI9/U1, folder 12, HFR, CAH. The Pittsfield clinic opened January 14, 1924, and was operated by William B. Terhune, one of Hogg's many correspondents. Books by Terhune and Riggs are listed on undated Bayou Bend book inventories (Archives, MFAH). See also Addams, *Child, Clinic* (210), for reference to these clinics.

67.	James Stephen Hogg to Ima, Mike, and Tom Hogg, July 22, 1904, reprinted in "James Stephen Hogg," Varner-Hogg dedication pamphlet (West Columbia, TX: Varner-Hogg Plantation State Historical Park, 1958), 11, folder 8, JSH, WRC.

68.	Menninger comments in "Condensed Notes," interview with Robert L. Sutherland, Nov. 21, 1961, 4W241, folder 4, IHP, CAH.

69.	Stevenson later became medical director of the National Association for Mental Health. Ima Hogg to George Stevenson, Dec. 1, 1952, 4W270, IHP, CAH.

70.	*Community* 1 (May 1919): 1; Ima Hogg to Robert Sutherland, March 8, 1962, interview, Bayou Bend, MAI9/U1, folder 12, HFR, CAH; "The Guidance Center of Houston," pamphlet in Box 5, folder 33, Sharp Papers, WRC. In November 1933 Stevenson returned to Houston to evaluate the clinic, and in November 1934 he helped organize the Texas State Mental Hygiene Society in Austin. Minutes, Nov. 21, 1933, Oct. 18, 1934, DCC.

71.	Ruth West, "The Root of Evil," *Gargoyle,* April 14, 1929, 12.

72.	Ruth West, "Young Habits and Hopes," *Gargoyle,* Oct. 20, 1929, 15.

73.	*Gargoyle,* April 14, 1929 (12), lists members of the steering committee: C. W. Areson of Faith Home, Walter Whitson of the Family Service Bureau, Dr. John Willis Slaughter, Ima Hogg, Nina Cullinan, Dr. Fred Lummis, and J. W. Mills from the Houston Independent School District, among others. Lists in board minutes, 1929, DCC; box 5, folder 33, Sharp Papers, WRC.

74. Financial records are not located at DePelchin Children's Center with the minutes, and archival sources are contradictory. A memorandum lists a $2,000 donation from Ima for 1929, but other evidence indicates that she probably pledged the entire $10,000. Memorandum, 4W235, IHP, CAH. Ima Hogg's cash book for 1929 lists three gifts totaling $1,000. Cash book, 2.325U514, IHP, CAH.

75. Bylaws, minute book, 1929, DCC; history of Guidance Center notes incorporation in May 1929, Oct. 22, 1951, 4W235, folder 6, IHP, CAH.

76. Memorandum, Nov. 11, 1930, 4W235, folder 1, IHP, CAH.

77. Minutes, Jan. 10, 1930, DCC.

78. Ruth West, "The Ounce of Prevention," *Gargoyle*, Nov. 10, 1929, 17; West, "A Pound of Prevention," *Gargoyle*, April 17, 1930, 16.

79. Pamphlet in minutes, March 11, 1957, DCC. In 1939 the name was changed to Bureau of Mental Hygiene, Child Guidance Clinic, Adult Clinic; in 1944 Guidance Center of the Bureau of Mental Hygiene of Houston was adopted; in 1949 the name was shortened to Guidance Center of Houston; and, finally, to Child Guidance Center of Houston in 1956.

80. Annual report, 1956, DCC.

81. Annual report, 1958, DCC.

82. Box 5, folder 33, Sharp Papers; Nina Cullinan, interview, WRC; Meyer, *Days of My Years*.

83. Correspondence in 4W235, IHP, CAH, does not clarify Ima's record of donations. A 1932 letter from Hogg Brothers to Ima Hogg lists these figures. Ima Hogg to George Stevenson, Jan. 29, 1932, 4W235, IHP, CAH. Cash book entries detail donations totaling $2,500 in 1929, $6,500 in 1930, $3,250 in 1931, and small gifts in 1932, 2.325U514, IHP, CAH.

84. Minutes throughout the 1930s discuss deficits and staff cuts; DCC.

85. Leopold Meyer to Margaret McCann, secretary to Ima Hogg, Nov. 16, 1944, acknowledging receipt of $250 to pay a guest speaker, 4W235, folder 1, IHP, CAH; Ima Hogg to William Hobby, Oct. 27, 1961, 4W235, folder 2, IHP, CAH.

86. Minutes, Sept. 10, Nov. 19, 1962, DCC; Ima Hogg to Ralph Yarborough and John Tower, Nov. 25, 1970, 4W235, folder 2, IHP, CAH.

87. *Houston Architectural Survey*, 4:931.

88. Lovett Peters to Ima Hogg, June 15, 1959, 4W235, folder 1, IHP, CAH.

89. Ima Hogg to John H. Freeman, June 14, 1960, 4W235, folder 1; Ima Hogg to William P. Hobby Jr., June 12, 1960, 4W235, folder 2, IHP, CAH.

90. *Gargoyle*, Dec. 14, 1930, 11.

91. *Gargoyle*, Nov. 10, 1929, 17.

92. Ima Hogg, interview, Oct. 2, 1974, oral history, HMRC, HPL.

93. Minutes, June 2, 22, 23, 1944; planning report, Nov. 9, 1945; Jan. 28, 1945, DCC; also in 4W235, folder 3, IHP, CAH; Ima Hogg to Beulah T. Wild, Nov. 28, 1944, 4W235, folder 3, IHP, CAH; Ima Hogg to Robert

Sutherland, Sept. 30, 1944, praising course outline; Robert Sutherland to Ima Hogg, Oct. 3, 1944, requests "quite frankly any rewording" and "give your opinion concerning any phase of the organization of the course," 4W235, IHP, CAH; Ima Hogg to Robert Sutherland, Aug. 10, 1945, MAI9/U1, folder 1, HFR, CAH ("galaxy of stars"); minutes, Nov. 4, 1945, 4W235, folder 3, IHP, CAH. In the 1960s Ima strongly supported affiliation with Baylor College of Medicine to place four or five residents on rotation at the center. Meeting minutes May 13, 1962, May 19, 1962, Nov. 19, 1962, April 27, 1965, 4W235, folder 4, IHP, CAH.

94. Minutes, Planning Committee, Oct. 30, 1945, 4W235, folder 3, IHP, CAH.

95. Minutes, March 14, 1930; June 2, 1939, DCC.

96. Minutes, Executive Committee, May 18, 1932, DCC.

97. Ima Hogg to George Stevenson, Jan. 29, 1932, 4W235, IHP, CAH; minutes, April 10, 1931, March 8, 1934, Dec. 11, 1936, May 12, 1939, DCC.

98. Minutes, annual meeting, Jan. 27, 1950, DCC.

99. Correspondence and minutes, 4W236, IHP, CAH; Mental Health Association of Greater Houston, History, www.mhag.org.

100. Henry A. Cromwell to Ima Hogg, Jan. 11, 1957, 4W235, folder 1, IHP, CAH. Also Texas Society for Mental Hygiene folders, 4W267, IHP, CAH.

101. Child Guidance Center Study Committee Report, May 4, 1959, 2, in Box 5, folder 33, Sharp Papers, WRC.

102. Joann Mitchell to the author, March 4, 1999, interview, DCC; DePelchin Children's Center brochures, 1999–2003.

103. The name change occurred at a December regents meeting; Robert Sutherland to Ima Hogg, Dec. 10, 1957, 4W235, folder 1, IHP, CAH.

104. *State of Texas v. Mike Hogg et al.*, in 3F389, Hogg Family Papers, CAH. Ima's brother Tom and her sisters-in-law left portions of their estates to the foundation, but they did not shape foundation programs.

105. Memorandum, 1940, MAI9/U1, folder 1; statement to regents, March 8, 1962, MAI9/U1, folder 4, HFR, CAH.

106. Will, 2J329; probated will, 2J330, folder 1, WHP, CAH.

107. "In Memoriam," MAI9/U14, folder 1, HFR, CAH; Report to the Board of Regents, March 1960, 4W241, folder 3, IHP, CAH.

108. Will, 2J329; probated will, 2J330, folder 1, WHP, CAH; Ima Hogg to Dr. H. L. Prichett, Southern Methodist University, Sept. 2, 1939, MAI9/U1, HFR, CAH; committee meeting with Homer Rainey, Jan. 30, 1940, MAI9/U25, HFR, CAH.

109. In 1939 foundation directories listed only 243 foundations nationwide. F. Emerson Andrews, *Philanthropic Foundations* (New York: Russell Sage Foundation, 1956), 14, 16. Homer Rainey recalled lengthy discussions: "I became enthusiastic about the possibilities in the program. I gave her all the encouragement that I could"; "The Hogg Foundation: A Personal Reminiscence," in Hogg Foundation for Mental Health, *The Hogg Foundation for Mental Health: The First Three Decades, 1940–1970* (Austin: University of Texas, 1970), 4.

110. July and August 1939, letters; Homer Rainey to Ima Hogg, Sept. 8, 1939, 4W239, IHP, CAH.
111. Memorandum for planning the foundation, MAI9/U25, HFR, CAH; report to the Board of Regents, March 1, 1960, 4W241, folder 3, IHP, CAH.
112. Draft of Hogg memorandum to regents, March 8, 1962, MAI9/U1, folder 4; annual report, 1967–1968; annual report, February 1950, MAI9/U25, HFR, CAH.
113. Homer Rainey, remarks, Feb. 11, 1941, 9 a.m., planning folder, MAI9/ U25, HFR, CAH. Speakers included Frank J. O'Brien, director of guidance clinics for New York City public schools; Daniel A. Prescott, director of the University of Chicago Collaboration Center on Child Development; George S. Stevenson, director of the National Committee for Mental Hygiene; and Dr. Muriel Brown, consultant on Family Life Education in the U.S. Office of Education. *Alcalde*, March 1941.
114. Robert L. Sutherland (1940–1970); Wayne H. Holtzmann (1970–1993); Charles Bonjean (1993–December 2002); King Davis (since March 2003).
115. Quotes, "In Memoriam," MAI9/U14, folder 1, HFR, CAH; *Hogg Foundation News* (Winter/Spring 1977), MAI9/U14, HFR, CAH; Robert Sutherland to F. Leland, Nov. 12, 1941, resume, MAI9/U14, folder 1, HFR, CAH. Information about Sutherland provided by Ralph E. Culler III, associate director, Hogg Foundation, to the author, March 15, 1999, in a telephone interview; Homer Rainey to Ima Hogg, June 21, 1940, MAI9/U25, HFR, CAH.
116. Wayne Holtzman, "The Hogg Foundation, Prologue and Promise," in Hogg Foundation for Mental Health, *Hogg Foundation for Mental Health*, 8.
117. Annual report, 1962–1963, MAI9/U225, HFR, CAH.
118. Clipping, *Post*, Nov. 19, 1940, scrapbook, 2J408, WHP, CAH.
119. Correspondence between Ima Hogg and Robert Sutherland in MAI9/U1, folders 1–4, 9, 13, 15, 17, HFR, CAH; 3B166, folder 1, 4W236, IHP, CAH.
120. Correspondence between Ima Hogg and University of Texas regents and President Homer Rainey, 4W239, 3B166, folder 1, IHP, CAH; MAI9/U1, folders 1, 3, 4, 5, 8, 13, HFR, CAH.
121. Ima Hogg to Leslie Waggener, April 8, 1941, MAI9/U1, folder 8, HFR, CAH.
122. Robert Sutherland to Ima Hogg, March 19, 1956, 3B166, folder 2, IHP, CAH.
123. Ima Hogg to Robert Sutherland, Jan. 6, 1958, 3B166, IHP, CAH. A long draft dated Jan. 5, 1958, is in MAI9/U1, folder 3, HFR, CAH.
124. Annual reports, MAI9/U22, 25, HFR, CAH.
125. Annual report, 1962–1963, MAI9/U25; memorandum, March 6, 1961, MAI9/U14, folder 5, HFR, CAH. Ima and Mrs. Ray Willoughby of San Angelo had lobbied legislators in 1950 for authorization and funding for the Graduate School of Social Work. Pat Folmar Robinson, "The School of Social Work Celebrates Its 25th Birthday," *Alcalde* (September/ October 1975), 20–25. In 1951 Ima sponsored a scholarship for a "Latin-American" student at the school. MAI9/U1, folder 2, HFR, CAH. Several

funds secure the Hogg Foundation, the most important of which are
the Will C. Hogg Fund and the Ima Hogg Endowment. Other funds
administered by the Hogg Foundation: Harry Estill and Bernice Milburn
Moore Fellowship Fund, Frances Fowler Wallace Fund, DeRossette
Thomas Fund, Varner-Bayou Bend Heritage Fund.

126. Robert Sutherland to Ima Hogg, Dec. 14, 1961, overview of other gifts,
MAI9/U1, folder 3, HFR, CAH. See for example Hogg Foundation for
Mental Health, *Philanthropy in the Southwest: Foundations Cooperate in
Community Programs; A Resume of the Years 1966–1968* (Austin: University
of Texas, 1969), 9–10. From September 1964 through August 1968,
forty-one Texas foundations assisted twenty-seven agencies to develop
thirty-eight demonstration projects through Ford and Hogg Foundation
cooperation.

127. Ralph E. Culler III and Wayne H. Holtzman, *The Ima Hogg Foundation:
Miss Ima's Legacy to the Children of Houston* (Austin: Hogg Foundation for
Mental Health, 1990).

128. Ibid., 3, 33, 8, 10.

129. "In Memoriam," MAI9/U14, folder 1, HFR, CAH.

130. *Post*, April 6, 1956, describes the dinner and presentation; clipping in
3B166, IHP, CAH.

CHAPTER 4

The title of this chapter is taken from Ima Hogg, talk to the Woman's Club, Civic
Department, March 23, 1943, typescript, 4W237, folder 3, IHP, CAH.

1. *Chronicle*, Oct. 9, 1912, Society page, listed seventeen hostesses (wives of
board and faculty members), eighty-nine female assistants for the institute
garden party following the Thursday lectures, and ninety-eight couples
and individuals at the Lovetts' farewell reception, Saturday, Oct. 12, 1912.

2. Edgar Odell Lovett, "The Meaning of the New Institution," in *Edgar
Odell Lovett and the Creation of Rice University*, with an introduction by
John B. Boles (Houston: Rice Historical Society, 2000), 127n10 (service of
song and prayer), 82–83 ("first alignment"). Original programme available
in Rice Institute, Opening Ceremony Files, WRC.

3. The original trustees were Cesar Maurice Lombardi, president of the
Houston School Board; Emanuel Raphael, president of the Houston
Electric Light Company and a trustee of the School Board; Frederick
Rice, the founder's brother and a banker and treasurer of the Houston
and Texas Central Railroad; James Everett McAshan, a banker; Alfred
S. Richardson, director of the Houston and Texas Central Railroad; and
Captain James Addison Baker, Rice's lawyer. By 1912 Frederick Rice and
Alfred Richardson, then both deceased, had been replaced by nephews
Benjamin Botts Rice and William Marsh Rice Jr., a graduate of Princeton;
Lovett took William Marsh Rice's seat on the board.

4. Federation of Women's Clubs, *Key to the City*, 18

5. Montgomery, *Houston as a Setting*, 26–38; Houghton et al., *Houston's
Forgotten Heritage*, 256, 304. Private schools: Jack Yates Academy for

African-American children (1884–1921), founded by white missionaries from the American Baptist Mission Women's Home Society of Chicago in cooperation with Antioch Baptist Church Pastor Jack Yates; Professor Christopher Welch's co-educational Houston Academy for white boys and girls (1896–1921); Margaret Kinkaid's (1904–present) college-preparatory tutelage; and all-girls St. Agnes Academy (1906–present) and all-boys St. Thomas High School (1900–present) for prosperous members of the Catholic community. *Houston* (February 1930, 22) reported 22,220 students in 1910, 26,015 in 1920, and 52,822 in 1929 at a cost per student that year of $87.11.

6. Ralph Adams Cram, *My Life in Architecture* (Boston: Little, Brown, 1936), 125–126.

7. *Houston*, June 1922, 18.

8. *Progressive Houston: A Monthly Publication for the Benefit of the Taxpayer and General Public* 2 (May 1910): 3, WRC.

9. Lovett, "Meaning of the New Institution," 57, 63–64, 112–114, 129, 133–134.

10. E. O. Lovett to William C. Hogg, March 16, 1927; memo to William C. Hogg, Nov. 19, 1928, 2J367, WHP, CAH. Each man paid $250 per year; Mrs. Sharp paid $4,000 per year. Incomplete records indicate that they continued support for many years.

11. "Negro hospital" box, folders 1, 2, Joseph S. Cullinan Papers, HMRC, HPL.

12. John Willis Slaughter Information File, WRC; River Oaks Garden Club Records, passim; Director's Records: James H. Chillman Jr., box 2, folder 19, Archives, MFAH.

13. *Gargoyle*, Sept. 21, 1930, 12.

14. *Gargoyle*, Dec. 8, 1929, 8.

15. *Gargoyle*, Nov. 8, 1931, 12.

16. Cotner, *James Stephen Hogg*, 6, 10, 12, 14; "Reminiscences of Life in the Texas Governor's Mansion," 3B168, folder 3, IIIP, CAH.

17. The 1836 Texas Constitution required the Congress of the new republic to "provide by law, a general system of education," and in 1839 more than 221,000 acres of land were set aside to endow two colleges or universities while in each county three leagues of land were set aside to finance public primary schools. The Texas State Constitution of 1876 mandated a university that included a branch for "the instruction of colored youths of the State" and an agricultural and mechanical college. In 1881 the state passed enabling acts that permitted classes to begin. Roger A. Griffin, "To Establish a University of the First Class," *Southwestern Historical Quarterly* 86 (October 1982): 135, 137, 140, 143.

18. Cotner, *James Stephen Hogg*, 581.

19. Lomax, *Will Hogg, Texan*; Robert C. Cotner, *Addresses and State Papers of James Stephen Hogg*, centennial edition (Austin: University of Texas Press, 1951), passim.

20. Founders list and speech to Alumni Association, June 12, 1911, box 2J311, folder 1, WHP, CAH. Information summarized in Lovett, "Meaning of the New Institution," 115–116, n8.

21. During 1913 reorganization, regents were assigned two-, four-, or six-year terms to achieve a rotation system.
22. William C. Hogg to James E. Ferguson, Sept. 30, 1914, Box 43, folder 10, Edgar Odell Lovett Personal Papers, WRC. Throughout his life, Will sent copies of his letters to selected friends. He categorized the subject matter, in this case "EDUCATION," by date.
23. William C. Hogg to James E. Ferguson, Dec. 11, 1914, box 43, folder 10, Lovett Personal Papers, WRC, concludes that the one-board plan is probably more feasible even though separation would be best "*with* permanent and adequate constitutional tax,*" a statement that Ferguson thought undercut his position.
24. Letters and pamphlets, 2J314, WHP, CAH; Record of Investigation, 2J316, WHP, CAH, contains all printed information about the Ferguson impeachment.
25. Lewis L. Gould, "The University Becomes Politicized: The War with Jim Ferguson, 1915–1918," *Southwestern Historical Quarterly* 86 (October 1982): 255–276.
26. Record of Investigation, 2J316, WHP, CAH.
27. William C. Hogg to Austin *Statesman*, Feb. 9, 1917, in 3D168, folder 1, Lomax Family Papers, CAH.
28. John Avery Lomax, "Random Recollections of the University 'Bear Fight'" in 3D 168, folder 3, Lomax Family Papers, CAH. For the conflict with Ferguson see letters, clippings, pamphlets 2J312, 2J316, WHP, CAH; and 3D157, 3D168, Lomax Family Papers, CAH. See also Norman D. Brown, *Hood, Bonnet, and Little Brown Jug: Texas Politics, 1921–1928* (College Station: Texas A&M University Press, 1984), 129–167, 352–354, for Will's continuing efforts to depoliticize the university.
29. Correspondence 2J312, WHP, CAH.
30. Lomax, *Will Hogg, Texan*; Cullen Thomas to William C. Hogg, Sept. 21, 1912, 2J376, Sundry folder, WHP, CAH; William C. Hogg to Ike Ashburn, executive secretary, Association of Former Students, A&M, June 11, 1924, 2J313, WHP, CAH.
31. By 1924 Will had helped the following institutions set up funds and write charters of incorporation: University of Texas, A&M College, College of Industrial Arts at Denton, Sam Houston State Normal College in Huntsville, West Texas State Normal College in Canyon, East Texas State Normal College in Commerce, Rice Institute, John Tarlton Agricultural College in Stephenville, Grubbs Vocational College in Arlington, North Texas State Normal College in Denton, Prairie View State Normal and Industrial College, Sul Ross College in Alpine, and Southwest State Normal College in San Marcos.
32. "The Rice Institute to the Memory of William Clifford Hogg," p. 1, President's Office Records, E. O. Lovett 1912–1945, ARI, box 35, folder 3, WRC.
33. T. R. Sampson, Conference for Education in Texas, to William C. Hogg, March 2, 1915; William C. Hogg to James E. Ferguson, May 3, 1915, 2J310, WHP, CAH.

34. "The Rice Institute to the Memory of William Clifford Hogg," 2; President's Office Records, Lovett, box 35, folder 3, WRC.

35. Correspondence with Jesse H. Jones, 1924, Houston Endowment archives, courtesy of Ann Hamilton; "An Encore for Hogg Auditorium," *Texas Tribute* (Spring/Summer 2005), recaps the history of the auditorium, "the historic home of the performing arts at the University."

36. Letters in MAI9/U1; U14, folder 6; U25, HFR, CAH; 2J325, folder 4; 2J367, 2J313, WHP, CAH; box 1, folder 10, Mike and Alice Hogg Papers, MS 19, Archives, MFAH; box 2, folder 2, Julia Ideson Papers, HMRC, HPL; Box 43, folder 10, Lovett Personal Papers, WRC.

37. During her lifetime, Ima used the Hogg Foundation as a conduit to fund scholarships and lectureships in the College of Education; the psychiatry, sociology, and psychology departments; and the School of Social Work. In 1951 she was named advisor to the Graduate School of Social Work. Ima and Alice Hogg established the Mike Hogg Memorial Fund for Mental Health to train visiting teachers. Will of Mike Hogg, no. 31,414, County Clerk's Office, Harris County, Texas, filed November 17, 1941, p. 239.

38. William C. Hogg to Edgar Odell Lovett, Dec. 4, 1923, box 24, folder 1, President's Office Records, Lovett, WRC. Support continued through the 1930s. David M. Picton to William C. Hogg, April 9, 1923, describes Ima's desire to set up a $25,000 trust and distribute $1,500 yearly. Correspondence about the lectureship in 4W271, IHP, CAH.

39. Box 24, folder 1, President's Office Records, Lovett, list of attendees at Powell lectures, April 5 and 6, 1923.

40. William C. and Mike Hogg to Edgar Odell Lovett, April 2, 1926, ibid.

41. *Chronicle*, April 1, 1929; *Post*, Sept. 27, 1928; clippings in John Willis Slaughter Information File, WRC.

42. Memorial Book, William C. Hogg to Wallace Pratt, Oct. 28, 1929, 2J367, Memorial Book folder, WHP, CAH. Minutes, William Marsh Rice Institute for the Advancement of Literature, Science, and Art, vol. 5, May 20, 1929, p. 319.

43. Typescript, March 13, 1951, 4W271, folder 7, IHP, CAH.

44. An earlier version of Ima Hogg's Board of Education service appeared in Kate S. Kirkland, "For All Houston's Children: Ima Hogg and the Board of Education, 1943–1949," *Southwestern Historical Quarterly* 101 (April 1998): 460–495.

45. BE, Minutes, April 5, 1943; also reported in *Chronicle*, April 6, 1943, B1.

46. In 1922 the Texas Legislature created independent school districts. Houston's tax department collected the school tax for the district but otherwise had no connection with schools in the district, which has never corresponded exactly to city limits. In 1924 the district taught 35,186 pupils in one black and two white senior high schools, four junior high schools, fifty-six elementary schools including eleven kindergartens, and two schools for "subnormal" children, reflecting both the city's progressive attitudes toward educational innovation and its acceptance of Southern de jure segregation. Norman Henry Beard, ed., *The City Book of Houston* (Houston: N.p., 1925).

47. Board member Mrs. O. C. Castle's letter to the editor, *Woman's Viewpoint*, April 15, 1924, 21, 29.
48. E. E. Oberholtzer, *Houston*, September 1931, 3. Of 1,605 classrooms available in June 1930, 942 had been built since 1924 (4). Oberholtzer noted that 1,000 parents attended child development classes and that special classes for tubercular, retarded, or deaf students and for children with speech defects and "social" diseases were included in the 105 schools. Howard Beeth and Cary D. Wintz, editors of *Black Dixie: Afro-Texan History and Culture in Houston* (College Station: Texas A&M University Press, 1992), point out that between 1921 and 1940, the district built eight elementary, three junior high, and two senior high schools for African-American students and renovated many older campus buildings (96).
49. *Gargoyle*, April 10, 1932, 9.
50. *Gargoyle*, April 3, 1932, 17.
51. Patrick J. Nicholson, *In Time: An Anecdotal History of the First Fifty Years of the University of Houston* (Houston: Pacesetter Press, 1977), 1.
52. Date book, week of February 5, 1945, 3B165, IHP, CAH. In BE Minutes, July 12, 1943, Ima was named chairman of the Lunch Room Committee and member of the New School Properties and Future Construction Committee. Other standing committees included Adult Education under Ray Daily and Rules and Regulations under Henry A. Petersen. Ima represented the board at the annual meeting of the Association of Texas Colleges in 1944, served as special liaison to the City Planning Commission in 1945 and 1946, and participated on six of the eight standing committees in 1948 and 1949. See BE Meeting folder, May 12, 1947.
53. Ima Hogg to B. F. Pittinger, April 7, 1943, 4W237, folder 4, IHP, CAH; Ima Hogg Oral History, typescript, 5, HMRC, HPL. Mills's brother J. W. Mills served as Harris County clerk. Hubert Mills was a teacher and principal (1913–1923).
54. Cables between the Hoggs and Hugh Potter, October 1928, 2J304, WHP, CAH. Will and the River Oaks Corporation purchased the land abutting River Oaks from the Dickey family and turned it over to the school system. Interview with Eva Margaret Davis, principal of River Oaks Elementary, May 3, 1978, by Walter L. Buenger Jr., Estelle Sharp Papers, interviews, WRC; William C. Hogg, memorandum regarding school site, Jan. 11, 1927; William C. Hogg to E. E. Oberholtzer, June 24, 1927, 2J368, WHP, CAH.
55. On Jeppesen see Ray K. Daily Oral History, typescript of interview with Don E. Carleton, 20, HMRC, HPL; Nicholson, *In Time*, 1, 8, 147. On elections see Records, Board Services files, BE. On Petersen see Nicholson, *In Time*, 150; Daily Oral History, 14–15; Don Carleton, *Red Scare! Right-Wing Hysteria, Fifties Fanaticism, and Their Legacy in Texas* (Austin: Texas Monthly Press, 1983), 158. On Werlein see Ewing Werlein Biographical File, Texas Room, HPL; Carleton, *Red Scare!*, 108–109, 162–163; obituary, *Chronicle*, Nov. 28, 1975.
56. Daily, Oral History, 2–6, 7, 13; box 1, folder 1, Ray K. Daily Papers, HMRC, HPL; *Gargoyle*, Dec. 13, 1931, 11. The *Gargoyle* strongly

supported Daily by running a long profile on her on Aug. 14, 1928 (10, 13), illustrated by a photograph of her and her smiling son. Daily was supported in 1952 by the anti-Mills, anti–Red Scare slate organized by the Parents' Council for Improved Schools. Daily was accused, fairly, of poor attendance at board meetings.

57. On Shepherd see *Post*, Feb. 15, 1945 (section 1, p. 8), and *Press*, Feb. 15, 1945. On Wilson see *Post*, Feb. 25, 1943 (section 2, p. 1), and "Juvenile Delinquency Aided by Symphony," *Houston*, March 1943 (36).

58. William G. Farrington Biographical File, Texas Room, HPL; *Chronicle*, Jan. 30, 1945, B1; *Post*, Jan. 30, 1945, sec. 1, p. 3; Feb. 24, 1948, sec. 1, p. 5; Jan. 25, 1949, sec. 1, p. 4.

59. *Post*, May 17, 1967, sec. 3, p. 18 (McPhail died May 16); Jan. 24, 1945, sec. 1, p. 1; *Press*, Jan. 24, 1945, p. 4.

60. Ima Hogg to Terrill Sledge, Kyle, Texas, July 5, 1946, 3B164, IHP, CAH.

61. Ima Hogg to Jesse E. Martin, March 1, 1943, 3B164, folder 1; several letters including Ima Hogg to Mayor Oscar Holcombe, Sept. 30, 1947, 4W235, folder 1, IHP, CAH.

62. Chamber of Commerce propaganda in *Houston*, March 1941, 2; February 1941, 3, 14; April 1943, 7–17, 28; "SS *James S. Hogg* Launched April 23," May 1943, 34.

63. Carleton, *Red Scare!*, 12–13. Paul Alejandro Levengood, "For the Duration and Beyond: World War II and the Creation of Modern Houston, Texas" (Ph.D. diss., Rice University, 1999).

64. *Post*, Feb. 21, 1943, sec. 1, p. 1. The story was carried by the *Press* on Feb. 20, 1943 (1). A full statement of Ima's position was printed by the *Post* on Feb. 25, 1943 (sec. 1, p. 7). See also folder 6, IHP, Archives, MFAH.

65. *Post*, Feb. 27, 1943, sec. 1, p. 6; April 3, 1943, sec. 1, p. 1. Rosella Werlin handled publicity for the Hogg-Daily campaign. Years later she described the campaign as "unusually heated." She found that her task "candidly was not at all an easy assignment." Rosella Werlin to Geraldine Styles, archivist for the Bayou Bend Docents, May 19, 1983, folder 5, IHP, Archives, MFAH.

66. "Radio Talk," KPRC, typescript, April 2, 1943; "Miss Hogg's Statement to the Newspapers," typescript, 4W237, folder 3, IHP, CAH. See also "Talk by Ima Hogg Before the Woman's Club," typescript, March 23, 1943, ibid.

67. *Post*, March 28, 1943, sec. 1, p. 15 (Taylor); *Post*, March 31, 1943, "Teachers Morale Discussed" (Hogg).

68. *Press*, March 31, 1943, 7; *Post*, March 26, 1943, sec. 1, p. 6.

69. *Chronicle*, April 1, 1943, A7. Minutes confirm Daily's assertion; comparatively few meetings mentioned curriculum.

70. Ray Daily to Ima Hogg, Feb. 16, 1943, 4W237, folder 3, IHP, CAH.

71. Leaflet, box 2, folder 1, Daily Papers, HMRC, HPL; leaflet, 4W237, folder 3, IHP, CAH.

72. Mrs. Milby Porter to Ima Hogg, March 8, 1943, and Ima Hogg to Mrs. Milby Porter, March 11, 1943, 4W237, folder 3, IHP, CAH.

73. Citizens in *Press*, March 31, 1943, 12; Sharp in *Post*, March 21, 1943, sec. 2, p. 7; Law in *Press*, March 24, 1943, 12; Hutcheson in *Post*, March 30,

1943, sec. 1, p. 17; Bates from Ima Hogg to Colonel William B. Bates, April 4, 1943, 4W237, IHP, CAH. Also box 2, folder 3, Daily Papers, HMRC, HPL; *Post*, March 30, 1943, sec. 1, p. 16; April 24, 1943, 4W237, folder 3, IHP, CAH. Advertisement, Box 3, folder 1, Daily Papers, HMRC, HPL.

74. *Post*, April 2, 1943, sec. 1, p. 6; *Press*, March 30, 1943, 10; *Chronicle*, April 2, 1943, A6; *Bellaire Breeze*, March 26, 1943, clipping in 4W237, folder 4, IHP, CAH.

75. Arthur J. Mandell to Ima Hogg, April 13, 1943, 4W237, folder 3, IHP, CAH.

76. *Informer*, March 13, 1943, 1; April 3, 1943, 8. Jesse O. Thomas's *Study of Social Welfare Status of Negroes in Houston* (1929) stated that in 1927–1928 sixty-eight white schools were valued at $16,544,902 and twenty-five "colored" at $278,068, a difference of $16,266,834; Thomas report quoted in Amilcar Shabazz, "One for the Crows and One for the Crackers: The Strange Career of Public Higher Education in Houston, Texas," *Houston Review* 18 (1996): 127.

77. J. B. Grigsby to Ima Hogg, Feb. 24, 1943, 4W237, folder 3, IHP, CAH.

78. *Press*, March 30, 1943, 10. Tally in BE Minutes, April 10, 1943.

79. Ima Hogg to Dr. Frank O'Brien, April 20, 1943; Ima Hogg to B. F. Pittinger, April 7, 1943; B. F. Pittinger to Ima Hogg, May 9, 1943, 4W237, folder 4, IHP, CAH. 4W237, folder 3 contains congratulatory letters and copies of her replies.

80. Michael Botson, "Jim Crow Wearing Steel-Toed Shoes and Safety Glasses: Dual Unionism at the Hughes Tool Company, 1918–1942," *Houston Review* 16 (1994): 115.

81. William Henry Kellar, "Make Haste Slowly: A History of School Desegregation in Houston, Texas," Ph.D. diss., University of Houston, 1994, 67–74, 76, 81, 91–93; William Henry Kellar, "Alive with a Vengeance: Houston's Black Teachers and Their Fight for Equal Pay," *Houston Review* 18 (1996): 89–99; *Informer*, March 6, 1943, 1, 8.

82. *Chronicle*, April 2, 1943, A10; *Press*, March 30, 1943, 2.

83. BE Minutes, April 5, 1943; *Post*, April 6, 1943, sec. 1, p. 6.

84. See for example "Economic Security for Teachers Asked by Miss Ima Hogg," *Press*, March 3, 1943, and "Miss Hogg Declares for Fair Wage to Teachers," April 1, 1943, clippings in folder 6, IHP, Archives, MFAH.

85. *Informer*, April 17, 1943, 1.

86. BE Minutes, May 3, 1943.

87. From 1927–1953 the school system managed the Houston Junior College and Houston Colored Junior College. After 1933 the University of Houston included the Houston College for Negroes. In 1936 Ben Taub and the Settegast Estate provided 112 acres in southeast Houston for the main campus of the University of Houston, and by 1937 Hare and Hare had developed a site plan of four linked quadrangles that retained dense tree cover. The Roy Gustav Cullen Memorial building opened in 1939. By 1946 the Houston College for Negroes had moved to its permanent campus on 53 acres donated by Hugh Roy Cullen.

88. Summary based on Nicholson, *In Time*, 149–220; BE Minutes during these years; Handbook of Texas Online, University of Houston, Main Campus, and Texas Southern University entries at www.tsha.utexas.edu/handbook/online.

89. BE Minutes, May 24, 1943; *Post*, May 25, 1943, sec. 1, pp. 1, 6.

90. Cullen spent more than $26 million on buildings for the university, including the 53-acre campus for the Houston College for Negroes. Although he failed to establish an endowment to stabilize institutional growth, he did place most of his fortune in the Cullen Foundation after establishing relatively modest trusts for his daughters. See Merle Curti and Roderick Nash, *Philanthropy in the Shaping of American Higher Education* (New Brunswick, NJ: Rutgers University Press, 1965), 129–130; Carleton, *Red Scare!*, 89–90; Edward W. Kilman, *Hugh Roy Cullen: A Story of American Opportunity* (New York: Prentice-Hall, 1954).

91. BE Minutes, July 26, 1943; H. R. Cullen to Board of Trustees, May 20, 1944, copy of letter and notes of discussion, BE Meeting folder, May 29, 1944; BE Minutes, May 29, 1944. The proposal also authorized the Advisory Committee to place the bill before the legislature in January 1945.

92. *Press*, March 13, 1945, 1; *Post*, March 13, 1945, sec. 1, p. 1.

93. Ima wrote experts about candidates and placed a letter in the press, but the board appointed Moreland at a special called meeting on June 29, 1945. The nomination was made official at the regular July 9 board meeting. BE meeting folders; *Post*, June 30, 1945, sec. 1, pp. 1, 2; Ima expressed disappointment in Ima Hogg to A. Y. Wilson, July 2, 1945, 4W237, IHP, CAH.

94. In subsequent years, the committee changed its composition and name, but its purpose of overseeing facility improvements remained the same. School population tapered off after war's end, reaching 84,866 in 1950. African-American students comprised about 22 percent of the population (14,145 in 1940 and 18,167 in 1950). Hispanic, Asian, and Native American students were not treated as discrete demographic groups at this time.

95. BE Minutes, July 12, 1943; Ima Hogg to Mary Gearing (University of Texas Home Economics Department), May 16, 1945; Ima Hogg to Lou Elva Eller, director of Lunch Rooms, Nov. 12, 1943, 4W237, folder 4, IHP, CAH.

96. Steven R. Strom, "A Legacy of Civic Pride: Houston's PWA Buildings," *Houston Review* 17 (1995): 103–121, discusses public buildings constructed with PWA funds, including $3,821,000 to build twenty-five elementary schools and sixteen high schools and to rehabilitate thirty-seven other school system structures. Top architects executed the school board commissions.

97. *Chronicle*, March 20, 1943, A1; *Post*, Nov. 30, 1945, sec. 2, p. 1.

98. *Post*, Nov. 21, 1943, sec. 1, pp. 1, 4; March 30, 1944, sec. 2, p. 17 (quote). BE Minutes, March 13, 1944; March 27, 1944; *Chronicle*, Oct. 15, 1945, p. 9; *Press*, Jan. 9, 1945, p.1.

99. Ima Hogg to Mrs. Erma H. Friede, St. Louis, Mo., June 7, 1946, 4W237, folder 5, IHP, CAH.

100. *Woman's Viewpoint*, May 1925, 7.
101. Ima Hogg to Dorothy Jarrett, March 26, 1945, 4W237, IHP, CAH.
     BE Minutes, April 28, 1947. Automatic increments stood at $100 per
     year from 1920 until the Depression, were eliminated in the 1930s, and
     were restored to $50 per year in 1936. Figures provided by the U.S.
     Department of Labor and quoted in a report to the board made by
     the Tax Research Association of Houston and Harris County Inc., BE
     Minutes, March 22, 1948.
102. BE Minutes, Aug. 9, 1943; Nov. 22, 1943; May 31, 1943.
103. Margaret Patrick to Ima Hogg, April 27, 1949; Houston Teachers
     Association President Eula Ware to Ima Hogg, June 3, 1948, 4W237,
     folder 5, IHP, CAH.
104. BE Minutes, Jan. 10, 24, 1944.
105. BE Minutes, Feb. 15, 1944.
106. BE Meeting folder, Feb. 26, 1945; BE Minutes, April 14,1947.
     Each program required separate discussion and approval.
107. Youth Services Committee member Mrs. Merrick W. Phelps, quoted in
     Post, Oct. 15, 1944, 5. Ima Hogg, "Vita," Dec. 6, 1967, typescript, 3B168,
     folder 1, IHP, CAH, gives Ima's account of her role in initiating the
     visiting teacher program.
108. BE Minutes, Oct. 9, 1944; *Press*, Oct. 15, 1944, 1, 4. Originally the
     committee included Oberholtzer and Mills; all board members were
     added after July 23, 1945.
109. Report to the board, Nov. 27, 1944, 4W237, folder 1, IHP, CAH. Also
     Ima Hogg to Sarah Gaskell, Ima Hogg to Mrs. Leonard P. White, Ima
     Hogg to Mrs. C. R. Latimer, Oct. 17, 1944, 4W237, IHP, CAH; BE
     Meeting folder Nov. 27, 1944.
110. Speech to the Houston Teachers Association, typescript, 4W237, folder
     1, IHP, CAH. "Last of October or first of November 1944" written in ink
     on report.
111. BE Meeting folder, Nov. 27, 1944. Dr. Petersen voted no, citing financial
     reasons. Ima Hogg to Mrs. Beulah T. Wild, Ima Hogg to Robert L.
     Sutherland, Ima Hogg to Carmelita Janvier, Nov. 28, 1944; Ima Hogg to
     Gladys E. Hall, School of Social Work, Tulane University, New Orleans,
     Oct. 3, 1945, 4W237, folder 2, IHP, CAH.
112. Ima Hogg to Robert Sutherland, Aug. 10, 1945, MAI9/U1, HFR, CAH.
113. BE Meeting folder, March 26, 1945 (figures); April 24, 1944; Sept. 21,
     1944; Sept. 25, 1944; BE Minutes, Sept. 25, 1944; *Post*, Sept. 26, 1944,
     p. 1.
114. *Post*, Aug. 29, 1945, sec. 2, p. 1; Oct. 9, 1945, sec. 2, p. 1; Oct. 26, 1945,
     sec. 2, p. 1. *Informer*, Aug. 25, 1945, p. 1; *Chronicle*, Oct. 9, 1945, A4.
115. BE Minutes, April 25, 1949.
116. Ima Hogg to Margaret Caillet, Aug. 4, 1943, 4W237, folder 4, IHP,
     CAH; BE Minutes, July 12, 1943; Aug. 9, 1943.
117. BE Minutes, Nov. 8, 1943; Ima Hogg to Mrs. W. L. Clayton, Oct.
     5, 1943, Nov. 4, 1943, 4W237, folder 4, IHP, CAH. Clayton served
     as chairman in absentia while living in Washington, D.C., during

her husband's term of government service as undersecretary of state administering the Marshall Plan.

118. Thank-you note from a student to Ima Hogg, Feb. 23, 1944; Ima Hogg to Mabel McBain, April 13, 1945, 4W237, folder 4, IHP, CAH. See Chapter 6 for more information about the pre–World War I project sponsored by the Houston Art League, forerunner of the Museum of Fine Arts, Houston.

119. Ruth Red to the author, telephone interview, March 24, 1997.

120. "Report on Music in the Houston Schools," undated, among 1945 minutes, 4W237, folder 5, IHP, CAH; BE Minutes, Sept. 22, 1947; Jan. 12, 1948; April 25, 1949, copy in 4W237, folder 5, IHP, CAH; Ima Hogg to Ewing Werlein, May 2, 1949, 4W237, folder 4, IHP, CAH.

121. BE Minutes, Dec. 30, 1946, Jan. 10, 1949, March 25, 1946. *Press*, Aug. 5, 1943, 13.

122. Ima Hogg to Mrs. Erma H. Friede, St. Louis, Mo., June 7, 1946, 4W237, IHP, CAH.

123. Ima Hogg, "Retirement Statement," typescript, 4W237, folder 4, IHP, CAH; resolution expressing appreciation, BE Meeting folder, May 9, 1949; *Post*, Feb. 2, 1949, sec. 1, pp. 1, 14; Feb. 4, 1949, sec. 1, p. 1; Feb. 18, 1949, sec. 1, p. 1; Feb. 20, 1949, sec. 1, p. 15; March 22, 1949, sec. 1, p. 4; April 1, 1949, sec. 1, p. 4.

124. Ima Hogg to Margaret Patrick, April 30, 1949, 4W237, IHP, CAH.

125. Lists of donations (1962, 1963) in 4W238, folders 1–4, IHP, CAH; inventory lists in IHP, Archives, MFAH.

126. See Carleton, *Red Scare!*, 277, for an extensive list of the anti–Red Scare, anti-Mills coalition; Don E. Carleton, "McCarthyism in Local Elections: The Houston School Board Election of 1952," *Houston Review* 3 (Winter 1981): 168–177.

127. Ima Hogg to Arthur Laro, director and managing editor, *Post*, Oct. 7, 1954; clipping from *Post*, Oct. 17, 1954, both in 4W237, folder 4, IHP, CAH. This summary resembles Ima's farewell speech to the Board of Education in which she also outlined qualities necessary for successful school board participation. Carleton, *Red Scare!*, 84–85, 220, 233.

128. Speech, April 18, 1956; Verna Rogers to Ima Hogg, April 23, 1956, letter, 3B168, folder 5, speeches, IHP, CAH.

129. James Stephen Hogg, in Cotner, *Addresses*, 122–123.

CHAPTER 5

The title of this chapter is taken from Ima Hogg, Feb. 15, 1952, Speech to Friends and Sponsors of the Houston Symphony, 3B168, folder 5, IHP, CAH.

1. *Woman's Viewpoint*, July 1, 1924, 21.

2. Rabbi Barnstein officially changed the spelling of his name to Barnston sometime in 1922. He is listed as Rabbi Henry Barnstein in the 1922 city directory and as Rabbi Henry Barnston in the 1923–1924 edition. Many U.S. citizens anglicized the spellings of their names during the

xenophobic 1920s. Henry Barnstein appears on Congregation Beth Israel letterheads in 1920, but the rabbi, who was in England at the time, signed his name Barnston. Letter of resignation, April 21, 1920, box 5, folder 1, Congregation Beth Israel Collection, MSRC, HPL.

3. Wille Hutcheson, *Post*, June 22, 1913, 20 ("everyone for it"). See also Hubert Roussel, *The Houston Symphony Orchestra, 1913–1971* (Austin: University of Texas Press, 1972), 16–19; Bernhard, *Ima Hogg*, 56–57; Pentimento, *Houston Symphony Magazine*, 1993–1994, 18.

4. Ima Hogg, November 1952, Speech, 3B168, folder 5, IHP, CAH.

5. Saengerbund pamphlet, May 1, 1917, scrapbook 3, IHPC.

6. Ima supported friends' Little Theatre activities (amateur independent forerunners of municipal repertory theater that enjoyed popularity in the 1920s and 1930s), attended opera in Houston, and opened her home for Music Guild performances after 1950, but family philanthropy focused on the Symphony Society and Museum of Fine Arts. The Music Guild, begun by music maven Elva Lobit, assembled five musicians from the symphony for chamber music concerts. Concertmaster Raphael Fliegel, violinist Andor Toth, cellist Marion Davis, violist Gaetano Molieri, and pianist Albert Hirsch performed for several years at the three-hundred–seat, acoustically perfect Playhouse Theatre in the round on Main Street. Playbills from New York, London, Paris, and Houston in IHPC; Raphael Fliegel to author, Oct. 4, 2003; Hubert Roussel, *Post*, Nov. 10, 1950, clipping in 2J413, Symphony Scrapbook, 1950, WHP, CAH.

7. Blair, *Torchbearers*, 32–38. See also Saengerbund pamphlet (scrapbook 3, IHPC), in which the author recognizes a "gradual awakening of the commercial interests to the fact that art is an essential of modern life" and links business support to future success of Houston's Symphony Orchestra. Johnston, in *Houston: The Unknown City*, analyzes these issues.

8. Lewis A. Erenberg, *Steppin' Out: New York Night Life and the Transformation of American Culture, 1890–1930* (Chicago: University of Chicago Press, 1981), 5.

9. Fred R. von der Mehden, ed., *The Ethnic Groups of Houston* (Houston: Rice University Studies, 1984), 160–171; B. H. Carroll, *Standard History of Houston, Texas: From a Study of the Original Sources* (Knoxville: H. W. Crew, 1912), 378.

10. Scrapbook 4, IHPC, contains programs for the May 5–7, 1913, Twenty-ninth Biennial State Saengerfest.

11. Mehden, *Ethnic Groups*, 171; Saengerbund pamphlet, scrapbook 5, IHPC. Larry Wolz, "Roots of Classical Music in Texas: The German Contribution," in *The Roots of Texas Music*, Clayton Lawrence and Joe W. Sprecht (College Station: Texas A&M University Press, 2003), 26. The German-Texan Singers League, a federation of singing societies, was formed in New Braunfels in 1852 and was a member of the German National Saengerbund.

12. *Post*, Nov. 23, 1914, 34.

13. Carroll, *Standard History*, 378.

14. Carroll, *Standard History*, 381; scrapbook 3, IHPC.

15. *Gargoyle*, May 25, 1930, 14, 15; *Civics for Houston*, May 5, 1929, 13.

16. *Gargoyle*, May 25, 1930, 15.

17. Federation of Women's Clubs, *Key to the City*, 149.

18. *Gargoyle*, May 25, 1930, 14.

19. Obituary, Mrs. W. Hutcheson, *Dallas News*, Feb. 11, 1924, Hutcheson Family Papers, WRC. Ione Allen Peden died in 1903, and Edward Andrew Peden married Cora Root (Peden), also a music enthusiast, in 1905. Cora's sister Stella Root was an accomplished violinist. My appreciation to Peden descendant William Conner for clarifying the family's genealogy.

20. Scrapbook 1, 1908–1909 program, IHPC. Hu T. Huffmaster became music director in 1909.

21. Scrapbook 4, IHPC.

22. Program, Fourth Annual Festival in scrapbook 5, IHPC; Box 53.8, Edgar Odell Lovett Personal Papers, WRC.

23. Comment Raphael Fliegel to author, Oct. 4, 2003. In 1911 Houstonians heard ten concerts by the Russian Symphony Orchestra and return engagements by Walter Damrosch and the New York Symphony.

24. Federation of Women's Clubs, *Key to the City*, 152; Carroll, *Standard History*, 378.

25. Carroll, *Standard History*, 379.

26. Ima Hogg to Mrs. E. J. Wheeler, March 19, 1969, Scrapbook 1, p. 71, IHP, Archives, MFAH: "Ever since I opened my eyes I have had a love affair with music!"

27. Recollection of the author; teenagers in Mary Ann "Muffy" McLanahan to Patricia Prioleau, *The Bridge*, February/March 2002, 12; scrapbook 1, p. 33, series 14, IHP, Archives, MFAH. When Ima moved to Inwood Manor during the last decade of her life, she took one piano with her. A piano she gave to the Symphony Society was ruined by Hurricane Allison in 2001.

28. Program, Dec. 10, 1897 (Schubert solo), May 17, 1898 (Raff *Fantasie*), 3B163, folder 10, IHP, CAH.

29. *Alcalde*, November/December 1975, 46–47.

30. Solo program, Feb. 12, 1900, 3B163, folder 10, IHP, CAH. Margulies taught Ima Hogg, Ima's lifelong friend Mary Fuller, and seven other Houstonians, including Ima's pupils Eloise Chalmers and Bessie Griffiths before 1931, when Ima and Mary Fuller arranged for their mentor to teach an eight-month master class for pianists and teachers in Houston, the first such offering in the Southwest. *Gargoyle*, March 29, 1931, 6; advertisement, Sept. 13, 1931, 19. Petitioned by her students, Margulies returned for another teaching season in 1932. *Gargoyle*, Feb. 7, 1932, 11. Ima helped Margulies financially and gave sheet music to the Houston Public Library in her honor (1949); 4W238, folder 1, IHP, CAH.

31. Scrapbook 1, IHPC. Ima found rising star Josef Hofmann "disappointing," was held "spellbound" by Richard Strauss's tone poem "Ein Heldenleben," and noted that "Saint-Saens even at his age played very brilliantly" after a November 1903 concert at Carnegie Hall. Ima Hogg kept hundreds of programs, many with handwritten comments in the margins, collected them in scrapbooks during the summer of 1965,

and donated them to the University of Houston archives sometime before May 1966; 3B175, folder 5, IHP, CAH.

32. Ima was in Europe from July 1907 through October 1908. She toured England, Scotland, Holland, France, Italy, and Germany for several months and, encouraged by a friend's recommendation, decided to remain in Berlin; 3B153, folder 1 (diaries), folders 2–4 (postcards), IHP, CAH. "Memo of Absences from the State of Miss Ima Hogg" gives dates, 2J328, WHP, CAH; dates confirmed in 3B118, folder 3, IHP, CAH. Ima once again noted her impressions on programs: Siegfried Wagner (February 1908) was "a puny imitation of his father"; popular performer Frederic Lamond was "very exaggerated and mediocre"; and Felix Mottl led the Philharmonie on March 13, 1908, in "the most inspiring interpretation of Eroica Symphony I have yet heard." Scrapbook 4, IHPC.

33. William Lee Pryor, a friend in her later years, believed Ima's standards must have been high if she felt inadequate despite Krause's encouragement (comment to author, June 2, 2003). Ima recalled that she studied for her own pleasure (interview, Oral History Collection, HMRC, HPL). Virginia Bernhard (*Ima Hogg*, 54) cites a confidence made to a close friend: "The great sorrow of my life is that I was never a concert pianist." These difficult choices may have contributed to her feelings of depression or melancholia of 1918–1923 and in later years.

34. Programs, scrapbook 4, IHPC. Student recital programs for Eloise Helbig (later Chalmers) and Florence Griffiths, who played Bach, Mozart, and Mendelssohn selections on Saturday, June 12, 1915, scrapbook 3, IHPC.

35. Constitution of the Girls Musical Club in 1919–1920 program and membership roster, article 3, sec. 1, and article 6, sec. 2, Tuesday Musical Club File, HMRC, HPL.

36. Ruth West, "Words and Music," *Gargoyle*, May 25, 1930, 14. The official history (1976) says "about forty young ladies" met. Audrey Kenyon Brown, "Our First Fifty Years," pamphlet in Box 26, folder 24, Marguerite Johnston Papers, WRC.

37. Girls Musical Club program and yearbook, 1919–1920. Ima, who was ill during that season, was no longer listed as a member. She began participating again in 1923, when she hosted a "reciprocity meeting" on March 6, and in 1924, when an open meeting was held in her home. Scrapbook 5, IHPC.

38. Box 2, folder 1, E. Richardson Cherry Papers, HMRC, HPL.

39. *The Stylus* 4, no. 1 (Jan. 13, 1912): 13.

40. Yearbook 1912–1913, IHP, Archives, MFAH.

41. West, "Words and Music," 15; Tuesday Musical Club file, clipping, Oct. 13, 1963, HMRC, HPL; program, Girls Musical Club, benefit concert, April 16, 1925, Main Street Auditorium, scrapbook 5, IHPC. The official history (Brown, "Our First Fifty Years") incorrectly places the concert at the Beach Auditorium.

42. Bernhard (*Ima Hogg*, 57) notes Ima's insistence that she was "a" founder. Hubert Roussel (*Houston Symphony*, ix) states that "the organization's earliest documents were destroyed" while in the home of an officer. In

2001 waters from Hurricane Allison flooded Symphony Society offices and ruined many valuable papers, scores, and instruments. See also Ima Hogg, Oral History, HMRC, HPL. Roussel acknowledges that much information in his 1972 study of the symphony comes from Ima's recollections and files. To date, Roussel's is the only published history of the Houston Symphony.

43. Ima Hogg, Dec. 7, 1953, 3B168, folder 5, IHP, CAH; Houston Symphony Society, program, Dec. 21, 1953, 31.

44. Ima Hogg, Remarks developed for Houston Independent School District bulletin boards, Aug. 12, 1968, 3B175, folder 5, IHP, CAH.

45. First quote from Ezra Rachlin to Ima Hogg, July 4, 1965, 3B175, folder 5; last two quotes from Speech to Friends and Sponsors of the Houston Symphony, Feb. 15, 1952, 3B168, folder 5, IHP, CAH.

46. Joseph S. Smith to Ima Hogg, July 29, 1935, 3B174, folder 2, IHP, CAH.

47. Ima Hogg to R. C. Kuldell, Hughes Tool, March 13, 1935 (quote); R. C. Kuldell to Ima Hogg, March 22, 1935, 3B178, folder 2, IHP, CAH.

48. Wille Hutcheson, "Upward Step of Houston Symphony," *Musical America*, May 22, 1915, clipping in Joanne Wilson Collection. In an interview for the Houston Public Library oral history project (Ima Hogg, Oral History, HMRC, HPL), Ima claimed Blitz "didn't want to" consult her but that "everyone sent him" to speak with her. Planning meetings at the home of Mrs. Gentry Waldo in *Post*, June 1, 1913.

49. *Post*, Nov. 9, 1913, 39. Many of Wille Hutcheson's articles were unsigned. Hutcheson wrote for numerous journals including *Musical America*, the major national publication.

50. *Post*, Oct. 26, 1913, 33; Wille Hutcheson, "The Symphony Orchestra Is Assured," *Post*, Nov. 23, 1913, 34; "Houstonians Backing Move for Symphony Orchestra," *Post*, Nov. 23, 1913, 51, lists 150 guarantors, including Will Hogg, and announces three concerts at the Majestic Theatre; undated clipping in scrapbook 3, IHPC. Roussel says the organizational meeting took place at Mrs. Parker's home, but the *Post* clearly distinguishes the meetings.

51. Symphony Association organization in *Post*, Nov. 23, 1913, 34, 51; Roussel, *Houston Symphony*, 13–27; Pentimento, *Houston Symphony Magazine*, Dec. 1993, 13–14; Programme of Houston Symphony Orchestra, scrapbook 2, IHPC. The Houston Symphony Society program magazine changed names over the years. Hereinafter "program" and date indicate a Society program publication. Programs from 1931 to the present are found in Alice Pratt Brown Fine Arts Library, Fondren Library, RU.

52. Clipping, *Chronicle*, Jan. 10, 1971, Miss Ima Hogg Vertical File, Archives, MFAH.

53. William C. Hogg to Bassett Blakely, Nov. 18, 1913, 3B118, folder 4, IHP, CAH.

54. Wille Hutcheson, "Houston Symphony Concert a Marked Success," *Post*, Dec. 20, 1913, 8.

55. Clipping of advertisement, Levy Brothers Dry Goods Co., Dec. 18, 1913, scrapbook 3, IHPC.

56. Wille Hutcheson, *Post*, Dec. 13, 1913, p. 8; B. R. Forman, *Chronicle*, Dec. 20, 1913, 5. Scrapbook 3 contains information about and critiques of the fall 1913 season; scrapbook 2 contains the inaugural program and list of early patrons. Years later (program, Dec. 18, 19, 1967, 21), Ima recalled the high goals of the 1913 founders: an orchestra for Texas; an "instrument of entertainment and education"; broad-based community support; free summer concerts; the best possible directors; a recording contract; national tours; and an "acoustically perfect, glamorous and convenient" civic music hall.

57. *Post*, clipping in Joanne Wilson Collection.

58. Scrapbook 3, IHPC.

59. Program, scrapbook 3, IHPC; *Musical America*, Oct. 14, 1916, 102.

60. Ima Hogg to William C. Hogg, Oct. 20, 1917 ("in a terrible rush"), 3B119, folder 1, IHP, CAH. The 1917–1918 program of the Girls Musical Club lists Ima as chairman of the Artistic Committee. Box 2, folder 1, Cherry Papers, HMRC, HPL. In 1917–1918 two of Ima's piano students received scholarships from the Texas Federation of Music Clubs; "History of the Texas Federation of Music Clubs," typescript in Joanne Wilson collection.

61. Wille Hutcheson, *Musical America*, April 20, 1918, 52.

62. Saengerbund pamphlet, scrapbook 5, IHPC.

63. *Musical America*, April 6, 1918, 11; Oct. 19, 1918, 181–182; Jan. 4, 1919, 9.

64. Program of Rice Institute Lectureship, Nadia Boulanger, Scottish Rite Cathedral, Jan. 27–29, 1925, scrapbook 5, IHPC. Isham Jones, composer, bandleader, and saxophonist wrote hits like "I'll See You in My Dreams" and "What's the Use" and enjoyed a long engagement on the Rice Roof during the summer of 1930 (*Gargoyle*, July 20, 1930, ad on inside cover; July 27, 1930, 9). During the decade of Symphony Association quiescence, Houstonians could hear, among numerous other offerings, Gluck, March 24, 1919, City Auditorium; Paderewski, Feb. 1, 1923, City Auditorium; the London String Quartet, May 7, 1924, Main Street Auditorium; Boulanger, Jan. 27–29, 1925, Scottish Rite Cathedral; tenor John McCormack, Feb. 6, 1926, Feb. 16, 1928, City Auditorium; New York Philharmonic, Oct. 14, 15, 1926; ballet and opera programs in January and February 1927; and a Chicago Civic Opera Company season, March and April 1927, scrapbook 5, IHPC.

65. Anna Clyde Plunkett, *Chronicle*, Nov. 31, 1922, 13.

66. *Chronicle*, Feb. 3, 1927, Our City column, 1; programs in IHPC. The 1920 *Blue Book* claimed Texas was musically "advanced" and noted professional orchestras in San Antonio (under Julien Paul Blitz), Dallas, Austin, and Waco. Clyde Whitlock, "Musical Texas," in *The Standard Blue Book Texas Edition* (San Antonio: N. S. Peeler, 1920), 140.

67. Claim made by Anna Clyde Plunkett, *Chronicle*, Nov. 3, 1922, 13; *Post*, March 4, 1930, 1, 2; March 5, 1, 5; March 6, 1, 4; March 7, 5.

68. *Post-Dispatch*, Feb. 15, 1927, 5; March 20, 1927, 1, 2; March 21, 1; March 22, 1, 2; March 23, 1; March 24, 4.

69. Ruth West, "The Music Masters," *Gargoyle*, July 10, 1928; Hubert Roussel, "Symphony in Silver," *Gargoyle*, April 28, 1929, Civics Section.

70. Mary Elizabeth Rouse, "Houston and Harmony," *Gargoyle*, Dec. 1, 1929, 25.
71. Rouse, "Houston and Harmony," 25. Julien Paul Blitz debunked jazz as "merely amusing," *Gargoyle*, Aug. 17, 1930, 16.
72. Horton Corbett, "Lifting Music's Curtain," *Civics for Houston*, December 1928, 18.
73. *Civics for Houston*, January 1929, 15 (touring); Rouse, "Houston and Harmony," 25 (lectures).
74. Ima Hogg to Mrs. Underwood Nazro, Feb. 5, 1929, 3B174, folder 1, IHP, CAH.
75. Roussel, *Houston Symphony*, 29, 30; "Houston Civic Opera Plans," *Houston*, Oct. 1930, 28.
76. Hubert Roussel, *Gargoyle*, Jan. 25, 1931, 8.
77. Roussel, *Houston Symphony*, 33, 37.
78. Hubert Roussel, "Unfinished Symphony," *Gargoyle*, March 15, 1931, 8.
79. *Gargoyle*, Dec. 20, 1931, lauds Dr. Mullen as supportive of all cultural movements in the city; he was Houston's first ear, nose, and throat specialist, advocated public health issues, and in retirement became a scholar of music and archeology.
80. Maxine Tindel, "Symphony Is Success Here," *Post-Dispatch*, May 7, 1931.
81. Hogg comment in Oral History Collection, HMRC, HPL. Mrs. Graham finally launched her Houston Civic Opera Association in April 1932 with a production of *Il Trovotore* at the City Auditorium, Hubert Roussel, *Gargoyle*, April 24, 1932, 22.
82. Hubert Roussel ("Unfinished Symphony," 32) said friends of the Philharmonic charged that association members called Philharmonic musicians and offered cash. Philharmonic members retaliated by threatening expulsion of any member who played with another group. Roussel omitted this rumor in his history.
83. Students were invited to attend the ten o'clock dress rehearsal on Thursday morning.
84. Roussel, "Unfinished Symphony," 32, and *Houston Symphony*, 34. Van Hoose made his opera debut in 1897 with the Metropolitan Opera Company and performed frequently with the Metropolitan and Chicago Operas. He introduced Handel's *Messiah* to Houston audiences and presented the oratorio for twenty seasons. King, *Except the Lord Build*, 77.
85. Roussel, "Symphony Week," *Gargoyle*, May 10, 1931, 23. In his history Roussel is more critical of Philharmonic concerts.
86. Roussel, "Symphony Week," 18; *Post-Dispatch*, May 7, p. 11; May 8, p. 7.
87. Tindel, *Post-Dispatch*, May 7, p. 11; Ima Hogg to Dr. Joseph Mullen, May 11, 1931, 3B174, folder 1, IHP, CAH. She itemizes union costs she will cover.
88. Subscribers list, 3B177, folder 1, IHP, CAH. Editorial, *Houston*, July 1931, 15.
89. Program, Nov. 16, 1931.
90. Program, Jan. 14, 1933, 3B163, folder 10; Mike Hogg to Ima Hogg, Arizona Inn, Tucson, Nov. 8, 1933, 3B174, folder 1, IHP, CAH. Long-widowed friend Estelle Sharp spent Christmas in Arizona with Ima that year. Maybelle McIntyre to Alice Hogg, Oct. 26, 1933, March 10, 1934,

Box 4, folder "O. O. McIntyre," Mike and Alice Hogg Papers, Archives, MFAH.

91.   First quote, Florence Hogue to Ima Hogg, Aug. 30, 1933, 3B174, folder 1, IHP, CAH. Radaslav A. Tsanoff, Rice Institute, to Ima Hogg, Oct. 9, 1933, ibid., makes clear that Ima was elected to the post, although official symphony rosters did not record this election. Mullen continued as president until succeeded by Joseph Smith in 1934. Tsanoff said in part: "Your enforced absence . . . at this season makes us realize anew the Symphony's great and constant need of your counsel and guidance. Your gracious letters of resignation as president were read at a meeting of the Executive Board, but of course we could only postpone action, hoping your convalescence may bring you back sooner than you at present expect. You are bound to know that your election as President of the Houston Symphony . . . was the effective recognition of the present needs of our organization and of our whole enterprise."

92.   Roussel, *Houston Symphony*, 47.

93.   R. C. Kuldell to Ima Hogg, March 22, 1935, 3B178, folder 2, IHP, CAH.

94.   *Press*, May 30, 1932, clipping, 3B174, folder 1, IHP, CAH; Hubert Roussel, *Gargoyle*, Nov. 22, 1931, 20–21; Dec. 20, 1931, 20.

95.   Letter, Uriel Nespoli to Houston, in *Gargoyle*, June 19, 1932, 4; "woefully underrehearsed" in Hubert Roussel, *Gargoyle*, May 1, 1932, 19. Roussel's account of Nespoli's dismissal, *Gargoyle*, July 31, 1932, and *Houston Symphony*, 53–55.

96.   Hubert Roussel, *Gargoyle*, July 31, 1932, 16.

97.   Raphael Fliegel to author, Oct. 4, 2003.

98.   *Chronicle*, "Music to Suit All," Dec. 11, 1934; *Post*, "St. Leger Leads City Symphony in New Triumph," Dec. 11, 1934, clippings in scrapbook 7, IHPC.

99.   Letters between Ima Hogg and Joseph S. Smith July 23, 27, 29, 30, 31, 1935, reveal that Ima had thought through the requirements for director and begun interviewing candidates. Joseph Smith to Frank St. Leger July 31, Aug. 16, letter and telegram, reveal reconsideration requests. The board decision to hire three guest directors was taken Sept. 9 and announced in letters Sept. 10, 1935, 3B174, folder 2, IHP, CAH. Hubert Roussel, *Press*, July 26, 1935, "Scouts Seeking New Symphony Conductor/Committee of Four in New York Asked to Look Out for Successor to Frank St. Leger," clipping in scrapbook 7, IHPC. Dr. Mullen was also in New York.

100.   Clippings in scrapbook 7, IHPC; "Three Famous Maestros," *Post*, Sept. 10, 1935 ("significant step"); Hubert Roussel, "Large Audience Back," *Press*, Nov. 5, 1935; Pat Barnes, "Verse Is Given Ovation by Colorful Audience," *Post*, Nov. 5, 1935; Pat Barnes, *Post*, Dec. 16, 1935 ("much improvement"); Pat Barnes, "Great Triumph Is Achieved By Symphony," *Post*, Jan. 14, 1936 ("replete with musical beauty"); Pat Barnes, *Post*, Feb. 18, 1936 ("new standards"); "Houston Symphony Orchestra Makes Notable Progress," *Dallas Times Herald*, Feb. 23, 1936; Hubert Roussel, *Press*, March 10, 1936 ("graceful and civilized performance"); "Disappointing Debut," Walter Dancy, *Chronicle*, March 10, 1936.

101. Roussel, *Houston Symphony*, 69–71.
102. Report of Committee on Selection of Conductor, July 1, 1936, 3B174, folder 3, IHP, CAH.
103. Letters, Ima Hogg to Dr. Nicolai Sokoloff, Federal Musicians Project, May 26, 1935; to Mary Fuller, May 26, 1936; to Mrs. Walter Walne, May 27, 1936; Walter Walne to Ernest [*sic*] Hoffman, June 16, 1936; Report of Committee on Selection of Conductor, July 1, 1936, in 3B174, folder 3, IHP, CAH; articles in *Post*, May 27, 1936, July 3, 1936; *Chronicle*, May 27, 1936, June 2, 1936, June 14, 1936, June 16, 1936, and numerous other clippings in Scrapbook 7, IHPC.
104. Roussel, *Houston Symphony*, 76–80; Raphael Fliegel to author, Oct. 4, 2003 (quote). Fliegel recalled that Hoffman was not "glamorous" and would set up chairs himself or do "whatever needed to be done."
105. Ima Hogg to Dr. Nicolai Sokoloff, Federal Music Project, May 26, 1935, 3B174, folder 3, IHP, CAH. Ima wanted names of musicians who might move to a city of 350,000; the symphony needed two violins, two violas, two double basses, one flute, one oboe, one English horn, two bassoons, and one French horn.
106. Charitable groups included the Catholic Women's Club, the Women's Cooperative Home, the Bellaire Home, Sheltering Arms, and the Young Men's Chamber of Commerce. See unsigned letter to Ima Hogg, Nov. 22, 1931; Bessie Oliver to Ima Hogg, Jan. 19, 1932; Bessie Oliver to Ima Hogg, Nov. 11, 1932, 3B174, folder 1, IHP, CAH. Ima purchased 148 tickets at $0.50 each, although most recipients were seated in the orchestra "to make a better balance of the house." Recipients received letters saying "a friend of the orchestra" was presenting the reserved tickets to them. Ima spent $1,782.75 on donated tickets in 1931 and 1932.
107. Form letter, 1937–1938 season in 3B174, folder 4, IHP, CAH.
108. Meyer, *Days of My Years*, 161–162. The term "pop concert" was used in the 1930s and 1940s. The term "pops concert" is current today.
109. Walter Walne, Report to City Council, Jan. 31, 1938. Pop concert tickets cost twenty-five to fifty cents.
110. Mrs. Robert Stuart to her daughter Francita Stuart Koelsch Ulmer, Program, Dec. 7 and 8, 1970, 21.
111. Program, April 2, 1951, 35; remarks, Mrs. Albert P. Jones, May 13, 1957, 3B175, folder 4, IHP, CAH.
112. *Post*, April 1, 1937, editorial, 4, scrapbook 7, IHPC.
113. Clippings, *Post*, March 5, March 30, April 13, May 2, 1937; *Chronicle*, March 30, 1937, April 13, May 2, 1937, scrapbook 7, IHPC. Extensive photograph spread in the *Chronicle*, Feb. 17, 1938, of women working in the Bayou Bend library. Committee report to Walter Walne, January 1938, established a goal of 8,000 names (3B174, folder 5, IHP, CAH). Also Nettie (Mrs. Albert P.) Jones, "Houston Women's Committee," program, April 2, 1951, 35. Campaign records indicate Ima underwrote secretarial costs of nearly $1,000 in 1938–1939 at $0.40 per hour, 3B177, folder 1, IHP, CAH.
114. Program, May 1994, 16–17; "50th Anniversary: Houston Symphony League," pamphlet, 1987.

115. "History of the Symphony Society," June 21, 1943, box 2, IHPC.
116. Symphony Society Minutes, Nov. 3, 1943, reprinted in Meyer, *Days of My Years*, 344.
117. Ima Hogg to Hugh Roy Cullen, Jan. 2, 1944, 3B176, folder 1, IHP, CAH.
118. See Meyer, *Days of My Years*, 157–158, 342–343 (appendix with reprint of minutes in which Meyer suggested Hoffmann be relieved of "all responsibilities not pertaining directly to the duties of conductor").
119. Hugh Roy Cullen to Major General Richard Donovan, May 25, 1943, letter explaining Wartime Youth Council, box 2, 1959–1964, IHPC.
120. According to Roussel (*Houston Symphony*, 107–108), NBC was stunned by this unusual request but agreed to move its entire engineering and production staff to Houston for the experiment.
121. Roy Cullen to President-Elect Joseph S. Smith, April 16, 1946, 3B176, folder 1, IHP, CAH.
122. Roy Cullen, resignation statement, April 23, 1946, 3B176, folder 1, IHP, CAH.
123. Roy Cullen to Joseph S. Smith, president-elect, April 16, 1946; Roy Cullen to Ima Hogg, president, May 18, 1946, 3B176, folder 1, IHP, CAH.
124. Gus Wortham to Ima Hogg, May 27, 1946; Ray Dudley to Ima Hogg, Dec. 27, 1946, 3B174, folder 6, IHP, CAH.
125. Cullen remained close to Hoffmann, persuaded him not to announce his resignation during a concert, and told him there were two unappreciated professions—clergy and conductors—and that congregations and audiences became "restless" and wanted change, "often without cause." Roy Cullen to Ernst Hoffmann, March 5, 1947, 3B176, IHP, CAH. Cullen was incensed by press reports that he had "thrown Joe Smith out of the Symphony," since he firmly believed Smith had caused the crisis. Roy Cullen to Gus Wortham, March 19, 1947, ibid.
126. Roussel, *Houston Symphony*, 116n3; Ernst Hoffman to Ima Hogg, letters, 1946–1948, 4W194, folder 1, IHP, CAH.
127. Ima Hogg to Tom Johnson, Dec. 1947, 3B180, IHP, CAH, welcomes Johnson to Houston and invites him to tea to meet volunteer women; 3B180 contains Hogg-Johnson correspondence; "A Bow to Tom Johnson," program, Dec. 17, 18, 1962, 21.
128. F. M. Law to Ima Hogg, June 29, 1949, telling her to enjoy her vacation because the affairs of the orchestra have "never been in such sound and promising condition," 3B174 , IHP, CAH.
129. Leonard Bernstein to Ima Hogg, March 11, 1948, 4W195, folder 3, IHP, CAH. Budgets confirmed the ambition; in 1950 symphony volunteers were given a $100,000 fund-raising goal; *Houston*, September 1950, 34.
130. Cullen exploded again when Ima and Wortham made overtures to Kurtz, although both believed Cullen had agreed to the search for a new man. See Roussel, *Houston Symphony*, 117–118. Ima Hogg to Roy Cullen, March 1947, 3B176, folder 1, IHP, CAH, indicates that Cullen's telegram threatening withdrawal of support if she and Wortham continued negotiations for a new conductor was a complete surprise.

131. Of the 103 performances, 20 were subscription, 5 were free Henke and Pillot Saturday-evening concerts, 10 were for students, 26 were radio broadcasts, 40 were touring spots, and 2 were special events.

132. Clipping, *Christian Science Monitor*, May 20, 1950, 2J413, Symphony Scrapbook, WHP, CAH.

133. Roussel, *Houston Symphony*, 124–140. Both Ann Holmes and Raphael Fliegel recalled that Kurtz fired many musicians in an effort to raise the level of performance. Conversations with author, May 8, 2003, Oct. 4, 2003. Kurtz later divorced his wife and married the flutist.

134. Pamphlet, 4W194, folder 6, IHP, CAH.

135. Ima Hogg to Andrew Schulhof, Fricsay's manager, Nov. 25, 1953 (folder 6); memorandum of conversation with Andrew Schulhof, Dec. 4, 1953, listing Fricsay's demands, which included a "big house" (folder 1); Ima Hogg to Mr. and Mrs. Ferenc Fricsay, Dec. 11, 1953, Jan. 5, 1954 (folder 6); memorandum announcing engagement, n.d.; Ferenc Fricsay to Tom Johnson, Jan. 20, 1954, letter (folder 6), all in 4W194, IHP, CAH. On Jan. 5, 1954, she thanked Nevenna (Mrs. Don) Travis for her enthusiastic letter about the Fricsays and confided that Houston wanted him for a few weeks so the city and musician could know each other better; both letters, ibid., folder 6.

136. Patrick J. Nicholson III to Ima Hogg, Dec. 23, 1953, mentions the importance of acceptance in the community and participation in the city's social life, 4W194, folder 6, IHP, CAH. In 1970 Ima continued to urge hiring a resident conductor despite the "fashion for conductors to flit from orchestra to orchestra." Program, Women's Committee page, Dec. 13–15, 1970, 21.

137. Quote in Ferenc Fricsay to Tom Johnson, Jan. 20, 1954, 4W194, folder 6, IHP, CAH.

138. Ann Holmes to author, May 1, 2003. Raphael Fliegel to author, Oct. 4, 2003, said Fricsay was a "wonderful" man and a "brilliant" musician.

139. Ann Holmes to author, May 1, 2003, said Ima "froze," and soon she and Fricsay could agree on nothing.

140. Ferenc Fricsay to board, statement, Nov. 20, 1954; statement of the board, Nov. 27, 1954, 4W194, folder 6. Although the storm burst after Fricsay arrived in Houston, Tom Johnson's letters to Ima in August indicate problems ahead. Johnson was "very discouraged" about Fricsay (Aug. 23, 1954) and believed he had "no conception of the American symphony audience" (Aug. 23, 1954), 3B180, IHP, CAH.

141. Ann Holmes, "Ferenc Fricsay Reported Out," *Chronicle*, Dec. 13, 1954, A1, A14, disclosed "unofficial reports" from musical circles that Fricsay's requested improvements had been rejected. Ima Hogg refused to comment. Holmes column, Dec. 15, 1954, F2, reported the "love and admiration of [Fricsay's] players and the gratitude of selective listeners." Holmes column, Dec. 20, 1954, A1, A13, re-explained the crisis. Clipping, Ann Holmes, Dec. 21, 1954, E6, saved in 4W194, folder 6, IHP, CAH, described Fricsay's departure and noted that "whether arrangements can be made to retain this very valuable man's services in this city where

hostility to his efforts lurks remains to be seen." Holmes, "Symphony
Airs Fricsay Issue," Dec. 22, 1954, F4, laid out both sides of the quarrel.
Hubert Roussel, *Post*, Dec. 14, 1954, sec. 4, p. 9, countered that now was
a "Good Moment to Keep Calm: A View of a Musical Agitato"; the article
mentioned an "impressive concentration of misunderstanding" caused
by talkative musicians "setting off fireworks" and claimed there was no
change in symphony policy. Roussel, too, stressed the "disparity between
the views of Mr. Fricsay and those of certain officials of the Symphony as
to what should be the immediate objectives." In his Dec. 15, 1954, review,
sec. 4, p. 7, Roussel reported an "organized demonstration" by a "claque"
at the Tuesday evening performance that rose for repeated long, "heated"
ovations.

142. Andrew Schulhof to Ferenc Fricsay, Dec. 6, 1954, memo, 4W194, folder
6, IHP, CAH. On Dec. 3, 1954, Schulhof had tried to rectify the situation
by stressing that Fricsay never saw his suggestions as demands and that
the director and his wife loved Houston; Schulhof to Tom Johnson,
Dec. 3, 1954, ibid. It is also possible that Schulof dropped Fricsay as his
client because he saw more opportunity for himself by maintaining good
relations with the Houston Symphony Board; he played a pivotal role in
bringing Stokowski to Houston in the fall of 1955. Letters and letter of
agreement signed by Stokowski, Schulhof, and Johnson March 7, 1955, in
4W194, folder 7, IHP, CAH.

143. Ima Hogg and Harmon Whittington to board, Dec. 20, 1954, enclosing
Ferenc Fricsay proposals, 4W194, folder 5, IHP, CAH.

144. Statement, 4W194, folder 6, IHP, CAH. Raphael Fliegel recalled that
Fricsay was, indeed, suffering health problems.

145. Betty, Lady Beecham, to Ima Hogg, Dec. 16, 1949, 4W194, folder 5, IHP,
CAH.

146. Ima attended numerous musical events during periods of recuperation
in Philadelphia in the early 1920s. Stokowski brought the Philadelphia
Orchestra to world-celebrated status during his 1912–1936 tenure and
himself gained renown as a musical interpreter and orchestra builder. See
Programs from Philadelphia Academy of Music concerts Nov. 19–20, 26–
27, Dec. 2–3, 1920; Jan. 21–22, March 12–13, 1921, and passim, IHPC.

147. Telegrams and letters, 4W194, folder 7, IHP, CAH.

148. Correspondence in ibid.

149. Roussel, *Houston Symphony*, 170.

150. Ibid., 154–175.

151. Ann Holmes to author, May 8, 2003; tribute to John Barbirolli, program,
Sept. 14, 15, 1970.

152. In Memoriam, Sir John Barbirolli, insert, signed by Mrs. Ray L. Dudley,
Miss Ima Hogg, Gen. Maurice Hirsch, Mr. Thomas Fletcher, Mrs.
Theodore W. Cooper, Dr. Charles F. Jones, Jan. 8, 1971, program, Feb.
28, March 1, 2, 1971.

153. Walter Walne to City Council, Jan. 31, 1938, 3B174, folder 5, IHP, CAH.

154. Houston Symphony Society, program, Dec. 19, 20, 1966, 33.

155. Carl Cunningham articles; Gus Wortham to Ima Hogg, July 7, 1969; Ima
Hogg to Sound-Off editor, *Post*, Oct. 6, 1969, all in 3B175, folder 5.

156. Roussel, *Houston Symphony* (213–231) covers the years to 1971.
157. Mrs. Joseph S. Smith Jr. to Ima Hogg, Oct. 8, 1968, 3B168, folder 5, IHP, CAH.
158. Leopold Stokowski to Mrs. Albert Burrage, Dec. 16, 1958, storage box 4, folder 23, River Oaks Garden Club records, Archives, MFAH.
159. Program, Oct. 30, 1956, 5.
160. Campaign literature, 3B177, folder 1, IHP, CAH.
161. Series 14, scrapbook 1, p. 33, IHP, MFAH.
162. Leopold Stokowski to Mrs. Albert Burrage, Dec. 16, 1958, storage box 4, folder 23, River Oaks Garden Club Papers, Archives, MFAH.
163. Program, April 18, 19, 20, 1971, 21.
164. Houston Symphony Society, program, Nov. 1, 1948, City Auditorium, box 1, IHPC.
165. Houston Symphony Society, program, Nov. 26, 1951, 33; program, Dec. 10, 1951, 33.
166. "The Symphony Story," a brochure prepared in 1953 for Maintenance Fund campaign workers explaining why a "top executive, or a housewife" should give, provided the following statistics: 40,000 students attended ten student concerts; 100,000 citizens enjoyed twenty-one free summer park concerts; 23,000 heard five free pop concerts; 60,000 attended twenty subscription concerts; 45,000 heard the orchestra on tour; and twenty-six broadcasts were heard by thousands on the radio. Brochure in symphony archives, courtesy of Terry Brown.
167. Houston Symphony Society, program, Oct. 30, 1956, 37, 39; program, March 25, 27, 1957.
168. Files in 4W195 and 3B175, IHP, CAH.
169. Correspondence in 4W195, folder 5, IHP, CAH.
170. Quote "eyes and ears" Ima Hogg to Mrs. E. J. Wheeler, March 19, 1969, scrapbook 1, p. 71, IHP, Archives, MFAH; Ima Hogg to Gus Wortham, Sept. 19, 1946, letter; speech with handwritten notes, n.d., seating plan for the head table, n.d., 4W194, folder 2, IHP, CAH. Houston Symphony program (November 18) lists Mozart, Beethoven's 7th Symphony, and three works by Chavez (program, 1945–1947, pp. 2273, 2304–2306).
171. Carlos Chavez to Ima Hogg, Feb. 24, 1948, 4W194, folder 2, IHP, CAH. In 1966, Ima invited Chavez to be her guest for the Jones Hall opening, which he was unable to attend.
172. Correspondence, 4W194, folder 3, IHP, CAH.
173. Ima Hogg, speech, Dec. 7, 1953, 3B168, folder 5, IHP, CAH.
174. Program, Dec. 20, 1955, 33.
175. Program, Dec. 13, 14, 15, 1970, 21.
176. Mrs. McClelland (Winifred) Wallace, secretary of the Executive Committee, tribute to Ima Hogg, program, Sept. 8, 9, 1975, 9.
177. Statement, Annual Report, May 16, 1956, Box 1, Programs 1948–1958, IHPC.
178. Ima Hogg to Mrs. Ralph E. Gunn, president, Women's Committee, letter, 4W195, folder 8, IHP, CAH; program, March 4, 1957, Women's Committee page.

179. Resolution of the Women's Council, n.d. (circa 1962), 4W195, folder 6, IHP, CAH.
180. Carl Cunningham, "Houston Symphony Competitions Evolve," *Houston Symphony Magazine*, May 2004, 16.
181. Raphael Fliegel used the words "icon" and "head of state" to describe Ima's role in the symphony's life from the 1940s until 1975.
182. Program, Dec. 20, 1954, 33 ("spiritual life"); other quotes, Ima Hogg speech, November 1952, 3B168, folder 5, IHP, CAH.

CHAPTER 6

The title of this chapter comes from the motto of the Museum of Fine Arts, Houston, carved on the lintel over the original main entrance overlooking the sculpture garden at the juncture of Main Street and Montrose Boulevard.

1. Homer St. Gaudens, "Functions of an Art Museum," pamphlet, box 5, folder 31, Estelle Sharp Papers, WRC. Detailed accounts of the opening in *Post*, April 13, 1924, front page, 24, and editorial, 32; William Ward Watkin Papers, box 6, folder 37, WRC, RU.
2. William C. Hogg to donors, April 11, 1924, 2J337, WHP, CAH; quotes from editorial, *Post*, April 13, 1924, 32.
3. Nathaniel Burt, *Palaces for the People: A Social History of the American Art Museum* (Boston: Little, Brown, 1977), 75, 86–89, 106.
4. Ima Hogg, *Look and Listen*, KPRC broadcast from Lamar Hotel, April 15, 1944, in Miss Ima Hogg Collection, Accessions File, Registrar's Office, MFAH.
5. William Cullen Bryant, quoted in Burt, *Palaces for the People*, 91.
6. Box 8, folder 10, E. Richardson Cherry Papers, HMRC, HPL; *Art Students League News* 8 (January 1955), box 8, Cherry Papers.
7. Federation of Women's Clubs, *Key to the City*, 75, found in Art League of Houston Records, scrapbook, pp. 36–40, Archives, MFAH, and in Estelle Sharp Papers, WRC, and in HMRC, HPL. The Nichols-Rice-Cherry House is now preserved as a house museum in Sam Houston Park by the Harris County Heritage Society.
8. Minutes of the March 17, 1900, meeting, Art League of Houston Records, scrapbook 1, p. 4, Archives, MFAH. The other man present was probably Dr. William Hayne Leavell, who opened the April 1924 dedication with a prayer. *Post*, April 13, 1924, 24, says Dr. Leavell "attended the organizing meeting of the league." The name of Dr. Henry Barnstein, the cultured rabbi so prominent in symphony activities, also appears on "founders" lists and histories elsewhere in the museum's archives. The other officers were Cara Redwood and Roberta Lavender, first and second vice presidents; Sibyl Campbell, corresponding secretary; Gussie Howard, recording secretary; and Edith House, treasurer. Mrs. Sherwood traveled across Texas for fourteen years giving illustrated lectures in schools, clubs, and town auditoriums. Stella Hope Shurtleff,

"Art Came to Texas," typescript, 129, Stella Hope Shurtleff Papers, WRC.

9. Federation of Women's Clubs, *Key to the City*, 72.

10. Minutes of the second annual meeting, March 1902, scrapbook 1, p. 8; folder 38, p. 7, Art League of Houston Records, Archives, MFAH.

11. Clipping, Emma Richardson Cherry Vertical File, Archives, MFAH.

12. Active members could sign on for $0.50, and life members (twenty-five of them in 1913) paid one-time dues of $15.00, which were set aside for an endowment fund. Folder 38, p. 13, Art League of Houston Records, Archives, MFAH.

13. Federation of Women's Clubs, *Key to the City*, 72–75.

14. Covington Collection, HMRC, HPL.

15. Shurtleff, "Art Came to Texas," 130, 134, 135. The Bayou Bend Collection includes *Portrait of the Jones Children of Galveston* (circa 1853) by Thomas Flintoff and *Hill Country Landscape* (1862) and *West Cave on the Pedernales* (1883) by Hermann Lungwitz.

16. Houghton et al., *Houston's Forgotten Heritage*, 81.

17. Hermann agreed to provide land free of rent for forty years if the Art League would pay taxes, should the property not qualify for tax exemption. The property designated by the committee was near the final site provided by Cullinan and the trustees of the Hermann Estate. James Lockett, lawyer for the Hermann Estate and the Houston Art League, "George H. Hermann, Philanthropist," in scrapbook 1, pp. 167–173, Art League of Houston Records, Archives, MFAH.

18. "Hermann, Philanthropist," scrapbook 1, pp. 169–70, Art League of Houston Records, Archives, MFAH.

19. Folder 38, p. 8; dedication program, April 12, 1917, scrapbook 5, Art League of Houston Records, Archives, MFAH; Founders' Day reviewed in *Bulletin*, Spring 1944, in 4W234, folder 1, IHP, CAH.

20. Watkin article and plan in William Ward Watkin Papers, WRC.

21. Ralph Adams Cram, publicity pamphlet, Box 6, Folder 37, William Ward Watkin Papers, WRC.

22. Scott in *Chronicle*, Nov. 2, 1922, 16; "drudgery" in scrapbook 2, p. 79, Art League of Houston Records, Archives, MFAH. Information about Florence Fall in "Who's Who of the Womanhood of Texas, 1923–1924" and "The Texas Woman, 1906," both in Mrs. Henry B. (Florence K.) Fall Vertical File, Archives, MFAH.

23. The *Post*, April 13, 1924 (24), reported that $1,000 sponsors also included Mrs. S. F. Carter, Mellie Esperson, the Farishes, Jesse Jones, H. F. MacGregor, Neill T. Masterson, Dr. Joseph Mullen, Cora V. Peden, Ross Sterling, the Harry Wiesses, and the Womacks. Will initially pledged $5,000 and Ima and Mike $2,500 each, making Hogg family support the largest single gift in 1923.

24. School Superintendent R. B. Cousins, *Chronicle*, Nov. 2, 1927, 16.

25. Henry Stude to John A. Lomax, June 21, 1939, 3D205, folder 3, John Avery Lomax Family Papers, CAH. John T. Scott to William Ward Watkin, July 29, 1924, says Will "volunteered" to raise money needed to

complete Watkin's original plan, 2J337, WHP, CAH. John Lomax claims Will called on Scott and "without hesitation, he at once expressed his willingness and desire to raise the necessary funds," 3D205, folder 2, John Avery Lomax Family Papers, CAH. Susan Clayton McAshan noted that her mother wanted to approach Will because he had asked the Claytons to support the YMCA. In McAshan's account, Will was "immediately distressed," and Ima called to say he was "horrified" and wanted to apologize. Mrs. Clayton was not interested in an apology. Susan McAshan to Marguerite Johnston, interview, Marguerite Johnston Papers, Box 3, folder 10, WRC, RU. Diary entries for 1918 (2J399, WHP, CAH) indicate that Will discussed museum issues with Mrs. Joseph Mullen, vice president of the league.

26. Editorial, *Post*, April 13, 1924, 32.
27. Burke Baker to William C. Hogg, April 14, 1924; Edgar Odell Lovett to William C. Hogg, April 13, 1924, 2J337, Art League of Houston, folder 1, WHP, CAH. A memo Nov. 15, 1925, lists the subscribers and shows Will at $35,000, Cullinan at $25,000, the Claytons at $30,000, and Mike and Ima at $7,500—all sums including earlier pledges. Memo in 2J337, Art League of Houston, folder 2, WHP, CAH. In a letter to the Levys, April 7, 1924, and in a memo to Treasurer John T. Scott, April 16, 1924, Will notes $30,000 from himself. Information about the fund drive is also found in box 38, folder 19, Joseph S. Cullinan Papers, HMRC, HPL.
28. William C. Hogg to Abe Levy in Hot Springs and to S. F. Carter in El Paso, telegrams, n.d., other letters, 2J337, folder 1, WHP, CAH.
29. William C. Hogg to John F. Dickson, telegram, April 9, 1924, William C. Hogg to Captain James A. Baker (Dear Captain Baker), April 3, 1924, 2J337, folder 1, WHP, CAH; list in file 10, pp. 90–91, Art League of Houston Records, Archives, MFAH.
30. William C. Hogg to Mike Hogg, Ima Hogg, Joseph Cullinan, and others, April 10, 1924, 2J337, folder 1, WHP, CAH.
31. William C. Hogg to William Ward Watkin, Aug. 31, 1924; William C. Hogg to subscribers, Dec. 14, 1925, 2J337; March 4, 1926, 2J339, WHP, CAH.
32. Comments, 3D205, folder 2, Lomax Papers, CAH.
33. William C. Hogg to Mrs. H. B. Fall, March 2, 1925, 2J337, Art League of Houston folder, WHP, CAH.
34. Exhibition File, Archives, MFAH; Neff, *Frederic Remington*, 34n66.
35. "Retrospective Exhibition of Gifts to the Permanent Collections, March 1 to 12 1933," Catalog Collection, Archives, MFAH.
36. James H. Chillman Jr. to Edsel Ford, Aug. 25, 1940, Box 1, folder 7, Director's Records: James H. Chillman Jr., correspondence 1924–1970, Archives, MFAH.
37. The perfume bottle collection, bequeathed to Alice Hogg Hanszen's niece Alice Simkins, was given to the Museum of Fine Arts, Houston, by Miss Simkins in 2003.
38. Scrapbook, Hogg Brothers Collection, Archives, MFAH.
39. Library inventories, Bayou Bend, IHP, Archives, MFAH. These inventories from the 1930s and 1940s specify room locations and suggest

that Bayou Bend was crammed with books. Will applied the same focused zeal to book buying that he did to collecting Remington. For example, in March 1920, Yale University Press acknowledged Will's purchase of the George Washington Edition of *The Chronicles of America*, a fifty-volume history bound in blue; in September 1920 Will purchased an extensive list of books on American decorative arts, china, rugs, and prints; and in December 1920 he ordered several books on "mental efficiency"; entries in 2J341, "Library Sept. 16, 1920–June 8, 1925," WHP, CAH.

40. "Frederic Remington Memorial Exhibit, October 1–October 28, 1925," Catalog Collection, Archives, MFAH. The bronze, now known as *Bronco Buster* (43.73), is listed as "Bronze Statuette, cowboy and pony." James Chillman to William C. Hogg, Oct. 29, 1925, 2J337, Art League of Houston folder, WHP, CAH, thanks Will for sharing his Remingtons and says they were "very much enjoyed . . . and . . . of particular interest to the school children."

41. "Loan Exhibition of the Works of Frederic Remington Lent Through the Courtesy of Hogg Brothers of Houston, January 3rd to 18th, 1931," Catalog Collection, Archives, MFAH. Categories reflect catalog language. Although records are not explicit, the wording in the catalog, itself a rarity in the museum's early years, confirms paintings curator Emily Neff's conjecture that the exhibit honored Will's memory. Emily Neff to author, email, July 14, 2003; *Post-Dispatch*, Jan. 4, 1931, clipping in Box 1A, folder 47, Registrar's Records, Archives, MFAH; Hubert Roussel, *Gargoyle*, Jan. 11, 1931.

42. H. E. Brigham to James Chillman Jr., Feb. 11, 1939, letter regarding Remington Exhibit Feb. 26–March 19, 1939, box 3, folder 62, Registrar's Records, Archives, MFAH. Exhibition files show loan exhibits in 1940 and 1941, Archives, MFAH.

43. *Chronicle*, May 29, 1943, clipping in Registrar's Records, box 1A, folder 47, Archives, MFAH. At this time, the collection was composed of 64 objects: 18 "oils in full color," 35 oils in black and white, 10 watercolors and drawings, and 1 large bronze. Subsequent study and authentication procedures reduced the current museum holdings to 41 works including 1 bronze, 16 color oils, 14 black-and-white oils, 7 watercolor and mixed media, 2 pen-and-ink sketches, and 1 graphite sketch. Until the 1960s, Alice kept *The Fight for the Water Hole*, and Ima retained *The Herd Boy* and *The Mule Pack*, which had been moved to Bayou Bend probably in the late 1920s. See Neff, *Frederic Remington*, checklist of works, 131–137.

44. Charles Muskovitch to Ima Hogg, Jan. 19, 1942, 4W234, IHP, CAH. He reported that many canvases were rotted and needed new linings but that the collection was in "excellent condition."

45. *Chronicle*, May 29, 1943, clipping in Box 1A, folder 47, Registrar's Records, Archives, MFAH.

46. Deed of gift, May 18, 1943, Accessions File, Registrar's Office, MFAH.

47. *Bulletin* 7 (Spring 1944), in 4W234, folder 1, IHP, CAH. *Cavalry Scrap* became Mike's property after Will's death and was bequeathed to the University of Texas in 1941. In 1943 Ima gave the large (4 feet 8 inches by 11 feet 4 inches) painting, which filled a wall in the Hogg Brothers office

beside the desk, to the university, where it is now displayed in the Jack S. Blanton Museum of Art.

48. Philippe de Montebello to Ima Hogg, Sept. 26, 1973, 4W234, folder 1, IHP, CAH. The collection was reinstalled when the Audrey Jones Beck Building designed by Rafael Moneo opened in March 2000.

49. Hogg Brothers Scrapbook, Archives, MFAH; Neff, *Frederic Remington*, 29–30.

50. Neff, *Frederic Remington*, 126–132.

51. Will collected works by several American landscape artists, and six remain in the Museum of Fine Arts, Houston, collection: *Sunlight and Shadow* (1888) by Willard Leroy Metcalf (41.28), *Two Soldiers* (n.d.) by Gilbert Gaul, *Sand Dunes, Lake Ontario* (1874) by Homer Dodge Martin (48.11), *The Storm* (1894) by Francis J. Murphy (48.12), and *Moonlight* (n.d., 48.13) and *Afterglow* (n.d., 51.29) by Ralph Albert Blakelock; Gifts of Hogg Family, Accessions report, April 25, 2003.

52. Diary, 1920, 2J399, WHP, CAH. Will saw two Remingtons at John Levy Galleries in New York on Jan. 27 and purchased the book on Feb. 4; while in Chicago he bought *The Transgressor* on Sept. 15 from J. W. Young American Art Gallery and acquired the first black-and-white oils on Sept. 17 at Thurber Art Galleries. Back in New York, he bought his only bronze and paintings and prints from George H. Ainslie Galleries (Sept. 21) and paintings from Howard Young (Sept. 25), Levy Galleries (Sept. 28), and Holland Galleries (Sept. 28). He also recorded purchasing prints and sketches on Sept. 23 and 24 but did not list galleries. On Sept. 29 he visited "my" Remingtons at Levy's and Young's galleries.

53. William C. Hogg to Ima Hogg, Oct. 7, 1920, 3B119, folder 3, IHP, CAH.

54. Ima Hogg to William C. Hogg, Sept. 22, 1920, 3B120, IHP, CAH.

55. Owen Wister, "Remington: The Man and His Work," *Collier's*, Jan. 8, 1910, clipping in Hogg Brothers Scrapbook, Archives, MFAH.

56. From November 1920 until his death, Will received information from dealers and others hoping to sell him Remington examples. Accessions files, MFAH.

57. Plaque, Lovett Hall, Museum of Fine Arts, Houston, now located on the Lovett Hall staircase wall, to the left.

58. Lucy Runnels Wright, "A Woman Extraordinary," *Texas Outlook* 21 (May 1937), in box 1, folder 3, Cherry Papers, HMRC, HPL.

59. James Chillman Jr. to Mrs. D. B. Cherry, May 23, 1924, box 8, Cherry Papers, HMRC, HPL.

60. Cherry painted numerous important Houstonians, including Mary McDowell, first president of the YWCA; Florence Fall, Art League president and president of the Texas Federation of Women's Clubs; Adele Looscan, founder of the Ladies' Reading Club. See clippings, box 2, folder 5; Wright, "Woman Extraordinary," box 1, folder 3, in Cherry Papers, HMRC, HPL.

61. Finnigan's friend, the librarian Julia Ideson, remarked, "She has the most thorough and brilliant mind of anyone I know," clipping Feb. 10, 1937, in Annette Finnigan Vertical File, Archives, MFAH.

62. Janelle D. Scott, "Local Leadership in the Woman Suffrage Movement:

Houston's Campaign for the Vote, 1912–1918," *Houston Review* 12 (1990): 7–9; Johnston, *Houston: The Unknown City*, 137; Betty Trapp Chapman, *Houston Women: Invisible Threads in the Tapestry* (Virginia Beach: Donning, 2000), 86–87, 133, 155, 162–163; Annette Finnigan Vertical File, Archives, MFAH, which includes an interview with James Chillman, March 6, 1968, and a paper given by Betty Chapman at the Texas State Historical Association, Lubbock, March 1989, as well as clippings from newspaper accounts of Finnigan's gifts to the museum.

63. James Chillman, interview, Annette Finnigan Vertical File, Archives, MFAH.

64. Ibid.

65. Clipping, *Post*, Jan. 15, 1937. Also *Post*, January 27, 1935, describing gift of seventeen Greek vases. Clippings in Annette Finnigan Vertical File, Archives, MFAH.

66. *Permanent Legacy: 150 Works from the Collection of the Museum of Fine Arts, Houston*, introduction by Peter C. Marzio (New York: Hudson Hills Press, 1989), 84.

67. *The Annette Finnigan Collection of Laces* (Houston: Museum of Fine Arts of Houston, 1940), n.p.

68. *Gargoyle*, Dec. 15, 1929, 3; Barbara Rose and Susie Kalil, *Fresh Paint: The Houston School; The Museum of Fine Arts, Houston* (Austin: Texas Monthly Press, 1985), 17.

69. Stella Hope Shurtleff Papers, Archives, MFAH. Manuscript in Stella Hope Shurtleff Papers, WRC.

70. *Woman's Viewpoint*, Nov. 1924, 31.

71. Director's Records: James H. Chillman Jr., box 3, folder 8, Archives, MFAH; Ruth West, "Lyres and Easels," *Gargoyle*, April 27, 1930, 28; "Retrospective Exhibition of Gifts to the Permanent Collections, March 1–12, 1933," Exhibition Files, Archives, MFAH.

72. *Gargoyle*, Sept. 15, 1929, 24.

73. Hubert Roussel, *Gargoyle*, Jan. 11, 1931, 32; "Loan Exhibition of Old Masters of the Seventeenth and Eighteenth Centuries, Museum of Fine Arts of Houston, Jan. 3–18, 1931," Catalog Collection, Archives, MFAH.

74. Rose and Kalil, *Fresh Paint*, 18; "Modern French and American Art" (1928); "Post-Modern French Painters" (1929); "Drawings and Lithographs of José Clemente Orozco" (1930), in Catalog Collection, Archives, MFAH.

75. Stephen Fox, "The Museum of Fine Arts, Houston: An Architectural History, 1924–1953," *Bulletin of the Museum of Fine Arts, Houston* 15 (Winter/Spring 1991): 45; Director's Records, James H. Chillman Jr., box 3, folder 16, Archives, MFAH.

76. Constitution and bylaws, Museum Guild, Feb. 19, 1940, folder 1, Art Museum Guild Papers, 1939–1944, Archives, MFAH.

77. Clipping, *Post*, June 13, 1941, in folder 3, Art Museum Guild Papers, Archives, MFAH.

78. Folders 4, 5, Art Museum Guild Papers, Archives, MFAH. By 1940 (folder 8) the program included eighteen speakers, some from New York,

Austin, and London. Ima Hogg spoke on the program April 15, 1944, about the "collective effort of many" who had created the museum and "paved the way" for the enjoyment of all. Miss Ima Hogg Collection, Accessions File, Registrar's Office, MFAH.

79. "Retrospective Exhibition of Gifts, 1933," Exhibition Files, Archives, MFAH.

80. Naomi Kroll, "Ima Hogg's Twentieth Century Collection," Bayou Bend Docent Organization Records, Docent Papers, Archives, MFAH. Ima replaced the Matisse with *Two Heads*, a gouache by Pablo Picasso.

81. H. E. Brigham, visa orders, June 12, 1929, 3B151, folder 1, IHP, CAH, visas for Russia, Norway, Finland, England, France, Spain; tour itinerary also included Scotland, Ireland, Switzerland, Germany, Belgium, Prague, Vienna, and Italy. William C. Hogg to Hermilla Kelso (a cousin), June 25, 1929, letter, 2J325, folder 1, WCH, CAH; Ima Hogg to Julia Ideson, letter, Aug. 23, 1929, Box 1, folder 2, Julia Ideson Papers, HMRC, HPL. Legend relates that Ima turned down a meeting with Soviet leaders in favor of a trip to art museums.

82. Miss Ima Hogg Collection, Accessions File 39.47–131, Registrar's Office, MFAH.

83. Summary in Miss Ima Hogg Collection, Accessions File 39.47–131, Registrar's Office, MFAH. See shipping order Hans Goltz, Munchen to James Chillman, Aug. 31, 1929, regarding a Puvis de Chavannes drawing and Corot landscape "we send you by order of Miss Hogg." Note that her works on paper collection includes two woodcuts (circa 1496–1497) by Albrecht Dürer and a handful of nineteenth-century examples.

84. Accessions File 39.47–131 records show 18 watercolors, 31 lithographs, 19 etchings, 9 drawings, 1 block print, 5 woodcuts, and 1 color reproduction, Registrar's Office, MFAH. *Permanent Legacy* lists "more than 100" works on paper.

85. Correspondence between George Hill Jr. and Ima Hogg, July 21, 1939, noting transfer on June 14, 1939; James A. Chillman Jr. to Ima Hogg, July 31, 1939, thanking her for donation; James A. Chillman Jr. to Ima Hogg, Ritz Hotel, Mexico City, Sept. 4, 1939, notifying her that the collection had been gratefully accepted by unanimous assent. Accessions File, 39.47–131, Registrar's Office, MFAH.

86. James A. Chillman Jr. to Ima Hogg, letter, July 31, 1939, Accessions file, 39.47–131, Registrar's Office, MFAH.

87. The American list included work by E. Richardson Cherry, Mary Bonner, and Wayman Adams and eight works by Mexican Roberto Montenegro, three by José Clemente Orozco, and one by Diego Rivera. Quote from summary prepared for the Accessions File, 39.47–131, Registrar's Office, MFAH.

88. Kroll, "Twentieth Century Collection."

89. Stella Shurtleff, *Post*, April 21, 1940, clipping in Accessions file, 39.47–131, Registrar's Office, MFAH; discussions 4W381, IHP, CAH; press clippings, correspondence, 4W382, folder 7, IHP, CAH.

90. Adaline Wellborn Bruhl, KPRC remarks, July 7, 1941, in Accessions File, 44.4–485, Registrar's Office, MFAH.

91. Deed of gift correspondence, Ima Hogg to John Bullington, president of Museum of Fine Arts of Houston, Aug. 16, 1943, ibid.
92. H. E. Brigham, secretary to Ima Hogg, to Museum of Fine Arts of Houston, check for $100 to cover lecture on Indian art, Feb. 6, 1930, Accessions File, 44.4–120, Registrar's Office, MFAH.
93. "Loan Exhibition of Houston-Owned Indian Handcrafts," Registrar's Records, box 1A, Archives, MFAH.
94. Dorothy M. Hoskins, "American Indian Pottery," *Gargoyle*, Feb. 16, 1930, 12. Hoskins had been editor of Will Hogg's *Civics for Houston*.
95. Letters, June 3, 1935, June 10, 1935, July 8, 1935, regarding payments and discount; correspondence, May 20, 1937, regarding 35 paintings loaned for a June 1936 exhibit; other correspondence, Southwest Indian (Miss Ima Hogg) Collection, Accessions Files, 44.4–485, Registrar's Office, MFAH.
96. Deed of gift letter, Ima Hogg to John Bullington, Aug. 16, 1943, Accessions Files, 44.4–485, Registrar's Office, MFAH. The collection was composed of 168 ceramics, 96 jewelry items, 5 photographs, 81 paintings, 123 Kachina dolls, 7 musical instruments, and 7 miscellaneous items. It seems hard to imagine how a donation labeled "Bayou Bend Collection" would remain "anonymous," but these instructions reinforce Ima's ambivalent attitude toward public recognition.
97. Inventory of goods, 2950 Lazy Lane, June 1, 1931, Box 3, folder 1, Mike and Alice Hogg Papers, Archives, MFAH. See also Ima Hogg to Alexander McLanahan, Feb. 16, 1970, Series 1, Box 1, folder 7, IIIP, Archives, MFAH, expressing delight to be an honorary life member of the board.
98. Loan information from Exhibition Files, Archives, MFAH.
99. James Chillman, Look and Listen program, May 25, 1941, folder 16; Ray L. Dudley, *Look and Listen* program, April 12, 1942, folder 22, Director's Records: James H. Chillman, Jr., RG 2:1, Series 1, Box 2, Archives, MFAH.
100. Headline, *Chronicle*, Dec. 7, 1941, "Magnificent Straus Collection of Art Given to Houston Museum/Works of Masters of Many Ages to Make City Great Art Center," 1, photo in *Permanent Legacy*, 16. Information on Straus Collection, *Permanent Legacy*, 15–17; MFAH Chronology, Archives, MFAH.
101. For in-depth analysis of the Straus collection see Carolyn C. Wilson, *Italian Paintings XIV–XVI Centuries in the Museum of Fine Arts, Houston* (Houston: Museum of Fine Arts, Houston, with Rice University Press and Merrell Holbertson Publishers, 1996).
102. Museum Chronology, Archives, MFAH. The wing conformed to Watkin's plan and was designed by architect Kenneth Franzheim (1890–1959), former associate of popular Houston architects Alfred C. Finn and John F. Staub.
103. "Retrospective Exhibition of Gifts to the Permanent Collections, March 1–12, 1933," now labeled *Holy Family with St. Catherine*, Catalog Collection, Archives, MFAH.

104. *Permanent Legacy*, 17–19; Museum Chronology, Archives, MFAH. Today twenty-six Kress paintings are part of the permanent collection.

105. *The Menil Collection: A Selection from the Paleolithic to the Modern Era*, foreword Dominique de Menil, introduction Walter Hopps (New York: Henry Abrams, 1997).

106. See Rose and Kalil, *Fresh Paint*, 21–24.

107. Campbell Geeslin, *Post*, cited in Rose and Kalil, *Fresh Paint*, 21.

108. Information about the Brown family in Joseph A. Pratt and Christopher J. Castaneda, *Builders: Herman and George R. Brown* (College Station: Texas A&M University Press, 1999), 264; Museum Chronology, Archives, MFAH.

109. During this campaign Ima lobbied successfully for an "extra" $500,000 allocation to Bayou Bend. The Campaign Steering Committee allocated $4 million to the Brown Pavilion, $500,000 to the Museum School, $4 million to Endowment, $1.5 million to Bayou Bend curatorship and building, and $5 million to the Accessions Endowment. Alexander McLanahan to Capital Campaign Steering Committee, November 1970, Series 1, Box 1, folder 7, IHP, Archives, MFAH.

110. Gifts and purchases of Alice Hanszen, Accessions file, Registrar's Office, Museum of Fine Arts, Houston; *19th and 20th Century French Painters in Houston Collections*, February 1957, Box 14, folder 2, Registrar's Records, Archives, MFAH; *Permanent Legacy*, 25 (Bol) 140, (Redon) 212. Bayou Bend items in David B. Warren, Michael K. Brown, Elizabeth Ann Coleman, and Emily Ballew Neff, *American Decorative Arts and Paintings in the Bayou Bend Collection* (Princeton: NJ: Museum of Fine Arts, Houston, and Princeton University Press, 1998); Lupp, M59, 298; Meeks, F219, 135–36; loo table, F215, 133–34.

111. *Pre-Columbian Art from Middle America*, Catalog Collection, MFAH, Archives; Scrapbook 3, IHP, Archives, MFAH; correspondence with James Johnson Sweeney in Series 2, Box 2, folder 14, Box 9, folder 10, Director's Records: James Johnson Sweeney, Archives, MFAH.

112. Ruth Pershing Uhler, *Look and Listen* program, April 28, 1940, Director's Records: James H. Chillman Jr., RG2:1, Series 1, Box 2, folder 9, Archives, MFAH.

CHAPTER 7

1. "Remarks," in "Bayou Bend Collection of the Houston Museum of Fine Arts," March 5, 1966, dedication pamphlet, 15, in Archives, MFAH, in WRC, and in other archival collections; description in Ann Holmes, *Chronicle*, March 6, 1966, sec. 1, p. 20; Helen Anderson, *Post*, March 6, sec. 1, p. 11.

2. Edward Rotan, master of ceremonies, "Remarks," 7; James Johnson Sweeney, "Remarks," 16; Dr. Harry Ransom, "Remarks," 22.

3. Clipping, *Chronicle*, "Society Today," March 7, 1966, Ima Hogg Vertical File, CAH.

4. "Remarks by Miss Ima Hogg," 11, in "Remarks." Bayou Bend volunteer docents named their publication *The Bridge*.

5. See *Houston*, August 1950, 6, 8–13 (population, academic building programs); December 1951, 41 (Gulf Freeway almost finished); May 1952, 6 (port).

6. Ima Hogg speech, November 1952, 3B168, folder 5, IHP, CAH.

7. Ima Hogg to S. I. Morris, Museum of Fine Arts board president, Aug. 16, 1960, Series 1, box 1, folder 9, IHP, Archives, MFAH; also Miss Ima Hogg Vertical File, Archives, MFAH; Ima Hogg to docents, July 5, 1961, series 1, box 4, folder 15, IHP, Archives, MFAH.

8. Guests at the house party included fellow collectors Katharine Prentis Murphy, Electra Webb, Henry Francis and Ruth du Pont, and Henry and Helen Flynt. Forum attendees in 3B154, IHP, CAH; series 1, box 1, folder 30, Director's Records, Lee Malone, Archives, MFAH. Archival correspondence and Ima's intense and deliberate collecting in the 1940s make clear that discussions at the 1956 house party could only have reinforced decisions she had already made. Note Michael Brown's analysis of Ima's collecting patterns that reinforce the importance of Ima's renewed interest in the 1940s. Brown, *America's Treasures*, 11–12.

9. In 1943 Ima purchased three important pairs of side chairs, one in the rococo (F84) and two in the Grecian mode (F192, F194). In 1946 she found a chest of drawers with the rare bombe contour (F137), a magnificent neoclassical bedstead (F190), and a handsome baroque dressing table (F76), among other items that show she was looking for specific, important examples of high-quality craftsmanship. In 1948 several important pieces of furniture entered the collection (F42, F45, F46, F89, F120, F121, F128, F135, F188). Numbers refer to catalog entries in Warren et al., *American Decorative Arts*; correspondence in Accessions File, Bayou Bend, accessed, with permission, by accession number. All the above items were accessioned to the museum in the 1960s.

10. Miss Ima Hogg Vertical File, Archives, MFAH.

11. Resolution, Dec. 23, 1953, 4W202, IHP, CAH; copy of resolution, dated Dec. 16, 1953, in Trustee Records: Full Board Meeting Minutes, folder 25, Archives, MFAH. This is the same resolution, although the dates differ. The trustees' resolution indicates a vote taken Dec. 16, 1953.

12. Ima Hogg, interview, Oct. 2, 1974, Oral History, HMRC, HPL; Edward Mayo to Marguerite Johnston, interview, Marguerite Johnston Papers, box 3, folder 6, WRC.

13. Francis G. Coates to Ima Hogg, Aug. 6, 1956, 4W202, IHP, CAH, revisits the property owners issue and notes that consent forms had been prepared and distributed two and one-half years earlier (early spring 1954). Trust agreement setting Homewoods apart from River Oaks signed April 10, 1926, between River Oaks Corporation and trustees, Mike Hogg, Hugh Potter, and F. C. Proctor, 4W201, folder 2, IHP, CAH.

14. Minutes, Sept. 17, 1956, Executive Session of the Board of Trustees, folder 30, Trustee Records, Archives, MFAH.

15. Ray L. Dudley to Ima Hogg, Sept. 12, 1956, 4W202, IHP, CAH.

16. Ima Hogg to Francis G. Coates, Sept. 4, 1956, 4W382, folder 1, IHP, CAH; excerpt from minutes, Sept. 17, 1956, folder 30, Trustee Records,

Archives, MFAH. Requirements included entrance from Memorial Drive over a footbridge, a guard, no structures but a guardhouse, and numerous other details.

17. 4W382, folder 1, IHP, CAH; E. L. Wehner, Memorandum of Trust, various deeds of trust and gifts over the years, 4W202, folder 2, IHP, CAH; trust activities described in 4W377–382, IHP, CAH. This fund also was used as a conduit for gifts to the Houston Symphony, the Hogg Foundation, the Child Guidance Center of Houston, Varner-Hogg, and Winedale. Correspondence 4W382, folders 3, 4, 7, IHP, CAH; Trustee Records, Nov. 17, 1959, Archives, MFAH; and series 1, box 1, folder 6, IHP, Archives, MFAH. Ima promised to make annual payments of at least $37,500 to defray maintenance and operations until the full endowment was in place.

18. Press release, Dec. 30, 1956, 4W202, IHP, CAH. The other collections were the American Wing at the Metropolitan Museum in New York and Winterthur Museum in Delaware. Trustee Records, Full Board Meeting Minutes, folders 30, 31, on legal challenges to gift from River Oaks Property Owners Association neighbors, Archives, MFAH.

19. Folders 30, 33, Trustee Records, Archives, MFAH.

20. Jan. 26, 1960, folder 34, Trustee Records, Archives, MFAH. Original members included Dorothy Dawes Chillman, Mrs. John Staub, Mrs. L. R. Bryan Jr., Hugo Neuhaus, and Thomas D. Anderson. These records also show that a special committee was appointed to present a testimonial "expression of appreciation" from the museum board to Ima. Theodore Swigart, president, to Ima Hogg, Feb. 2, 1960, folder 17.

21. Gift deed for furniture and accessories, May 1962, in Trustee Records, folder 37, Archives, MFAH. David B. Warren accepted the post of curator on Feb. 18, 1965 (folder 42).

22. Quotes from Ima Hogg, Remarks to the River Oaks Garden Club, Nov. 5, 1963, Docent Papers, Box A, Archives, MFAH. Entries in Will Hogg's diary, 2J399, 1920, and correspondence confirm that Ima knew at once that she wanted to form a collection for a public institution.

23. "Circumstances and events" from Ima Hogg, remarks, Bayou Bend dedication, March 5, 1966, pamphlet, WRC (printed version); "greater respect," in remarks to River Oaks Garden Club, Nov. 5, 1963, Docent Papers, box A, Archives, MFAH; "learned to respect" from Ima Hogg in *Texas Magazine*, Feb. 20, 1966, clipping of extensive article on Bayou Bend in Miss Ima Hogg Vertical File, Archives, MFAH; also in vol. 25, River Oaks Collection, HMRC, HPL.

24. David B. Warren in "Inaugural David B. Warren Symposium: American Culture and the Texas Experience," Feb. 9–11, 2007, *The Bridge*, April/ May 2007, 5.

25. Ima Hogg quoted in *Texas Magazine*, Feb. 20, 1966.

26. Bayou Bend dedication pamphlet, 16.

27. Ima Hogg, remarks to River Oaks Garden Club, Nov. 5, 1963, Docent Papers, box A, Archives, MFAH.

28. Neff, *Frederic Remington*, 10–11, 16.

29. Bayou Bend dedication pamphlet, 15; remarks to River Oaks Garden Club, Nov. 8, 1963, Docent Papers, box A, Archives, MFAH; Ima Hogg, oral history, HMRC, HPL. In an interview published in *Texas Magazine* on Feb. 20, 1966, Ima said, "I never felt that anything here belonged to me. I always bought with the idea that everything would one day go to a museum." Clipping, Miss Ima Hogg Vertical File, Archives, MFAH.

30. Stephen Fox, "Bayou Bend," typescript, 2000, p. 27; in the author's possession. See Stephen Fox, *The Country Houses of John F. Staub*, color photography by Richard Cheek (College Station: Texas A&M University Press, 2007), 78–100; for Fox's analysis of Bayou Bend as the "tangible" expression of the Hoggs' urban ideal see p. 99.

31. This beautiful house was razed in 2005.

32. Correspondence in series 1, box 1, folder 1, IHP, Archives, MFAH.

33. Original paneling from the Metcalf Bowler House had been installed in the American Wing of the Metropolitan Museum of Art, New York, shortly before the Hoggs designed their Bayou Bend interiors. Ima often celebrated Christmas in this room, now called the Pine Room.

34. Fox, *Country Houses*, 78 ff.; Neff, *Frederic Remington*, 16–19; Fox, "Bayou Bend," 5, 6; Mark A. Hewitt, *The Architect and the American Country House, 1890–1940* (New Haven, CT: Yale University Press, 1990), 234–236.

35. Staub insisted that Ima invented the term "Latin Colonial"; Barnstone, *Architecture of John F. Staub*, 28. He told Howard Barnstone that Bayou Bend was based on Homewood, a Baltimore country house of 1803 (Fox, *Country Houses*, 94).

36. Barnstone, *Architecture of John F. Staub*, 12.

37. Ibid., 10, 57n30, 77–78, 81.

38. William C. Hogg to Ima Hogg, Jan. 10, 1926, telegram, indicates that Ima had chosen a homesite by that date. 3B119, folder 4, IHP, CAH.

39. Barnstone, *Architecture of John F. Staub*, 57n34. Historian Dorothy Knox Howe Houghton, a Briscoe descendant, affirms this split as family lore; conversation with author, February 2004.

40. Payments in 4W203, IHP, CAH.

41. Neff, *Frederic Remington*, 19; see 17–19, 35nn78, 80, for an in-depth analysis of the Varner project. For correspondence see letters 1926–1928, 4W203, Bayou Bend folder, IHP, CAH.

42. Ima Hogg to William C. Hogg, Feb. 8, 1926, 3B119, folder 5, IHP, CAH. Also instruction book from John F. Staub and Birdsall P. Briscoe, associate architects, Feb. 7, 1927, in series 1, box 1, folder 3, IHP, Archives, MFAH; William C. Hogg to Ima Hogg, Aug. 25, 1927, 3B119, IHP, CAH, in which Will comments that "Mr. Briscoe and I" feel cast ironwork should be used on all balconies and grill details. By 1957 Ima remembered Staub as the architect and Briscoe as "consultant." Ima Hogg to Francis G. Coates, Jan. 7, 1957, series 1, box 1, folder 5, IHP, Archives, MFAH. "The house is truly the work of John Staub."

43. Ima Hogg to William C. Hogg, Feb. 8, 1926, 3B119, folder 4, IHP, CAH.

44. The moth room was a closet to store furs and woolens, often cedar-lined to protect against moths and other wool-loving pests.

45. Diary, Nov. 19, 1926, 2J399, WHP, CAH. Memories differed about how the site was selected. John Staub told docents the house was placed on the only possible location and remembered that he, Ima, and Briscoe had chosen the site together. Ima recalled that Will turned the house ninety degrees (better to avoid hot afternoon sun) while she was traveling. Will was still complaining about the site in March 1927. Sarah Shaw, "William Clifford Hogg and His Relationship to Bayou Bend," Docent Papers, box C, Archives, MFAH; William C. Hogg to Briscoe and Staub, March 20, 1927 (site), 4W203, folder 1, IHP, CAH. Dorothy Knox Howe Houghton recalled Briscoe family stories that Staub could not be present when the site was staked out, and so Briscoe oversaw that critical process; conversation with author, February 2004; Dorothy Knox Howe Houghton to author, Sept. 7, 2007.

46. William C. Hogg to Briscoe and Staub, March 22, 1927, instructions, 4W203, Bayou Bend folder, IHP, CAH; Shaw, docent paper. See also William C. Hogg to Mr. and Mrs. O. O. McIntyre, March 29, 1927, in which Will laments the "mass of detail in building a new house that you can't even imagine until you get down to finalities," 2J342, McIntyre file, WCH, CAH.

47. William C. Hogg to Ima Hogg, June 16, 1937, 3B119, folder 5, IHP, CAH.

48. "'Bayou Bend'—A Georgian Residence in Texas," *House and Garden*, March 1931, 63–65, and *Southern Architecture Illustrated* (Atlanta: Harman, 1931), 34–38; these publications, cited in Warren et al., *American Decorative Arts*, xx n10, were only the first of numerous references and articles in magazines and general works.

49. "Bayou Banks" guest book, Hogg Family Personal Papers, Memorabilia Series, box 15, folder 6, Archives, MFAH. The "informal" dinner included Estelle Sharp, Florence Fall, O. S. Carlton, F. Proctor, and one illegible entry. In 1957 Ima told Frank Coates the house was completed in December 1928. Either she misremembered the date, or there were still a few finishing touches to complete in the ensuing month. Ima Hogg to Francis G. Coates, Jan. 7, 1957, Series 1, Box 1, folder 5, IHP, Archives, MFAH.

50. The "Bayou Banks" guest book records gatherings for Nov. 6–13, 1928, in Hogg Family Personal Papers, Archives, MFAH.

51. Objects in the collection accessioned through the mid-1990s are detailed in Warren et al., *American Decorative Arts*. Note that about 4,500 objects comprised her collection in 1975 and about 1,700 objects have been added since her death.

52. Inventory and Appraisement of Furniture and Furnishings at Bayou Bend, June 25, 1933, Series 10, Box 2, folder 17, Bayou Bend Collections, Archives MFAH; photographs in MS21, series 14, scrapbook 1, p. 28, IHP, Archives, MFAH.

53. William C. Hogg to Ima Hogg, June 16, 1927, 2J329, folder 1924–1928, WHP, CAH. Neff, *Frederic Remington*, 24–23, also analyzes the collecting interaction between Will and Ima. In January 1921 Will told Ima to furnish the living room at the office "just as you want it." William C. Hogg to Ima Hogg, Jan. 29, 1921, 3B119, IHP, CAH.

54. B.65.9, Hepplewhite-style card table, purchased Jan. 24, 1920; B.20.1, New England armchair (1735–1790), Accessions file, Bayou Bend. The table is F173 and the chair F50 in Warren et al., *American Decorative Arts*.

55. William C. Hogg to Ima Hogg, Feb. 28, 1921, 3B119, folder 3, IHP, CAH. "You haven't got any thing on me when it comes to auctions. . . . I bought a mess of stuff, particularly sixteen varieties of Windsor chair."

56. B.65.12 (tambour desk), B.69.361.2–9 (chairs), B.69.361.361.1 (settee), Accessions file, Bayou Bend; Warren et al., *American Decorative Arts*, 48, F81; 58, F99; 110–111, F178. Legend relates that Henry Francis du Pont was rushing to New York from Delaware to inspect the settee and chairs when Will Hogg entered the store and scooped up the rare find. In 1956 du Pont is said to have entered the room where they were placed to see "his" settee. Collectors never forget! Accounts vary as to the purchaser, Will or Ima; correspondence indicates the purchase was made by Hogg Brothers "for Miss Ima," and Will initialed invoices and payments. Correspondence B.69.361.1–9, Accessions File, Bayou Bend. The settee and side chairs were placed in the Massachusetts Room when the house was reorganized for public viewing.

57. H. E. Brigham to Ima Hogg, July 26, 1926, inventory of dealers, 3B158, folder 1, IHP, CAH.

58. Summary of the antique-collecting movement based largely on Elizabeth Stillinger, *The Antiquers: The Lives and Careers, the Deals, the Finds, the Collections of the Men and Women Who Were Responsible for the Changing Taste in American Antiques, 1850–1930* (New York: Alfred A. Knopf, 1980).

59. B.65.12, Accessions file, Bayou Bend; Warren et al., *American Decorative Arts*, 110–111, F178.

60. *Press*, April 1936, clipping in Box of Newspaper Articles and Clippings, 1927–1947, River Oaks Garden Club Records, Archives, MFAH.

61. *Houston*, March 1937, 21.

62. Photograph of Alice Hogg in the Clock Garden, *Chronicle*, March 29, 1936, 12. Ima opened her gardens in 1934 and 1935, but 1936 marked the first official Azalea Trail. David B. Warren, *Bayou Bend Gardens: A Southern Oasis* (Houston: MFAH, 2006), provides a beautifully illustrated, detailed chronology of the development of Bayou Bend Gardens under Ima Hogg's aegis.

63. Correspondence in 4W203, folder 1, IHP, CAH, shows activity for house and garden in 1926.

64. See garden books and extensive correspondence with nurseries and garden experts in series 1, box 3, folders 11–20, IHP, Archives, MFAH.

65. Harry L. Daunoy, Metairie, La., to Ima Hogg, Dec. 4, 1939, Series 1, Box 3, folder 11, IHP, Archives, MFAH.

66. Warren, *Bayou Bend Gardens*, 3, citing David F. Hood, "The Renaissance of Southern Gardens in the Early Twentieth Century," *Journal of Garden History* 16, no. 2 (April–June 1996): 129.

67. Information about River Oaks Garden Club activities, by permission of the River Oaks Garden Club president, is found in River Oaks Garden Club Papers, Archives, MFAH. See Nina Cullinan to Ima Hogg, March 9, 1939, 4W270, folder 5, IHP, CAH, enclosing a check for $250 to

cover expenses for a tea at Bayou Bend during the annual meeting of the Garden Club of America.

68. Club records do not mention the pilgrimage after 1938.

69. Hare and Hare Collection, RGD 26, box 4, folder 16, and box 3, folder 17, MSRC, HPL; landscape plan February 1928, 2.325/D31a, IHP, CAH.

70. List of disbursements, 4W203, IHP, CAH (Teas, Blume System, B. P. Briscoe, and J. F. Staub, etc.); some disbursements as early as 1926; garden party in Will Hogg diary, May 17, 1929, 2J399, WHP, CAH;

71. London designs for a green garden (June 27, 1932), a peach garden (n.d.), and an azalea garden (July 26, 1934), 2.325/D31a, IHP, CAH. Other garden sketches in this box. Ima, Mike, and Alice made payments to Studio Gardens in 1931 and 1932, box 7, folder 10, Estelle Sharp Papers, WRC.

72. Rogers, *Landscape Design*, 396–397.

73. I am indebted to Stephen Fox for this information. A payment of $100 plus expenses to Mrs. Shipman suggests Ima discussed broad concepts with Shipman but basically created her own design. Notes compiled by landscape historian Joanne Wilson on Shipman's Houston work do not include Ima Hogg as a major client (papers courtesy of Joanne Wilson).

74. Correspondence 1929–1934, 3B151, folder 1, IHP, CAH.

75. Series 1, box 4, folder 2, IHP, Archives, MFAH.

76. Garden books in series 1, box 4, folder 2, IHP, Archives, MFAH; Bayou Bend library lists, IHP, Archives, MFAH.

77. "Bayou Bend Collection and Gardens," brochure, Museum of Fine Arts, Houston, 1997, contains a map, a description of purpose and plantings, and photographs of each garden. Analysis based on author's observation and correspondence in series 1, box 3, folders 11–20, box 4, folder 2, Archives, MFAH.

78. The Bicentennial Garden received the Houston Bicentennial Commission Certificate and the Janie Briscoe Award in the Governor's Community Achievement Awards Program.

79. Ruth London to Henderson's Iron Works, New Orleans, April 19, 1935, ordering garden furniture, series 1, box 3, folder 11, IHP, Archives, MFAH; Waterfall Garden in "Plan for Preservation . . . of Bayou Bend Gardens," 121.

80. Diana is pictured in "Gardens at Houston and River Oaks, Texas, Visited by the Garden Club of America in February, 1939," *Landscape Architecture* (July 1939): 184, 185, courtesy of Joanne Wilson.

81. See for example Shipman's Diana Garden at the Henry Croft Garden in Greenwich, circa 1928, replicated in Rogers, *Landscape Design*, 397.

82. See Warren, *Bayou Bend Gardens*, 42–54.

83. Series 1, box 3, folder 11–16 (1940s, 1950s), IHP, Archives, MFAH.

84. Ima Hogg to Mrs. E. Conway Broun, Nov. 26, 1957, Mrs. Wesley West to Ima Hogg, Reports folder (1957–1958), box 2, River Oaks Garden Club Records, Archives, MFAH.

85. May 18, 1961, folder 36, Trustee Records, Archives, MFAH; Ima Hogg to Mrs. J. Griffith Lawhon, May 17, 1961, 4W202, folder 2, IHP, CAH; Ima

Hogg, Remarks to the River Oaks Garden Club, Nov. 5, 1963, Docent Papers, box A, Archives, MFAH.

86. Minutes, Dec. 2, 1966, approve Endowment Fund; River Oaks Garden Club history, Year Book 1971–1972, pp. 10–13, River Oaks Garden Club Records, Archives, MFAH.

87. River Oaks Garden Club, President's Report, 1975–1976, and passim, River Oaks Garden Club Records, Archives, MFAH detail expenditures in the 1960s and 1970s.

88. James H. Chillman Jr. to Joseph Downs, Sept. 10, 1946, Sept. 14, 1948; Downs to Chillman, Aug. 31, 1948, RG 2:1, series 2, box 1, Chillman Papers, Archives, MFAH.

89. Brown, *America's Treasures*, 13. While his primary allegiance lay with the Metropolitan, Andrus examined items Ima was considering for purchase, surveyed the collection, and sometimes steered her to objects appropriate for Bayou Bend.

90. Janet Fayle, "A Circle of Friends," *The Bridge* (December 2002/January 2003): 1, 2, 10, 14; "Address by Charles F. Montgomery," senior research fellow, Henry Francis du Pont Winterthur Museum, in "Bayou Bend Collection of the Houston Museum of Fine Arts," dedication pamphlet, March 5, 1966, pp. 18–19.

91. "How Ima Hogg Met Katherine [*sic*] Prentis Murphy," typescript in series 14, scrapbook 1, p. 1, IHP, Archives, MFAH. Lillian Cogan, an antiques dealer in Hartford, Connecticut, recalls sending Ima and a companion to meet Katharine at her Westbrook, Connecticut, summer home. Directions were confusing, and Ima drove slowly and got lost. Mrs. Murphy closed her kitchen and sent the cook home at eight o'clock in the evening. When the wayfarers arrived, whiskey sours cooled heated tempers and sealed a friendship.

92. Harold Sack to Max Wilk, "Miss Ima Hogg," *Art and Antiques*, February 1986, 64, in Miss Ima Hogg Vertical File, Archives, MFAH.

93. Many examples of this dealer strategy could be cited, but see correspondence with New York dealer Bernard Levy about a Baltimore sofa ("At last I have succeeded in getting the Baltimore sofa for you"), B.61.13; John S. Walton regarding a Newport secretary bookcase ("exactly the same as Du Ponts [*sic*] but finer interior behind the doors"), B.69.22, Christmas gift, December 1964, B.64.50, 1–2, Accessions Files, Bayou Bend.

94. See Warren et al., *American Decorative Arts*, 142–50, for detailed information about Belter and the objects Ima collected.

95. Michael Brown, Curator of the Bayou Bend Collection, conversations with the author, spring 2003.

96. David B. Warren, interview, *The Bridge* (December 2003/January 2004), 4.

97. See Rudolf G. Wunderlich to Michael K. Brown, Dec. 8, 1992, in B.60.69, Accessions file, Bayou Bend.

98. Ima Hogg to Margaret Adams, Jan. 25, 1960, Feb. 19, 1960, in 68.3, Accessions file, Bayou Bend.

99. Israel Sack to Ima Hogg, Dec. 3, 1951, Correspondence, B.69,362, Accessions file, Bayou Bend.
100. Ima Hogg to James V. McMullan, Oct. 22, 1959, 60.47, Accessions file, Bayou Bend.
101. Correspondence, worksheets, series 1, box 4, folder 8, IHP, Archives, MFAH.
102. Ima Hogg to S. I. Morris, Aug. 16, 1960, letter, series 1, box 1, folder 9, IHP, Archives, MFAH.
103. Correspondence, series 1, box 4, folder 10, September 1960–January 1961, to the Honorary Advisory Committee: Ralph Carpenter, Henry Francis du Pont, Mr. and Mrs. Henry Flynt, John Graham II, Maxim Karolik, Charles F. Montgomery, Katharine Prentis Murphy, Donald Shelley. Electra Webb, who gave Ima the Mr. and Mrs. H delft charger, died before she could serve on the committee.
104. Series 1, box 4, folder 9, IHP, Archives, MFAH.
105. List of "Gifts of Mrs. Katherine [*sic*] Prentis Murphy," July 30, 1962, Accessions file, Bayou Bend; Ima Hogg, remarks, cited in Jonathan Fairbanks lecture (p. 9), series 1, box 4, folder 4, IHP, Archives, MFAH.
106. Ima Hogg to Katharine Prentis Murphy, April 7, July 3, July 30, Aug. 21, Oct. 6, Dec. 4, 1959, 3B149, folder 3, IHP, CAH.
107. Museum of Fine Arts Trustee Records, Full Board Meeting Minutes, folders 33–39, Archives, MFAH.
108. Correspondence in B.54.21, Accessions File, Bayou Bend (plotting for the 1954 Lockwood sale). In 1954 Ima also acquired *Portrait of a Boy* (circa 1758–1760) from Vose Galleries, Boston; *Portrait of Mrs. Paul Richard* (1771) from M. Knoedler and Co., New York; and several studies from Childs Gallery and the Lyndhurst Library Sale. See Warren et al., *American Decorative Arts*, 177–186, for detailed discussion of Bayou Bend's Copley holdings. In May 1954 Ima learned that she had beaten Henry Flynt for the Sarah Henshaw portrait, and, feeling a twinge of conscience because Flynt was a Henshaw descendant, she suggested that he purchase another pastel that was "not nearly as beautiful," and she would make a trade with him. Flynt replied that he was happy Sarah "found such a good home." Correspondence May 17, 19, 1954, between Ima Hogg and Henry Flynt, in B.54.25, Accessions file, Bayou Bend.
109. For detailed information about the silver collection at Bayou Bend see Michael K. Brown, "American Silver at Bayou Bend," *Museum of Fine Arts, Houston, Bulletin* (Fall 1987): 22–32; Warren et al., *American Decorative Arts*, 268–347.
110. *Intelligencer*, January 1969, in a memorial to Dorothy Dawes Chillman, describes her "most recent contribution to Bayou Bend . . . as consultant for the new Empire Suite," in 4W202, folder 3, IHP, CAH. David B. Warren, in "David Warren Looks Back," *Intelligencer* (Winter 2003–2004, 6), recalls discussions with Miss Hogg about the importance of including an Empire-style room, "something she had planned to skip" until he urged her to develop the suite. Denominated "Grecian" in Warren et

al., *American Decorative Arts* (120), this style is also known as Empire or Greek Revival.

111. Mary Ann "Muffy" McLanahan to Patricia Prioleau, *The Bridge* (February/March 2002): 2, 12–13; Docent Meeting Oct. 26, 2001. Original class list in series 14, scrapbook II, p. 3, IHP, Archives, MFAH.

112. Talk to docents, Feb. 7, 1962, and Fairbanks information in series 1, box 4, folder 7, IHP, Archives, MFAH. Fairbanks spent the month at the home of Charles and Faith Bybee. She was president of the Harris County Heritage Society at the time. In the morning Fairbanks taught the docents; in the afternoon he consulted with members of the Heritage Society about restoring the Kellum-Noble and Nichols-Rice-Cherry houses. Mrs. Bybee and Miss Hogg were rival collectors with many common interests. See Jonathan L. Fairbanks's introduction to *American Furniture in the Bybee Collection*, by Charles L. Venable (Austin: University of Texas Press, 1989), xv, xvii.

113. Jonathan Fairbanks lecture, March 20, 2007, in *The Bridge*, June/July 2007, 3.

114. Jonathan Fairbanks, introduction to Brown, *America's Treasures*, 4.

115. Ima Hogg, "Remarks," 9; Box 9, folder 36, Director's Records, James Johnson Sweeney, Archives, MFAH.

116. Information about the Bayou Bend Docent Organization based on experiences of the author, who has been an active docent since 1971. Ima Hogg attended monthly docent meetings until her death in 1975.

117. Ima Hogg was a founding member of the society in 1954, served on its board 1957–1959, and gave a chest of drawers to the Noble House. The society, created to save the Sam Houston Park from highway encroachment and preserve Houston's heritage, has moved period homes from Harris County locations to the park and furnished them in period styles of 1830–1910. 4W238, folder 9, IHP, CAH.

118. See Neff, *Frederic Remington*, 22–26, for analysis of the office furnishings.

119. 3B130, folders 1, 2, IHP, CAH.

120. On Oct. 9, 1939, Ima wrote officials in Quitman about her interest in preserving what became the Honeymoon Cottage, and later that year Mike was named to the Jim Hogg Memorial Shrine Commission. Correspondence, 4W262, IHP, CAH.

121. The park is currently administered by the City of Quitman as the Governor Hogg Shrine Historic Site.

122. Speech, Ima Hogg, opening of James Stephen Hogg House, Quitman, March 23, 1952, in 4W263, IHP, CAH.

123. Ima Hogg speech, May 25, 1969, 4W263, folder 4 (nestled, coming home); T. C. Chadick, remarks, dedication of Stinson House, Nov. 2, 1974, folder 3 (turned wilderness), IHP, CAH. Information about the restoration at Quitman is found in 4W263, IHP, CAH, and in clippings in scrapbook 1, MS 21, Series 14, pp. 4–7, IHP, Archives, MFAH.

124. Information about the Rusk park in 4W263, IHP, CAH. By House Bill No. 110, the state accepted the Hogg family gift and agreed to beautify

the land as a park, April 29, 1941, Governor Hogg Shrine State Historical Park Vertical File, CAH.

125. Ima Hogg to A. J. Bond, June 23, 1942, 4W256, IHP, CAH. Will of Mike Hogg, no. 31,414, County Clerk's Office, Harris County, Texas, filed Nov. 17, 1941, courtesy of Michael K. Brown.

126. Lomax, *Will Hogg, Texan*, 6.

127. Rains delayed completion of the Varner project, but plumbers and electricians finished work in January 1920. William C. Hogg to Ima Hogg, Nov. 8, 15, 1919, folder 2; Mike Hogg to William C. Hogg, folder 3, 3B119, IHP, CAH. Varner information in 2J307, WHP, CAH. Ima's dismay in Ima Hogg to Mrs. Clifford Braden, Sept. 20, 1948, 4W256, IHP, CAH. She recalled the interiors during her father's lifetime and said Will had done "a great deal . . . which I later regretted" in 1920 when Ima was away from home. See Neff, *Frederic Remington*, 16–19, for analysis of Will's attachment to Varner and its place in the colonial revival canon.

128. Kaye Northcott, "Former Slaves Remembered," *Texas Co-Op Power*, May 2001, 15–18.

129. Letters in 4W256, IHP, CAH. Ima noted that it was "always . . . the intention of my brothers and myself to some day offer the Varner house and a small park to the State." Ima Hogg to Gordon K. Shearer, May 4, 1953, 4W256, IHP, CAH. Furnishings include her mother's sewing box in the upstairs hall and an oversize rocker made by Huntsville prisoners for Governor Hogg.

130. T. C. Chadick, remarks, dedication of Stinson House, Nov. 2, 1974, 4W263, folder 3, IHP, CAH.

131. Quote, "laboratory," Series 14, Scrapbook III, p. 35, IHP, Archives, MFAH. Lonn Taylor, interview with Martha Norkunas, Feb. 28, 1996, Winedale Oral History Collection, CAH.

132. James Dick, an Ima Hogg protégé, moved the classical music festivals to a separate facility adjacent to Winedale after a funding dispute. Chancellor Harry Ransom insisted Ima provide an endowment for Winedale (originally about $500,000) before he would accept Ima's gift. Ima funded Wayne Bell, a University of Texas employee, and all workmen until restoration of the first structures was complete. Wayne Bell, lecture, Bayou Bend Docent Organization, March 17, 2003. Winedale is administered by the Center for American History at the university.

133. Development Guidelines for the Winedale Properties, Round Top, School of Architecture, University of Texas, Austin, 4W245, folder 1, p. 9, IHP, CAH.

134. Program, box 11, folder 11, Marguerite Johnston Papers, WRC.

135. Ima Hogg to Robert Sutherland, May 10, 13, 1967, MAI9/U1, HFR, CAH.

136. Information about Winedale is found in 4W243–4W245, IHP, CAH; Interviews with Wayne Bell, professor of architecture, University of Texas, June 14, 1995; and Lonn Taylor, former curator Winedale, Feb. 28, 1996, Winedale Oral History Collection, CAH. Wayne Bell, lecture to Bayou Bend Docent Organization, March 17, 2003.

137. Bayou Bend curator Barry Greenlaw wrote Winedale curator Lonn Taylor May 6, 1975, "I tried to explain to her that she couldn't just give things and then take them back, but as they were in storage and not being used, she was insistent, and as you know it's difficult to contradict her under these circumstances." Taylor replied sympathetically, "Short of physically preventing her from moving them, there seems to be no way to deal with it." In June 1975, Museum of Fine Arts curator Katherine S. Howe and Diane Taylor corresponded about "wandering candlesticks." Correspondence in Winedale Archives, CAH.

EPILOGUE

1. Museum of Fine Arts Director Peter Marzio to Museum Friends, letter, Jan. 20, 2006, p. 1, copy in author's possession.
2. Sara M. Evans and Harry C. Boyte, *Free Spaces. The Sources of Democratic Change in America* (New York: Harper and Row, 1986), viii.

Works Consulted

ARCHIVAL SOURCES

DE PELCHIN CHILDREN'S CENTER, HOUSTON

Board Minutes (Houston Child Guidance Center)

HOUSTON INDEPENDENT SCHOOL DISTRICT, ADMINISTRATION BUILDING

Board of Education Minutes, Board Services Department

HOUSTON METROPOLITAN RESEARCH CENTER, HOUSTON PUBLIC LIBRARY

Bayland Orphans Home File
Chautauqua File
Cherry, E. Richardson, Papers
City of Houston, Department of Planning, Collection
Committee on Inter-Racial Cooperation File
Community Chest Files, 1928–1931
Congregation Beth Israel Records
Covington Collection
Cullinan, Joseph, Papers
Daily, Ray K., Oral History
Daily, Ray K., Papers
Democratic National Convention, 1928, Collection
Downtown Club File
Ethel Ransom Art and Literary Club Collection
Farrington, William G., Biographical File
Federation of Women's Clubs File
Hare and Hare Collection
Heiser, J. M. Jr., Environmental Collection
Hogg, Ima, File
Hogg, Ima, Oral History
Holcombe, Oscar, Papers
Houston Little Theatre File
Houston Open Forum Records
Houston Social Service Bureau Records

Houston Street and Newsboys Club File
Houston Subdivision Collection
Ideson, Julia, Papers
Junior League of Houston File
Ladies Reading Club File
Map Collection, Texas Room
Married Ladies Social, Art, and Charity Club File
Mayors Book (Houston)
Ring, Elizabeth Fitzsimmons, File
River Oaks Collection
Tuesday Musical Club File
United Way and Community Chest Pamphlets
Werlein, Ewing, Biographical File
Yates, Jack, Family Collection
YWCA Collection

MUSEUM OF FINE ARTS, HOUSTON, ACCESSIONS FILES, REGISTRAR'S OFFICE

North American Indian General File
Pre-Columbian Collection
Southwest Indian (Miss Ima Hogg) Collection
Works on Paper Collection

MUSEUM OF FINE ARTS, HOUSTON, ARCHIVES

Art League of Houston Records
Art Museum Guild Papers (1939–1944)
Bayou Bend Docent Organization Records, Docent Papers
Catalog Collection
Cherry, Emma Richardson, Vertical File
Cullinan, Nina J., Papers, 1953–1981
Directors' Records: James H. Chillman Jr.; Lee Malone; James Johnson
    Sweeney
Exhibition Files
Fall, Mrs. Henry B. (Florence K.), Vertical File
Ferguson, William Booker, "Hogg Family Financial History," Vertical File
Finnigan, Annette, Vertical File
Garden Club of Houston Records
Hanszen, Mrs. Harry C., Vertical File
Hogg, Ima, Papers
Hogg, Mike and Alice, Papers
Hogg, Miss Ima, Vertical File
Hogg, William Clifford, Vertical File
Hogg Brothers Collection
Hogg Family Personal Papers
Museum of Fine Arts, Houston, Chronology
Registrar's Records
River Oaks Garden Club Records

Shurtleff, Stella Hope, Papers
Trustee Records

MUSEUM OF FINE ARTS, HOUSTON, BAYOU BEND

Bayou Bend Accessions Files

RICE UNIVERSITY, ADMINISTRATIVE OFFICE, HOUSTON

Board of Trustees Minutes

RICE UNIVERSITY, WOODSON RESEARCH CENTER, FONDREN LIBRARY, HOUSTON

Autry, James L., Papers
Axson, Stockton, Papers
Blayney, Lindsey, Information File
Chillman, James H. Jr., Papers
Clayton, William Lockhart, Papers
DePelchin, Kezia (Payne), 1828–1893, Papers
Dillingham Family Papers
Guérard, Albert Léon, Information File
Hogg, James Stephen, Papers
House, Edward M., Correspondence, 1896–1927
Hutcheson Family Papers
Jameson, W. G., Letter File
Johnston, Marguerite, Papers
Lovett, Edgar Odell, Personal Papers
Lovett Family Papers: Series I, Correspondence
President's Office Records, Edgar Odell Lovett, 1912–1945
Rice University Opening Ceremony, Files
Ryon, Lewis B., Information File
Sharp, Estelle (1883–1965), Papers, Interviews
Sharp Lectureship/Lectures Information File
Shurtleff, Stella Hope, Papers
Slaughter, John Willis, Information File
Tsanoff, Radoslav A., Information File
Tsanoff Chair of Public Affairs, Information File
Watkin, William Ward, Papers, 1903–1953

UNIVERSITY OF HOUSTON, SPECIAL COLLECTIONS

Hogg, Ima, Symphony Programs Collection, 1900–1978

UNIVERSITY OF TEXAS AT AUSTIN, CENTER FOR AMERICAN HISTORY

Board of Regents Records
Hogg, Ima, Papers

Hogg, James Stephen, Papers
Hogg, William Clifford, Papers
Hogg Family Papers
Hogg Foundation for Mental Health Records
Lomax, John Avery, Family Papers
Winedale Archives
Winedale Oral History Collection

NEWSPAPERS AND MAGAZINES

Alcalde (University of Texas)
Bellaire Breeze
Bridge, The (Bayou Bend Docent Organization publication)
Civics for Houston
Community, The: A Review of Philanthropic Thought and Social Effort (Houston)
Houston (Chamber of Commerce magazine)
Houston Chronicle
Houston Daily Post
Houston Gargoyle
Houston Informer and Texas Freeman
Houston Labor Journal
Houston News: The Junior League of Houston
Houston Post
Houston Post-Dispatch
Houston Press
Houston Symphony (Program)
Intelligencer (Friends of Bayou Bend publication)
Musical America
New York Times
*Progressive Houston: A Monthly Publication for the Benefit of the Taxpayer and
   General Public*
Telegraph and Texas Register
Woman's Viewpoint

PUBLISHED SOURCES

Addams, Jane, ed. *The Child, the Clinic, and the Court.* New York: New
   Republic, 1927.
———. *Democracy and Social Ethics.* New York: Macmillan, 1916.
———. *The Second Twenty Years at Hull-House: September 1909 to September 1929.*
   New York: Macmillan, 1930.
———. *Twenty Years at Hull-House.* New York: Macmillan, 1920.
Agatha, Sister M. *The History of Houston Heights, 1891–1918.* Houston: Premier
   Printing, 1956.
Alexander, Charles C. "Crusade for Conformity: The Ku Klux Klan in Texas,
   1920–1930." *Texas Gulf Coast Historical Association Publication Series* 6
   (August 1962): 1–62.

Allen, Frederick Lewis. *Only Yesterday: An Informal History of the Nineteen-Twenties*. New York: Harper and Brothers, 1931.

———. *Since Yesterday: The Nineteen-Thirties in America, September 3, 1929–September 3, 1939*. New York: Harper and Brothers, 1940.

Allen, O. Fisher. *The City of Houston from Wilderness to Wonder*. Temple, TX: O. Fisher Allen, 1936.

Allied Arts Association. *Seventy-Five Years of Sculpture in Houston*. Houston: Museum of Fine Arts, 1953.

Annette Finnigan Collection of Laces, The. Houston: Museum of Fine Arts of Houston, 1940.

Barnstone, Howard. *The Architecture of John F. Staub: Houston and the South*. With Stephen Fox, Jerome Iowa, and David Courtwright. Foreword by Vincent Scully. Austin: University of Texas Press, 1979.

Baron, Steven M. *Houston Electric: The Street Railways of Houston, Texas*. Lexington, KY: Steven M. Baron, 1996.

Barr, Alwyn, and Robert A. Calvert, eds. *Black Leaders: Texans for Their Times*. Austin: Texas State Historical Association, 1981.

Barthelme, Marion K. *Women in the Texas Populist Movement*. College Station: Texas A&M University Press, 1997.

Bartholomew, Ed. *The Houston Story: A Chronicle of the City of Houston and the Texas Frontier from the Battle of San Jacinto to the War Between the States*. Houston: Frontier Press of Texas, 1951.

Bath, Alan. "Enlightened Investment: Rice Institute and the Growth of Houston, 1900–1915." *Cornerstone* (Summer 2001): 6–7.

Beard, Norman Henry, ed. *The City Book of Houston*. Houston: N.p., 1925.

———. *The Municipal Book of the City of Houston, Illustrated, 1922, Containing an Analysis of Houston and a Brief Survey of the Activities of the Various City Departments*. Houston: N.p., 1922.

Beck, Audrey Jones, comp. *The Collection of John A. and Audrey Jones Beck*. Houston: Museum of Fine Arts, Houston, 1986.

Beeth, Howard, and Cary D. Wintz, eds. *Black Dixie: Afro-Texan History and Culture in Houston*. College Station: Texas A&M University Press, 1992.

Bernard, Richard M., and Bradley R. Rice, eds. *Sunbelt Cities: Politics and Growth since World War II*. Austin: University of Texas Press, 1983.

Bernhard, Virginia. *Ima Hogg: The Governor's Daughter*. St. James, NY: Brandywine Press, 1984, 1996.

Big Town, Big Money: The Business of Houston. Houston: Cordovan Press, 1973.

Blair, Karen J. *The Clubwoman as Feminist: True Womanhood Redefined, 1868–1914*. New York: Holmes and Meier, 1980.

———. *The Torchbearers: Women and Their Amateur Arts Associations in America, 1890–1930*. Bloomington: Indiana University Press, 1994.

Boles, John B. *University Builder: Edgar Odell Lovett and the Founding of the Rice Institute*. Baton Rouge: Louisiana State University Press, 2007.

Bonjean, Charles, and Bernice Milburn Moore. *Miss Ima: 1882–1982. Centennial Celebration*. Austin: Hogg Foundation for Mental Health, 1982.

Botson, Michael. "Jim Crow Wearing Steel-Toed Shoes and Safety Glasses: Dual Unionism at the Hughes Tool Company, 1918–1942." *Houston Review: History and Culture of the Gulf Coast* 16 (1994): 101–116.

Boyer, Paul. "The Ideology of the Civic Arts Movement in America, 1890–1920." *Houston Review: History and Culture of the Gulf Coast* 2 (Winter 1980): 5–20.

Bradford, Ernest S. *Commission Government in American Cities*. New York: Macmillan, 1919.

Breckinridge, Sophonisba P. *Women in the Twentieth Century: A Study of Their Political, Social and Economic Activities*. New York: Arno Press, 1972. First published in 1933.

Bremner, Robert H. *American Philanthropy*. 2d ed. Chicago: University of Chicago Press, 1988.

———. *Giving: Charity and Philanthropy in History*. New Brunswick, NJ: Transaction, 1994.

Brooks, Elizabeth. *Prominent Women of Texas*. Akron, Ohio: Werner, 1896.

Brown, Dorothy M. *Setting a Course: American Women in the 1920s*. Boston: Twayne, 1987.

Brown, Michael K. "American Silver at Bayou Bend." *Museum of Fine Arts, Houston, Bulletin* (Fall 1987): 22–32.

———. *America's Treasures at Bayou Bend: Celebrating Fifty Years*. London: Scala Publications, in association with the Museum of Fine Arts, Houston, 2007.

Brown, Norman D. *Hood, Bonnet, and Little Brown Jug: Texas Politics, 1921–1928*. College Station: Texas A&M University Press, 1984.

Brownell, Blaine A. *The Urban Ethos in the South, 1920–1930*. Baton Rouge: Louisiana State University Press, 1975.

Buchanan, James E., ed. *Houston: A Chronological and Documentary History, 1519–1970*. Dobbs Ferry, NY: Oceana, 1975.

Buckle, D., and S. Lebovici. *Child Guidance Centres*. Geneva: World Health Organization, 1960.

Buenger, Walter L., and Joseph A. Pratt. *But Also Good Business: Texas Commerce Banks and the Financing of Houston and Texas, 1886–1986*. College Station: Texas A&M University Press, 1986.

Bullard, Robert D. *Invisible Houston: The Black Experience in Boom and Bust*. College Station: Texas A&M University Press, 1987.

Burlingame, Dwight F., ed. *The Responsibilities of Wealth*. Bloomington: Indiana University Press, 1992.

Burt, Nathaniel. *Palaces for the People: A Social History of the American Art Museum*. Boston: Little, Brown, 1977.

Caram, Dorothy F., Anthony G. Dworkin, and Nestor Rodriguez, eds. *Hispanics in Houston and Harris County, 1519–1986: A Sesquicentennial Celebration*. Houston/Harris County: Texas Independence Community, 1989.

Carleton, Don E. *A Breed So Rare: The Life of J. R. Parten, Liberal Texas Oil Man, 1896–1992*. Austin: Texas State Historical Association, 1998.

———. "McCarthyism in Local Elections: The Houston School Board Election of 1952." *Houston Review: History and Culture of the Gulf Coast* 3 (Winter 1981): 168–172.

———. *Red Scare! Right-Wing Hysteria, Fifties Fanaticism, and Their Legacy in Texas*. Austin: Texas Monthly Press, 1985.

Carnegie, Andrew. "The Best Fields for Philanthropy." *North American Review* 148 (December 1889): 682–698.

———. "Wealth." *North American Review* 148 (June 1889): 653–664.

Carroll, B. H. *Standard History of Houston, Texas: From a Study of the Original Sources*. Knoxville: H. W. Crew, 1912.

Chafe, William H. *The Paradox of Change: American Women in the 20th Century*. New York: Oxford University Press, 1991.

Chamber of Commerce, City of Houston. *Illustrated City Book of Houston*. Houston: Cumming and Sons, Art Printers, 1916.

Chapman, Betty Trapp. *Houston Women: Invisible Threads in the Tapestry*. Virginia Beach: Donning, 2000.

Chernow, Ron. *Titan: The Life of John D. Rockefeller, Sr*. New York: Random House, 1998.

Cheung, Monit, Jennifer Levit, and Carole R. Linseisen. "Children's Services in Houston: The First One Hundred Years of DePelchin Children's Center." Pamphlet. Houston: DePelchin Children's Center, Feb. 20, 1996.

City of Houston, Texas. New York: Blyth, 1946.

Coben, Stanley. *Rebellion Against Victorianism: The Impetus for Cultural Change in 1920s America*. New York: Oxford University Press, 1991.

Collection of John A. and Audrey Jones Beck: Impressionist and Post-Impressionist Paintings. Catalog. Houston: Museum of Fine Arts, Houston, 1974.

Comey, Arthur Coleman. *Houston: Tentative Plans for Its Development; Report to the Houston Park Commission*. Boston: Press of Geo. H. Ellis Co., 1913.

Cook, Charles Orson, and Barry J. Kaplan. "Civic Elites and Urban Planning: Houston's River Oaks." *East Texas Historical Journal* 15 (1977): 29–37.

Coryell, Janet L., Martha H. Swain, Sandra Gioia Treadway, and Elizabeth Hayes Turner, eds. *Beyond Image and Convention: Explorations in Southern Women's History*. Columbia: University of Missouri Press, 1998.

Cotner, Robert C. *Addresses and State Papers of James Stephen Hogg*. Centennial edition. Austin: University of Texas Press, 1951.

———. *James Stephen Hogg: A Biography*. Austin: University of Texas Press, 1959.

Cram, Ralph Adams. *My Life in Architecture*. Boston: Little, Brown, 1936.

Crawford, Audrey Y. "'To Protect, to Feed, and to Give Momentum to Every Effort': African American Clubwomen in Houston, 1880–1910." *Houston Review of History and Culture* 1 (Fall 2003): 15–23.

Crocker, Ruth. "From Widow's Mite to Widow's Might: The Philanthropy of Margaret Olivia Sage." *American Presbyterian* 74 (Winter 1996): 253–266.

Culler, Ralph E. III, and Wayne H. Holtzman. *The Ima Hogg Foundation: Miss Ima's Legacy to the Children of Houston*. Austin: Hogg Foundation for Mental Health, 1990.

Curti, Merle. "The History of American Philanthropy as a Field of Research." *American Historical Review* 62 (January 1957): 352–363.

Curti, Merle, and Roderick Nash. *Philanthropy in the Shaping of American Higher Education*. New Brunswick, NJ: Rutgers University Press, 1965.

Daniels, A. Pat. *Texas Avenue at Main Street: The Chronological Story of a City Block in Houston*. Houston: Allen Press, 1964.

Dauphin, Sue. *Houston by Stages: A History of Theatre in Houston*. Burnet, TX: Sue Dauphin, 1981.

Davidoff, Leonore, and Catherine Hall. *Family Fortunes: Men and Women of the English Middle Class, 1780–1850*. Chicago: University of Chicago Press, 1987.

Davidson, Chandler. *Race and Class in Texas Politics*. Princeton, NJ: Princeton University Press, 1990.

Davidson, John, and Robert Fisher. "Social Planning in Houston: The Council of Social Agencies, 1928–1976." *Houston Review: History and Culture of the Gulf Coast* 18 (1996): 1–28.

Davis, John L. *Houston: A Historical Portrait*. Austin: Encino Press, 1983.

Davis, Stephen. "Joseph Jay Pastoriza and the Single Tax in Houston, 1911–1917." *Houston Review: History and Culture of the Gulf Coast* 8 (1986): 56–78.

Day, Barbara Thompson. "The Heart of Houston: The Early History of the Houston Council on Human Relations, 1958–1972." *Houston Review: History and Culture of the Gulf Coast* 8 (1986): 1–31.

Donald, James. *Imagining the Modern City*. London: Athlone Press, 1999.

Downs, Fane, and Nancy Baker Jones, eds. *Women and Texas History: Selected Essays*. Austin: Texas State Historical Association, 1993.

Dreyer, Martin. "The Way We Were: Houston's Culture in the 1940s." *Houston Review: History and Culture of the Gulf Coast* 1 (Spring 1979): 27–31.

Dunbar, Clarence Peckham, and William Hunter Dillard. *Houston: 1836–1936: Chronology and Review*. Houston: Business Research and Publications Service, 1936.

Egerton, John. *Speak Now Against the Day: The Generation before the Civil Rights Movement in the South*. New York: Alfred A. Knopf, 1994.

Ehrlich, George. *Kansas City, Missouri: An Architectural History, 1826–1990*. Rev. ed. Columbia: University of Missouri Press, 1992.

Ellis, L. Tuffly. "The University's Centennial: A Commemoration." *Southwestern Historical Quarterly* 86 (October 1982): 125–134.

Ellis, Susan J., and Katherine H. Noyes. *By the People: A History of Americans as Volunteers*. Rev. ed. San Francisco: Jossey-Bass, 1990.

Elshtain, Jean Bethke. *Jane Addams and the Dream of American Democracy: A Life*. New York: Basic Books, 2002.

Emmott, Sarah H. *Memorial Park: A Priceless Legacy*. Houston: Herring Press, 1992.

Endelman, Sharon Bice. "The Open Forum, 1926–1938: The Lecture Platform and the First Amendment in the Bayou City." *Houston Review: History and Culture of the Gulf Coast* 4 (Winter 1982): 5–18.

Engler, Robert. *The Politics of Oil: A Study of Private Power and Democratic Directions*. Chicago: University of Chicago Press, 1961.

Enstam, Elizabeth York. *Women and the Creation of Urban Life, Dallas, Texas, 1843–1920*. College Station: Texas A&M University Press, 1998.

Erenberg, Lewis A. *Steppin' Out: New York Night Life and the Transformation of American Culture, 1890–1930*. Chicago: University of Chicago Press, 1981.

Evans, Meredith M. "Emma Richardson Cherry: American Art Pioneer." Research practicum, University of Denver, November 20, 2000.

Evans, Sara M., and Harry C. Boyte. *Free Spaces. The Sources of Democratic Change in America*. New York: Harper and Row, 1986.

Feagin, Joe R. *Free Enterprise City: Houston in Political-Economic Perspective*. New Brunswick, NJ: Rutgers University Press, 1988.

Federation of Women's Clubs. *The Key to the City of Houston*. Houston: State
Printing Company, 1908.

Fehrenbach, T. R. *Lone Star: A History of Texas and the Texans*. New York:
Macmillan, 1968.

Ferguson, Cheryl Caldwell. "River Oaks: 1920s Suburban Planning and
Development in Houston." *Southwestern Historical Quarterly* 104 (October
2000): 191–228.

Fisher, Robert. "'Be on the Lookout': Neighborhood Civic Clubs in Houston."
Houston Review: History and Culture of the Gulf Coast 6 (1984): 105–111.

Fox, Stephen. "Bayou Bend." Typescript. 2002.

———. "Big Park, Little Plans: A History of Hermann Park." In *Ephemeral City:
Cite Looks at Houston*, ed. Barrie Scardino, William F. Stern, and Bruce C.
Webb, 117–132. Austin: University of Texas Press, 2003.

———. *The Country Houses of John F. Staub*. Color photography by Richard
Cheek. College Station: Texas A&M University Press, 2007.

———. *Houston Architectural Guide*. 2d ed. Houston: American Institute of
Architects, Houston Chapter, and Herring Press, 1999.

———. "The Museum of Fine Arts, Houston: An Architectural History, 1924–
1953." *Bulletin of the Museum of Fine Arts, Houston* 15 (Winter/Spring
1991): 3–45.

———. "Planning in Houston: A Historic Overview." In *Ephemeral City*, ed.
Scardino, Stern, and Webb, 34–40.

———. "Public Art and Private Places: Shadyside." *Houston Review: History and
Culture of the Gulf Coast* 2 (Winter 1980): 37–60.

———. "River Oaks: A Distinguished Experiment in Fine Living." Typescript.
2002.

———. "Spanish-Mediterranean Houses in Houston." Pamphlet. Houston:
Rice Design Alliance, 1992.

Freeman, J. H. *The People of Baker Botts*. Houston: Champagne Fine Printing
and Lithographing, 1992.

Friedman, Lawrence J. "Philanthropy in America: Historicism and Its
Discontents." In *Charity, Philanthropy, and Civility in American History*,
ed. Lawrence J. Friedman and Mark D. McGarvie. Cambridge, England:
Cambridge University Press, 2003.

Friedman, Lawrence J., and Mark D. McGarvie. *Charity, Philanthropy, and
Civility in American History*. Cambridge, England: Cambridge University
Press, 2003.

Fuermann, George. *Houston: Land of the Big Rich*. Garden City, NY: Doubleday,
1951.

Garden Book for Houston, A. Houston: Forum of Civics, 1929. Reprinted and
revised after 1945 by River Oaks Garden Club.

"Gardens at Houston and River Oaks, Texas, Visited by the Garden Club of
America in February, 1939." *Landscape Architecture* 29 (July 1939): 183–
191.

Gilbert, Charles E. Jr. *A Pictorial and Factual Look at Houston: Space City U.S.A.
What to See—What to Do in the South's Largest City*. Houston: Gilbert,
1963.

————. *A Pictorial and Factual Story of Houston Today: And a Pocket Guide to the City with a Brief History of the Early Days of Texas and Houston*. Houston: Gilbert, 1955.

Glass, James L. "The Original Book of Sales of Lots of the Houston Town Company from 1836 Forward." *Houston Review: History and Culture of the Gulf Coast* 16 (1994): 167–187.

Glenn, John M., Lilian Brandt, and F. Emerson Andrews. *Russell Sage Foundation, 1907–1946*. 2 vols. New York: Russell Sage Foundation, 1947.

Goodwin, Lawrence. *The Populist Moment: A Short History of the Agrarian Revolt in America*. New York: Oxford University Press, 1978.

Goodwyn, Lawrence. *Texas Oil, American Dreams: A Study of the Texas Independent Producers and Royalty Owners Association*. Austin: Texas State Historical Association, 1996.

Gould, Lewis L. *Progressives and Prohibitionists: Texas Democrats in the Wilson Era*. Austin: University of Texas Press, 1973.

————. "The University Becomes Politicized: The War with Jim Ferguson, 1915–1918." *Southwestern Historical Quarterly* 86 (October 1982): 255–276.

Goyen, William. "While You Were Away (Houston Seen and Unseen, 1923–1978)." *Houston Review: History and Culture of the Gulf Coast* 1 (Fall 1979): 81–90.

Grantham, Dewey. *Southern Progressivism: The Reconciliation of Progress and Tradition*. Knoxville: University of Tennessee Press, 1983.

Green, Elna. *Southern Strategies: Southern Women and the Woman Suffrage Question*. Chapel Hill: University of North Carolina Press, 1997.

Greene, Casey. "Guardians Against Change: The Ku Klux Klan in Houston and Harris County, 1920–1925." *Houston Review: History and Culture of the Gulf Coast* 10 (1988): 3–15.

Griffin, Roger A. "To Establish a University of the First Class." *Southwestern Historical Quarterly* 86 (October 1982): 135–160.

Griswold, Mac, and Eleanor Weller. *The Golden Age of American Gardens: Proud Owners, Private Estates, 1890–1940*. New York: Henry Abrams, 1991.

Grob, Gerald. *From Asylum to Community: Mental Health Policy in Modern America*. Princeton, NJ: Princeton University Press, 1991.

————. *Mental Illness and American Society, 1875–1940*. Princeton, NJ: Princeton University Press, 1983.

Gunter, Jewel Boone Hamilton. *Committed: The Official 100-Year History of the Women's Clubs of Houston, 1893–1993*. N.p., n.d. Texas Room, Houston Public Library.

Handbook of Texas Online. www.tsha.utexas.edu/handbook/online.

Hart, James P. "Oil, the Courts, and the Railroad Commission." *Southwestern Historical Quarterly* 46 (January 1941): 303–320.

Hartmann, Susan M. *The Home Front and Beyond: American Women in the 1940s*. Boston: Twayne, 1982.

Hatch, Orin Walker. "Lyceum to Library: A Chapter in the Cultural History of Houston." *Texas Gulf Coast Historical Association* 9 (September 1965): 1–63.

Haynes, Robert V. *A Night of Violence: The Houston Riot of 1917*. Baton Rouge: Louisiana State University Press, 1976.

Henderson, Archie. "City Planning in Houston, 1920–1930." *Houston Review: History and Culture of the Gulf Coast* 9 (1987): 107–136.

Hewitt, Mark A. *The Architect and the American Country House, 1890–1940*. New Haven, CT: Yale University Press, 1990.

Hewitt, Nancy, and Suzanne Lebsock, eds. *Visible Women: New Essays on American Activism*. Urbana: University of Illinois Press, 1993.

Hobbs, Nicholas. *Mental Health: An Interest of Miss Hogg*. TAMU Docs T Doc.

Hogg Foundation for Mental Health. *The Hogg Foundation for Mental Health: The First Three Decades, 1940–1970*. Austin: University of Texas, 1970.

———. *Philanthropy in the Southwest: Foundations Cooperate in Community Programs; A Resume of the Years 1966–1968*. Austin: University of Texas, 1969.

Holmes, Ann Hitchcock. *The Alley Theatre: Four Decades in Three Acts: A History of One of the Nation's Oldest Resident Theaters*. Houston: Transco Energy Company, n.d.

———. *Joy Unconfined: Robert Joy in Houston, A Portrait of Fifty Years*. Houston: San Jacinto Museum of History Association, 1986.

Horn, Margo. *Before It's Too Late: The Child Guidance Movement in the United States, 1922–1945*. Philadelphia: Temple University Press, 1989.

Horowitz, Helen Lefkowitz. *Culture and the City: Cultural Philanthropy in Chicago from the 1880s to 1917*. Chicago: University of Chicago Press, 1976.

Houghton, Dorothy Knox Howe. *The Houston Club and Its City: One Hundred Years*. Houston: Gulf Printing, 1994.

Houghton, Dorothy Knox Howe, Barrie M. Scardino, Sadie Gwin Blackburn, and Katherine S. Howe. *Houston's Forgotten Heritage: Landscape, Houses, Interiors, 1824–1914*. Houston: Rice University Press, 1991.

Houston: A History and Guide. Work Projects Administration Writers' Program American Guide Series. Houston: Anson Jones Press, 1942.

Houston Architectural Survey. Southwest Center for Urban Research and Rice University School of Architecture. Vols. 1–5, Houston: Texas Historical Commission and City of Houston, 1980. Vol. 6, Houston: City of Houston, 1981.

Houston Area Survey: 1982–Present. www.houstonareasurvey.org.

Houston Blue Book: 1896: A Society Directory. Houston: J. R. Wheat, 1896.

Houston, City of. *The Illustrated City Book of Houston, Containing the Annual Message of Ben Campbell, Mayor of the City of Houston*. Houston: Cumming and Sons, Art Printers, 1916, 1917.

———. *The Municipal Book of the City of Houston*. Houston: City of Houston, 1922.

"Houston in 1910: A Photographic Essay." *Houston Review: History and Culture of the Gulf Coast* 1 (Spring 1979): 44–54.

Houston Symphony League. "50th Anniversary: Houston Symphony League." Pamphlet. Houston: Houston Symphony League, 1987.

Hunter, Joel D. "The History and Development of Institutes for the Study of Children." In *The Child, the Clinic, and the Court*, ed. Jane Addams. New York: New Republic, 1927.

Hurley, Marvin. *Decisive Years for Houston*. Houston: Houston Chamber of Commerce, 1966.

Hutton, Jim, and Jim Henderson. *Houston: A History of a Giant; A Pictorial and Entertaining Commentary on the Growth and Development of Houston, Texas.* Houston: Continental Heritage, 1976.

Inaugural Exhibition: Amon Carter Museum of Western Art. Selected Works Frederic Remington and Charles Marion Russell. Catalog. Fort Worth, TX: Amon Carter Museum, January 1961.

Isaacs, I. J., ed. *Industrial Advantages of Houston, Texas, and Environs, The; Also a Series of Comprehensive Sketches of the City's Representative Business Enterprises.* Houston: Akehurst, 1894.

Iscoe, Louise Kosches. *Ima Hogg, First Lady of Texas: Reminiscences and Recollections of Family and Friends.* Austin: Hogg Foundation for Mental Health, 1976.

James, Marquis. *The Texaco Story: The First Fifty Years, 1902–1952.* Houston: Texas Company, 1953.

Johnston, Marguerite S. *A Happy Worldly Abode: Christ Church Cathedral, 1839–1964.* Houston: Cathedral Press, 1964.

———. *Houston: The Unknown City, 1836–1946.* College Station: Texas A&M University Press, 1991.

Jones, Howard. *The Red Diary: A Chronological History of Black Americans in Houston and Some Neighboring Harris County Communities—122 Years Later.* Austin: Nortex Press, 1991.

Jones, Julia. *Houston: 1836–1940.* Houston: N.p., 1941.

Josiah Macy, Jr. Foundation, The, 1930–1955: A Review of Activities. New York: Josiah Macy Jr. Foundation, 1955.

Justice, Blair. *Violence in the City.* Fort Worth: Potishman Fund, 1969.

Kalil, Susie. *The Texas Landscape, 1900–1986.* Houston: Museum of Fine Arts, Houston, 1986.

Kellar, William Henry. "Alive with a Vengeance: Houston's Black Teachers and Their Fight for Equal Pay." *Houston Review: History and Culture of the Gulf Coast* 18 (1996): 89–99.

———. "Make Haste Slowly: A History of School Desegregation in Houston, Texas." Ph.D. diss., University of Houston, 1994.

Kelley, Mary L. *The Foundations of Texan Philanthropy.* College Station: Texas A&M University Press, 2004.

———. "From Spindletop to Round Top: Texas Oil and the Hogg Family Legacy in Philanthropy." *Texas Gulf Historical and Biographical Record* 36 (November 2000): 46–57.

Kelly, Thomas. "Free Enterprise, Costly Relief: Charity in Houston, Texas, 1915–1937." *Houston Review: History and Culture of the Gulf Coast* 18 (1996): 29–62.

Kiger, Joseph C. *Philanthropic Foundations in the Twentieth Century.* Foreword by Sara L. Engelhardt. Westport, CT: Greenwood Press, 2000.

Kilman, Edward W. *Hugh Roy Cullen: A Story of American Opportunity.* New York: Prentice-Hall, 1954.

King, John O. *Joseph Stephen Cullinan: A Study of Leadership in the Texas Petroleum Industry, 1897–1937.* Nashville, TN: Vanderbilt University Press, 1970.

King, Judy. *Except the Lord Build . . . : The Sesquicentennial History of First Presbyterian Church, Houston, Texas, 1839–1989.* Houston: The Church, 1989.

Kirkland, Kate S. "For All Houston's Children: Ima Hogg and the Board of Education, 1943–1949." *Southwestern Historical Quarterly* 101 (April 1998): 460–495.

———. "A Wholesome Life: Ima Hogg's Vision for Mental Health Care." *Southwestern Historical Quarterly* 104 (January 2001): 416–447.

Kiser, Clyde V. *The Milbank Memorial Fund: Its Leaders and Its Work, 1905–1974.* New York: Milbank Memorial Fund, 1975.

Klineberg, Stephen L. *Houston's Ethnic Communities.* 3d ed. Houston: Rice University, 1996.

Knight, Robert P., and Cyrus R. Friedman. *Psychoanalytic Psychiatry and Psychology: Clinical and Theoretical Papers.* New York: International Universities Press, 1954.

Lane, Ann J. *To Herland and Beyond: The Life and Work of Charlotte Perkins Gilman.* New York: Pantheon Books, 1990.

Lasswell, Mary. *John Henry Kirby: Prince of the Pines.* Austin: Encino Press, 1967.

Lawrence, Clayton, and Joe W. Specht. *The Roots of Texas Music.* College Station: Texas A&M University Press, 2003.

Léon, Arnoldo de. *Ethnicity in the Sunbelt: A History of Mexican Americans in Houston.* Mexican American Studies Monograph Series No. 7. Houston: University of Houston Mexican American Studies Program, 1989.

———. "Whither Tejano History: Origins, Development, and Status." *Southwestern Historical Quarterly* 106 (Jan. 2003); 349–364.

Levengood, Paul Alejandro. "For the Duration and Beyond: World War II and the Creation of Modern Houston, Texas." Ph.D. diss., Rice University, 1999.

Linn, James Weber. *Jane Addams: A Biography.* Introduction by Anne Firor Scott. Urbana: University of Illinois Press, 2000.

Linsley, Judith Walker, Ellen Walker Rienstra, and JoAnn Stiles. *Giant Under the Hill: A History of the Spindletop Oil Discovery at Beaumont, Texas, in 1901.* Austin: Texas State Historical Association, 2002.

Lipartito, Kenneth, and Joseph A. Pratt. *Baker and Botts in the Development of Modern Houston.* Austin: University of Texas Press, 1991.

Loan Exhibition of Old Masters of the Seventeenth and Eighteenth Centuries Lent Through the Courtesy of the Reinhardt Galleries of New York, Jan. 3–18, 1931. Catalog. Houston: Museum of Fine Arts of Houston, 1931.

Lomax, John Avery. *Will Hogg, Texan.* Reprint, Austin: University of Texas Press for the Hogg Foundation, 1956. First published in *Atlantic Monthly*, 1940.

Longstreth, Richard. "J. C. Nichols, the Country Club Plaza, and Notions of Modernity." *Harvard Architecture Review* 5 (1896): 120–135.

Looser, Don. "A Musical Renaissance: The Growth of Cultural Institutions in Houston, 1929–1936." *Houston Review: History and Culture of the Gulf Coast* 6 (1984): 135–155.

Lovett, Edgar Odell. *Edgar Odell Lovett and the Creation of Rice University: The Meaning of the New Institution.* Introduction by John B. Boles. Houston: Rice Historical Society, 2000.

Marchiafava, Louis J. "Oil! A Reservoir of Houston History." *Houston Review: History and Culture of the Gulf Coast* 2 (Fall 1980): 134–143.

Matthews, Harold J. *Candle by Night: The Story of the Life and Times of Kezia Payne de Pelchin, Texas Pioneer Teacher, Social Worker and Nurse*. Boston: Bruce Humphries, 1942.

Mays, Fayrene Neuman. "A History of Public Library Service to Negroes in Houston, Texas, 1907–1962." Master's thesis, Atlanta University, School of Library Service, 1964.

McArthur, Judith. *Creating the New Woman: The Rise of Southern Women's Progressive Culture in Texas, 1893–1918*. Urbana: University of Illinois Press, 1998.

McAshan, Marie Phelps. *A Houston Legacy: On the Corner of Main and Texas*. Houston: Hutchins House, 1985.

McCall, Perry McAshan. "A Progressive City During the Frivolous Decade: A Study of Social Concern in Houston, Texas, During the 1920s." Master's thesis, Texas A&M University, 1971.

McCarthy, Kathleen D. *Lady Bountiful Revisited: Women, Philanthropy, and Power*. New Brunswick, NJ: Rutgers University Press, 1990.

———, ed. *Women, Philanthropy, and Civil Society*. Bloomington: Indiana University Press, 2001.

McComb, David G. *Houston: The Bayou City*. Austin: University of Texas Press, 1969. Revised 1981.

McElhaney, Jacquelyn Masur. *Pauline Periwinkle and Progressive Reform in Dallas*. College Station: Texas A&M University Press, 1998.

McGerr, Michael. *A Fierce Discontent: The Rise and Fall of the Progressive Movement in America, 1870–1920*. New York: Free Press, 2003.

Mehden, Fred R. von der, ed. *The Ethnic Groups of Houston*. Houston: Rice University Studies, 1984.

Meiners, Fredericka. *A History of Rice University: The Institute Years, 1907–1963*. Houston: Rice University Studies, 1982.

Menil Collection, The: A Selection from the Paleolithic to the Modern Era. Foreword by Dominique de Menil; introduction by Walter Hopps. New York: Henry Abrams, 1997.

Meyer, Leopold L. *The Days of My Years: Autobiographical Reflections*. Houston: Universal Printers, 1975.

Mollenkopf, John H. *The Contested City*. Princeton, NJ: Princeton University Press, 1983.

Montgomery, Julia Cameron. *Houston as a Setting of the Jewel: The Rice Institute, 1913*. Reprint, Houston: Rice Historical Society, 2002. First published in 1913 by Julia Cameron Montgomery.

Morrison and Fourmy Directory Company. *Houston City Directory*. Houston: R. L. Polk and Co., Compilers and Publishers, 1907, 1918.

Muir, Andrew Forest. *William Marsh Rice and His Institute: A Biographical Study*. Ed. Sylvia Stallings Morris. Houston: William Marsh Rice University, 1972.

Muncy, Robyn. *Creating a Female Dominion in American Reform: 1890–1935*. New York: Oxford University Press, 1991.

Neeley, Gwendolyn Cone. *Miss Hogg and the Hogg Family*. Dallas: Hendrick-Long, 1992.

Neff, Emily Ballew, with Wynne H. Phelan. *Frederic Remington: The Hogg Brothers Collection of the Museum of Fine Arts, Houston*. Princeton, NJ: Princeton University Press, 2000.

New Handbook of Texas. Ron Tyler, Douglas E. Barnett, Roy R. Barkley, Penelope C. Anderson, and Mark F. Odintz, eds. 6 vols. Austin: Texas State Historical Association, 1996.

Nicholson, Patrick J. *In Time: An Anecdotal History of the First Fifty Years of the University of Houston*. Houston: Pacesetter Press, 1977.

Northcott, Kaye. "Former Slaves Remembered." *Texas Co-Op Power* May 2001, 15–18.

Norvell, James R. "The Railroad Commission of Texas: Its Origin and History." *Southwestern Historical Quarterly* 68 (April 1965): 465–480.

O'Kane, Elisabeth. "To Lift the City Out of the Mud: Health, Sanitation and Sewerage in Houston, 1840–1920." *Houston Review: History and Culture of the Gulf Coast* 17 (1995): 3–27.

Ostrower, Francie. *Why the Wealthy Give: The Culture of Elite Philanthropy*. Princeton, NJ: Princeton University Press, 1995.

Papademetriou, Peter. "Urban Development and Public Policy in the Progressive Era, 1890–1940." *Houston Review: History and Culture of the Gulf Coast* 5 (Fall 1983): 115–131.

Park, Robert E., Ernest W. Burgess, and Roderick D. McKenzie. *The City*. Chicago: University of Chicago Press, 1967. First published in 1925.

Payton, Robert L. "Philanthropy as a Right." In *The Citizen and His Government*, ed. W. Lawson Taitte. Dallas: University of Texas at Dallas, 1984.

Pen and Sunlight Sketches of Greater Houston. Houston: N.p., circa 1913.

Perkins, Howard. "Caught on Camera: Images of Spindletop." *Texas Gulf Historical and Biographical Record* 36 (November 2000): 31–37.

Permanent Legacy: 150 Works from the Collection of the Museum of Fine Arts, Houston. Introduction by Peter C. Marzio. New York: Hudson Hills Press, 1989.

Platt, Harold L. *City Building in the New South: The Growth of Public Services, in Houston, Texas, 1830–1910*. Philadelphia: Temple University Press, 1982.

Pratt, Joseph A., and Christopher J. Castenada. *Builders: Herman and George R. Brown*. College Station: Texas A&M University Press, 1999.

Pryor, William Lee. "'The Fate of Marvin': An Epic Poem of the Civil War by a Texas Soldier." *Texas Quarterly* (Summer 1977): 6–12.

Putnam, Robert D. *Bowling Alone: The Collapse and Revival of American Community*. New York: Simon and Schuster, 2000.

Red Book of Houston: A Compendium of Social, Professional, Religious, Educational and Industrial Interests of Houston's Colored Population. Houston: Sotex Publishing, circa 1915.

Report of the City Planning Commission, Houston, Texas. Houston: Forum of Civics, 1929.

Rice, Bradley Robert. *Progressive Cities: The Commission Government Movement in America, 1901–1920*. Austin: University of Texas Press, 1977.

Richardson, Theresa. *The Century of the Child: The Mental Hygiene Movement and Social Policy in the United States and Canada*. New York: State University of New York Press, 1989.

Riddle, Don, comp. "River Oaks: A Pictorial Presentation of Houston's Residential Park." Pamphlet. Houston: River Oaks Corporation, n.d.

Riggs, Austen Fox. *Intelligent Living*. Garden City, NY: Doubleday, Doran, 1934.

———. *Play: Recreation in a Balanced Life*. Garden City, NY: Doubleday, Doran, 1935.

Rogers, Elizabeth Barlow. *Landscape Design: A Cultural and Architectural History*. New York: Harry N. Abrams, 2001.

Rosales, Francisco Arturo. "Mexicans in Houston: The Struggle to Survive, 1908–1975." *Houston Review: History and Culture of the Gulf Coast* 3 (Summer 1981): 224–246.

Rosales, Francisco Arturo, and Barry J. Kaplan, eds. *Houston: A Twentieth Century Urban Frontier*. Port Washington, NY: Associated Faculty Press, 1983.

Rose, Barbara, and Susie Kalil. *Fresh Paint: The Houston School; The Museum of Fine Arts, Houston*. Austin: Texas Monthly Press, 1985.

Rose, Warren. *The Economic Impact of the Port of Houston, 1958–1963*. Houston: University of Houston Center for Research in Business and Economics, College of Business Administration, 1965.

Rothman, David J. *The Discovery of the Asylum: Social Order and Disorder in the New Republic*. Rev. ed. Boston: Little, Brown, 1990.

Roussel, Hubert. *The Houston Symphony Orchestra, 1913–1971*. Austin: University of Texas Press, 1972.

Rundell, Walter Jr. *Early Texas Oil: A Photographic History, 1866–1936*. College Station: Texas A&M University Press, 1977.

Rybczynski, Witold. *A Clearing in the Distance: Frederick Law Olmsted and America in the Nineteenth Century*. New York: Scribner, 1999.

Saarinen, Aline B. *The Proud Possessors: The Lives, Times and Tastes of Some Adventurous American Art Collectors*. New York: Random House, 1958.

Savage, Charles C. *Architecture of the Private Streets of St. Louis: The Architects and the Houses They Designed*. Columbia: University of Missouri Press, 1987.

Scardino, Barrie. "A Legacy of City Halls for Houston." *Houston Review: History and Culture of the Gulf Coast* 4 (Fall 1982): 154–164.

Scardino, Barrie, William F. Stern, and Bruce C. Webb, eds. *Ephemeral City: Cite Looks at Houston*. Foreword by Peter G. Rowe. Austin: University of Texas Press, 2003.

Scharf, Lois, and Joan M. Jensen. *Decades of Discontent: The Women's Movement, 1920–1940*. Westport, CT: Greenwood Press, 1983.

Schmidgall, Gary. "Can Do: Houston, a City That Thinks Big, This Month Officially Christens the Wortham Theater Center, a Sterling New Home for Opera." *Opera News*, October 1987, 12–20, 66–67, 70.

Schultz, Stanley K. *Constructing Urban Culture: American Cities and City Planning, 1800–1920*. Philadelphia: Temple University Press, 1989.

Schuyler, David. *The New Urban Landscape: The Redefinition of City Form in Nineteenth-Century America*. Baltimore: Johns Hopkins University Press, 1986.

Scott, Anne Firor. *The Southern Lady: From Pedestal to Politics, 1830–1930*. Charlottesville: University of Virginia, 1970. Revised 1995.

Scott, Janelle D. "Local Leadership in the Woman Suffrage Movement: Houston's Campaign for the Vote, 1912–1918." *Houston Review: History and Culture of the Gulf Coast* 12 (1990): 3–22.

Scott, Mel. *American City Planning Since 1890.* Berkeley: University of California Press, 1969.

Seaholm, Megan. "Earnest Women: The White Women's Club Movement in Progressive Era Texas, 1880–1920." Ph.D. diss., Rice University, 1988.

Sealander, Judith. *Private Wealth and Public Life: Foundation Philanthropy and the Reshaping of American Social Policy from the Progressive Era to the New Deal.* Baltimore: Johns Hopkins University Press, 1997.

Seymour, Charles, ed. *The Intimate Papers of Colonel House.* Vol. 1, *Behind the Political Curtain, 1912–1915.* Boston: Houghton Mifflin, 1926.

Shabazz, Amilcar. "One for the Crows and One for the Crackers: The Strange Career of Public Higher Education in Houston, Texas." *Houston Review: History and Culture of the Gulf Coast* 18 (1996): 125–138.

Shelton, Beth Anne, Nestor P. Rodriguez, Joe R. Feagin, Robert D. Bullard, and Robert D. Thomas. *Houston: Growth and Decline in a Sunbelt Boomtown.* Philadelphia: Temple University Press, 1989.

Sibley, Marilyn McAdams. *The Port of Houston: A History.* Austin: University of Texas Press, 1968.

Siegel, Stanley E. *Houston: A Chronicle of the Supercity on Buffalo Bayou.* Woodland Hills, CA: Windsor Publications for Harris County Historical Society, 1983.

Sloan, Anne. "Altering the Fine Edge of Respectability: Business Women in Houston, 1880–1920." *Houston Review of History and Culture* 1 (Fall 2003): 37–46.

Smith, C. Calvin. "The Houston Riot of 1917, Revisited." *Houston Review: History and Culture of the Gulf Coast* 13 (1991): 88–101.

Sorelle, James M. "'An De Po Cullud Man Is in de Wuss Fix uv Awl': Status in Houston, Texas, 1920–1940." *Houston Review: History and Culture of the Gulf Coast* 1 (Spring 1979): 15–26.

———. "The Darker Side of 'Heaven'": The Black Community in Houston, Texas, 1917–1945." Ph.D. diss., Kent State University, 1980.

Spell, Lota M. *Music in Texas: A Survey of One Aspect of Cultural Progress.* Austin: N.p., 1936.

Spratt, John S. *The Road to Spindletop: Economic Change in Texas, 1875–1901.* Dallas: Southern Methodist University Press, 1955.

Sproul, Kathleen. "James Stephen Hogg: March 24, 1851–March 3, 1906." Pamphlet. West Columbia, TX: March 24, 1958.

Standard Blue Book, The: Texas Edition. San Antonio: N. S. Peeler, 1920.

Standard Blue Book of Texas Who's Who, The. Edition deluxe of Houston. Houston: Who's Who Publishing, 1907.

Stillinger, Elizabeth. *The Antiquers: The Lives and Careers, the Deals, the Finds, the Collections of the Men and Women Who Were Responsible for the Changing Taste in American Antiques, 1850–1930.* New York: Alfred A. Knopf, 1980.

Strom, Steven R. "A Legacy of Civic Pride: Houston's PWA Buildings." *Houston Review: History and Culture of the Gulf Coast* 17 (1995): 103–121.

Taitte, W. Lawson, ed. *The Citizen and His Government*. Introduction by Andrew R. Cecil. Dallas: University of Texas at Dallas, 1984.

Taylor, Lonn. "Miss Ima Hogg." *Texas Observer*, Sept. 5, 1975, 11.

Texas Blue Books: Houston, 1900. Houston: Mrs. Corra Bacon Foster, 1900.

Thompson, Marjorie S. *Frederic Remington: Selections from the Hogg Brothers Collection*. Catalog. Houston: Museum of Fine Arts, Houston, 1973.

Timmons, Bascom N. *Jesse H. Jones: The Man and the Statesman*. New York: Henry Holt, 1956.

Tinsley, James A., ed. *Growth of the Business of Anderson, Clayton, and Co.* Publication Series 10, Texas Gulf Coast Historical Association. September 1966, 1–13.

Turner, Elizabeth Hayes. *Women, Culture, and Community: Religion and Reform in Galveston, 1880–1920*. New York: Oxford University Press, 1997.

Unibook Staff. *Houston: City of Destiny*. New York: Macmillan, 1980.

Venable, Charles L. *American Furniture in the Bybee Collection*. Introduction by Jonathan L. Fairbanks. Austin: University of Texas Press, 1989.

Wall, Joseph Frazier, ed. *The Andrew Carnegie Reader*. Pittsburgh, PA: University of Pittsburgh Press, 1992.

Warren, David B. *Bayou Bend: American Furniture, Paintings and Silver from the Bayou Bend Collection*. Foreword by Miss Ima Hogg. Houston: Museum of Fine Arts, Houston, 1975.

———. *Bayou Bend: The Interiors and Gardens*. Houston: Museum of Fine Arts, Houston, 1988.

———. "Bayou Bend: The Plan and History of the Gardens." *Bulletin of the Museum of Fine Arts, Houston* 12 (Winter–Spring 1989): 67–95.

———. "Bayou Bend Gardens." Curator's Choice Lecture, March 2, 2003, Museum of Fine Arts, Houston.

———. *Bayou Bend Gardens: A Southern Oasis*. Introduction by Mac Griswold; photographs by Rick Gardner, Don Glentzer, and Rob Muir. Houston: Scala Publishers with Museum of Fine Arts, Houston, 2006.

———. "A Great Texas Collection of Americana: The Bayou Bend Collection at the Museum of Fine Arts, Houston." Reprint, *Connoisseur*, September 1971.

———. "Ima Hogg and Bayou Bend: A History." *Bulletin of the Museum of Fine Arts* 12 (Fall 1988): 2–12.

———. "Ima Hogg, Collector." *Magazine Antiques*, January 1982, 228–243.

Warren, David B., Michael K. Brown, Elizabeth Ann Coleman, and Emily Ballew Neff. *American Decorative Arts and Paintings in the Bayou Bend Collection*. Princeton, NJ: Museum of Fine Arts, Houston, and Princeton University Press, 1998.

Warren, David B., and Katherine S. Howe. *Houston Collects Nineteenth-Century American Decorative Arts: An Exhibition of American Furniture, Silver, Glass and Ceramics from 1830 to 1914*. Houston: Museum of Fine Arts, Houston, 1978.

Weber, Bruce J. "Will Hogg and the Business of Reform." Ph.D. diss., University of Houston, 1979.

White, William. *The Mental Hygiene of Childhood*. Boston: Little, Brown, 1923.

Whitlock, Clyde. "Musical Texas." In *The Standard Blue Book Texas Edition*. San Antonio: N. S. Peeler, 1920.

Wilson, Michael E. "Alfred C. Finn: Houston Architect." *Houston Review: History and Culture of the Gulf Coast* 5 (Summer 1983): 65–79.

Wilson, William H. *The City Beautiful Movement in Kansas City.* Columbia: University of Missouri Press, 1964.

Wolz, Larry. "Roots of Classical Music in Texas: The German Contribution." In *The Roots of Texas Music*, Clayton Lawrence and Joe W. Sprecht (College Station: Texas A&M University Press, 2003.

Worley, William S. *J. C. Nichols and the Shaping of Kansas City: Innovation in Planned Residential Communities.* Columbia: University of Missouri Press, 1990.

Young, S. O. *True Stories of Old Houston and Houstonians.* Galveston, TX: Oscar Springer, 1913.

Zelden, Charles. "Regional Growth and the Federal District Courts: The Impact of Judge Joseph C. Hutcheson, Jr., on Southeast Texas, 1918–1931." *Houston Review: History and Culture of the Gulf Coast* 11 (1989): 67–94.

Index